The Educational Tasks and Content of the Steiner Waldorf Curriculum

Edited by Martyn Rawson and Tobias Richter

Waldorf Resource Books No. 4

ISBN 1 900169 07 X

Steiner Schools Fellowship Publications 2000
Reprinted 2001
Reprinted 2005
Reprinted 2008

Steiner Waldorf Schools Fellowship
Kidbrooke Park
Forest Row
East Sussex RH18 5JA

Telephone: 01342 822115 • Facsimile 01342 826004
E-mail: mail@swsf.org.uk
www.steinerwaldorf.org.uk

Charity number 295104
Company Registered in England number 519230

Publications Department
Steiner Schools Fellowship Publications
Telephone: 01342 825005 • Facsimile 01342 826004
E-mail: info@steinerschoolbooks.com
www.steinerwaldorf.org.uk/publications

Printed and bound in Great Britain by
Imprint • Crawley Down • Sussex RH10 4LQ

The Educational Tasks and Content
of the
Steiner Waldorf Curriculum

This research document has been produced on behalf of
the Pedagogical Section of the School for Spiritual Science
at the Goetheanum, Dornach, Switzerland,
in co-operation with the
Steiner Schools Fellowship Publications

The Educational Tasks and Content of the Steiner Waldorf Curriculum

CONTENTS

FOREWORD

Caroline von Heydebrand's achievement in piecing together the many suggestions that Rudolf Steiner made to the teachers of the first Waldorf School in the form of lectures or during meetings and forming them into a comprehensive curriculum for Steiner Waldorf schools amounted almost to a work of genius.[1] In a style that was both precise and concise, and having the courage to leave gaps, she painted a picture with many facets.

Nevertheless, given the developments in education and cultural life generally that have occurred over eight decades, it seemed time to review, update and extend the work. Furthermore the increasing demand from the authorities for schools to document their curricula has led more and more Steiner Waldorf schools to present their own versions. Waldorf education has of course not only moved on in time, it has moved to other places too, each with its own geographical and cultural educational influences. Translating the original Waldorf Curriculum in time and space raises many interesting questions about the nature of child development and the cultural role of any curriculum. In an age in which nothing can be taken for granted, no traditions can remain living without full consciousness, it seemed right to reformulate the Waldorf Curriculum for a new age.

This was discussed in the Hague Circle, a group of experienced teachers and teacher trainers from the Steiner Waldorf schools movement in Europe and America, who meet twice annually to review the development of the movement. The conclusion reached was that such an undertaking would require a balancing act. On the one hand there would be the need to explain and confirm the freedom every school must have if it is to succeed in taking full account of the developing child (who is, after all, the foundation on which the curriculum must rest). On the other hand it should be possible to document the fruitful and sensible educational practice which goes on in these schools. By giving examples, rather than stating norms, there would be general directions to illustrate the substance of the education as envisaged by Rudolf Steiner in relation to children of different ages, while at the same time proper account would be taken of the requirements of the different subjects.

This was quite a tall order. By way of making a realistic start it was decided to base the work on a presentation compiled by Tobias Richter with Austrian colleagues, who had already prepared such documentation for the Vienna (Mauer) school. A number of colleagues from the international Steiner Waldorf schools' movement shared in this initial task. Tobias Richter, Georg Kniebe (Germany), Bengt Ulin (Sweden) and Shirley Noakes (Scotland) belonged to the working group, together with Dr. Heinz Zimmermann, leader of the Pedagogical Section at the Goetheanum in Switzerland.

This group produced a draft of which a limited number of copies were distributed to the schools in Germany for discussion both in their internal meetings and at the larger conferences to which the schools send delegates. Quite considerable objections and also very productive and stimulating suggestions were the result, all of which enabled the work to move on to the next stage. Some of these observations referred to the subjects, others to the different ages of the children, and yet others to the overall concept. It became obvious that this initial effort did not as yet go far enough towards meeting the requirement that the document should, on the one hand, take account of the freedom of the individual teacher while at the same time offering descriptions of how individual teachers actually set about their tasks. Led by Georg Kniebe, the *Pädagogische Forschungsstelle* (German education research group) then undertook to sift all the suggestions and, where necessary, have specialist groups work out further ideas. This having been done, two more colleagues, Dietrich Esterl (Germany) and Christof Wiechert (Netherlands), once again made a critical assessment of the whole manuscript. They took care to ensure that it contained nothing that could be interpreted as requiring an adherence to any norms (this remained the most vociferous objection to the whole undertaking).

A limited edition of the curriculum *Pädagogischer Auftrag und Unterrichtsziele einer Freien Waldorfschule*, was published in manuscript form by the *Pädagogische Forschungsstelle* in 1995, so that further experiences and improvements could be collected and later incorporated into the whole. The reception was initially controversial, though the arguments of many of the detractors seemed to remain consistent and essentially theoretical. Little attention seems to have been paid to the major revisions that were undertaken and little respect was shown for the authority and experience of those responsible for the project. In the meantime, the book has become a fact of life and seems to provide many, if not most practising Waldorf teachers with a useful orientation. There is now a Spanish translation and one has recently appeared in the Czech language. I know of a Russian version in the pipeline.

A translation or a new version for the English-speaking world?

Following the 'twists and turns' of debate that the German edition generated, persuaded me that any English language edition should be no mere translation, but a further step in the direction of a broad yet coherent presentation of the Waldorf Curriculum.

This edition was accompanied by widespread consultation with colleagues working within the British schools. I reluctantly took the decision to limit the consultations to the UK for practical reasons, having discovered that, even in the age of global communication, busy Waldorf teachers rarely respond to letters or even e-mail requests for comments on aspects of the curriculum. It is remarkable how often I have received the reply, "actually we have to go right back to the drawing board and build the curriculum up from scratch, unfortunately I don't have time to do so at present, unless you can fund my sabbatical." UK colleagues were closer at hand to badger.

The objection, however, is interesting. I interpret it as follows. No, the Steiner Waldorf Curriculum does not need rethinking from scratch. It does not need wholesale revision, or nine tenths of it throwing out as out of date. But it does need re-living and working through at a new level. Every Waldorf hero has the wish at heart to re-write Steiner's *Philosophy of Freedom* in their own words. Presumably the re-working of the curriculum would then follow that. This reluctance to be pinned down on the curriculum, however, betrays a healthy wish to derive the actual curriculum, that is to say, what occurs in the teaching setting, from insight into the children; a noble and fundamental Waldorf ideal. Anyone who attempts to write anything down about the curriculum is suspect of betraying that ideal.

On the other hand those involved in teacher training, those involved in presenting Waldorf ideas to a wider world, those involved with schools in countries with no previous history of Waldorf education, continuously call for some kind of accessible guidelines. We are damned if we do and damned if we don't.

To my mind there are a number of far more fundamental questions relating to the curriculum, than whether one can write down what people actually do. Without some written documentation, it will be difficult to address the following questions in any scientific way. The questions I have in mind can be briefly formulated as follows.

- How much of the Waldorf Curriculum is universally applicable and how much can and should be adapted to local cultural circumstances?
- How much of the Waldorf Curriculum is essentially focused on supporting actual child development and how much is there for external cultural reasons?
- What minimum constitutes the Waldorf Curriculum? What is the bottom line, below which a curriculum cannot in all honesty be considered Waldorf?
- In what specific or general, long or short-term ways do the subjects and experiences of the curriculum actually support the child's development and how can this be observed and evaluated?

With these thoughts in mind, I decided that it was necessary to do an English edition, not merely as a reference for the 28 schools at present in the UK and Ireland, but as an example to schools in any country who wished to have a thoughtful reference work to base their own research on. For that ultimately is the purpose of a written curriculum. It provides a benchmark to measure *oneself* against. Not, as some governments seem to believe, as a yardstick to make external judgments of quality and merit against (with punitive consequences for failure!). The central educational activity belongs clearly in the realm of the free cultural domain, which can only be freely assessed by its practitioners in self and peer assessment. As public institutions, schools have a responsibility to be accountable to pupils, parents and society at large. But that accountability must meaningfully be *self-accountability*, which includes the informed judgment of one's peers and listening to the views of parents and pupils.

The fundamental difference between the Waldorf Curriculum and the English National Curriculum (or its equivalents elsewhere) is the intention that lies behind them. The latter claims to be an enabling instrument that guarantees common standards of attainment for all children. It aims to achieve this by setting out what must be taught by when and by setting a range of standards for pupil attainment. These are demonstrated by regular standardised testing. The results of such tests are made public and drawn up in published league tables, on the principle of 'name and shame'. This essentially introduces a punitive and competitive element into education, aimed at raising standards. Inspections and ultimately interventionist strategies by central or local government reinforce this. The funding of schools is directly pegged to the delivery of the National Curriculum. Parents have the choice as discerning consumers to choose the right school for their children, by moving them from failing schools to successful schools (assuming they have the mobility and that the successful schools have any free places left). Parental choice, except for the wealthy who can afford to pay their taxes *and* pay for private education, is reduced to choosing from a range of schools that offer the same education in detail, in slightly different surroundings. It is like saying, you can shop anywhere you like as long as it's at a branch of Marks and Spencers. One asks oneself, was state education really so bad that government ministers had to take total control of it to save the nation from disintegration?

The Waldorf Curriculum also claims to be an enabling instrument. It maps out a series of routes through the school learning process, just as the National Curriculum does. In fact the two documents cover much of the same ground. It would be surprising if they didn't. Both concern themselves with the development of key skills and the acquisition of knowledge deemed necessary by contemporary society. There is little disagreement there. In fact a two-year study by the British (Waldorf) Curriculum Research Group presented to the Department for Education and Employment [2] concluded that the Waldorf Curriculum fulfilled the aims and intentions of the National Curriculum fully by the end of Key Stage 4. Indeed the good public exam results attained by Steiner Waldorf pupils in the UK confirm this. Actual convergence with National Curriculum learning outcomes and attainment levels would be unproblematic for Key Stage 3, with minor differences by Key Stage 2. Only for Key Stage 1 were problems apparent, and these largely due to the later introduction of formal learning in Steiner Waldorf. From a curriculum point of view the differences are essentially about methodology.

4

One thing of course that distinguishes the Waldorf from the National Curriculum is that the former justifies itself from an educational point of view and attempts to explain the development of each subject from the point of view of child development. The National Curriculum offers no such justification. Indeed it seems strangely oblivious to the concept that any educational approach must be based on some philosophy of education, some understanding of the nature of the human being that underpins, justifies and explains the steps that have to be taken. Education without theory is like sailing with a map but no compass. The National Curriculum is a fully illustrated and detailed map with no inner orientation. Every part of the map has its own internal logic. The purpose of the map is clear – the government is determined to ensure that its ships don't stray off course – captains will be demoted to the ratings if the ships wobbles off course, rations will be cut etc. But what is the map a map of and what is its inner orientation? Is the map *creating* the underlying geography or reflecting it?

The metaphor has over-reached itself. A curriculum is a map of a living process, not a fixed and permanent entity. The Waldorf Curriculum is not prescriptive but descriptive, it seeks to describe where children typically are at the various ages. It relates the particular qualities of the various subjects to the developmental processes and maps out the intrinsic progression of child and subject as a correlation.

Any Steiner Waldorf school can say, this is how *we* interpret the ideas of Waldorf education, this is *our* rationale and these are *our* reasons for doing so. The existence of a book such as this gives any school the freedom to teach its own curriculum, because now it can read here what is good practice, what is usually done, when and why. Thus the assertion of its own identity, if it chooses to distance itself from the guidelines and examples given here, will be all the stronger and clearer. Clearly each school must set its own targets for attainments in whatever way it feels appropriate. Having done so, it is then accountable to its parents and the world.

Another factor which decided me to proceed with this edition was the recognition that the original attempt to present an overview of the educational tasks, objectives and content of the Waldorf Curriculum in language that was accessible to non-insiders was only partly successful. I felt that it was imperative to present the ideas in such a way that anyone familiar with education would be able to follow the presentation without being alienated by strange terminology.

So what of the original book edited by Tobias Richter has remained?

Initially we commissioned Johanna Collis to translate the whole of the original, which she did with her usual professional competence. We had to call on specialist assistance to deal with physics and chemistry, since not even Johanna's excellent command of the language goes that far! This was then sent in sections to colleagues to review and comment on. The British Curriculum Research Group of John Burnett, Trevor Mepham, Shirley Noakes, Dorothy Salter, Anne Tandree and myself then produced a new introduction on the Steiner Waldorf Approach, which essentially forms Sections 3, 4 and 5.

Other colleagues helped from a distance. They are listed in the areas of their contribution at the end of this Foreword.

From Tobias Richter's original, only parts of the horizontal curriculum remain along with the core work on the subjects. Where we have re-written, in some cases entirely, the vertical subject curricula, it was not because we thought they were in any sense wrong from the point of view of content, but rather because we felt the presentation needed changing for the English language. This was often easier when another colleague equally versed with the material put it into his or her words. This is not meant in any sense disrespectful to the original authors, some of whom have international reputations. It was a stylistic necessity. All the sections have been worked over by myself as English editor.

In several other respects, we have broadened the scope of Tobias Richter's original German edition. We have interpreted the concept of curriculum to include more of the *way* something is taught, as well as the content of the lessons. The *'how'* constitutes the Steiner Waldorf approach as much as the 'what'.

We have therefore added an explicit section on the Steiner Waldorf approach, specifically for the benefit of students, academics or educational officials and inspectors who may need a brief introduction. This includes short descriptions of the main-lesson, the structure of the teaching day, the use of narrative, the rhythm of learning and memory and so on. We have also added a section on evaluation and assessment.

Furthermore, we have added a section on Early Years education. This assumes that the roots of the curriculum and formal learning, the foundation for literacy, numeracy, social competence, healthy physiological development, co-ordination and orientation, as well as moral values, grow in the pre-school period. The Kindergarten (and pre-Kindergarten provision) is very much an integral part of the curriculum and has therefore been included.

A companion volume of this book is being prepared which outlines curriculum variations that have been developed in the different parts of the world. I have asked colleagues in those countries to note ways in which the curriculum has been modified and adapted in response to the different needs of children. Here we were not so much looking for individual innovation, though happily there is always much of that, but rather tried and tested curriculum elements that seem to be right for children in a particular place. We hope in subsequent editions to expand the supplement to show the particular curriculum developments in all countries where Steiner Waldorf Schools work. Further research is being undertaken into the way different subjects and teaching methods influence children's development. The descriptions of the subject curricula vary considerably in detail and presentation. We hope in subsequent editions to expand and, where necessary, clarify. This applies most to the teaching methods.

In conclusion I would like to include a few words that Tobias Richter wrote in the original Foreword to the German Edition, as it expresses my own views too.

By fixing these things in writing, anyone involved in the living flow of teaching cannot help experiencing the limitations of a project that by its very nature inhibits and restricts what ought to remain fluid. So the suggestions laid down here resemble a line that is the track left behind by movement; they are like movement that has been brought to a standstill.

Nevertheless, we venture to present this attempt at depicting the aims of the education and the possible content of lessons in the hope that every 'artist in the teaching profession' will succeed in creating life out of a dead form by shaping and developing his or her own sculpture of the curriculum, her or his own painting of the curriculum.

Intensive study of Rudolf Steiner's contribution to education never fails to kindle the enthusiasm so much needed in education when it is seen as a force for renewal. First and foremost, therefore, it is to Rudolf Steiner that our thanks are due.

Though many colleagues (their names are listed below) contributed to parts of this curriculum, the editors take overall responsibility for what finally reached the printer.

The following colleagues contributed in parts to this book:

Kevin Avison (checklists for class teachers), Martin Baker (Movement curriculum), John Burnett (Curriculum Research Group – CRG), Judy Byford (Eurythmy), Elena Christie (Eurythmy), Linda Churnside (Spelling Checklists and Maths), H. David (Handwork), Michaela Devaris (Eurythmy), Vivien Easton (Geography and Maths), William Forward (German), Bernard Graves (Crafts), Helene Jacquet (Eurythmy), Sally Jenkinson (Early Years), Graham Kennish (Biology and Chemistry), Ewout van Manen (Literacy and Learnin g Support), Dr. Brien Masters (Music), Monika McGovern (German), Trevor Mepham (CRG), Jenny Milne (Handwork), Shirley Noakes (CRG), Deborah Pike (French), Ken Power (History), Dorothy Salter (CRG), Martine Scott (French), H. Seufert (Crafts), Rob Sim (Movement curriculum), Jan Swann (quality development and administration), Anne Tandree (CRG), David Urieli (Maths and Physics), Dorothee von Winterfeldt (Foreign Languages), Richard Zienko (Philosophy).

Martyn Rawson

ACKNOWLEDGEMENTS

The editors would especially like to thank the following people who helped with this book:

Johanna Collis	Translation
Anne McNicol	Layout and typesetting
Sue Sim	Typing and proof reading
Brien Masters	Proof reading
Wilma Rawson	Proof reading
David Urieli	Translation

ABBREVIATIONS

In the lists of references, abbreviations used include:

AP	Anthroposophic Press, Hudson, New York
GA	Gesamtausgabe, German volume of Steiner's complete works. Given where no translation is known
RSP	Rudolf Steiner Press, London
SSF	Steiner Schools Fellowship Publications
n.d.	No date known

1   Translated into English and modified for the English-speaking world by Eileen Hutchins and Tilda von Eiff. This may be a belated moment to name and thank Tilda von Eiff, whose name never appeared in the SSF editions. As, at time of going to press, she is still hale and hearty, the editors take this opportunity to thank her for her contribution.
2   *Steiner Waldorf Education in the UK, aims methods and curriculum*, ed. M. Rawson, SSF, 1997.

INTRODUCTION: The Tasks of Steiner Waldorf Education

The tasks of the education can be summarised succinctly as follows:
- Fostering healthy development in each individual child
- Enabling children to realise their potential
- Helping children to develop the skills they need to contribute to society

Each of these tasks requires a high degree of skill and insight on the part of the teachers. Being able to fulfil these tasks also requires that teachers can work responsibly in an environment of institutional freedom, free from prescribed curricula and targets and imposed methodology. In order to meet both the needs of the developing individual and an evolving society, education must occur in a context of accountable and self-critical autonomy. Paradoxical though this sounds, higher development always requires a minimum of restraint and a maximum of consciousness.

Fostering Healthy Development

The Waldorf Curriculum aims not only to match the key developmental stages of childhood and adolescence but also to stimulate important developmental experiences. A certain topic taught in a specific way can awaken new faculties, new ways of seeing, new ways of comprehending. Rudolf Steiner also intended that the curriculum would work in a harmonising way, right down into the physical organism and into the bodily rhythms and processes. In this sense, the Waldorf Curriculum has a fundamentally therapeutic task in that it enables and supports the healthy development of the whole person. Health in this sense means a dynamic balance of the forces within the child and that the individual can relate to other people and the world in a balanced way. It also means that the realisation of each child's potential is fostered in an optimal way.

The Archetype of Human Development

But are children everywhere the same? Do they all have the same developmental needs and maturational timetable? The answer obviously is, clearly not. Diversity is a primary characteristic of the human being.

Whilst there are numerous ways in which we can usefully apply character typology to understanding people, such as recognising temperaments, constitutional types, psychological types, cultural characteristics, geographical differences and so on, the most dominant characteristic is always the individuality. It is the core of individuality, the 'I' or 'Ego' of the human being that comes to expression through interaction with the influences of both the genetic inheritance and the natural and human environment. It is the 'I' which strives to hold the balance between those two legacies (see also section 1.0 on anthroposophy).

A further human trait is the fundamentally heterochronous nature of human development in which we encounter many variations in the rhythms within the spheres of physical, behavioural, emotional, cognitive, social and spiritual maturation. Some of these are sequential, progressive and essentially predictable, the one following on from the other. Obvious examples include the way children learn to walk and speak, or when they become sexually mature. Other patterns of development, however, are more irregular, elliptical and individual. Within broadly similar patterns of unfolding, individual variation can be unpredictable and highly revealing of individuality.

Human development can be seen as the interaction between the spiritual core of the person striving to come ever more fully to expression within and through the organism he or she has inherited and must individualise. This body must first become a home for the soul and spirit, and one with windows and doors to the world. Then it must become the means through which the individual engages the world. And this interaction always occurs within a social, cultural and environmental context.

Steiner Waldorf education assumes that there is an archetypal human developmental timetable which is healthy in that it integrates physical, psychological and spiritual development. The Waldorf Curriculum is a cultural process, which reflects and supports this archetypal development by providing the right challenges and support at the right times. If children can tune into this rhythm of development, their own development can be harmonised.

This concept of a universal pattern of child development is no simplistic model but a subtle and richly complex process. Each individual developmental path has its own trajectory, which we usually refer to as an individual's biography or destiny. Each individual meets, joins and departs from the common path at various times and in specific places. We often experience such moments as crises or periods of critical learning opportunities. Such crises often occur in children at particular ages, at the ages of 9, 12 or 16 for example, though not necessarily so. We can also observe that each new learning step needs to be followed by a period of consolidation and maturing. Whilst on the common path provided by the curriculum, children can acquire much that is of use to them, that nourishes their inner development, that helps them build capacities, and equips them with the knowledge of the world that they need.

Though the variables are many and individual variation vast, there are also clearly factors such as ethnicity, language, social structures, climate and geography which influence large numbers of individuals in similar ways. To invoke the metaphor used above, one could say that the common path runs through a variety of different cultural and geographical landscapes. This makes it possible for schools or even whole regions to have broadly similar curricula. Yet no curriculum can remain fixed in time or place. Education has to work with both the common factors and the individuality, addressing the one through the other in rhythmical exchange. The rain falls on all but it is the individual who gets wet.

How do we know what the archetype is? Continuous observation, research, comparison and reflection enable us to discern the living archetype of human development. This also reveals to us that the archetype is no static entity, no absolute but a changing and evolving constellation. There is, for example, a clear sense amongst experienced observers that children have changed over the past few generations. The patterns of maturity have certainly changed, typified by earlier sexual maturity with delayed psychological readiness to take the responsibilities that being an adult entail. Cultural change drives human evolution along at an increasingly faster pace than biological evolution, thus exaggerating the inherently heterochronous nature of human development.

Yet other changes are more difficult to define. It may be the case that children today have a different inner relationship to questions of higher meaning, which is reflected in their spiritual development. In a world in which higher meaning is not necessarily any longer intrinsic to our culture, do children have a greater need to find meaning? And does this express itself in greater anxiety and insecurity? Are they more awake in their senses and thus more prone to sensory overload? Do they have higher expectations of the adult world with correspondingly greater sense of disappointment when their longing for certainty and direction is not met with appropriate nourishment?

What are the consequences for child development in an 'Age of Information'? It is difficult to assess whether children have to learn more today than at the turn of the last century. The *increase* in information today may replace the *quality* of information children had to deal with in previous periods of history. Perhaps people in the past knew more about fewer things, whereas today we know less about more things! At any rate, it is evident that children are presented with more unconnected units of information than ever in the past. The nature of information communicated by electronic media is that it is largely devoid of real, direct experience. This poses major questions about the nature and needs of learning.

All these questions highlight the need for a comprehensive and holistic understanding of the nature of the human being, what I have termed the living archetype. For without this we lack a sound basis for understanding the individual child.

Recognising the Individual

The thorough observation of children also enables us to recognise the symptoms of the individuation process, which generally proceeds not smoothly and continuously but is often punctuated by crises of one kind or another. Children often develop through a series of transformations, in which something held back suddenly breaks through. We may notice instability, frustration, anxiety, a blockage in learning, behaviour difficulties and so on. We may also notice that a child returning after a holiday, an illness, after a school trip or an important personal experience may seem somehow different in themselves. We see that the child has taken a new step, relates to us in a new way, thinks and speaks with greater maturity, is suddenly freer in her movements, or may simply have grown by several centimetres.

The individual reveals him- or herself most clearly when we have a picture of the archetype to measure our judgment against. In this sense the archetype is fundamentally different to a statistical average. The archetype provides a picture of how the 'I' integrates into the whole human being in an organic way at a given age, within a given phase of development. For the individual, the archetype provides an inner model against which to measure, indeed to shape their individuality.

We could say that life itself provides the individual with resistance. Each child must individualise her own bodily organism, establish her own habits, her own ways of seeing and being. The process is often not easy. With resistance comes friction, abrasion, pressure, which are all defining qualities, which shape, wear and form. In a sense development needs resistance. In its absence we would get non-specific, undirected growth. At the psychological level we would get passivity, apathy and ultimately sleep. Where there is resistance, individuals are called upon to assert themselves, awaken, become conscious – in short, to develop.

One task of education is therefore to provide the right kind of resistance or challenge at the right time. Another task is to offer supportive structures, which provide the child with both security and the opportunity to develop new abilities. This balance enables what the Russian psychologist Lev Vygotsky termed the child's 'zone of proximal development',[1] to expand. Based on what the child can do, support is given to enable the child to reach beyond into the realm of her potential. This technique of 'scaffolding'[2] in age-appropriate ways is fundamental to Waldorf education.

The central task of education, however, is to strengthen the 'I', the spiritual core of each individual child. Education seeks to assist the 'I' to integrate itself into its bodily organism, its rhythms and processes and to establish faculties with which to express itself and help it to relate to the world and other people in a socially fruitful way. The spiritual core of the individual and his or her life of thinking, feeling and willing have to grow together with the organism, in what Steiner referred to as the path of incarnation. This central task therefore is to stimulate and direct the child's self-activity within the learning process. Its goal is to support individuals as they progressively learn to direct and take responsibility for their own learning processes.

Education is such a familiar and obvious task in our society, that we rarely stop to consider why we educate children in the first place. If asked, most people would give the following reasons: children need certain essential skills and knowledge, which empower them to take their place in modern society. Further reasons may include the need for children to learn about culture and to cultivate their minds. Government has become increasingly interested in adding to the list of essential skills and knowledge, and dictating through legislation levels of attainment and their achievement. They often prescribe, on the advice of academics, the content of what should be learned.

Waldorf education sees a further and more basic reason for providing children with education. This addresses what is fundamentally human within us.

The young child follows her bodily instincts, her urges and drives, whose wonderful intelligence provides the inner impetus to stand upright, find equilibrium, move about, and learn language. However, if these will forces were deprived of close human example to imitate, the child's movements would be undirected and proto-language would never transform into full syntactical linguistic competence. Through imitation the forces of will within the young child are directed in such a way that they learn to adopt life rhythms, behaviour patterns, attitudes, ways of being and thinking that free the individual from the merely instinctive realm.

The school age child must apply her will to thinking, to the formation of memory, to forming of concepts and to all those important skills that the human being needs. Why then cannot children do this through continuing to observe and imitate what their elders do? Rudolf Steiner put this aspect into perspective by comparing the human being with the higher animals:

> *Insofar as we belong to the human kingdom and not to the animal kingdom, we must ask ourselves: why do we educate? Why do animals grow up to fulfil their tasks without having to be educated? Why do human beings have to bring up and educate human beings? Why do human beings not gain what they need for life simply by observing and imitating? Why must an educator, a teacher, interfere in a child's life? These are questions that usually remain unasked because the matter appears totally obvious.*
>
> *In actual fact the matter is this: between the child's seventh and fourteenth years we have to bring about the right relationship between thinking and the will. Otherwise it is possible that this might go wrong. With animals, in so far as they have a dreamlike kind of thinking and in so far as they have a will, these come together of their own accord. But with the human being thinking and will do not come together of their own accord, so that is why we educate. With animals it is a natural activity. With human beings it must become a moral activity. Human beings can become moral beings because here on earth they have the opportunity to bring thinking into their will. The whole character of the human being – in so far as it arises from within – rests on the proper harmony being established between thinking and will as a result of the individual's own efforts.* [3]

Thus we can see that the self-activity of the child has to be directed, initially through imitation and then through education.

The Task of the Teacher

The study of children is the heart of teacher development and therefore of curriculum development. Such study requires a continual broadening and deepening of our powers of observation. Just as reading reveals the thoughts of another person, so 'reading' the nature of a child reveals something of his or her inner being. In observing many children, we also discover what they have in common. Thus in learning to 'read' and understand the child, the archetype of human development reveals itself to the careful observer. Teaching is therefore a balance between knowing what supports the general development of children at a particular age and knowing what *this* child needs *now*. In this sense the Waldorf Curriculum is not so much 'child-centred', as centred on an understanding of child development.

Teachers have to familiarise themselves with the common path, the archetype of child development. They must be aware of the cultural and geographical landscape in which the school is embedded and observe how and when the children join or leave the common path. The curriculum is a means of making the common path visible.

The curriculum consists of subjects and experiences. The teacher has to understand what it is in each subject, in each school activity, that nourishes the child's development. The content of the curriculum works in different ways on the children at different ages. By their nature, the various subjects each represent a certain one-sidedness, hence the importance of the subjects complementing and supporting each other in interdisciplinary ways. This is the significance of developing transferable skills; abilities acquired in one realm of experience enhance those in another. The most profound of these correspondences is the inner link between manual, practical skills and cognitive development – nimble fingers really do make for nimble minds, but there are many such correspondences to be researched.

But content alone is a crude instrument. Far more subtle and effective is the teaching method. It is the task of the teacher and teachers working together, to research how the way we teach affects the children in their development. Steiner frequently indicated that how we teach can not only have immediate effects on the child's sense of well being but could also establish a long-term predisposition to ill health. [4] The corollary is of course equally true. Good teaching informs not only the mind but also supports bodily well being too. As far as I know there is, as yet, little empirical evidence to support this assertion. However, common sense tells us that one would only need to investigate the long-term health effects of stress, alienation or lack of engagement in education, to see the significance of this.

Thus we can see that flexible teaching methods can respond to individual needs through differentiation and through focus of emphasis on one or other aspect of the curriculum. Though this is very much a question of reviewing and planning lessons, it can also be necessary in the moment. It is this, which makes teaching a lively art.

The teacher can select from the educational tools at his or her disposal the right experience or teaching method for the child. Doing the right thing at the right time is only partly a question of considered preparation and empathetic observation. It is also sometimes a question of acting in the moment out of intuition. The insight needed to guide such intuition is the fruit of the individual teacher's own inner development. The Waldorf

Curriculum can therefore never be a prescribed curriculum based on outcomes deemed to be desirable by academics, or officials – or worse by politicians. What it can do, is provide a range of possible responses within the framework of the archetype of human development. Each step taken by the teacher can be observed and evaluated in terms of the children's response and this in turn is related to the developmental picture. The vital quality in this process is that it is a living, artistic, intuitive activity and never a mechanical, causal or predetermined one.

The Self-activity of the Teacher

Crucial to the task of stimulating the self-activity of the child is the teacher's own self-activity. This takes many forms but from a specifically educational perspective, one can see that the different phases of childhood and adolescence require this of the teacher in different ways.

In the Early Years period, the child assumes in an unreflected way that the world is good and filled with meaning. Everything the young child experiences works formatively on the processes of growth and maturation, especially movement and co-ordination, language development and the integration of sensory perception. The task of the adult and educator is to ensure that the child's learning environment is consciously structured in a meaningful way and that the sense impressions the child is exposed to are appropriate to her developmental needs. This 'nourishment' has therefore to be prepared and contextualised. This means, for example, that the materials the child comes in contact with should be of good and richly varied quality. This also means experiences should be real rather than virtual. The language a child hears should be natural, both in the sense of being live rather than electronically reproduced and in the sense of being rich in colloquial texture and clearly spoken. The activities should involve the child in practical ways related to everyday life and the changing seasons within daily and weekly rhythms that give the child a sense of continuity and orientation.

The young child's nature is to participate not reflect; therefore it is not the intellectual skills, which need to be stimulated, but the child's whole being through activity. This activity needs to be embedded in a meaningful context, rather than be random, non-sequential or abstract – in other words, out of context. The implicit teaching method is creating a context in which everything has its given time, place and purpose and which draws upon the child's innate faculty of imitation.

It is the teacher who provides coherence and meaning for the child's learning environment. The thought behind the rhythm is given by the teacher and intuitively rather than consciously taken in by the child. The self-activity of the teacher consists of careful preparation of the setting into which the child enters and the cultivation of a calm, caring attentiveness, including the appropriate tone of voice and gesture. In such an environment the child can feel secure and free to unfold through creative play in her own time. The supportive presence and presence of mind of the teacher are what the young child needs most.

The Role of the Teacher in the Lower and Middle Schools

The school age child assumes that the world can be explored, experienced and discovered and wants to know that the world is interesting, beautiful and ordered within an integrated whole. It is the teacher's task to present and represent such a world. From the age of 7 onwards, but particularly from the ninth year onwards, the child can increasingly form a more conscious inner relationship to the world. In this period, which leads up to puberty and adolescence, it is the child's soul life that most needs new nourishment. The formative processes that were active in forming and maturing the bodily organism and its reflection in the neural structures of the brain, now increasingly become active in forming and differentiating the child's inner experience. The nature of the child's mind in this stage of life is essentially pictorial and imaginative – indeed the first signs of the child's ability to form mental pictures independently of outer sensory stimulation through memory, mark the beginning of this period.

It is the teacher's task to provide the child with experiences that both cultivate and strengthen this process. Learning to use symbols, as in writing, reading and arithmetic, is an important aspect of this. So too is the conscious development of memory through repetition and recall. The cultivation of conceptual and later logical or deductive thinking, are stages in the progression of this process, up to and beyond the twelfth year. Yet in all these processes, the pictorial and narrative nature of the child's inner life has to be nurtured, the parts have to relate to the whole, and the child's own being is always the point of reference for the whole.

This means, especially in the period between the seventh and twelfth years but also in modified form throughout schooling, that the world has to be initially understood in anthropomorphic terms, since that is what the child can best relate to. This means not only fairy tales, fables, legends and myths in which archetypal human experiences are clothed in images, but also that in discovering the animal, plant and mineral worlds, the children discover the animal, plant or mineral qualities in themselves. Nature has, in a sense, to be humanised in order that the child can form a relationship to it.

The teacher exemplifies and directs this process of 'humanising' the world. Just as the infant needs a humanised nourishment in the form of milk, the young child needs a humanised environment such as that provided by the structured and rhythmical activities in the Kindergarten and the school age child needs the world to be presented in humanised form.

That means the teacher has first to form a strong and living connection to the subjects she teaches, not merely know about them, but make them a part of herself. This is not the same as being an expert. It means having immersed herself in the subject to the point where she has formed a personal connection to it. In terms of knowledge, the teacher of children of this age needs only to know *somewhat more* than the children will be taught. Adolescents require that their teachers are subject specialists. More importantly, however, the teacher must have grasped something of the essential quality of the subject.

How is this acquired? There are two fundamental points of access. Firstly the teacher is expected to have an experiential basis in the subject, that is to have worked with it, literally *done* it before, and also to have a good overview of its scope. Furthermore, this experience has to have had time to mature (i.e. not read up the previous weekend). Secondly the teacher must have a good idea why it is that this subject needs to be taught in a certain way to certain age children. This approach asks: what effect does this subject have on these children? Why should I teach it? The answer to these questions is the counterbalance to questions like: what is there to know about the Middle Ages, granite, compound interest, past tense etc.? It is obviously not the teacher's task to know and then teach everything there is to know about these subjects. It is the teacher's task to make these subjects relevant to the children and to do so in such a way that they learn to form a relationship to them. The children need to learn how to use the knowledge that belongs to these subjects to understand the world. Above all, the children need to develop abilities that enable them in later life to direct their own learning.

The teacher has to prepare, one could almost say 'pre-digest' knowledge and present experiences which engage the children's own self-activity and interest. Even when the children are to learn through their own direct experience, which should be encouraged, the teacher still has to prepare the experience by having done it herself so that the subsequent process of making the experience conscious through discussion, recalling, relating, forming concepts and so on, can be directed by the teacher. This is the basis for the teacher's authority.

Whilst the young child imitates the teacher's inner and outer activity in an unreflected way, the school age child has to learn how to learn from the teacher. The main advantage of having a class teacher and a group of subject teachers over many years in this period of schooling, is that the children can experience how their teachers progressively translate the world and show them how to enter it. In the first primary classes this is essentially a very teacher-led process. As the children grow older, their own self-directed activity becomes stronger. The input of the teacher in the classroom becomes less and less, though her preparation certainly increases.

The Role of the Teacher in the Upper School

The transition to Upper School involves a shift of focus in the activity of the teacher. If the soul of the child has to be nourished in the class teacher period, it is the thinking spirit that needs to be awakened in the Upper School. The students seek ideas that can lead them through their own activity to ideals. The Upper School students not only expect their teachers to be experts in their fields but they need to know that the teachers draw their own ideals from their work, indeed from their lives. The students do not expect their teachers necessarily to reveal the truth in any absolute sense, but they do expect the teachers to show them that the truth *can* be found. And they want to know, in each subject, *how* higher meaning and relevance can be discovered. What this requires in terms of the inner activity of the teacher is on-going research. When the students experience that their teachers are continuously deepening both their understanding of their subject and their understanding of the nature of the human being, their own inner activity receives encouragement, recognition and stimulus.

Naturally, being able to teach, which means enabling children to learn, is the primary skill teachers need. Students and pupils of all ages usually have a very good sense for what constitutes good teaching. Yet being a good teacher is not only about being proficient in the classroom, it means having the inner qualities, which address the children's development in equally real, though less visible ways.

The Social Task

Naturally, any curriculum drawn up by educationalists will have broad areas of commonality since there is much intrinsic logic within a given field of knowledge. It would be surprising if there were not broad areas of overlap between different curricula. How and when an experience is brought to children, however, has to be an area of judgment by teachers who know their children. The Waldorf Curriculum is essentially aimed at supporting the healthy balanced development of the individual. The outcome of this process is to equip the individual to participate in and contribute to society. It is not primarily driven by learning outcomes, which are merely subject- or skills-orientated.

While the teaching approach can and should respond to individual needs, the curriculum content is aimed at peer groups. Since one of the crucial factors in human development is the role of social processes, no curriculum can be wholly individually orientated. Children learn with and from each other. Sharing experiences with others at broadly the same stage of development is more productive and enriching than learning alone. Thus Waldorf education's emphasis is on whole class mixed ability learning groups. Each lesson and learning process requires a balance of primary experience, social interaction – through discussion, listening, working together and so on – and working alone. Each of these elements is essential; their balance will depend on the given situation.

Thus it is helpful for a group of 20-30 children of the same age to share major learning experiences in a class together. Within such a group there will be a very wide range of responses. Perceiving and appreciating this spectrum is deeply rewarding for the learning individual in helping to provide insight into other individuals' ways of relating to the lesson content. In such a group the living archetype of development is present in the richly diverse expressions of the children.

Those key phases of childhood development, such as school readiness and the change of teeth, the ninth year, the twelfth year transition, puberty and so on, are all marked by significant shifts of emphasis and the introduction of new activities and learning methods within the Waldorf Curriculum. Within this framework the teacher has many possibilities to accelerate or slow down the tempo, to vary the balance of cognitive, emotional or willing elements, to choose narrative material with specific individuals in mind and to differentiate the tasks.

Guidelines

The teacher is artist and professional educator. As artist the teacher is responsible to the being of the child. As a professional, he or she has a wider responsibility to the requirements of parents, authorities and the State. Society rightly has expectations of outcomes and standards, of accountability and comparison, not merely if it is paying for it. As long as learning outcomes, and more particularly the time-frame for such expectations, are based on an understanding of normal child development, they are perfectly legitimate. Where learning outcomes run counter to the nature of childhood and may for some children even be harmful – the premature introduction of formal literacy skills for example – then education has lost its way. The crucial question is who determines learning outcomes and what criteria are used? Clearly classroom experience is essential and an objective study of how children develop and learn.

The purpose of writing down guidelines for the Waldorf Curriculum is also to set out a framework for developing appropriate attainment targets and their range of levels. This feature should in no way be confused with the living archetype of human development, which can only be observed through children as intuitive knowledge. As professional teachers, we need both our intuitive insight based on experience *and* guidelines that benchmark in a formal way the parameters for evaluation. For this reason this curriculum describes aims and objectives and then gives possible teaching content through which those goals can be achieved. Within those guidelines there have to be minimum expectations of both content and levels of attainment. Those given here are of a provisional nature since the entire curriculum is conceived of as a working document. We have provided guidelines for basic skills levels and attainments for numeracy and literacy in the Lower School, ages 7-14. The selection of these two subjects, and the exclusion of all others, is simply because they are the most readily comparable with other educational approaches. It is of course equally possible to draw up similar guidelines for minimum skill levels in movement, in musical ability, in crafts, in the natural sciences and even social skills. Every teacher has expectations of his or her pupils when they teach them. The difficulty is how to define and evaluate skills which can be less easily observed. We have addressed the question of evaluation in a special section 4.

The editor and the advisory group expect and look forward to comment, especially on these areas.

Tasks for the Future

The challenge of curriculum research is on-going. The rapid growth of Waldorf schools in the Eastern European countries of the former Soviet Bloc, Asia and Africa has highlighted an issue that has actually been there since the very first schools were founded in Europe after the 'Mother School' in Stuttgart. How does a curriculum get transferred from one place to another? However faithful the new school is to the tradition, there are bound to be changes simply by virtue of the fact that different people are doing it in a different place.

In the first two generations of the Waldorf schools movement and during the initial expansion to other European countries, to South and North America, what we actually saw on the whole, was local variation within fairly strongly traditional forms. This trend was indeed enhanced by the arrival before and during the Second World War of Waldorf teachers escaping as refugees from the Nazi regime. Many of them brought with them to their new adopted countries passionate memories and a wealth of experience of Waldorf. Their contribution to the development of Waldorf education in South Africa, Brazil, the United States and Britain has been profound. Wonderful though their contribution was, it also had something of an inhibiting factor.

Even up until the last decade or so there were schools half a world away that aspired to a version of Waldorf education that their founders had brought with them from Middle Europe. European, even Germanic curriculum content such as Norse mythology, Goethe and Schiller, continued to be taught, rather than literature arising out of the vernacular and local culture. Pioneers always tend to have something of the missionary about them. Without the conviction they would never achieve the impossible founding of Waldorf schools in unlikely places. The irony in many ways is that the Stuttgart Mother School and the whole generation of Waldorf schools re-founded in Germany after the Second World War have probably evolved further than those at the periphery (seen from the Middle European perspective). What passed as the original tradition or way of doing things had long since been superseded in the heartland.

There has of course been a counter reaction, as one would expect within a movement of creative individualists such as one finds typically working in Waldorf education. In some countries, notably Australia, Waldorf schools have been founded that have radically turned their backs on the entire European heritage and rigorously built their curriculum on native Australian myth and legend, on working rhythms that reflect the specific climate and landscape of that part of the world. In schools in which the celebration of the Christian festivals plays such an important role in the life of the community, how can one celebrate the redemptive, renewing character of spring in association with Easter, when nature is doing something else, let alone sing 'In the Bleak Midwinter' on the beach? Of course, the inner aspect of this problem is far subtler.

Another issue related to the growth of new Waldorf schools in countries without an established tradition is the increasing demand made by the State that the new education prove itself. This means documenting the curriculum, providing evidence of its effectiveness. Where only a handful of schools have maintained a precarious existence, starved of resources with often few trained staff, the understandable tendency is to ask abroad for help. Faced with a sceptical Ministry of Education, such young schools are forced to import, as it were, a curriculum that been evolved and developed elsewhere, into a different society with entirely different preconditions as regards training and so on. What is actually needed is time for a curriculum to evolve out of the local culture.

These and other problems simply highlight certain fundamental questions which Waldorf education needs to address within its on-going process of inner renewal. I would like to identify the following questions which are already being worked on to some extent but which need to find a broader basis within the work of schools and teacher training.

1. The documentation of good practice in Waldorf education in different countries. This volume has been an attempt to do this for Britain and Europe (since the original research was done in Austria and Germany). Similar work needs to be done in other countries with one or more generations of schools. This would be helpful in many ways, not least in showing which curriculum contents are typically appropriate at which ages. Are there regional variations in the pattern of cognitive development, for example? Can one introduce the 'rule of three' (if, then, therefore) at the same age all over the world? One can find many other fruitful questions of this nature.

2. Another aspect of this task would be to collect and review narrative content, stories, fables, legends and myths which are typically told to certain age groups in different countries, other than those recommended by the European curriculum. Comparison would show what they had in common. If children go through similar stages of psychological development all over the world and benefit from certain narrative motifs at certain ages, we would expect to find similar elements in myths from different cultures. What would the South African equivalent to Norse myths at the age of ten years be? It may well be that certain aspects of Norse mythology are universal and may be told anywhere. It may be that it is only the stories of the Gods that have these qualities, the myths of the heroes having more local folk-soul relevance. Again, one could pose many other similar questions at different points of the curriculum.

3. A subtle aspect of this question is the relationship of European based or influenced cultural mentality, ways of seeing, patterns of thinking in non-European contexts and the actual native heritage. Clearly white, black or coloured South African children have to deal with both cultural elements. They live in a world whose dominant cultural patterns are Western and American-European, yet whose environment is African. Each child belongs to a people, a language group, a cultural (or culturally fragmented) context. Each has to find their way in the modern world. Yet each sleeps under an African sky and walks on African earth. Finding the balance between the culture that arises out of the *spirit of the place* and that which arises out of the *spirit of the times* is a challenge for every Waldorf school, no matter where it is.

4. Research is also needed into ways in which the teaching approach and the different activities within the curriculum actually work on the children's development. It is clear that Steiner in his discussions with the teachers of the first Waldorf school was concerned that these effects be understood and very consciously worked with. This is an area which requires far more study.

5. There is also need for research into the techniques and methods of individual child study and in particular into approaches which can take account of the child's developmental potential.

6. We also need to find better ways of bringing all these research questions into school based study in ways which enhance the on-going process of educational development, so that the insights gained from the classroom can flow back into to teaching quickly and effectively.

These and many other questions form the process of educational renewal and it is intrinsic to Waldorf education that they are not only dealt with in specialist groups separated from real school life: each school must become a research institute in its own right. It may be that specialist groups, say within the Pedagogical Section of the School for Spiritual Science, or within national Waldorf associations, can help co-ordinate and publish the results of such work, but the core activity must live within the schools themselves.

Martyn Rawson
Forest Row, September 1999

References
1 Vygotsky, L., *Thought and Language*, MIT Press, 1962.
2 This term was coined by the American psychologist Jerome Bruner to describe the support adults give during phases when a child is acquiring new skills.
3 Steiner, R., *A Modern Art of Education*, lecture of 8th August 1923, RSP 1981.
4 Steiner, R., *Conferences with Teachers*, 4 volumes, meeting of 6th February 1923, SSF 1989-92.

1.0 ANTHROPOSOPHY AS THE BASIS FOR STEINER WALDORF EDUCATION

Steiner Waldorf education is founded on Rudolf Steiner's (1861-1925) understanding of the human being, which was based on empirical study and observation, enhanced by his direct insight into psychological and spiritual realities. This body of knowledge has been supplemented and supported by considerable research done within the Waldorf movement over the past 80 years and which is described in an extensive secondary literature in various languages.

Steiner's understanding of the nature of the human being formed the central part of a philosophy and cosmology that he called *anthroposophy*. [1] Steiner was asked by the industrialist Emil Molt to establish the first Waldorf School in Stuttgart in 1919, initially for the children of the workers at the Waldorf Astoria cigarette factory. He was the school's director until his death in 1925. During this time he gave a number of courses to the teachers, visited lessons and regularly attended teachers' meetings. The original curriculum was developed and introduced by Steiner and then underwent further development under his guidance and through the initiative of the teachers at the Stuttgart school. Since then, what has become known as the Waldorf Curriculum, has naturally evolved and been adapted to changing cultural and geographical circumstances and is now used in over 780 schools in some 40 countries.

Anthroposophy forms the epistemological and anthropological basis for Steiner Waldorf education, though its content is not taught in the schools. Its insights and ethos, however, inform the curriculum and provide the teachers with a body of ideas with which they as individuals work and from which they derive inspiration. Steiner himself described anthroposophy as *"a path of knowledge that seeks to lead the spiritual in the human being to the spiritual in the universe."* [2]

A central aspect of anthroposophy is the possibility of the spiritual development of the individual. Steiner published a number of guidelines for individuals who wish to undertake such a path of moral and spiritual development, designed to enable individuals to enhance their moral strength, sharpen their perceptive faculties and extend their thinking capacities and powers of judgment. Fundamental to this path of knowledge is meditation, by which Steiner meant that the individual should establish a rhythm in his or her daily life of regular concentration and focus of consciousness in *"devotion to a particular mental image, thought-feeling or act of will"*. [3] Such discipline in thinking is intensified through various concentration exercises in the direction of a selfless, unrestricted and alert form of pure thinking. The preconditions for such inner development by the individual were described by Steiner as: *"(self-)control over the direction of his thoughts, control over his impulses of will, equanimity in the face of pleasure and pain, positivity in his attitude to the world around him, readiness to meet life with an open mind"*. [4] The moral and personal qualities that accompany such disciplined thinking are patience, calm, respect, reverence, devotion to the truth, honesty with regard to facts, enthusiasm for work, interest in the world, love and gratitude towards others and responsibility for one's deeds.

Steiner maintained that spiritual insight, such as he himself possessed, can be developed by any individual to a greater or lesser extent. He always insisted that the spiritual insights that he spoke of publicly and described in his books were all verifiable by anyone who schooled their powers of thinking and observation in an appropriate way. His consistent recommendation to the teachers was to work with the ideas he suggested and use them only if they proved to be fruitful through experience.

Since many of Steiner's ideas and insights were radical and often unfamiliar, he developed a specific terminology to describe the phenomena recognised by anthroposophy. Much of this terminology is unconventional and is often used only in anthroposophical circles. Some of it is difficult to translate from the German. Such terms are of course only labels, the phenomena they describe being more important. In this book the authors have attempted to use conventional language wherever possible.

Anthroposophical anthropology

Whilst it is not within the scope of this book to give a detailed account of the anthroposophical anthropology that underpins Steiner Waldorf education, some essential aspects need to be briefly explained.

Steiner Waldorf education starts from the premise that each human being comprises body, soul and spirit. The process of human maturation and individuation is essentially one in which the individual spirit, referred to as the 'I' or Ego, seeks to fashion a bodily vessel in which it can live and experience the physical world and through which it can express itself. As Steiner himself put it, the human being is a citizen of three different worlds: *"In body, we both belong to and perceive the outer world; in soul, we build up our own inner world; and in spirit, a third world that is higher than both of the others reveals itself to us"*. [5]

The physical body is that part of the human being that is directly sense perceptible and through which the individual is connected with and embedded in the material world. In the soul, the human being builds an inner world of personal experience which relates the individual to the outer world and which expresses itself in the form of thinking, feeling and willing. Through the spirit or 'I', the world reveals its real or complete nature to the individual.

Steiner made an even more specific differentiation than the traditional threefold distinction between body, soul and spirit in describing a fourth discrete part or body. The body of formative forces (also referred to by him variously as the temporal body, habit body, body of formative forces, life body or etheric body) comprises all those forces which enable the physical body to function as an organism and which regulate the life rhythms, growth, regeneration and reproductive processes. As well as these organic functions, the body of formative forces also supports certain activities within the soul and is the bearer of patterns of habitual behaviour, constitutional characteristics, memory and the activity of mental picturing. The body of formative forces also constitutes the activity of thinking, mediating between the physical organs of the nervous system and the experience of the soul, thus enabling these organs to function as instruments of the soul and spirit.

Within the soul itself Steiner distinguished between various levels or modalities, namely sensation (the sentient body) and experience (sentient soul). The first is the realm of bodily sensation produced through the activity of the sense organs, the second is the inner experience felt by the individual in relation to the sensation. The sentient body organises sensory processes to the point at which sensation arises. In the sentient soul the individual experiences those sensations.

The sentient soul is also the bearer of urges, drives such as hunger, self defence, aggression, sexual arousal, and emotions such as fear, pleasure, aversion, desire, satisfaction and so on, which have their origin in bodily and instinctive processes. As human beings we do not have to blindly react to our drives, instincts and passions. We can think about them and thus set about gratifying or ignoring them. Most of our material culture is the result of thought power applied to meeting the needs felt by our sentient soul.

Through the activity of thinking we have access to higher meaning, to laws and principles that are inherent in the world beyond our personal lives. In seeking knowledge and truth we make a connection to that which has an independent existence beyond our experience of it. If something is true, it is not merely true for me in this moment but has a universal validity. As Steiner put it: *"We must realise that the truth, in itself, endures, even though our thoughts are only transient manifestations of eternal truths".* [6] This is also true of moral values: *"what is morally right, like what is true, has an intrinsic eternal value that it receives from the spiritual soul".* [7] Where the human soul is ennobled or enlightened by eternal truth, spiritual reality comes to expression. Only at this level is the soul freed from biological determination, the compulsion of self-orientated desires, such as grasping or aversion and the emotions of sympathy and antipathy.

Though consciousness obviously exists at the mundane level of sensation of pain and pleasure, full consciousness is only present in the human mind when it raises its focus of attention beyond the awareness of bodily states or emotional, subjective content.

Through consciousness of self, the individual achieves a sense of identity. We use the word 'I' to describe the totality of this experience. Just as the brain is the integrating centre for the physical organism as perceived through the senses, so the 'I' is the focus for the soul. The body and soul react to stimulation from outside. However, through the process of individuation, the 'I' increasingly becomes the centre from which the individual directs intentional action. *"We are justified in seeing the 'I' as our true being, and may therefore describe body and soul as the 'garments' in which we live, as the bodily conditions under which we act. In the course of our development we learn to use these instruments more and more as servants of our 'I'."* [8] Through the 'I', spirit lives and comes to expression in the human being.

Individuation

The individuation process, in which education plays a very significant, supportive role, involves a progressive shift of the activity of the 'I' in integrating into the other bodies described above. At birth the 'I' is primarily active within the physical body. At around the age of 7 some of the forces of the life body gradually become superfluous to their organic functions and emancipate themselves from the physical organism. They thus become available to support the emergence of a distinctive inner life and particularly to enable the process of mental picturing and the formation of memory, two processes essential to learning. Before this emancipation has occurred, the child learns through imitation rather than through understanding, since sense experience passes relatively unmediated by the mind into the activity of the child. Once the formative forces of the life body begin to free themselves, the child can increasingly form and structure an inner life of experience. Whilst memory is still closely bound to the organism it will be situational rather than independent. Only once memory can function independently of sensory stimulus, is abstract thought possible.

At puberty the soul activities of thinking, feeling and willing, which have hitherto been integrated into the processes of the physical organs and subsequently within the body of life processes, begin to emancipate themselves. The 'I' becomes active within the soul in aiding the young person to make judgments, form independent concepts and gradually direct their own behaviour according to conscious intentions motivated by ideals.

It will be clear from even this very brief characterisation that it is a central task of education to support the self-activity of the 'I' in each child in integrating the various bodies in such a way that healthy, harmonious development can occur. Supporting the self-activity of the individual is essential in realising his or her potential to the fullest extent. All aspects of education serve that aim.

Rudolf Steiner made the relationship between anthroposophy and Waldorf education very clear when he addressed parents at the newly founded first Waldorf School:

> You absolutely do not need to be afraid that we are trying to make this school into one that represents a particular philosophy, or that we intend to drum any anthroposophical or other dogmas into the children. That is not what we have in mind. Anyone who says that we are trying to teach the children specifically anthroposophical convictions is not telling the truth. Rather, we are trying to develop an art of education on the basis of what anthroposophy means to us. The 'how' of education is what we are trying to gain from our spiritual understanding. We are not trying to drum our opinions into the children, but we believe that spiritual science differs from any other science in engaging the entire person, in making people skilful in all areas, but especially in their dealings with other human beings. This 'how' is what we are trying to look at, not the 'what'. The 'what' is the result of social necessities; we must apply our full interest to deriving it from a reading of what people should know and be able to do if they are to take their place in our times as good, capable individuals. The 'how', on the other hand, how to teach the children something, can only result from a thorough, profound and loving understanding of the human being. This is what is meant to work and to prevail in our Waldorf School. [9]

---

* Please note: references 1 – 9 are on page 31.

2.0 THE STAGES OF DEVELOPMENT IN RELATION TO THE CURRICULUM

> *The ideal curriculum must be modelled on the changing image of the human being passing through different phases while growing up. But like any ideal it is confronted by the reality of life and must accommodate itself accordingly. This reality comprises many things: the individuality of the teacher, the class itself with all the peculiarities of every pupil in it, the moment in history, the education authorities and education laws prevailing at the place where the school wanting to implement the curriculum is located. All these factors modify the ideal curriculum and call for transformation and discussion. The educational task with which the growing human being confronts us can only be achieved if the curriculum remains mobile and pliable.*
>
> Caroline von Heydebrand

Steiner Waldorf education recognises three basic stages in child development: 0 to 7 years, 7 to 14 years and 14 to 21 years. In educational terms this covers the Early Years period of 3 to 6 years, the Lower School period from 6 to 14 years and the Upper School from 15 to 19 years. Each of these stages is marked by significant and specific developments in physical, psychological and spiritual maturation. The following descriptions are of necessity only a summary.

Whilst each stage represents a phase of life, integral and distinct in its own right, each metamorphoses into the next. Processes coming to a certain culmination in one phase transform into faculties in the subsequent stage of development.

The Early Years stage, for example, is seen as a valid state of being *in its own right*, and not merely a preparation for the following stages of life. In fact since so much depends on the healthy development of the young child's whole being, Early Years education is viewed with increasing importance in education as a whole. For this reason, Early Years education has a high profile in Steiner Waldorf education where practitioners have always been accorded equal status within the teaching profession. Given the increasing pressures on young children and the loss of many traditional forms of nurture and support in the contemporary environment, Early Years education needs greater research, teacher development, parent education and resources than ever before.

2.1 Ages 0-7 Early Years

In the first three years, the infant is actively growing and adapting his or her organism to the demands of its needs. This wonderfully complex process may be encapsulated in the achievement of balance and upright walking, the acquisition of language and the establishing of the basis for cognition. If we add to this, the equally important task of learning to relate to other people and becoming members of society as represented by the extended circle of family and friends, one can only relate to these achievements with the profoundest respect. What the very young child needs most of all is healthy nutrition, care and, above all, love. As interactive beings from the very start, children thrive on loving attention, communication and the security of being an integral part of human society.

In this phase, the young child learns primarily through imitation and play. Children absorb and digest their experiences in a largely unconscious way. Learning is *caught rather than taught*, that is to say, through implicit rather than explicit teaching methods. Children need a secure, caring and structured environment where activities occur in a meaningful context. What they experience is turned into activity, which in turn plays a part in forming their organism as a whole. In this way imitation actually educates the physical organism as well as establishing the mother tongue, habits and patterns of behaviour.

Play is a serious and vital activity of early childhood. Through play the powers of creativity, imagination and initiative are cultivated. In play children learn to relate. In the Early Years phase the task of education is to provide an environment in which good habits of behaviour, such as memory, reverence, orderliness, listening and enjoyment of the natural world can be established.

2.2 School Readiness

During their first six or seven years children are immensely active in their senses, while at the same time having little ability to filter their sense impressions. They are uninhibitedly open to their surroundings and accept anything they find there. They therefore need adults and an environment that can set worthy examples for them. Once this formative process has reached a certain degree of completion, especially in the brain, the forces that have shaped the organs and established the rhythm of their processes are gradually released. They have a potential beyond the establishment and maintenance of the life rhythms and organic processes. This potential emerges around the age of six. On being emancipated from the physical organism, these formative forces progressively become accessible to education. This is the moment when children can be considered ready for formal school learning. These formative forces are now active in enabling the child to form mental pictures, in establishing memory, learning and the focusing of attention. If these forces are prematurely called upon by formal learning of literacy or numeracy, for example, it can lead to a loss of vitality and a narrowing of the experiential basis for subsequent learning to build on.

Likewise if children do not have the opportunity between the ages of 5 and 6 years to apply their imaginative will to the social tasks of being with and helping others in an unreflected and intuitive way, their subsequent social competence may be limited in its development. Up until the age of around 4 years, young children tend to play *alongside* other children. From this age on they tend to play increasingly with their peers and engage, given the right encouragement, in constructive social interaction through creative play. This marks a significant development, which needs time to mature and become structured. Many children are quite capable of applying their intelligence to tasks such as learning to read and write. The question is: Shouldn't this intelligence be given time to develop a social awareness of others through creative play? Without this, literacy can become an anti-social activity, rather than a means of communicating and sharing. The listening and oral language skills, the social interaction and initiative that children can develop at this age in a structured Kindergarten setting should not be underestimated. If the early years period is essentially characterised by the child's will in activity, this last part of the first seven year phase is important for the development of will in the social and feeling realm.

One external sign that the main bodily organs are more or less established in their functions and that the integration of these functions is to a great extent harmonised, is the onset of the second dentition in which the milk teeth are replaced by the far more substantial (and individually distinct) permanent teeth. This must be distinguished from the actual completion of the full second set of teeth, which can take years.

There is a whole range of other symptoms indicating the freeing of the formative forces which show that the child is ready to make the transition to formal learning in school, the change of teeth being only one of the more obvious but by no means determining criteria. These include co-ordination of movement, certain memory abilities such as the ability to perceive, recall and reproduce shapes and figures that have been shown to the child as well as the emotional independence and strength to leave the security of the parents and Kindergarten teacher. Nowadays it is becoming increasingly difficult to assess children's readiness for school and it is by no means an automatic question of chronological age, maturity or ability. Long-term factors need to be borne in mind and the advice of a group of professionals including Kindergarten teacher, class teacher and school doctor is often sought. Delaying school entry can sometimes be as unhelpful as pushing precocious children.[10]

Ultimately how we understand the nature of the curriculum proves decisive. Asking: Is the child ready for Class 1? is one perspective. Saying the child needs Class 1 in order to begin the process of maturation that comes with formal schooling and its introduction to literacy and numeracy, is a completely different perspective on the function of the curriculum. It is the difference between asking is she ready to do this or that and asking does she now need to do this or that in terms of her whole development. Such decisions can only be taken on an individual basis.

2.3   Ages 7 – 14 Childhood

During this stage, children begin formal learning; and the intellectual development of the child is fostered through the establishment of basic learning skills and the development of memory in a way that is firmly rooted in practical life. All learning at this stage seeks to engage the feelings of the child so that a strong personal identification with the subject matter can occur. Learning is essentially experiential; and strong and continuous narrative structures with an element of personification are used to enhance direct experience. Imagination is the key quality, and pictorial imagery is a vital factor in making learning a personal inner experience. Art and music play an important role in engaging the child's feelings. This period has distinct sub-phases: up to the age of 9, between 9 and 12 and from 12 to 14. These stages are marked by, among other things, specific cognitive developments and the changing relationship of self to the world.

2.4   Ages 7 to 9

One of the main characteristics of children between the seventh and ninth year is their desire to learn, without any need to form their own judgments. Memory, imagination, enjoyment of rhythmical repetition and a desire for universal concepts presented in picture form, are a part of this stage. Unquestioning acceptance of adults remains strong but now it changes from being a matter of imitating what their senses tell them to concentrating on a particular role model who affects the child not only through words but also by the way he or she acts in life. A child's inner question to the teacher is: 'Can you really see who I am?' and: 'Can you help me encounter the world?' This determines the teacher's position and relationship in regard to the child. These basic questions are answered in and through the lessons which aim not only to teach about experiencing the world but also to let the children actually experience the world. The teacher who succeeds in meeting these expectations set by the children will be accepted by them as an authority.

The first two or three years of school still retain an echo of the age of imitation. The children do not yet have any strong desire to make a distinction between 'me' and the world; and there is as yet no sharp distinction between what is inanimate and what is alive. The teaching takes account of this and the lessons therefore provide sufficient space for learning through direct experiencing. Cognitive abilities are not valued more highly than social, emotional and volitional learning. The period between 7 and 9 is still characterised by strong forces of imitation and situational memory. From 9 onwards the children increasingly stand back and question given authorities.

2.5   The Ninth Year

The first experience of separation comes at around nine years of age i.e. in Class 3. Now the children notice a stronger division between themselves and the grown-ups. Unconsciously at first, they begin to question the teacher's authority, which they have hitherto accepted unquestioningly as being almost like a law of nature. They now want to know whether what the teacher says really is securely based on a wide-ranging experience of the world and of life. On the whole this question remains at the sub-conscious level and is rarely put verbally. The children now want to admire a person where formerly they loved in a childlike way, but they want to know that their admiration is justified. This means that a new teaching method is called for. The aspects of the world presented in school have to take account of this distancing process, while at the same time the children need to be accompanied and supported in the right way as they step out of the golden background of childhood into the colourful reality of a world differentiated by a new, if naive, perspective. In other words, confronting them with the world as it really is does not mean that they must immediately be presented with cold or sobering scientific facts entirely detached from human life. As the 'loss of paradise' is increasingly felt, each individual child needs to be shown how he or she is a unique centre relating outwards to the environment. Between the ages of 9 and 12, rhythmical memory is at its strongest and children can learn a great deal at this age if the teaching method draws on the child's natural interest in the world and structures the content rhythmically.

2.6   Ages 10 to 12

Children begin a new phase of development between their tenth and twelfth years. By the ages of 12 their harmonious physical proportions typical for the middle period of childhood have usually been lost. The limbs begin to predominate and the muscular system becomes increasingly important. Psychologically there is an obviously critical attitude, and the children's newly won capacity to think causally must now be taken into account. The intellectuality now preparing to claim its right to be heard must be pointed in the appropriate direction by the teacher. The pupils' questioning, searching attitude should be directed increasingly towards inanimate nature and its laws. They want to find out about laws which exist independently of humanity and remain valid in spite of this. It is important, however, that a strong personal and subjective element is retained, with the children knowing that those who are doing the searching and discovering are still human beings and not some incomprehensible instruments. The children sense that not only space but also time has to be structured. This means that they need to learn about historical processes. History is shown to have been shaped by human beings who are in turn changed by historical forces, and not merely peopled by two dimensional historical figures attached to dates in the abstract. History can be both causal and passionate!

2.7   From 12 to 14

The final third of this second seven year phase is characterised by the range of symptoms we label puberty. The visible physiological changes and rapid growth are accompanied by psychological upheaval at least as disorientating and often more so. In both realms the child loses whatever balance and equanimity they have acquired in the heart of childhood. Teachers and parents come up against the limits of their abilities to directly influence the children. Much that has been adopted in terms of behaviour, attitudes or habits is lost or becomes ambivalent. As their inner life and self-experience becomes increasingly introspective and self-centred, the young adolescent increasingly needs a new, more objective orientation from teachers and parents. From 12 onwards children are increasingly able to form abstract concepts and understand causal relationships. This phase sees the introduction of exact observation and the transition from myth to history.

In this first phase of puberty the children have a strong urge to take hold of, even to 'conquer' the world around them. This essentially aggressive gesture is, however, on the whole a rough kind of playfulness. Challenging them physically can help them extricate themselves from this. The class teacher will endeavour to direct their attention away from themselves and towards the way the natural (and technical) world around them functions. Technology, profession and work become important themes.

> *The most important aspect of educating young people of this age is to educate their will. If this can be achieved, the youngsters can find their home in the 'outside world' step by step. Only by focusing on specific activities in the world can they gain ever new experiences about the partial sovereignty of their own inner being over this world. They also learn that this sovereignty can be extended, although each extension is only achieved as the result of considerable effort.*[11]

When young people seeking to find a new orientation in the world discover that other, older individuals are also engaged in inner battles, it can help them considerably to appreciate the other's questions, ideals, frustrations and limitations. But they must be left sufficiently free if these discoveries are to be a help to them. The more isolated young people feel in the world, the more they will long for and seek for an holistic view of the world to provide their orientation. They now have a growing interest in the interrelation of the traditional disciplines of science. These needs and experiences must govern the teacher's decisions as to method and teaching approach.

In Classes 1 to 3 the teacher had to be a master of the 'language of the universe' and make it audible for the children. In the second phase he or she had to articulate the dialogue between world phenomena and the human being. Now, as the youngsters fall silent outwardly in the third phase, the teacher must develop the capacity to hear their inner speech, the young people's hidden words.

2.8   Adolescence

In this phase the adolescent is developing the powers of independent judgment and the striving towards truth. The worlds of culture and nature need to reveal their inner principles in clear, objective and inspiring ways. Adolescents need to nurture their emerging inner selves with ideals worthy of their attention. Teaching methods become increasingly conceptual and cognitive. While independent inquiry and self-directed tasks are promoted throughout the entire curriculum, the focus now shifts to a more analytical and self-determined approach to learning. Students should learn to view the world from a range of different perspectives. The Upper School curriculum provides a broad basis of learning and prepares the students for access to further and higher education.

2.9   School Structure

The school structure reflects the major developmental phases.

Fully developed Steiner Waldorf schools are integrated pre-school, primary and secondary schools, usually on one site, under a single management. They comprise:

- PRE-SCHOOL
  Parent and Child groups
  Playgroup/Nursery provision   3-4 year-olds
  Kindergartens   Up to 6 year-olds
                                       Groups of up to 20 children with Kindergarten teacher and assistant.
  Afternoon Care Provision

- LOWER SCHOOL   Classes 1-8 ages 6-14

- UPPER SCHOOL   Classes 9-12 ages 14-18/19

Children enter Class 1, age 6. In many smaller schools two age groups are combined in one class, e.g. Class 2/3 are aged 7-9. All classes are of mixed ability and gender. Class sizes range from 12-30 pupils per class.

3.0   THE STEINER WALDORF APPROACH

This section describes key aspects of the SW approach, focusing primarily on the Lower School (ages 6-14).

3.1   The Class Teacher

Each class has a class teacher who moves up the school with the class. Ideally the class teacher remains with the class for eight years, though sometimes circumstances dictate otherwise.

The class teacher teaches the main morning lesson comprising the first two hours of each day and normally some other lessons with his or her class. Specialist teachers teach foreign languages, music, games and movement, eurythmy, handwork etc. to each class.

The class teacher provides a focus for the class and continuity over many years of development. He or she aims to be a figure of moral authority based on commitment, care for the children and a close relationship with the parents.

A curriculum that, from the outset, lays down the timetable and all sorts of other things completely eliminates the art of teaching... The teacher must be the driving and stimulating force in the whole education system. [12]

3.2   The Structure of the School Day

Each day begins with a two-hour period known as the main-lesson. This teaching unit is integrated and cross-curricular and includes activities to awaken and focus the children's attention, oral and written practice of basic skills, mental arithmetic, music and drawing, presentation of new material, recall and discussion of the previous day's (or earlier) work, individual working, conversation, narrative and practical work.

This is followed by 40-45 minute subject lessons, often doubled for art and crafts.

Priority is given in the morning to the more academic subjects and the afternoons are usually used for arts and crafts, outdoor activities, sport and practical work. Subjects such as music, eurythmy and foreign languages, which benefit from regular practice, are evenly spaced throughout the middle of the day whenever possible. In making up a school timetable, priority is given to the younger classes for whom a balanced rhythm of lessons and activities is especially important. The older classes are usually more able to cope with less than ideal conditions.

3.3   The Main-Lesson

The main-lesson (also referred to as the 'morning lesson' in some schools) is a central feature of the Steiner Waldorf approach. This lesson begins each school day and is normally about two hours in length. Subjects are taught in blocks of several weeks. All classes (Classes 1-12, ages 6-18), follow a main-lesson programme.

Principles and Features

The main-lesson embraces and addresses a varied and progressive range of skills, competencies and faculties in mathematics, English, the arts, science and humanities. Each day's main-lesson is viewed as an integrated and organic whole. Meaningful connections are made across subject areas and between main-lesson themes.

The class teacher chooses material, presentation and activities to suit the requirements of the curriculum and the needs of the specific class. Considerable care is given to preparation. Following a daily review process, the class teacher makes adjustments to the lesson plan as needed. It is the aim of the class teacher to make each lesson an artistic whole in which the parts relate to the whole; and the whole is permeated with rhythm, structure and purpose, as opposed to being a mere chain of events, however purposeful each link may be. This artistic approach is thought to have a beneficial effect on the children's learning.

The main-lesson incorporates activities and content which address the children's intellectual-cognitive, aesthetic-affective and practical modes of learning.

Each lesson is structured to contain a range of the following activities:

First part   – a morning verse, recitation of poetry, singing, musical instrumental work, mental arithmetic and recall of previous material.
Second part – presentation of new material and discussion.
Third part – individual working, narrative, practice of basic skills.

Assessment and Learning Outcomes

The assessment of learning through the main-lesson programme is a continuing process as the teacher endeavours to draw up a detailed profile, or child study, of each pupil, which conveys a picture of the child's learning and behaviour in the practical, emotional and cognitive realms, while seeking to understand and develop each child's skills, capacities and faculties (see section 7.1).

Assignments are on-going and arise out of work covered or introduced in classroom presentations. Projects, essays, tests and artistic/practical tasks indicate the range of assignments which are given.

In the course of the main-lesson the pupils' work is assessed in a variety of modes and recorded and used to build up individual pupil profiles, known as School Reports (see section 7.1 on Pupil Evaluation and Assessment). This information is included in the personal profile and used to define points of progression, intervention strategies or appropriate remedial support.

Records that are kept are shared with subject teachers, parents and, from the Middle School upwards, with pupils. [13]

The teachers plan their main-lessons and define their aims and expected learning outcomes. This is done individually and shared with the team of other class and subject teachers in regular weekly teachers' meetings.

3.4   Rhythm in Learning

The Steiner Waldorf approach sees rhythm as a vital element in learning.

The school day and the school year are structured in an organic way, which establishes a healthy balance of experience between concentration and relaxation, mental and practical work, movement and rest, listening and participating, looking and doing. Each lesson should contain a balance between the engagement of the child's thinking, their feeling and their willing. Each day has its own structured rhythm, as does each lesson.

Rhythm enables repetition to occur with renewed interest. By changing activities regularly, interest and attention can be maintained as well as being physiologically stimulating. The teacher can plan a variety of activities to suit the attention span of a given class and can vary this spontaneously according to need.

Such rhythms are flexible and can be directed by the teacher in response to the needs of the children e.g. Monday morning has a different quality to Friday morning. These factors actively play into lesson planning.

The celebration of the seasonal festivals gives the whole school year a balance and a sense of continuity as well as helping to form a strong community experience.

3.5   Forgetting and Remembering

The learning process itself benefits from a rhythmical approach.

Steiner Waldorf differentiates between skills needing regular practice (foreign languages, music, maths, spelling etc.) and the introduction of new content. New experiences or teaching content are often best introduced after a period during which the assimilation of previously taught material can occur. Acquiring new skills and practising them until they become ability are two different processes requiring different rhythms

Following a period of concentration on a given topic, say 3-4 weeks, this is then dropped and allowed to rest before being explicitly raised to consciousness again later. Experience shows a significant 'settling' effect, during which knowledge becomes faculty. This can be recalled at a later stage and built upon in a subsequent main-lesson. The 're-membering' or re-integrating of personal experience into a wider context is an important part of the learning process.

The nature of memory itself undergoes metamorphosis, evolving from situational, reflex memory to abstract memory. Steiner Waldorf draws strongly on these different memory types. Situational memory is strengthened by healthy routine in the younger classes, rhythmical memory is cultivated by such oral work as learning multiplication tables, number bonds, poems, proverbs, songs and foreign language vocabulary by heart. Active recall is a major skill practised daily in most lessons, as is the remembering and reviewing of complex shared situations. Good memory is based on the individual forming a strong bond of identification to his/her experiences. This is best achieved by engaging the pupils' interest and stimulating their feeling response. The other key to memory is context. All knowledge needs to be bedded in a context meaningful to the pupil. Imaginative teaching is crucial in the sense that pupils are enabled to imagine or form mental pictures in relation to what is being taught. Lack of tension is also a help to active memory, and the teacher attempts to create a mood of relaxed awareness in the class.

3.6   Learning in Stages

In the main-lesson programme and in the subject lessons where appropriate, three broad phases of learning can be identified. Stage one generally takes place over one day – the *first day*. Stage two usually occurs on the next day – the *second day*. The third stage, or phase, may take place over the following days, weeks or, in some cases, years, since the guiding aim of the third stage is to explore and consider concepts that are not *fixed* and *finished*, but *fluid* and *alive*. By focusing on concepts that are *unfinished* and *organic*, the pupils have the time and the space to *make them their own* through a process of digestion, assimilation and growth. In this manner, the lesson content can be understood by the individual in a differentiated and meaningful way. The teaching is thus transformed into learning.

STAGE ONE

The teacher presents new material or guides the children to specific learning experiences. The children receive the new content, they experience it and then, at the end of the lesson, it is hoped that they will let it sink from focused consciousness to the deeper layers of memory. Teaching content that is too abstract may prove 'indigestible'; and teaching that is too unstructured or chaotic may not have sufficiently engaged the pupils' attention – as is the case in boring, tedious lessons.

STAGE TWO

On the second day, after 'sleeping on' the previous day's content, the children are called upon to remember what was previously presented. In a process of discussion, recall and 'weighing up', the pupils are now invited to express creatively individualised and differentiated learning outcomes. The content is now 'owned' by the pupils and has been transformed. On a feeling level, a process of judgment-forming has taken place.

It is felt that the literal process of sleep is an essential part of learning. Clearly the brain processes sensory information in significant ways during REM and phases of deep sleep. On the following day such experiences often have a far more integrated character.

STAGE THREE

As the children move through the Lower School years, towards the development of analytical, causative thinking capacities, this third stage becomes more important as a consciously-sought element in the lesson. In this stage there is a further development of understanding towards the conceptual realm. Through a guided synthesis of different experiences, judgments and perspectives, the pupils are led towards the identification of a concept, or a scientific law. The seeds of the first stage have now developed and metamorphosed through a process of experiencing, forgetting, creative remembering and individual expression towards the flowering of concepts which are lively, mobile and founded in reality. Living concepts, introduced pictorially to younger children, are re-visited as the children grow up. The inner structure of the curriculum facilitates this spiral learning by building on earlier experiences.

3.7   Whole Class Teaching

The Steiner Waldorf approach is centred around whole class teaching. The teacher is a focus for the learning experience. This form is complemented by group work, differentiation into ability groups for maths, reading etc. However, such differentiation always goes from the whole class to groups which are then re-integrated back into the whole class.

A class of mixed ability children is a model for community. The task of the class teacher is to foster social awareness and cohesion within the class group. This process is enhanced by the long-term continuity offered by the class teacher.

There is much emphasis on children learning from and with each other, learning to appreciate each other's gifts and developing an understanding of each other's limitations and weaknesses.

The cultivation of such social awareness, empathy and the daily experience of individual and group problems being tackled constructively helps prepare pupils for life (see Social Skills curriculum).

3.8   The Importance of Narrative

Another key feature of the Steiner Waldorf approach is the emphasis on narrative.

Narrative gives children a conceptual framework within which they can orientate themselves and understand their experiences. Narrative contains beginnings, development and consequences or outcomes. It has sequence which conveys meaning, crisis which reaches resolution and it directs attention to personal experience.[14]

Listening to stories being told by a teacher in his/her own words is a powerful experience which engages the child. Not only are linguistic and listening skills enhanced through oral work but a strong sense of identification is encouraged.

> *Knowledge through narrative rather than mere transmission is constructed afresh by each individual knower on the basis of what is already known and by means of strategies developed both inside and outside the classroom.* [15]
>
> Gordon Wells

Furthermore, through storytelling children become participants in their community and culture. It encourages collaborative learning. Storytelling also enables children to 'digest' their experiences. Painful and difficult experiences such as grief, loss, anger and anxiety can often be clothed by the teacher in story form, thus enabling individuals and groups of children to come to terms with their own feelings. Conflict or tensions between individuals can often be worked through in this indirect way. Paradoxically, story is often more objective than the direct or moralising approach.

Children are told stories from a range of sources: fairy and folk tale, legend, fable, parables, mythology, history, literature. Teaching content is also related in oral form. For younger children this may involve personification and anthropomorphism e.g. 'number gnomes', dialogue between animals or plants, colours relating to each other in watercolour painting lessons etc. For older children biography is an important element in history as a means to strengthening identification.

With older pupils there remains a strong element of oral description in all presentations with emphasis on processes, sequences of events and outcomes. Communicating, exchanging viewpoints, dialogue and debate all have their place in lessons. The groundwork for such abilities is laid down in the younger classes. Narrative furthers this by exemplifying dialogue structure, by helping to shape experience into communicable form and by cultivating listening, perhaps the key skill in the classroom.

3.9   Pictorial and Imaginative Language

Throughout the primary years (ages 6-12) the pictorial element is preferred to abstract terminology. Imaginative concepts have the capacity to grow with the child's changing understanding of the world. The teacher uses imagery wherever appropriate in speaking to the children. Young children up to the age of 8 or 9 require concrete images that evoke strong sensory impressions on the imagination: *"Hot, salty tears ran down Cinderella's cheeks, making streaks like rain on dusty windows, dripping from her chin and making dark, damp patches on her grey dress."*

Children progress from an imaginative, picture consciousness to more abstract intellectual thought processes. The transition occurs after the age of 10 when the ability to think in abstract, and later causal, terms begins to emerge. From this age until puberty, language changes in character from literal to a more metaphoric and moral tone in description. Simile, metaphor and comparison create images in which physical detail is transformed into evocative mood: *"The north wind cut like a fish gutter's knife. The sea swelled darkly, fraying the wave crests like torn flags. His cheeks aglow with youthful enthusiasm, the young James Cook gripped the rail of the Whitby collier with pride and daring."*

In adolescence, imagery must build on the layers of language to create a level of symbolic meaning: *"In an image that would later be faked by the photographic department of* Pravda (Truth), *Lenin climbed onto the giant hulk of a locomotive derailed in the shunting yards of Finlandia Station. Unlike later icons, Lenin did not stand with feet firmly apart, left shoulder forward, chest proudly inflated, jowl jutting, the lapels of his greatcoat flapping in the biting wind. He was in fact hunched forward, feet unsteady on the icy metal, cheeks white, eyes dark and bloodshot, the famous beard wispy, his lips cracked. Someone had thrust a straggly bunch of red carnations into his hands. As he tried to clear his head and address the group of ragged railwaymen below, he absent-mindedly plucked the heads off the flowers one by one."*

The pictorial element is not only relevant for stories. Instructions and directions in classroom contexts can often be given in pictorial form.

> *We should educate children so that all their concepts are capable of growth, that their concepts and will impulses are really alive. This is not easy. But an artistic education succeeds in doing it. And the children have a different feeling when we offer them living concepts instead of dead ones, for they unconsciously know that what is given them grows with them, just as arms grow with the body.* [16]
>
> Rudolf Steiner

3.10   The Place of Textbooks

The teaching in a Steiner Waldorf school comes essentially 'through' the teacher and not via text books. The teacher chooses the material and presentation to suit the particular group of children. This is the case in all subjects.

Imaginative, oral and practical presentations of lesson material, thoroughly prepared by the teacher, engender interest and enhance the authority of the teacher in the eyes of the children.

The fundamental mode of delivery for lesson content is the immediate and direct interface between pupils and teacher, with the latter supported by appropriate materials and resources, including prepared work sheets, texts, vocabulary lists, maps, diagrams etc.

Reference books, such as dictionaries, atlases and other reference material are made use of as appropriate, but always in support of the teacher's main presentation.

Likewise, assignments and projects arising out of the lesson theme require that the pupils develop competence in a range of reading techniques and manual information-retrieval skills by the time they reach age 12 (Class 6).

3.11   The Authority of the Teacher

In the Early Years/Kindergarten period, the presence of inner authority working through the teacher's gestures, speech, actions and mood allows the young child to imbibe a living example of authority, the essence of which may be emulated in later years. The inner attitude of the teacher is reinforced by strong rhythms and routines which quieten behaviour.

In the Lower School period, children need clear guidance and boundaries. It is the role of the class teacher to provide these and to exemplify models of conduct. This authority manifests in the presentation of lesson material and in the whole social and pedagogical life of the class.

In adolescence the emphasis on authority as a pedagogical gesture shifts to the teacher as an authority in a given subject field. Based on his or her own integrity and search for truth, the teacher can lead the young person towards enthusiastic enquiry into what is true. The focus now moves to the development of independent judgment based on sound observation.

Together these three broad approaches, or aspects, of authority – imitation, guidance and respect for expertise – provide a setting in which ethical individualism and individual morality may flourish.

3.12   Discipline

Early Years

Young children imitate. It is in their nature to do so. The young child is sensitive to the environment in all its aspects – the material and the human – the physical, emotional and spiritual.

In order to cultivate discipline in the early years, it is incumbent on teachers and parents to create a healthy environment for a child to imitate. Children unconsciously respond to the moods created by adults. The extent to which conscious activity has structured this environment in a meaningful – as opposed to a haphazard – way is important. Children notice whether adults are sincere in their gestures, speech and general bearing. Adult relationships are observed, and children have a deep need to know that the world is good. Educators and parents have a responsibility to strive towards an honest morality. In many life situations this may be the only 'good' available – yet it is the most important. Time and again this has been demonstrated in times of war and social disaster: love is the absolute essential in Early Years education.

By consciously working with rhythm – daily, weekly and the yearly cycle through the seasons and the festivals – and using rhythmical repetition as a pedagogical tool, the teacher promotes and provides discipline for the young child.

Lower School

In the Lower School, rhythm, form, boundaries and teacher-authority unite to provide a meaningful structure within which the children are held and nurtured.

Well-prepared lessons, employing a suitable range of teaching strategies, foster a mood of positive discipline. When pupils are inspired and encouraged to develop specific skills and capacities, while working at a suitable pace and level, conditions are present in which good discipline can flourish.

The teacher's quest for self-development and professional excellence provides an important role model for pupils.

When authoritative guidance inspires the teaching, independence is conferred on the child and conditions are laid down for the development of self-discipline in later years.

The approach to discipline seeks to follow what may be called an 'artistic' approach. In presenting lesson material, setting of tasks and assignments, the teacher has the responsibility to create and inspire structure in classroom management and classroom life. In consciously providing a space, the teacher offers freedom. In this creative space there is room for dynamic interplay between absorption and assimilation, guidance and discovery, teaching and learning.

Upper School

In the Upper School classes, the process of cultivating and developing discipline continues and the focus now shifts towards conscious self-discipline, taking responsibility for one's actions and accepting the consequences of one's behaviour. When infringements occur, students are guided to understand the full consequences of their actions and given the opportunity to redress the harm done. Exclusion is very much a last resort since dialogue is crucial and youngsters need to come to terms with their responsibilities within the context of the social group. Alienation through rejection or humiliation can only make matters worse.

Young people clearly need to test the boundaries they are given and they should be given every opportunity to do this in a positive and constructive way. They also need to learn how to discuss such matters and in particular to understand complex situations from a variety of perspectives.

Rules and codes of conduct are designed to promote care and respect for the people and objects in the child's environment.

Social harmony, health and safety and a positive, creative learning environment are the guiding motives of school rules. Rules and codes of conduct should be clear, transparent and comprehensible to teachers, parents and pupils, in principle and in detail. Rules and the consequences deriving from their infringement should be age-appropriate.

Where infringements do occur, the incidents are looked at on a case by case basis. The emphasis is on the deed that has been done and attention is given to making good what has been harmed.

Sanctions are not applied in an automatic, 'fixed penalty' manner. Rather, individuals and individual situations are considered and appropriate sanctions and consequences are applied.

Codes of behaviour are regularly reviewed in the weekly staff meeting and are discussed with older pupils and parents.

3.13   Values

Steiner Waldorf education seeks to make the questions of human values the central element of the curriculum.

The children in any class come from varied social and cultural backgrounds. These groups of mixed religious, ethnic and national elements coalesce into one social group which stays together for the entire school time. The class is thus a microcosm of the society around them and here they learn to respect and understand differing individual gifts and weaknesses both in academic and social terms.

> *The wish for a selective, elitist education has no place in a Steiner Waldorf school. Parents who want such an education are in the wrong place. The rights of all children to the highest quality education is not only a social ideal but a social necessity.*
>
> Rudolf Steiner, *A Social Basis for Education*

Social harmony is dependent on an integrated, multi-cultural, mixed ability educational environment with equal chances for all. Children are not streamed for ability, though some differentiation occurs in some subjects, usually after age 14. Continuity is fostered. The class ethos is usually strong and enables the class to both carry and deal with the kind of crises that occur as part of normal child development. When social difficulties arise these are faced and addressed in age-appropriate ways. Kindness, sharing and the ability to listen to others are actively encouraged. An understanding that deeds have consequences is likewise engendered in age-appropriate ways.

In a non-competitive environment the children are encouraged to take pride in their work and achieve the highest standards they are personally capable of. Pupils are also encouraged to evaluate their own and fellow pupils' achievements in an objective, though positive and constructive way. [17]

The teachers try to impart to the children a sense of wonder and reverence for natural phenomena and for other people, and this forms a basis in the young child for interest, respect and the desire for knowledge in the adolescent. With such a foundation, young people can cultivate their own inner voice of conscience and sense of justice and responsibility.

Team work and problem solving are learned through many artistic and practical projects. Through comprehensive work-experience, ecological and social practicals, the students gain not only insight into the world of work but they also learn to empathise with others and to recognise the necessity for mutual support in all realms of life.

In their contacts with the pupils, the enthusiasm of the teachers is a moral force which arises out of their own personal development and growth. Teachers are effective and influential not only in what they know but equally in who they are and what they stand for.

Children are taught to form judgments on the basis of sound observation and to transfer these skills to the personal, social and moral domain.

The school community as a whole reflects these principles, not as a belief system but rather as a recognition of the inherent idealism in all people. The involvement, commitment and not least the work and sacrifice made by the parents, have an exemplary and motivating influence on the pupils. Vandalism, truancy and bullying are rare in Steiner Waldorf schools, which probably reflects pupils' identification with the ethos of the school.

Much time is given to the resolution of social difficulties in the classroom or school context. Schools have effective bullying and conflict resolution policies which are regularly reviewed in the weekly teachers' meetings and which are implemented as and when difficulties occur. The adult school community likewise seeks to address issues of grievance and conflict in a constructive manner. Both parents and teachers contribute to this process.

> *The question to be asked is not: What does an individual need to know and be capable of doing so as to fit into the existing social order? but rather: What potential does an individual have and what can be developed in him or her? When this is taken into account each new generation can bring forces of continuous renewal to the social order. In this social order there will then live all that the fully mature human beings in it cause it to be. For the existing social order to mould the coming generation in its own image is something that must not happen.* [4]   Rudolf Steiner

4.0   EVALUATION AND ASSESSMENT

General Principles

Assessment is *"clear seeing, rich understanding, respectful application."* [18]
Assessment is implicit in the whole Waldorf approach. Good practice occurs when the self-reflective teacher assesses his or her own teaching and its outcome with individual children and shares this with colleagues on a regular basis. This insight should feed directly back into the classroom. The Steiner Waldorf approach sees assessment as a means of gaining knowledge of, insight into and understanding for the child. The more accurate and comprehensive the observations, the richer the understanding. Increased understanding can lead to positive development in the child. In ideal circumstances, the outcome of an assessment of a child is that meaningful help is offered and new developmental opportunities are created. Assessment can lead to transformation in teaching and learning.

Assessment serves two essential functions: supporting learning and establishing standards. The former provides pupils and parents with feedback, identifies areas that need to be focused on, sets appropriate tasks for teacher and pupil, characterises the pupil's approach, attitude, behaviour and abilities within the context of their overall development. This form of assessment is formative, ongoing, responsive and qualitative. The second form of assessment provides quantifiable data relating to specific achievements, states what a pupil can or cannot do, enables selection and is usually used by forms of external moderation. Both formative and summative forms of assessment have their place, and either applied inappropriately, can stifle development.

Formative assessment plays a central role in the Steiner Waldorf approach. It is an expression of the core ethos of the Kindergarten or class teacher, who provides long-term continuity for the child's development. Each teacher works on the assumption that the child before them possesses greater reserves of potential than reveal themselves in the present. A child's entire biography is a picture of a path of progressive individualisation and realisation of the child's potential. This potential expresses itself in the way a child enters into the key developmental stages, how a child learns and encounters the difficulties with which life presents him or her. Observing this developmental path, and responding to it, is the prime objective of formative assessment.

Too much bureaucratic assessment stifles teacher initiative and intuition; too little of any assessment and there is a danger of subjectivity and arbitrariness.

4.1   Record Keeping

There are two levels of assessment; on-going observations made by the teacher and formal records. On-going observations made by the teacher on a daily or weekly basis include: attendance/punctuality, completion of classroom or homework tasks given, grades given (where appropriate), behavioural evaluation, unusual occurrences (untypical behaviour, domestic or social crises, illness/injury) and the child's level of participation in lessons. These points are recorded using lists and symbols accompanied by notes where necessary. On a monthly or termly basis records are kept on each child's progress in subject-specific skills, numeracy, literacy, gross and fine motor co-ordination and social skills.

Guidelines for attainment levels in language, literacy and numeracy in the form of checklists are included in the subject curricula in the following sections.

Records are expected to be kept on the following in the pupil's file:

* summaries of child studies done in the teachers' meetings;
* school doctor's reports;
* learning support reports, including results of screening tests;
* record of probationary periods;
* notes on disciplinary situations and outcomes and reviews;
* pastoral care reports;
* copies of termly, annual reports, student profiles;
* documentation from previous schools.

It is essential that schools have a clear policy and procedures for maintaining records, including having the form of and access to such records.

Annual (and in the Upper School termly) reports are written for the parents (see below). In some schools Student Profiles are written (see below).

4.2   Monitoring [19]

Class teachers regularly monitor and record the children's progress in literacy, numeracy, co-ordination and social skills, using checklists, records and screening.

Teachers plan their lessons and record the performance of the children. These plans are shared and integrated into the whole school curriculum through the regular teachers' meetings. Children's on-going work is evaluated and reflected to the children and used as a guide to lesson planning and as a diagnostic tool.

4.3   School Reports

A summary of these evaluations is given to parents in the form of an annual school report, which is often personalised by the teacher in style and design. This document normally includes:

- A characterisation of the child as a whole person, highlighting their strengths and weaknesses, written by the class teacher.
- An evaluation of the child's participation (attention span, co-operation, response), progress and ability in the various subjects (including comprehension, verbal and written attainments), age-appropriate ability to work independently, social behaviour (listening, working with others, co-operation), activity (presentation of work, tidiness, completed tasks), level of involvement and response and affective-aesthetic progression.
- A summary of the curriculum for the year.
- A record of attainments in all subjects.
- For younger children, a part of the report is addressed personally to them, offering praise, guidance and challenges for the coming year.
- Older pupils at some schools (such as Michael Hall, UK) now receive Student Profiles for each subject and bi-annual reports.
- Students graduating from Steiner Waldorf schools receive a detailed Leaver's Report, sometimes called a Record of Achievement.

4.4   Student Profiles

In some Upper Schools (ages 14-19) Student Profiles are written at the end of each main-lesson block for each arts/crafts/life skills course, and termly for on-going subjects. These profiles summarise both formative and summative aspects and include some element of student self-evaluation. As well as a description of the course and outline of its objectives, there usually follow two sections, one covering behaviour and motivation, the other covering subject-specific attainments. Each criteria is given both written comment and a grade (usually A-E) ranging from very good, good, satisfactory, unsatisfactory, to cause for serious concern, whereby satisfactory means that the student has attained the objectives set, no more or no less. Anything above satisfactory means that greater effort was made and above average attained. Each subject establishes its own specific criteria for evaluation. The Profile concludes with a summary by the teacher highlighting possible areas of future development.

4.5   Child Studies

Child studies are done on children who need special consideration e.g. learning or behavioural difficulties, exceptional qualities, or who typify a condition. These studies involve all the teachers who teach the child and may involve specialists such as a school doctor or therapist. The parents' involvement and support is important.

Observations are made of physical constitution, movement, behaviour in class and outside (home), results of any tests done, artistic work, social interaction with other children and adults, work habits, home circumstances, school and homework, willingness, participation, the child's relation to different subjects and school activities.

These Child Studies are often shared with the whole teachers' group. Sometimes it is enough that the staff's heightened awareness of a particular child has a beneficial effect on the child, though usually the study leads to some action and always requires regular follow-up.

4.6   Class Studies

Class studies can be helpful at developmental nodes e.g. end of Classes 3, 6, 8, or after a new teacher has taken on the class or if there is a consensus among subject teachers that a class is in need of a specific focus of attention. Class studies can focus on different aspects such as levels of attainment or social dynamics. Major reviews of a class are done when they enter the Upper School.

5.0   SELF MANAGEMENT IN STEINER WALDORF SCHOOLS

The founding of the first Waldorf School in Stuttgart 1919 was intended by its founders, Dr Rudolf Steiner and the industrialist Dr Emil Molt, to be a cultural deed that would bring about reforms and even revolutionise education. The organisational structures in the new school and in all subsequent Steiner Waldorf Schools were to reflect this radical approach.

The Waldorf School was founded on two fundamental sets of principles. The first was the curriculum and the study of the developing human being that informs it. The other foundation was to be provided by the functional principles of the Threefold Social Order. A central objective of Steiner Waldorf education is social renewal. The main means towards achieving a healthier social life is the cultivation of social responsibility based on individual insight through a broad and holistic education.

The Threefold Social Order is a way of understanding the dynamic and fundamental interaction between the main areas of social life, the economic sphere, the sphere of rights and politics and the cultural-spiritual sphere. Steiner saw these three primary realms as co-existing in mutual interdependence. Each realm has its functional principle. The guiding principle in spiritual or cultural life is freedom; in the sphere of rights and politics it is that of equality and justice; and in economic life the guiding principle should be mutuality. When each of these principles is applied in their appropriate sphere, there can be healthy social development. Applied in an inappropriate way, these principles lead to social imbalance and conflict. Unrestrained freedom applied in the economic sphere leads to exploitation and environmental destruction. Equality enforced on spiritual or cultural life leads to the denial of individuality and uniformity and blandness within the cultural life. Where justice and equality are absent or weakened in political or institutional life, the loss of respect for human rights leads to all manner of oppression.[20]

Naturally, the healthy balance of functioning principles within society or even within a social organism or institution is a subtle and complex process. Yet a recognition of these basic principles is crucial.

The principles of the Threefold Social Order were reflected in the organisational structures of the Waldorf School and, in numerous local variations, still form the basis for management structures in all Steiner Waldorf schools.

Steiner's primary concern was to protect the curriculum and educational approach from the prescriptions of politicians and bureaucrats or from the influence of commercial interests. In his view education should both be free of these influences and be freely accessible to those parents who choose it for their children.

A healthy relation exists between school and society only when society is kept constantly supplied with the new and individual potentials of people whose education has allowed them to develop unhampered. This can only be realised if the schools and the whole educational system are placed on a footing of self-administration within the social organism. The government and the economy must receive people educated by the independent spiritual-cultural life; they must not have the power to prescribe according to their own wants how these people are to be educated. [21]

Steiner further argued that the demands of self-administration would ensure that a free cultural institution like a school could not produce people who were unworldly. Indeed real social renewal requires that society take the risk that an education system which is independent and based on on-going research into human nature, would produce free-thinking individuals of initiative. To this end he argued for a complete disassociation of education from government bureaucracy and industry.

The place and function of educators within society should depend solely upon the authority of those engaged in that activity. The administration of the educational institutions, the organisation of courses of instruction and their goals should be entirely in the hands of people who are simultaneously either teaching or otherwise productively engaged in cultural life. In each case, such people would divide their time between actual teaching (or some other form of cultural productivity) and administrative control of the educational system. [22]

Having said that, at the founding of the first Waldorf School, Steiner spoke of the need to make compromises. The Waldorf school must avoid being isolated, becoming an elitist or minority schools movement. Its social task can only be achieved within the mainstream of society. He himself struck a deal with the local education authorities about pupil attainments at key stages. The real role for Waldorf education is as an active part of the cultural landscape, taking part, representing its view of child development, yet not relinquishing its identity.

A Teacher Republic

At the founding of the first Waldorf School, Steiner pointed out that given the need to find a healthy balance between the ideals of Waldorf education and the need to be flexible *"to conform to what lies far from our ideals"*, [23] it would be necessary for everyone to...

use their full strength from the beginning. Therefore, we will organise the school not bureaucratically, but collegially, and will administer it in a republican way. In a true teachers' republic we will not have the comfort of receiving directions from a head teacher, rather we must bring our own contributions towards the solution of problems and take full responsibility for what we have to do. Each one of us must be completely responsible.

We can replace the supervision of a departmental administration with this preparatory course, and through the work, receive what unifies the school. [24]

The way this principle applies in individual schools varies considerably. Practically all schools beyond the initiative stage, work with the delegation principle, which sees individuals or groups given responsibility for specific areas of decision making or management within overall agreed aims.

All Steiner Waldorf schools are established as non-profit making charitable foundations with Boards of Trustees (sometimes referred to as the Council of Management). The trustees delegate day to day management of all areas of the education to the College of Teachers, who appoint a chairperson for a short term of office on a rotating basis. The College of Teachers usually comprises all teaching staff on permanent contracts. The College of Teachers carries the educational ethos of the school and is responsible collectively (or via delegation) for all the areas normally the remit of a Head Teacher.

The College of Teachers collaborates closely with the Trustees on matters of planning, policy and monitoring of quality. The Board of Trustees has overall responsibility for the school as a public institution. Their chief role is to provide the means of support for the educational provision. This includes finance, legal and contractual matters, buildings, maintenance, administration, materials, health and safety, insurance etc. The College of Teachers, on the other hand, is primarily responsible for the teaching, educational research and curriculum development, staffing and staff development, admission of children, pastoral care, the timetable, celebration of the festivals and the general cultural life of the school.

Schools usually have administrative staff in a variety of support and management roles. Such administrators need to be part of, or at least work in close liaison with, the College of Teachers in order that the link to the education is a closely integrated one.

5.1 Parents and Teachers Working Together

Close collaboration between parents and teachers is essential in a Steiner Waldorf school. The education needs the support and interest of the parents and the children always benefit when this collaboration is mutually supportive.

Parents are involved at many levels. Some parents may become trustees; others will join groups or mandates on a voluntary basis within the school, with specific areas of responsibility such as financial management, building development, outreach and so on.

Schools often provide various forms of adult education including parenting classes, artistic groups, induction courses into the education, study groups and even part-time teacher training.

Many schools have PTAs or their equivalent which provide a forum for parent-teacher feedback, discussion of whole school issues or general educational themes.

Class parent evenings are held, at least once a term for each class, at which the teachers can present aspects of the curriculum or child development. Matters of concern can be discussed and support for the children in a wide variety of ways can be generated. Steiner Waldorf schools have a policy of home visits in recognition of the importance of the home situation in the child's development. Most schools enable regular access to teachers through parent surgeries and appointment times.

The life of the whole school community is enlivened by the celebration of the seasonal festivals, occasions at which parents and friends can often participate.

Much effort is devoted to informing parents through outreach materials, open days, 'school for parents', induction courses, parent handbooks, newsletters and school magazines. Access to information and transparency of organisation structures help to answer people's questions. When communication breaks down, or individuals are not able to resolve outstanding issues, schools have formal mediation and grievance procedures (which are outlined in the Parents Handbook). Indeed, in the UK, Steiner Waldorf schools follow a detailed Code of Practice which outlines basic procedures and describes best practice in a whole range of areas within the life of a school community.

5.2 Quality Development

The fundamental assumption of quality development is that there is always room for improvement. This goes hand in hand with the recognition that the process of planning and review, research and reflection should be experienced as creative, fruitful and effective. Work on quality development is best seen as a natural extension of existing work, rather than the imposition of extra procedures. In fact, outside of the teaching itself, most other school activities and meetings are devoted to the development of quality.

Perspectives

One of the central tasks of education is to meet the changing and developing needs of the children. This requires on-going study of children, curriculum development and continuous reviewing of the teaching approach. Furthermore this has to be done in a spirit of mutual respect and collegial recognition. This is actually the central task of the teachers' meetings. These meetings are, as Steiner put it in Ilkley (17/8/23) to be:

> *living adult education – a permanent training academy... for the reason that every practical experience gained by the teacher in school becomes, in turn, part of his own education. And he who derives such self-education for himself from his teaching work, gaining on the one hand a profound psychological insight into the practical side of the education and on the other into different qualities, characters and temperaments of the children, will always be finding something new, for himself and for the whole College of Teachers (the Faculty). All the experience and knowledge acquired from the teaching should be 'put into the pool' at these meetings. In this way the College of Teachers in spirit and soul becomes a whole where each member knows what the other is doing, what experience has taught him and what progress he has made as the result of his teaching with the children in the classroom.*

[It is important to stress that the differences in terminology should not confuse the issue. When Steiner is translated as referring to the College of Teachers he clearly meant all the teachers and not just some smaller group within the body of teachers. In the US the term 'faculty' usually includes all teaching staff.] He goes on to extend the metaphor of the teachers' meeting as heart organ, to include organs of perception at the periphery in the form of parents' evenings: *"...the echoes that reach the teachers when we have these parents' evenings, bring life to what the teachers especially need to maintain their own inner vitality."*

One could quote many more references [25] from Steiner to show that he considered the practical review of actual lessons, the study of children and classes and the involvement of all teachers in educational research as crucial to the development of quality in the educational provision. When Steiner refers to the self-development of the teacher or the group of teachers, this self-development includes learning to do things better. Development without the process of feedback and adaptation, without reference to outcomes and without aims, is no development in the full sense of the word.

A Spiritual Framework

The central aim of those responsible for leadership in Waldorf schools is to serve the 'spirit of the school' and thus to work to realise the intentions of those spiritual powers that inspire Waldorf education. The guiding spirit of each school needs organs through which it can perceive the life of the school and through which it can work in an inspirational way to support the endeavours of teachers and co-workers and to support the individual children in their development. That is the spiritual task of the school's management (who may consist of teachers, or teachers and administrators) and it is the inspiration for leadership. The Imagination or College Meditation, [26] which Steiner gave at the founding of the so-called Mother School, is the framework through which this activity can be focused. Quality development is an aspect of this work that needs to be embedded within this framework.

Responsibility and Accountability

Whilst each individual is existentially responsible for his or her deeds, institutional responsibility and accountability for quality development in the education rests with the College of Teachers. Administrative and organisational responsibility lies with the Board or Council of Management or equivalent legal body within the school. The question of formal accountability is an important one, and it is often lack of clarity in this area that is the source of problems, particularly in relation to parents.

Whilst the individual is responsible for his or her actions, the College of Teachers is collectively responsible that the individual as a teacher and the outcomes and quality of his or her work, conform to the collectively agreed standards. At the end of the day (usually Thursday!), the College is responsible for saying that the quality is or is not good enough. Within the school as an institution, the legally responsible body (the Board, Trustees, Council of Management, etc.) is accountable not for educational quality as such (they would usually be unqualified to judge it), but it is their responsibility to see that quality development occurs in appropriate ways, and for providing the resources necessary to enable it to happen.

This in no way contradicts the autonomy or freedom of the teachers, or indeed of the individual within the sphere of the cultural life. Indeed, this is exactly the kind of administrative responsibility within the free cultural life that Steiner foresaw in his work on the *Threefold Social Order.* [27] Judgments made about quality in education can only be made by educators. To a lesser extent those being educated, their parents and guardians can form judgments from their own personal perspective, but such judgments certainly cannot be made by bureaucrats or government officials on a theoretical basis.

However, the question of whether quality development takes place or not, and how it takes place is a question within the rights sphere. It concerns contractual agreements, social arrangements and must be characterised by the qualities of fairness, transparency and a respect for the rights of the individual. I would even argue that every child has the right (and by extension the parents) to the active commitment of his or her teacher to quality development. It is the school board's/council's role to ensure that these rights are respected.

Evaluation

There can be no real quality development or accountability without evaluation or assessment (the words are taken here as being synonymous). Assessment is *"noticing, finding out, leading forward... It is the attempt to gain knowledge, insight and understanding... Increased understanding can lead to positive development."* [28] Evaluation can be either qualitative (sometimes called formative) or quantitative (summative). The former monitors processes (e.g. a child's development, the working mood in a group of teachers, a consultation and decision-making process, the developmental stage of school). The latter measures outcomes (e.g. exam results, pupil recruitment numbers, achieving financial targets, all things that can be quantified or definitively ascertained). The former is more future orientated, the latter reflects on what has occurred. Both forms require there to be stated goals, appropriate criteria, evidence and feedback from different sources and, crucially individual judgment. There are several levels of evaluation.

SELF-EVALUATION is an on-going process involving (for teachers) making lesson plans which are reviewed on a daily, weekly, monthly and annual basis. The 'buddy system' is an extension of self-evaluation in which colleagues mutually agree to support and give feedback to each other. Mentoring provides informal evaluation though the emphasis is on support and development.

Departmental self-evaluation involves a group (say, the eurythmy teachers) meeting regularly to review their work and periodically to report to the rest of the teachers. Key questions would be: *Are we meeting the needs of the pupils? What do we teach and why? How do we evaluate the children's progress?* What practical resources and organisational support do we need (e.g. better floors, more lessons, more integration with other subjects)?

PEER EVALUATION AND ASSESSMENT involves individuals being assessed by colleagues of broadly the same professional standing, qualifications and experience. This is best done internally within a school but external assessors can be used by mutual consent. All parties involved should agree the procedures and consequences used beforehand.

ISSUE FOCUS. Specific areas of school life can be the subject of evaluation, such as the quality and effectiveness of a school's leadership, administration, communications, policies (e.g. gender or equal rights policies, bullying policies, school exclusion policies, salary structures etc.). Each area needs to be well defined and the objectives and follow-up procedures of the review need to be clearly defined. Whole school appraisals can also be undertaken, though these will be time-consuming and complex, but can on occasion be necessary and helpful.

Criteria

Obviously no evaluation procedure can be effective if there are no clear guidelines or criteria against which to measure the person or activity being assessed. In fact, working out criteria is as important and useful an activity as the evaluation itself. Since education is essentially a transformative process, general standards cannot be determined externally in any detail, though this does not preclude consensus on *minimum* standards. Criteria are agreed by the consent of those responsible in the field concerned and need themselves to be the subject of on-going review.

This is also the most difficult aspect of the whole issue of quality development. No-one wants to be told what to do and nobody wants to be restricted by prescribed conditions. Therefore consent is important. Consent depends upon mutual respect and recognition of competence. Furthermore, no criteria have absolute value. Neither, of course, can they be considered negotiable, unbinding or transient. Clearly, useful criteria arise out of the best considerations under the circumstances, and therefore should be given some credence and permanence whilst also being subject to regular review.

Educational criteria cannot be determined by external agencies that are not working out of the insights of Waldorf education. Therefore the Waldorf schools movement is called upon to create criteria through self-regulation. This can be done through the consent of a body of schools, for example, in appointing experienced colleagues to research, consult on and draw up guidelines for quality criteria appropriate to the various age groups, subjects and activities within the schools. Such criteria would then be available as guidelines for self-evaluation within the individual schools. Schools wishing to create their own criteria would be free to do so, though mutual recognition by other schools is an important moral authority, especially when quality is questioned, by parents for example. *It is not a question of imposing standards and establishing an inspectorate. It is a question of self-evaluation and peer recognition.*

Aims and Objectives

Aims are ideals, by nature unrealisable, yet they represent something to strive towards. Objectives are specific targets deemed to be realisable within a defined time limit. Quality development requires that there should be a common shared vision held by all the teaching staff, arrived at by consent and sustained by collaborative working practices. Furthermore these aims and objectives need to be communicated to and understood by the parents, older pupils and where necessary outside bodies such as the Government. The more parents can support the aims and objectives of the school the better it will be for the education.

Educational Development

The quality of educational provision in relation to the stated objectives can be evaluated in many ways (including, teachers having checklists providing guidelines, exam results, career achievements of former pupils, testimony of former pupils etc.) Regular surveys of the parent body and older students can also be helpful in providing feedback. Such results and feedback need to be taken into account in planning and policy development.

The development of the education involves:
- Lesson planning and reviewing by individual teachers.
- Groups of teachers teaching the same class sharing their observations, the contribution of their own subject and creating a unity of approach for this class at this time (e.g. for the coming term).
- Departmental reviews of the subject curriculum and its staffing, deployment and resources implications (see above).
- Child studies and class studies. On-going research on general educational themes e.g. learning support needs, rhythm in teaching, homework etc.
- Whole school discussions about policies and programmes for the coming year or more, out of a shared vision of the educational needs of the pupils and the school's ability to meet them.

All these levels of review and planning should constitute a coherent educational development plan, which will formulate the aspirations of the teachers for educational development. Such plans should be detailed and practical enough to influence organisational planning (e.g. spending more money on teacher development, new facilities, taking on new staff, starting an Upper School). Experience shows that schools often develop in a haphazard way, influenced either by strong individual visions or hindered by the lack of any coherent plan. In some cases educational aspirations are at odds with the organisation's ability to meet those needs; or the school's administration may have different priorities. It may be that the teachers (or some of them) have one set of educational objectives and the parents (some of them) another.

An educational development process is not merely a luxury that can be addressed when time permits. It could actually be a focus for all the non-teaching activities of the teachers. Such study, review and planning is not *on top* of the work teachers do in their meetings, it is the work teachers do in their meetings. This is the primary function of the self-administration of Waldorf schools and it requires a higher level of individual responsibility than in schools which have directors, departmental heads and so on.

A sense of common purpose and cohesion cannot be developed by exhortation or by organisational structures alone. Both of these qualities can only arise out of working together in fruitful and constructive ways.[29] Shared purpose needs to be consciously and systematically worked out in discussion and through mutual perception. It is our view that trust, the prerequisite of collegial working, can grow when colleagues work together on the one task which unites them all, the development of the educational quality. The pedagogical value of the trust between colleagues is unmeasurable but potent.

Development of Ability

One of the primary objectives of quality development is to recognise the abilities of individuals and to provide opportunities for those individuals to develop further. Such development is all the more relevant when it has a whole school focus – after all the purpose of school is not the self-development of the teachers! The greater the responsibility taken in this field, the greater the individual freedom and creativity in the service of the education.

Quality development encompasses many fields of work. The UK Waldorf schools have been working for some years on these issues. The work so far on mentoring, teacher and pupil assessment, quality development within the school organisation, educational guidelines for pupil attainments, curriculum documentation, self-management in Waldorf schools has been documented and is in an on-going process of review. Whilst paperwork is useful, obviously the real process involves dialogue and discussion. Schools wishing copies of the paperwork can get these from the Steiner Waldorf Schools Fellowship in Forest Row, UK.

References

1   See Steiner, R., *Intuitive Thinking as a Spiritual Path: A Philosophy of Freedom*, 1995, and *Theosophy: An Introduction to the Spiritual Processes in Human Life and in the Cosmos*, 1994, both published by Anthroposophic Press, for an introduction to anthroposophy. For an introduction to his educational ideas see *The Education of the Child* and *The Child's Changing Consciousness and Early Lectures on Education*, 1996 and *Waldorf Education*, 1996, both AP.

2   Steiner, R., *Anthroposophical Leading Thoughts*, p11, RSP 1985.

3   Steiner, R., GA 62, *Die Ergebnisse der Geistesforschung*, lecture 21/11/1912, p122 (M.R. translation).

4   Steiner, R., *Occult Science*, p250, RSP 1969.

5   Steiner, R., *Theosophy*, p25, AP 1994.

6   Ibid, p44.

7   Ibid, p45.

8   Ibid, p49.

9   Steiner, R., *Rudolf Steiner in the Waldorf School, Lectures and Addresses to Children, Parents and Teachers*, p79, AP 1996.

10   See Avison, K.A., *A Handbook for Waldorf Class Teachers*, section on School Readiness, 2nd edition, SSF 1998.

11   Steiner, R., *A Social Basis*, SSF 1994.

12   Steiner, R., *Practical Advice to Teachers*, p163.

13   For examples of record keeping see Avison, K.A., *A Handbook for Class Teachers*, 2nd edition, SSF 1995.

14   See Engel, S., *The Stories Children Tell*, 1995 and Whitehead, M., *Language and Literacy in the Early Years*, 1997.

15   See Wells, G., *The Meaning Makers*, 1987.

16   Steiner, R., *The Younger Generation*, p148, AP 1967.

17   A recent survey in Germany put the question: "What should national educational policy prioritise: the encouragement of high achievement by a minority or equal opportunities for all?"; 82% chose equality for all. (Spiegel 22-12-97, p34). Similar research for the UK is not known, but we would hope for a similar result.

18   Drummond, M.J., quoted in Mepham and Rawson: see below.

19   See *Pupil Assessment and Record Keeping in Steiner Waldorf Schools*: an information pack compiled by Trevor Mepham and Martyn Rawson, SSF 1998.

20   See Steiner, R., *Towards Social Renewal*, RSP 1977. See also 'Working together in a Waldorf School', a special number of the journal *Paideia*, SSF 1999, which contains a series of articles on the subject in relation to school organisation.

21   Steiner, R., *The Threefold Social Order and Educational Freedom in the Renewal of the Social Organism*, RSP 1985.

22   Ibid.

23   Steiner, R., *The Foundations of Human Experience*, p30.

24   Ibid, p30.

25   See Gladstone, F., *Republican Academies*, SSF 1997, for a compilation of Steiner's comments on self-management and pedagogical study in Waldorf schools. See also Manfred Leist, *Parent Participation in the Life of a Waldorf School*, AWSNA.

26   See Steiner, R., *The Foundations of Human Experience*, pp45 to 48. See also the author's article, "What is the Spirit of the School Trying to Tell Us", in *Paideia* No. 16, April 1998.

27   See Steiner, R., *The Renewal of the Social Organism*, published in *Paideia* No. 16. *Freie Schule und Dreigliederung*, 1919.

28   Mepham, T., in Mepham, T. and Rawson, M., *Pupil Assessment and Record Keeping in Waldorf Schools*, SSF 1998.

29   See Zimmermann, H., *Speaking, Listening, Understanding*, Lindisfarne Press, 1996.

6.0 EARLY YEARS CURRICULUM

6.1 The Kindergarten (3-6 years)

Children enter the Kindergarten between the ages of three and six. Parent and Toddler Groups and Play-groups are provided for younger children. Group sizes vary. Traditionally, five morning sessions per week are offered, each session lasting for approximately four and a half hours. Children take up provision according to age and need. Afternoon care is often available if required. Increasingly, providers are exploring the need for a wider Early Years provision with Waldorf nurseries and all day Kindergartens. A fine and flexible balance has to be maintained between parental needs and what is healthy for the young child.

6.2 General Principles

Cognitive, social, emotional and physical skills are accorded equal value in the Kindergarten and many different competencies are developed. Activities reflect the concerns, interests and developmental stages of the child and the carefully structured environment is designed to foster both personal and social learning.

Teaching is by example rather than by direct instruction and is integrated rather than subject based. The curriculum is adapted to the child. In recognition of its vital role in early education, children are given time to play.

Emphasis is given to regular patterns of activities both within the day and over each week. A cyclical pattern is reflected in themes of work related to seasons of the year.

6.3 The Nature of the Early Years

Physical, emotional and cognitive development are subtly and inextricably linked. This view underpins and informs the Early Years curriculum which is tailored to meet the child's changing needs during each phase.

At each developmental stage, the child presents a particular set of physical, emotional and intellectual characteristics which require a particular (empathetic) educational response in return. This is the basis of a child-centred education. The formative period before second dentition, is seen as the period of greatest physical growth and development. Structures in the brain are being refined and elaborated, a process which is not completed until after the change of teeth, and until that time the young child's primary mode of learning is through doing and experiencing – he or she 'thinks' with the entire physical being.

The nature of this early learning should be self-motivated, allowing the child to come to know the world in the way most appropriate to his or her age – through active feeling, touching, exploring and imitating, in other words, through doing. Only when new capabilities appear, at around the seventh year, is the child physically, emotionally and intellectually ready for formal instruction. Through experiential, self-motivated physical activity the small child 'grasps' the world in order to understand it – an essential prerequisite for the later activity of grasping the world through concepts. Children are encouraged to master physical skills before abstract intellectual ones.

6.4 Early Years Education – Aims and Objectives

*   *Providing opportunities for children to be active in meaningful imitation*

To complement the maturational timetable, imitation is acknowledged as the prime Waldorf means of children's learning – hence adults in Kindergartens teach by imitation and most of what children learn at this stage is imparted by example. The child learns for life from life (the acquisition of the mother tongue for example, takes place largely through imitation) and children model their behaviour on what happens around them. Adult activities stimulate direct responses in the young child, and teachers carry out their daily tasks in such a way as to be worthy of imitation.

The Kindergarten is a community of 'doers' supported through meaningful work, for example by baking bread. The children are welcome, but not required to help. The activity of the teacher may inspire the children to become independently active, finding their own learning situations in play. Children perceive and register everything the adults do – it isn't only *what* one does before the young child but also *how* one does it. Teachers are conscious of their own moral influence upon the child and of the development of good habits through imitation. One would expect to see a range of suitable activities for imitation taking place in the Kindergarten. These might include domestic tasks such as baking, cooking, cleaning, caring for the room etc. – all activities with a social, practical, moral and educational basis.

The forces of imitation, which are so important in helping the young child to know and understand the world in this first phase, naturally diminish and give way to a new kind of knowing which appears at around the time of second dentition. This is the time when teaching 'by example' moves into more formal teaching by instruction. The curriculum changes as one phase of child development comes to a close and another begins. (There is a similar shift in our curriculum at age 14 which corresponds to the changes which occur at puberty.)

- *Working with rhythm and repetition*

Steiner Waldorf Kindergartens identify rhythm as an important educational principle. Children need the reassurance of continuity and regular events mark the Kindergarten year, week and day. Seasonal activities celebrate the cycles of the year – autumn in Kindergarten might be a time for threshing and grinding and spring a time for planting. A 'seasonal area' in the room or wider environment reflects the changing natural world throughout the year, as do the themes of songs, stories and poems. In addition, each week has its own regular rhythm of recurring activities i.e. baking day, painting day, gardening day.

Every day has its own smaller rhythms which support the day's activities. These daily rhythms help the child to feel secure and to know what to expect, a tidy up song, for example, might signal the end of one activity and the beginning of another. The day is structured so that there is a varied pace – with periods of contraction and expansion – providing a balance between times of activity and times of rest. In practice, this might mean that creative play would be followed by a more concentrated circle time, or energetic outdoor activity by a quiet story. There is a rhythmic alternation between the 'child's time' (creative play, outside time) and the teacher's time (ring-time, story), the teacher's time being comparatively short at this age. Working with rhythm helps children to live with change, to find their place in the world, and to begin to understand the past, present and future. It provides a very real foundation for the understanding of time – what has gone before and what will follow – and helps children to relate to the natural and the human world. Attention to rhythm promotes healthy development and leads to a balanced life later.

Repetition also plays a key role in establishing continuity and in the healthy development of memory. Children's memories are strengthened by recurring experiences; and daily, weekly and yearly events in Kindergarten are remembered and often eagerly anticipated a second time around. Stories are told not just once, but many times: repetition brings the opportunity for children to familiarise themselves with the material and to deepen their relationship to it.

- *Encouraging personal, social and moral development*

Children learn, through their creative play and through their daily social activities, to interact with each other. In Kindergarten they learn to share, to work together, and to co-operate. They know and trust their teachers and are able to establish effective relationships with other children and adults. Teachers and children care for and respect each other.

Much emphasis is placed on caring for the environment – both inside and out. Wooden toys, for example, can be polished and mended, unlike their plastic counterparts. Where possible, gardening and composting activities introduce children to the idea of ecology and form an important part of the curriculum.

There are moments of reverence each day, and teachers lovingly create opportunities for children to experience joy, awe and wonder. Kindness is practised by teachers and encouraged in the children. Festivals provide rich cultural and religious experiences for the child. Traditional fairy tales and nature stories address the feeling realm and gradually awaken a fine moral sense for knowing right from wrong. The teacher sets the example and has certain expectations of the children.

- *Providing an integrated learning experience*

The learning experience of children under seven should be integrated and not compartmentalised. Young children need to experience the relevance of their world before they separate themselves from it and begin to analyse it in a detached way. Consequently learning in Kindergarten is integrated rather than subject based. Mathematics and use of mathematical language, for example, might take place at the cooking table, where food is prepared (thinly sliced carrots make wonderful natural circles and have the added virtue of being able to be eaten later in soup!) and concepts such as addition and subtraction (or more or less), weight, measure, quantity and shape are grasped in a practical manner as part of daily life. Mealtimes offer an opportunity for the moral, social and mathematical to work together as children engage in place-setting and the sharing of food which has been prepared earlier for everyone to eat.

Through movement games, children recognise and recreate patterns – in, out, alternate, in front of, behind. Natural objects such as acorns, pine cones, conkers and shells are sorted, ordered and counted, as part of spontaneous play. Children in Waldorf Kindergartens are directly involved in mathematical experience and use mathematical language in a natural way which is usually embedded in a social and moral context. Learning experiences for the young child are not separated from the business of daily living: learning gains meaning by its relevance to life.

As indicated above, a similar approach is taken to the teaching of language and literacy. Children develop competence in talking, listening and in the ability to use words with confidence they speak freely and learn to listen to others. Good speech and the development of aural skills are promoted. Concentration is on the oral tradition and the children listen to many wonderful stories – which belong to the literary heritage of the culture of childhood.

A well told story creates an appreciation for the human voice and the beauty and rhythms of language. It also helps to extend vocabulary and to aid the development of a good memory. Children leave Kindergarten with a rich and varied repertoire of songs, stories and poems; this might also include verses in French or German. Much of this learning will have taken place in the integrated way described – although story time is always a very special event.

Children engage in many activities, such as sewing, which develop hand to eye co-ordination, manual dexterity and orientation (useful preparation for reading print from left to right). Children also discuss their own drawings and take great delight in telling stories by 'reading' their pictures. This activity promotes the development of verbal skills and frees the narrative from the printed text, thus encouraging children to use their own words. Many children also act out or perform puppet shows and develop dramatic skills through working with narrative and dialogue. Painting and drawing help with balance and symmetry and most five year-olds are able to write their own name. Children experience the musicality of language and its social aspects through playing ring games and doing eurythmy, a form of movement which works with language and music.

The combination of these activities cultivates a love of language, promotes fluency and allows children time to become really familiar with the spoken word – the best preparation and foundation for the subsequent development of literacy. Use of language also affects cognitive development as well chosen words and good syntax support clear thinking.

- *Encouraging learning through creative play and supporting physical development*

Children are able to exercise and consolidate their ability to understand and to think through their play. Creative play supports physical, emotional and social development and allows children to learn through investigation, exploration and discovery. It also gives scope for the use of imagination – an essential aspect of human intelligence. Play encourages the child to become inventive and adaptable, and to work with initiative and flair. In addition it develops and strengthens concentration.

Studies [30] show that children who score highest in socio-dramatic play also demonstrate the greatest gains in a number of cognitive areas such as higher intellectual competence, longer attention span, and more innovation and imaginativeness. Good players also show more empathy toward others, less aggression, and in general more social and emotional adjustment. Time and space is given to creative play and a selection of suitable objects, for instance cloths, shells, logs, domestic toys and dolls, is provided in order to support a variety of play situations. *

- *Encouraging children to know and love the world*

As mentioned in the section on rhythm and repetition, children develop a good relationship to the natural world. They learn to value its gifts and to understand its processes and patterns of change. Domestic tasks provide opportunities for elementary experiences in science and good use is made of the four elements. Children make toys from sheep's wool, wood, felt, cotton and other natural materials. Many items are made as gifts for family members. Family participation is encouraged and teachers, working with parents, create 'birthday stories' which are based on the child's personal biography and are told at special ceremonies to which families are invited.

People in the community who practise a particular craft, or who have special skills, are often invited to visit Kindergarten, and many teachers take their children for short local walks.

- *Providing a safe child-friendly environment*

The Kindergarten should be a warm and welcoming place, an artistically shaped free space which serves as the setting for what the day's impulse brings. This 'impulse' is a mixture of child-motivated play experiences and teacher-structured activities. There are few 'finished' toys which demand to be used in a predetermined way. Furniture is small-scale and child-friendly and, as mentioned, the day is structured so as to provide the child with periods of activity and periods of rest. Groups are usually of a mixed age range; and older children, who are familiar with the rhythm of the particular Kindergarten, are able to help the younger members of the group to feel secure.

- *Working with parents*

Waldorf teachers are committed to establishing good relationships with parents and to the process of developing parenting skills. The importance of a happy, smooth transition from home to school is recognised, teachers working closely with parents to achieve this end. The majority of Kindergartens hold parent and toddler sessions and have a good rapport with the family before the child enters Kindergarten. Teachers promote and emphasise the importance of close partnerships with parents and provide a focus for parent support. Links are also created with parents through a range of social and school-based events and activities. Close liaison between parent and teacher is encouraged.

6.5   An Example of a Kindergarten Session

Perhaps the best way to exemplify the integration of the above educational aims is to describe a typical Kindergarten morning session. This example, of course, only highlights one range of activities. Normally each day of the week would have its own main focus and these vary with the changing seasons.

The Kindergarten staff spend hours in their Kindergartens both before the children arrive in the morning and after they have gone. There are activities and materials to prepare, of course, but more

*   Please note: references 30 – 42 are on page 62.

importantly there has to be the right mood in the place. The staff often meet in the morning to say a verse together before going to their rooms to be there when the children arrive.

As the children begin to arrive, the Kindergarten leader is already busy so that the children, having hung up their coats and changed their shoes, can be given a homely welcome. At first there may be a period of free play with small groups of children choosing their area, perhaps getting the dolls up and dressed, building with small logs or driving a bus made from an upturned chair. The adults are usually engaged in some task, such as preparing the dough if it is baking day. There is conversation and some of the children may prefer to be around the adults, as children traditionally have been, watching, 'helping', while adults work, asking questions and so on. These informal moments are vital, not least in a world in which every one is often so busy.

The adults initiate the next phase by beginning to clear the things away and the children join in helping each tool or object to find its place on shelf or in basket. The forces of imitation are strongest at this age and can be most easily directed when the adults perform their tasks in a conscious and careful way, repeating the gestures of each action in a rhythmical and natural way. Children can learn to do quite complex practical tasks, even involving sharp or awkward tools or equipment, if they see them regularly performed with love and care.

Tidying up is an important task and it is done in such a way that it does not occur to the children that this is something which spoils their fun or is a tedious chore. Once things have been put back in their places, the children gather for ringtime during which traditional songs are sung, and rhythmical verses spoken and acted out. Sometimes the eurythmist or foreign language teacher may visit and contribute to the circle's activities. These activities help focus the children's attention and especially strengthen their linguistic skills. Listening and clear articulation can be exercised through this kind of rhythmical recitation. Afterwards, the children go to the toilet and wash their hands. Some of the older ones who are first back help lay and set the table with place-mats, cutlery and perhaps a vase of flowers. Bread is cut and everyone gathers to say a grace and sing some seasonal songs. There is no deliberate effort to teach the children in any formal sense. The conscious activity of the teacher is imitated by the children.

Following the morning snack, some of the children help clear up while others go off to a second period of free play or another artistic or handicraft activity. Here the children follow by example and may paint or model for as long as their interest lasts. This might be the time to go outdoors into the garden or sandpit, or may even involve a walk to a nearby park. Once more everyone returns, coats and scarves are hung up, things are carefully put away and then all gather, perhaps around a chair in the 'story corner'. The morning concludes with the Kindergarten teacher telling a fairy story. By then the parents are waiting outside to collect the children. Some Kindergartens include afternoon sessions as well. In this case lunch is eaten, followed by a rest and then further periods of play.

Each day of the week has its own artistic or handicraft activity, such as a baking day. While most Kindergartens offer water colour painting and drawing with wax crayons, or beeswax modelling and eurythmy, the handicrafts vary according to the facilities or the particular skills of the adults concerned. In all these activities the children learn by example, finding their way in to the experiences at their own pace. In this way the children learn to explore and be creative whilst acquiring a love of work. This manifests itself in an increasing mood of self-reliance and calm industriousness when the children are engaged. The same mood is carried over into creative play. A strong and lively rhythm helps give the children a deep sense of security.

6.6 Introduction to Formal Learning

Many years of experience confirm that literacy and numeracy, as formal skills, are best taught when the child has reached a point of maturation which corresponds to the emergence of the second teeth .The principled approach of Steiner Waldorf practitioners to not forcing early literacy and numeracy leads to Class 1 pupils (at 6+) learning to read and to work formally with number with such enthusiasm and alacrity because:

a)   they have reached a point of developmental readiness;
b)   the diversity of lively hands-on experience, which they have encountered in their Kindergartens, supports and enriches this learning process;
c)   they are motivated learners, unburdened by early failure.*

*   For guidelines on school readiness see: Avison, K., *A Handbook for Waldorf Class Teachers*, SSF 1995.

7.0 A HORIZONTAL CURRICULUM

> *I myself have witnessed in the Waldorf School how the teacher and his class have become a unity and by this I do not mean the sum total of pupils plus teacher. This wholeness is the matrix out of which the development of the children can grow. According to each teacher's individuality, outer forms of teaching may vary enormously in the different classes, and yet the fundamental qualities are retained. In a Waldorf school outer forms do not follow set patterns, so that it is quite possible for one teacher to teach his class of nine year olds well while another, who takes a completely different line, may be an equally good teacher. In this way we plan the curriculum for each year in accordance with the nature of the growing child. As long as the teacher feels in harmony with the underlying principles and with the methods employed, he must be given freedom in his work instead of being tied to fixed standards. No matter whether he happens to be teaching a Class 1 or a Class 8, he should feel part of the whole school so that already in Class 1 he will lay the foundations for what will find a certain completion in Class 8.*
>
> Rudolf Steiner, *The Renewal of Education*, 24th April 1920

By 'horizontal curriculum' is meant the various subjects that are taught to children in any one class, which means children of the same age. The 'vertical curriculum', which follows this section, shows how each individual subject develops from year to year and from the youngest age groups to the oldest. The horizontal curriculum shows us the integration of the various subjects in meeting the age groups' needs in interdisciplinary ways. It also enables us to give typical developmental pictures of the children in the different age groups. The vertical curriculum shows us the spiral nature of the path of learning, in which new skills are built on existing skills and topics can be revisited from new and age-appropriate perspectives.

What neither of these forms of presentation can easily show is the 'diagonal curriculum', which would reveal cross-links between different skills and abilities at different ages. It would show, for example, the relationship between knitting in the first two classes and mathematical skills in the Middle and Upper School, or between folk tales and fables in Classes 1 and 2 and ecology in the Upper School, or indeed between grammar in the Middle School and the ability to form judgments in life after school! The diagonal curriculum is just as essential to the educational tasks of Waldorf education as the other two dimensions. It has to be said that this third curriculum remains to be thoroughly researched though there are many references to it within the curriculum descriptions given in this book.

Each teacher adapts the curriculum to meet the needs of the children. Therefore it is important to bear in mind that in the main-lesson blocks and subject lessons mentioned below, qualitative differences of approach are as important as the actual lesson content. These variations keep the content in tune with the spiritual, psychological and physical stage of development the children have reached. Every teacher at a Steiner Waldorf school has a duty to shape the curriculum or, better still, to re-create it anew to suit every situation. The following constitutes guidelines based on typical good practice.

The following sections give an overview and summary of the teaching content and methodology for each age range. The classes are grouped into three sections, 1 to 3, 4 to 6 and 7 and 8, since these stages mark significant developmental stages and distinctive teaching approaches. For reasons of space, the choice of examples is of necessity selective. A developmental profile is given for each age group.

7.1 The Lower School – Classes 1 to 3

Class 1 (Age 6-7)

Developmental Profile

The seventh year sees the commencement of 'formal' schooling in the Steiner Waldorf method. During the first seven years, the young child learns to be at home in the physical body, developing an orientation in space and acquiring the initial, fundamental developmental capacities of uprightness, speech and thought. The content of the child's whole environment is the learning context; the child 'imitates' the people and the agencies that are in his/her environment. This imitating gesture serves to imprint on the child's will the content and the quality of what is learnt. In the Nursery/Kindergarten, experiential learning, discovery through creative play and intensive social interaction with peers and teacher constitute the main educational themes. Awareness of the complexities of the mother tongue and number is acquired through informal play and social interaction. This is not taught didactically.

Around the seventh year the child completes the process of forming the second dentition sufficiently for forces that have been concentrated on growth and physical upbuilding to become active in developing the facility for independent, representational, pictorial thinking. 'Formal' methods of teaching – in literacy, numeracy and other disciplines – are introduced. The child is still in a mood of dreamy wholeness, more able to bring broad awareness than focused concentration to learning settings. Much learning is continued through activity and imitation through which the child receives an image, internalises it, recalls it, generalises it into a concept which can be applied e.g. the letter 'R' or times 'x'. What was experienced practically, though not conceptually, in the pre-school years is raised to a feeling relationship through mental picturing. The child's holistic experience of the world is nourished by archetypal pictures such as those reflected in fairy tales and well thought out nature stories.

Aims and Objectives

In this year the children make the important transition from the Kindergarten to school where they begin formal learning. The children are led by their teacher to a first experience of the forms, sounds and sequencing of letters and number symbols by using pictures, rhymes and stories.

The children learn to recognise and memorise these with lots of practice involving movement, verses, drawing and writing. During this first year the class acquires the good habits of classroom life and work, which will form the basis of their time together in the Lower School and indeed for all subsequent learning at school. Cultivating reverence for nature, care for the environment, respect for others, interest in the world and a feeling of confidence in their teachers – these are the moral aims for Class 1 and the following classes. The teachers aim to lead the children into becoming a socially cohesive group who care for and listen to each other.

Class 2 (Age 7-8)

Developmental Profile

The eight year-old child continues to reside in a largely self-created psychological landscape, which derives from the child's faculty for developing individualised thought-pictures from the realms of their inner life. The events and experiences of the outside world are filtered through the child's imagination and rearranged to accord with the child's homogenous world-picture. The children show greater alertness in noting what happens around them at this age. The mood of wholeness differentiates into contrasts such as a deeper, more conscious feeling for the religious element alongside a tempting awareness of the mischievous.

The curriculum content for this age serves to cultivate in the child a sense for the breadth and richness of the language of the feelings and emotions.

Cognitively the child continues to be at home in a learning context where pictorial thought content is to the fore. Concepts are best understood meaningfully when they are mobile and organic in quality. The pupils continue to familiarise themselves with the fundamentals of numeracy and literacy, while in gross and fine motor movements – whether through skipping, catching and throwing a ball, or knitting, crocheting or flute-playing – they develop a repertoire of skills and competencies, that were initially introduced in Class 1. Thus the intellect is allowed to awaken through the artistic approach.

In Class 2 pupils, the adult teeth continue to push through, laterality and dominance are firmly established and during this year, specific learning needs and difficulties are observable. The range of abilities within a class becomes clearly discernible. Much of the confidence and sense of belonging which Class 2 pupils exude is clearly due to the fact that the child is building on the foundations laid in Class 1.

Aims and Objectives

The initial experiences of the first year are deepened and enhanced in Class 2. This time is used primarily for practising and developing all the new skills from the previous year. Whereas in Class 1 a lot of energy goes into forming the class into a social cohesive group where children are supported by the wholeness that they experience, in Class 2 a mood of contrast or polarisation often surfaces, which can be observed in the way children relate to each other. To help the children go through this stage they are told stories where contrasting human qualities and characteristics are found portrayed by holy people and saints in legends and by animals in the fables. This class needs strong leadership from the teachers through consistency of approach and through the power of imagination. The children derive direction and form from the images they are given.

Class 3 (Age 8-9)

Developmental Profile

Class 3 in the Steiner Waldorf Curriculum is the equivalent point of entry into Key Stage Two in the National Curriculum guidelines. In Class 3 the pupils enter their tenth year. At this point, noticeable physiological, psychological and cognitive changes take place in the child. These changes, referred to as the ninth/tenth-year threshold, may begin as early as 8.5 years or as late as 9.5 years and may last from between six months and one year.

The child develops a firmer, more balanced gait; speech sounds are increasingly formed in the middle of the mouth and articulated more directly and the child focuses on the 'middle distance'. The child's constitution is noticeably stronger. The heart increases in size and is capable of receiving a larger volume of blood and a new breath/blood pulse ratio is established in the region of one breath to four pulses. Growth begins to focus more on the limbs and metabolism and there is a growth in the breadth of the trunk. In some children this developmental phase is marked by symptoms including weariness, tummy and head pains, nausea, dizziness, a variable appetite, asthma, eczema and disturbed sleep patterns.

Steiner talks about a metamorphosis in the child's feeling life. At seven years, there is a metamorphosis in the child's thinking. In Class 3, the child experiences a duality in perceiving the world, in his or her feeling. A process begins to unfold through which the child experiences with increasing strength, a sense of objectivity, alongside growing subjectivity. Subjective inner experience and objective world reality stand at odds within the child's soul. Questioning, doubt, aloneness and a dawning tendency to criticise are emergent features in the child's psychological landscape.

Sometimes a little earlier, sometimes a little later, but for most children a very significant step in self-awareness occurs during this year. It is experienced as an awareness of being separate from the surroundings both human and physical, and of a distinction between an inner and an outer world. Contrasting emotions of the sense of loss of the previous unity with the world and a sense of wonder at seeing the world in a new way often lead to confusion and insecurity. These can be expressed in marked changes of behaviour that vary considerably according to temperament and personality.

The images of the Old Testament, its laws and guidance foster inner security during the unsettled period and the main lesson blocks on farming, building etc. help the children to engage in a new relationship with their surroundings.

Aims and Objectives

As the Class 3 children become more aware of themselves and the physical environment in which they live, a new interest in the practical, material world emerges. After practising their literacy and numeracy skills in Class 2 they can now apply these in a wide range of everyday situations which require measuring or weighing, solving simple problems and the writing of simple formal letters.

By involving the whole class in the experience of working together in building, farming and other examples of work projects, the class teacher helps to transform the initial feeling of separateness from the physical world into a feeling of responsibility for it. It is important for the teachers to lay down clear guidelines for behaviour and to give the children confidence in the authority of the teachers, not only the class teacher. The children should have a strong sense of the social unity of the class, an experience of 'we'.

Curriculum Classes 1 – 3

The Steiner Waldorf curriculum usually begins with a subject unknown in other schools. This is 'form drawing' or 'dynamic drawing'. Basic straight and curved lines and shapes are made and drawn by the children, preferably making the shapes with their whole body to begin with (walking, running, sweeping movements of the arms and hands) and later using crayons or pencils on paper. Having been experienced in movement, these shapes and rhythms are then brought to rest by drawing them on paper. All this requires the children to make purposeful, concentrated efforts in movement, a medium ideally suited to them. The shapes have no outer meaning, neither do they depict anything in particular, rather they make the dynamic of movement and shape visible in space. The children learn to experience, feel (with their fingers, for example) and understand the inherent quality and nature of different shapes and movements. Experiencing the inner nature of something through movement is one of the basic themes in Classes 1 to 3. Form drawing is also an excellent preliminary exercise to writing. In Classes 2 and 3 such exercises stimulate the activity of forming mental pictures, an activity which both engages the will and stimulates the feelings. In a sense the life of feeling is used as an organ of perception. The child *feels* the balance, proportion, symmetry, integration and character of the forms and the dynamic movements they embody.

In English language lessons the children are introduced to the letters of the alphabet. Initially the aim is to lead the children to experience the qualities of the spoken sounds and sentence melody, whilst the shape, name and meaning of the capital letters of the alphabet are taught. By allowing the shape of a capital letter to emerge from a picture that stands for the character of the sound, the children can develop their own relationship to the individual letters and later to the whole activity of writing. Consonants are evolved out of pictograms, vowels out of interjections and expressions of feeling. The process proceeds from pictorial representation of the letters to formal writing, with the children initially copying examples written by the teacher and later through dictation. The exploration of the relationship of sound and symbol includes the use of emergent writing. From capital letters the children proceed to lower case cursive handwriting, usually in Class 2.

The content of written work is related to main-lesson themes and the children's own experiences. As a general guideline, about a third of writing is composed by the children, the other two thirds comprising texts prepared by the teacher and copied from the board or dictated by the teacher. By Class 3 the children write longer, more complex compositions. Instruction and practice in formal letters, diaries and description of nature moods supplement this. Neat legible handwriting is encouraged.

Reading proceeds from writing and in Class 1 the children read familiar texts which the teacher has written on the board and which they themselves have written in their exercise books. An integrated combination of whole word, phonic and contextual methods is used to develop reading, though with an emphasis on whole sentences/whole phrases. Reading books are not normally used until Class 2. A differentiated approach to reading is used including whole class reading, child to child and child to adult reading and supported with regular practice in the recognition of auditory, visual and kinesthetic patterns. Spelling is based on a whole language approach reinforced by contextual, phonic and kinesthetic methods. By Class 3 reading progresses to a differentiation of material for different purposes, including understanding instructions and tasks, finding information and reading timetables. Reading aloud is practised with an awareness of content and punctuation. Children are directed to a wide range of reading material according to ability.

Oral work plays an important role throughout the classes with equal emphasis on both speaking and listening. Good skills at both are prerequisites for the development of all literacy skills. As well as the daily recitation of poetry and verses, many of which are designed as speech exercises to strengthen pronunciation and articulation, the children are encouraged to describe their experiences and recall the stories they have heard. The teacher's own language serves as a model for the use and form of spoken language. This emphasis on oral work provides a basis for the subsequent understanding of grammatical structures and punctuation as well as exemplifying the linguistic expression of emotional qualities such as surprise, curiosity, denial, enthusiasm, willing affirmation and so on.

The work on writing, reading and speaking and listening in the first two classes provides a basis for introducing children to a systematic exploration of grammatical qualities in Class 3, starting with nouns, verbs, adjectives and adverbs. The aim is not only to make conscious principles that have hitherto been learned pragmatically but to school the child's thinking and awareness of the real relationships which grammar and syntax express and define.

Foreign language lessons are as important as those focusing on the mother tongue. From Class 1 onwards the children learn two foreign languages by the direct method of listening and speaking. Writing and grammar are not touched on during Classes 1 to 3. The children are immersed in these languages by means of poems, stories and fairy tales and dialogue, all learned by heart and enacted in context. Through the other languages they experience a different way of describing things, a different way of looking at things, a different way of approaching the world. This is one of the most important prerequisites for a lively ability to form concepts and also for achieving a more universal view of the world that encompasses more than one perspective, in that it broadens the one-sided orientation of the mother tongue. During the first three years the children acquire orally an extensive vocabulary of everyday things and situations and a practical usage of most of the main grammatical structures of the language. In the succeeding years the children will draw on this reservoir of oral language and experience as they begin to learn to become literate in the foreign language.

The stories told in this phase are those which describe 'the child's path down to the earth'. In Class 1 the oneness of humankind, animals, nature and the heavens is experienced in an archetypal way in traditional fairy tales and local folklore. Stories are also chosen which portray the cycles of the natural world and especially the seasonal changes. In Class 2 differentiation between these kingdoms begins to be demonstrated through fables and legends. In Class 3 the human being's responsibility towards the earth and God is shown in the creation stories of Genesis and other Old Testament material. (This applies chiefly to schools in countries with a European tradition. Steiner Waldorf schools where Buddhist, Hindu, Islamic, Hebrew or other cultures predominate choose other suitable material.) The essential elements in these myths are the creation of the heavens and earth, the plant and animal kingdoms, the divine origin of humankind: the tasting of the Tree of Knowledge, the origin of human community and the laws which govern it.

In Class 3, through the themes of farming and house-building, the children's journey is brought literally down to earth. They carry out practical farming and building activities. The actual topics chosen depend on the locality so that, for example, in coastal regions fishing may feature in the lessons. Such practical activities, tailored to the children's age and capabilities contain long-term pedagogical elements that prepare them for later insight into economics and ecology. Learning how natural raw materials are transformed into products, which serve real needs in the world, sows the seeds for a real experience of mutuality and service.

Arithmetic also involves movement. In Class 1 the children experience the totality and the individuality of numbers. Whole numbers are introduced with emphasis on their archetypal character – one means unity, two is a duality and so on, using pictures familiar to the child's world (the sun, parts of the body, petals of flowers etc.). Then come the four basic arithmetical operations and their different qualities, always going first from the whole to the parts. The symbols are introduced in a pictorial way. Rhythmical counting, recitation of tables, number bonds up to 20 and mental arithmetic are all practised intensively in the early years. This gives the children an experience of movement in mental activity, which complements the way the letters of the alphabet are introduced.

By Class 2 there is a shift of emphasis from manual operation to mental computation and the exploration of various forms of appropriate notation and algorithm and their application to problem solving. In Class 3 measurement moves from the oral realm, which is comparative, qualitative and contextual (this is bigger, there are more here etc.) to the use of formal units. Starting with traditional measures based on body proportions, the children are introduced to standard units of linear, liquid, weight, time, money and music measurement and notation.

In painting with watercolours the inner qualities of a colour are explored. What feelings does this colour generate? What soul qualities are linked to the three primary colours: blue, yellow and red? The aim of these painting lessons is not to copy external objects or make illustrations but to experience and 'listen' to the inner language of colours. The children illustrate their main-lesson books with pencils and crayons, an activity which unites the dynamic of line drawing with the mood and feeling expressed by the colours. In this way the children bring their powers of imagination to what they have perceived with their senses.

While in painting the 'sounds' of the colours are explored, in the music lessons during the first three years of school the inner 'colours' or character of the notes are explored. In these first school years, however, it is important that the children do not yet focus on musical moods that are as yet unfamiliar to their experience, such as those connected with the musical scales or the tonalities of major and minor. Their inner life is not yet mature or differentiated enough to empathise with such qualities. At this age the children still need to experience the tones and the space they fill in a free way, for example through the pentatonic mode. The music they play with their simple wooden flutes, recorder, child's harp or lyre is initially related to the songs they have learnt. This can perhaps be compared with the way they learn to write, by beginning with what they already know by heart.

There is an emphasis on active listening through singing, often accompanied with movement and gesture in response to melody. Through Class 2 the children expand their range of tunes, and individuals take the step to small solo parts within the context of the class as a choir. In Class 3 the transition is made to music that relates to a keynote or diatonic perspective, when the children meet with an early 'grammar' or 'spelling' (notation) of music. The recorder is an instrument that shapes and differentiates the stream of the breath. Bowed instruments bring in a new important element. With the recorder both hands are involved in shaping the stream of air. With a bowed instrument the right hand wields the bow, the left hand selects the notes and the listening ear makes sure that the result is in tune. An almost craft-like skill is needed for this, but it remains within the realm of feelings and sensations in the soul. It leads to a sense for the qualitative shaping of time.

Eurythmy lessons provide the link between space and time: the sounds of speech and the sounds of music are made visible through movement in space. This art helps the children harmonise their actions through the balance between the alert perception of the senses and bodily movement by filling both with feeling. Eurythmy helps the children become aware of the qualities of the spatial dimension in an artistic way.

During the first three years at school the children are led gently through movement to an experience of their own bodily orientation and mobility within their surrounding space. Traditional movement and ring games are learnt and practised, which develop skills and co-ordination as well as having a strong social component. The transition to more formal gymnastic exercises comes in the third year. The harmonious movement sequences already practised become more target-oriented.

Handwork lessons are also aimed at training manual skills. All children learn to knit and sew and use basic handicraft tools (scissors, craft knives, adhesives, string etc.) and work with a range of materials. The children produce useful articles such as recorder cases, potholders, shopping nets and so on. This schooling of fine motor skills, co-ordination combined with the artistic and practical element provides a sound basis for the subsequent basis of practical intelligence.

Summary:

The first three years of school can perhaps best be described as helping the children find their way into the world while taking into account their basic need to experience the 'inner side' of nature, language and music. The children also acquire a range of basic skills. It is important for the children to gain a sense of respect and reverence for what they learn about as well as for the people whose skills they admire. Then, in addition to learning to feel at home in the world, they will strengthen their desire to be good at things, which is an important stimulus to self-activity in learning. This feeling of wanting to be good at things forms the basis for the children's love for the authority of their teachers.

In their pre-school years the children had a strong urge to move; their movement was space-oriented and directed into exploring the world around them. In the early school years new developmental forces have to be taken into account, which seek to find an orientation in the qualities of their inner life. A start is made in achieving an interplay between external activity and inner reflection. In this sense it is the teacher's task to help the children acquire a healthy balance between the inner and outer worlds, between taking in and taking part, in bringing the child's own individuality into the right relationship to her own body and environment. This process of finding a healthy balance between the inner experience and the bodily organism is what Steiner referred to as teaching the children to breathe, [31] the breath being the archetype of inner-outer exchange. The metaphor also infers that the exchange is not fixed but rhythmical, with breathing in, a transformation of substance and breathing out.

7.2   Classes 4 to 6

Class 4 (Age 9-10)

Developmental Profile

In Classes 4 and 5 when the pupils are 10 and 11 years-old, the mid-way point of the class teacher years is reached. The transition from early childhood is complete, the transition towards puberty has not yet begun. This centre-point of the class teaching period coincides with the middle of the second seven-year period of life, and is referred to in Steiner Waldorf pedagogy as the 'heart of childhood'.

The self-activity of the child brings about a harmonising of the relationship of the breathing to the blood circulation.

Confidence in their new state is expressed in a quality of vigour and an eagerness to look at and learn about the world. A start is made on natural science with a phenomenological study of the animal kingdom in relation to the human being from a morphological point of view. Also a thorough study of the local surrounding and developing the process of map-making.

Aims and Objectives

The aim of Class 4 is first and foremost to channel positively the powerful energy which ten year-olds bring to the classroom. Pupils need to be challenged and stretched in every possible aspect of their work. "Work, work and lots of it" is the best motto for Class 4.

The teachers aim to meet, through imaginatively presented lessons, the growing interest of the children in more concrete areas of knowledge and to provide them with opportunities for more independence in their work. Individually the children need to find a new relationship to their work, to their peers and teachers. The narrative content of the lessons aims to respond by offering stories in which a multiplicity of personalities contributes to the social whole (e.g. stories of the Norse Gods) and in which darkness and evil become more concrete. The children should begin to identify individual 'badness' in contrast to social or communal 'goodness'. The children should form a sense of where they are in relation to their environment, in both a social and geographical sense.

Class 5 (Age 10-11)

Developmental Profile

At this age the child attains a certain ease and grace of movement intrinsic to the age. Movement that is co-ordinated, balanced and harmonious is a key-note of the developmental phase. Psychologically, the 'I'/world differentiation develops, the individual 'will' element begins to grow, the awareness of 'self' strengthens and socially, a powerful group dynamic can surface within a class, although the individual ego is very much a fledgling. Cognitively, children are more able to understand questions and phenomena in a realistic and reasoning manner. The pictorial element in thought processes remains an important element in the child's consciousness, although the understanding and formulation of concepts are beginning to depend less on the development of individualised images and thought pictures and more on the development of a faculty for comprehending clear, matter-of-fact, sense-free concepts.

Out of the growing memory powers, the sense for time has developed. Memory allows for looking back and planning the future and, combined with deepening feeling, for the emergence of conscience and responsibility.

This age is a time of rapidly flowering capacities. The child experiences a growth in length; sustained physical effort is within his or her group. Musically, a child has the capacity to master a musical instrument. In the basic skills of numeracy, literacy and linguistics pupils exhibit the emergence of independent creativity founded on a confident group of the basic rules, processes and structures.

Intellectually and morally the child is ready for new challenges. Foundations for the basic skills in numeracy and literacy have been set down by the tenth year. Elementary notions of personal responsibility and a faculty for understanding 'right and wrong' in a 'reasoning' spirit may be grasped from this age.

This year marks the pivotal point between childhood and puberty and for a short moment each child is poised at the crest of the wave, marking the end of the first part of their school years. They reach standards of work hitherto never dreamed of. They identify totally with their work, they spend time embellishing it, bringing it closer to perfection. They are often proud of their work, whereas in Class 4 they could easily be dismissive about it.

Towards the end of this year the teacher will begin to experience her pupils' emergent intellectual faculties, ready to be used more consciously. They bring with them a new detachment and their accompanying critical standpoint. The harmony is lost, to be found again at the end of the Upper School years.

Aims and Objectives

In this year the aim is to make the transition from myth to history and its emphasis on the individual. The children should develop a greater consciousness of the interrelatedness of life and environment – particularly through the study of botany. There will be an emphasis on the original Olympian ideal in which group distinctions are subservient to the greater whole and in which qualities such as beauty are as valued as speed and distance. The children should be encouraged to strengthen their memory by learning such things as vocabulary and by visualising spaces through the use of maps.

Class 6 (Age 11-12)

Developmental Profile

Class 6 in the Steiner Waldorf school is the equivalent point of entry into Key Stage Three in the National Curriculum guidelines. In the mainstream this age constitutes the first year in secondary education. There is a clear difference in methodology between the Steiner Waldorf curriculum and the National Curriculum as regards the age that it is appropriate for pupils to be introduced to the conscious development of deductive thinking, logical thought processes and analytical-critical faculties.

In Steiner's pedagogical indications there is common ground with the work of Piaget, Vygotsky and others, in the understanding that abstract thinking, or 'formal operations', begins around the thirteenth year, and not in Key Stage One.

Generally, the child's growth begins to express itself in the skeleton. The limbs begin to lengthen; the child develops a tendency for awkward, angular movements. The 12 year-old experiences the strength of gravity through the skeleton. The physical change is accompanied by the first experience of causation in the thinking realm, while psychologically, the child enters a phase which may be characterised as the 'changeling' period. The 12 year-old witnesses what may be described as the death of childhood and the birth-pangs of the individual.

In the final third of the second seven-year period, the child begins to anticipate adolescence. In the various curriculum topics indicated – sequential, recorded history, the geography of Europe, formal geometry, business maths, phenomenological science, gardening, woodwork and organised games – the child's changing physical, psychological and cognitive make-up is acknowledged and tended.

Aims and Objectives

At this age the teacher aims to work with the children's growing orientation towards the outer world. Their dawning critical faculties should be directed towards observing the natural world from a scientific standpoint and their increasing interest in social relationships should provide many opportunities for the children to take responsibility for their own class community. The aim is to forge a new social relationship between each other and their teacher.

As new capacities for thinking emerge, the children can be led to understand causal relationships at work in the world. The children's awareness should be directed towards the world they will live and work in as adults. The pupils should be challenged and are capable of high standards in their school work.

Curriculum Classes 4 and 5

In Classes 4 and 5, when the pupils are 10 and 11 years-old, they enter a period that can justifiably be called the heart of childhood. They have left early childhood behind them but have not yet entered puberty. The intensification of self-consciousness, which began during the ninth year, continues into Class 4 and the teacher increasingly experiences the power of the group of young individualities emerging in the class. Each child appears as a strong personality with distinctive gifts, talents and challenges but this is still essentially childlike in its manifestation. The children still respond well to imaginative stories and well-formed rhythms in teaching. The teaching needs to be challenging and lively if it is to engage the strengthening will of the children. Physiologically the self-activity of the child strives to bring about a harmonisation of the relationship of the breathing to the blood circulation.

At the latest by Class 4 the children enter into a psychological situation that differs from that of the preceding three years. Their relationship to nature and to their fellow human beings has become more distant. The 'world of which they are a part' has become 'the world that is around them'. As Steiner put it:

The time after the completed ninth year is particularly important because it is a significant turning point in the children's lives. Questions dart into their consciousness, you could say whole heaps of questions, all of which relate to differentiating on the feeling level between themselves and their environment, also between themselves and their teacher ... These questions need not necessarily be expressed, but they are there. In their feeling life the children question whether the teacher is skilful in the way he leads his life, above all whether the teacher has a firm foothold in life, whether he knows what he wants; above all they have a sure sense of the overall situation of the teacher's soul. [32]

Having lived hitherto in a totality of space and time, the children now want to begin to structure this totality in their thinking. They do this by differentiating both in space and in time. 'Before' and 'after' are more strongly felt and also related to one another and this reflects the child's growing ability to form independent mental images and recall them at will. Cognitively, the children are more able to understand questions and phenomena in a realistic and reasoning way, though the pictorial element in thinking remains important. Combined with greater capacity for empathetic feeling, this new clarity of thinking enables the cultivation of notions of personal responsibility and reasoned sense of right and wrong.

Around the age of 11 the child attains a certain ease and grace of movement which is co-ordinated, balanced and harmonious. By Class 6 (age 11-12) the children begin to undergo significant physical change commensurate with the onset of puberty. Growth usually begins to express itself in the skeleton, which becomes longer and heavier, leading to a tendency to awkward and angular movements.

These important physical changes are accompanied by a growing interest in the factual and sense perceptible world on the one hand and a psychological turbulence on the other. By about the twelfth year (Class 6) the moment will have arrived when the children no longer merely ask about causes, but actively look for them or actually create them in order to observe what effect they have. This applies equally to social relationships.

The trust shown up until now by children towards their teachers is now put to the test through challenging, silly and sometimes sharply critical behaviour. Peer values become increasingly significant in children's development, leading often to clearly distinguishable roles within the group, including leaders, bullies, victims, jokers, those who are deemed 'cool' and those who are marginalised.

The teachers must establish a new relationship to the class, one which can deal with the mood swings of the children and which can assert a new 'lawful' authority. Rules and parameters with clear consequences are essential at this age, though the teacher will also need to be able to defuse tension with humour.

In language lessons (both mother tongue and foreign) a new consciousness needs to be awakened for different linguistic qualities. *"Before their ninth year children have an entirely emotional relationship to language. However, they would be unable to develop an awareness of themselves if we did not bring an element of thought into language. That is why it is so important to bring in the thought element by means of grammatical rules, sensibly taught, mainly in the mother tongue but then also perhaps in a foreign language. However, the language must be learnt before the rules are introduced."* [33] For the foreign languages writing and reading in those languages must precede this.

The verb tenses bring an experience and understanding of how time is expressed in language. In English lessons the children learn about how the various parts of speech express different qualities and this responds to their increasing variety of inner experience. Declension, sentence structure, punctuation, prepositions etc. help articulate different standpoints and varying relationships, while distinguishing between direct and indirect speech or active and passive modes defines the speaker's own position (Class 5). In Class 6 comes the added facet of reality to be gained through using the subjunctive mode to indicate the difference between wish, intention and fact. Exercises in writing business letters brings in a further aspect of the real world and cultivates a sense for appropriate use of language in different contexts. The corresponding phase in foreign languages involves conversation exercises on situations in everyday life.

Music lessons now also involve the 'grammar of music'. Linked to what is going on in arithmetic lessons in which fractions are introduced in Class 4, note lengths and time value are now added to the notation begun in Class 3. The intrinsic laws of music are not studied theoretically but by playing music. The relationship of the subsidiary keys to the main key leads to the discovery of the cadenza. In keeping with the need to link everything to the level of the children's emotional development the difference between major and minor is practised by using the major and minor third (this refers particularly to Class 6). In keeping with this, singing and playing in unison now leads to rounds in several parts and then to simple polyphony.

Eurythmy lessons must be seen in connection with language and music. In speech eurythmy the various grammatical forms are practised while in tone eurythmy the scales and (in Class 6) the major and minor moods are worked on. Stepping in different rhythms and beats links to arithmetic through the values of the notes, while moving in geometrical forms supports the introduction of geometry that begins in Classes 5 and 6.

In the arithmetic lessons of Class 1 the unit was taken as the basis from which to experience the different numbers. Now, in Class 4, a similar principle comes into play again. The unit, the totality, splits up, but the parts have a regulated relationship with the whole through fractions. In the music lessons analogous discoveries are made. Fractions not only depict a 'spatial' differentiation but can also be comprehended in a dynamic and temporal way. Via decimals (Class 5) the path leads towards a preparation for logical, causal thinking, to percentages and thus to the first mathematical discovery of causes.

Form drawing now gains a strongly constructive component in intertwining, interlacing ribbon motifs, particularly in Celtic knotwork and patterns. Beauty now combines with accuracy. Attentiveness and alertness are required. In Class 5 form drawing includes freehand geometrical drawing, initially without compasses or ruler. Having done form drawing for four years, the children have gained a thorough sense of the circle, the straight line and the angle. These components are now taken separately and drawn as accurately as possible. Only once hand and eye have had enough practice is compass geometry introduced in Class 5 to draw shapes and in Class 6 to construct geometric forms.

Cause and effect can be experienced in the observation of the play of light and shadow in chiaroscuro or black-and-white shaded drawing. In Class 6 this subject complements painting with watercolours. As with free-hand geometry, the children search for and feel exactly how a shadow falls before shading it in charcoal.

Thus geometry emerges out of form drawing, and drawing with charcoal emerges from painting with watercolours. In each case the process is one of continuity. In the same way the practical experience of nature and human work in farming and building lessons is now extended and differentiated both spatially and temporally. Local studies lead on to geography and history on the one hand, and to nature studies on the other. From Class 6 onwards the latter also involves the practical aspect of gardening.

In local studies (Class 4) the children learn about the geography and above all the economic situation of their immediate surroundings. They discover how much depends on the type of soil and the lie of the land and learn what influences have been brought to bear during the course of history. The children also learn to make the transition from pictorial drawing to symbolic representation in map-making. When regional geography begins in Class 5, the whole country is studied, including its geographical and economic relationships with other countries. Finally a brief view of the whole world is given. Even at this age it is very important to go into the social aspects of geography both with regard to how the different peoples live together and with regard to caring responsibly for the environment.

Astronomy also appears on the horizon! At this stage the approach is phenomenological i.e. the children study what they can actually observe with their own eyes, especially the relationship between the earth and sun but also including the phases of the lunar cycle and visible constellations. Now the children come to understand that what they observe in the sky has a direct influence on the climate and vegetation all over the earth.

In the language lessons, mother tongue and foreign, the children have been writing business letters in the former and practising conversation in the latter. The same principle is brought to bear in geography, where, on the one hand, they study how human beings live together and, on the other, experience how we are all economically interdependent. In English the children learn how to write accurate descriptions of what they observe, as well as imaginative accounts of historical episodes they have heard about. In both the mother tongue and foreign languages there is an emphasis on accuracy of meaning through the correct use of words and declensions.

In nature study the animal kingdom is taken first because of its closeness to the human being. This aspect is emphasised through a comparison between the human being and various animal types. From an anatomical point of view, the human being is generalised and unspecialised, whereas each animal species has specific, one-sided anatomically based skills that have often developed at the cost of others e.g. one particular sense, specialised locomotion and so on, involving specific organs (eyes, nose, teeth, limbs etc.). The children learn about animals grouped by their chief characteristics in this regard, such as species with powerful metabolic systems (herbivores), animals that hunt and use their claws, strength and teeth (carnivores such as the big cats), animals with highly developed visual abilities (birds of prey) and so on. Human beings potentially have all these capacities, but each remains in balance with all the others, so that they can be seen as both synthesis and archetype of the whole animal kingdom. The children discover that *humans have what animals are*. We have technology and culture whereas they have specialised anatomy.

In plant studies the evolutionary path from lower to higher plants relates to the developmental stages of the child and young person. The sequence of plant forms growing ever more differentiated and expressive provides a visible image of the children's psychological development as more and more capacities develop. The children are shown how plants relate to the earth and sun, how they change during the course of the year and, in broad outlines, how they are distributed over the whole globe. In a manner comprehensible to children (but not in a childish manner!) the two important themes of evolution and ecology are thus present as an inner thread running through biology from the start. In nature studies in Class 6 the children enter for the first time the world of mineralogy in a block period devoted to this subject.

In the history lessons the children step out of the immediate present and imagine time processes in a concrete way with the help of vivid images from the past. The time for this falls between the eleventh and twelfth years. Psychologically the children are ready to move from myth and legend to history and biography. In Class 5, history involves giving the children historical images of Asian and Middle Eastern peoples i.e. the culture of Ancient India, China, Ancient Persia, Mesopotamia, Egypt and Greece. The culture of these early civilisations is characterised through story material. With Greece myth becomes history. In Class 6 they are introduced to Roman history and the Middle Ages. They learn about cultural changes throughout history e.g. what changes were brought about for Europe through contact with Islam. Here again the aspect of causality is taken into account. Europe lagged far behind the Orient. Then, thanks in part to contact with Islam and the East, new technological and industrial progress developed in European towns, particularly in Italy. The monastic settlements and the growth of urban cultures as well as the early influence of technology such as water wheels, building techniques, advancements in navigation and shipbuilding are important themes. The end of feudalism can, for example, be graphically characterised by events such as the Battle of Agincourt, which revealed a microcosm of social change.

Physics also begins in Class 6, and with it comes an experience of causality. The lessons are not yet concerned with the theories and hypotheses of physics: rather the children are helped to experience the basic phenomena of acoustics, optics, heat, magnetism and static electricity. Mechanics is held over for Class 7. Two of the reasons for this are as follows. Mechanics requires the study of gravity (unless you remain entirely in the neutral realm of theory), and it provides opportunities for the children to experience this force consciously. As the pupils enter puberty, they become 'ready for the earth'.[34] The growth associated with puberty has the effect of literally burdening the youngster with a new sense of physical weight. They have a need to explore the new strength that comes with this muscle and bone growth though they often lack an orientation both in their movements and in their emotional instability. They can be helped by discovering how the force of gravity can be employed in mechanics and made serviceable in life.

The second reason that mechanics is deferred until age 13, is that it provides examples for the application of physical law to technology, the consequences of which one can see most clearly in the industrial developments during the 19th Century. Practical applications of mechanical principles are the central theme. It is impossible to stress too strongly the importance of letting experience precede knowledge.

The practical subjects within the curriculum are now also expanded and differentiated. Gardening enables the child to encounter the consequences of work in a practical and necessary sphere of life. By providing opportunities to observe plant growth, gardening affords experiences of how time relates to space.

Three-dimensional space is now explored in handwork. The children knit gloves and socks on five needles and sew stuffed animals that require them to have a clear idea of the animal's shape when they design and cut out the pattern (the cause and effect aspect can also be seen here). The skills learned in cross-stitch are developed further to include the embroidery of interlacing ribbon motifs, such as those learned in form drawing.

'Soft' handwork is now joined by 'hard' craftwork, which is pursued by boys and girls alike. Working with wood provides a wonderful experience of what 'expertise' really means. Together, wood and tool are a unit when handled expertly. The skills of sawing, carving, rasping and filing are practised. In textile handwork, with the exception of leather, the resistance offered by the material is slight. Wood provides a considerably greater challenge so that form can be created by the practical activity of exercising 'expertise'.

Gym lessons provide a similar theme. The movement games are now replaced by various kinds of running game, such as relay races, which have a specific aim. Achieving this is the challenge. The same goes for apparatus work, which begins now, as well as athletics and swimming. In each case the children have to learn to move using the appropriate technique in the given medium.

The themes chosen for the narrative content of the lessons during these three years help the children experience their own psychological and spiritual steps in development, through examples which span the transition from myth and legend to history.

Summary:

During this period of development, in which the children begin to distance themselves from their surroundings, it is extremely important that their connection with the world be strengthened and renewed by means of direct and differentiated experience supported by understanding. To work in the world means to understand the world. The new subjects introduced during this phase make this possible. In working out of an understanding that has a moral foundation, the children learn to work in service for the sake of the world. Turning towards the world in this way can also be described as loving it in an active and concrete way. Class 6 marks an important transition in the class teacher period. With the onset of puberty the children are ready to develop a causal understanding of the world, yet given the emotional and subjective nature of their experience, it is important that this causal aspect be clothed in imaginative and pictorial language.

7.3 Classes 7 and 8

Class 7 (Age 12-13)

Developmental Profile

In Class 7 the pupils turn 13 and become teenagers. Two fundamental gestures characterise this phase of life: an outer, active principle and the stirring of a dynamic, inner, psychological state. An appetite for knowledge of, and about, world phenomena, mingles with a budding capacity for reflection and the first promptings of self-reflection. In this picture of emerging forces, the physical changes which establish sexual identity and capacity begin to manifest more clearly. The physical changes tend to be somewhat in advance of the psychological development. While a feeling and yearning for independence and solitude may be experienced, a certain anxiety, emotional sensitivity and embarrassment can run alongside. Sporadic bursts of energy and an appetite for expanding outer horizons vie with periods of lethargic heaviness and subdued introspection.

Generally, there are significant differences in the manner in which boys and girls face up to and deal with the challenges of this age. Curriculum themes which mirror the pupils' outer exploration of the world and the inner journey include: the journeys of exploration in history, the focus on mood and style in English, the areas of combustion and mechanics in chemistry and physics and the health, nutrition and hygiene main lesson block.

Aims and Objectives

The teachers should provide the adolescents with new perspectives, particularly by directing their attention into the world. The pupils should be encouraged to take initiative and to appreciate ideas which have an abstract and logical character. They should be encouraged to challenge attitudes and assumptions which formerly they accepted on authority and be shown how to formulate their own points of view as well as accepting that others may see the world differently. The teacher should increasingly appeal to the individual judgment of the children and should lead them gradually to the exercise of social responsibility within the context of their class community. At this age it is important for the class to experience themselves both as world citizens but also as individuals who have social responsibilities.

Class 8 (Age 13-14)

Developmental Profile

Class 8, during which the pupils pass their fourteenth birthday, signals the end of the class teacher period. Historically, this used to be the school-leaving age for many pupils and the entry point for an apprenticeship in a trade or craft. As such, Class 8 was seen as a 'rounding off' of the child's schooling. With the establishment of 'upper schools' and the raising of the school-leaving age throughout Europe over the last fifty years, it is no longer the case that children leave school at 14. However, 'Class 8' today continues to represent a certain 'completion' of a picture of the world and humanity's place within it.

At 14, the pupils are 'into' adolescence; bodily and psychological changes are well under way, so that in general, the young person seems more robust and the tenderness of the previous two years has lessened somewhat. Growth in height and sexual development are clearly established, with the onset of the 'breaking voice' in boys and the establishing of the menstrual cycle in girls. At this age, the world of ideas begins to take on meaning for the young adolescent and the critical faculties of the 14 year-old are noticeably sharper and parts of the accepted framework – particular rules for example – are subject to questioning scrutiny. Counter-balancing this critical tendency is the emergence of a reasoning or 'reasonable' side in the child.

The emergence of an independent life of feeling enters the 'labour and delivery' phase and the emotional turbulence which may attend this birth presents an important challenge to parents and teachers – how to accompany this birth or beginning of the emancipation of an individualised and independent inner life of thinking, feeling and intention without either being overwhelmed or swamped by the waves and tides of emotions, while being able to recognise that the state of crisis is part of a development.

While girls may spend much time and energy in discussing and sharing their feelings and the social and emotional aspects of life in small, cohesive groups, boys generally tend to respond rather differently to the hormonal and soul changes. Seemingly rather behind their female counterparts in terms of social behaviour and emotional maturity, boys can appear uncommunicative, emotionally illiterate and tend towards the brash or the sullen. Regardless of the outer manifestations, both genders now stand before new and unknown vistas with sharpening minds, tender hearts and limbs that struggle to reach an accommodation with gravity. By the end of this class, the pupils are already searching for new authorities and role models.

Aims and Objectives

The children should be led to bring together all that they have learnt into a meaningful world-picture in which the human being as a striving ethical individual has central significance.

Independence of working should be brought to a certain culmination in the Class 8 projects in which each pupil chooses a theme, researches it throughout the year and then makes a public presentation. The pupils should be prepared for the different style of teaching they will encounter in the Upper School.

Curriculum Classes 6 – 8

The children have now reached a critical period in their development that may be experienced negatively as a crisis and is often described as such in many publications on puberty. It is important, however, for educators to treat this challenge more as an opportunity than a crisis. Between the ages of 12 and 14 the pupils have indeed come into quite a new relationship with the world. Physically they undergo a second change of shape, often growing much taller, but their 'inner shape' also changes noticeably. Hitherto, habit and upbringing have governed their behaviour more than their own choices and inclinations. Now their soul life erupts into the world outside them.

The human being works his way through via the breathing system and the circulatory system right into the part where the muscles are attached to the bones. He works right to the edge of being human and at puberty breaks out into the outside world. Not until this moment does he arrive fully in the outside world. [35]

Steiner's choice of words here shows the drama of this situation. Often the sheer force of the children's inner tumult shocks those around them so much that they forget that the children are equally shocked. But the children do not want their alarm, which is very deep and disturbing, to be noticed by those around them. They don't want to reveal their individuality in this 'new territory' until they have gained some sense of security. Until they have achieved this they hide in many ways behind masks and 'difficult' behaviour.

"The pedagogical task for the middle of childhood is to understand that the children enter in their own time into the rhythm of a past that can be thought and a future that can be sensed." [36] There is even something of an existential feel about this future that can be sensed. The young people feel they are both solitary and a part of humanity as a whole. Sexual maturity makes this even clearer. Having become fully a part of the human race in their ability to reproduce, they also long for an extension of their own individual responsibility towards the world. Steiner described this as follows: *"One of the principles in the Waldorf School is to educate young people so that, on the one hand, they can bring to the fore in the right way the whole of their human potential, and, on the other hand, what they need to enable them to take their proper place in the world."* [37] What is referred to as a 'lack of discipline' or descriptions of the pupils 'just hanging around' can also be seen as a sign that these young people are searching to find their way within a new psychological situation and thus also within the new sense they have of the physical world.

In addition to the changes of physical and psychological 'shape', there is now also a change in the young people's consciousness. Conceptual thinking comes more to the fore as they endeavour to make links between isolated phenomena and thus leave their isolation behind them to take hold of a new totality. Whatever they experience must be transformed into original thinking, otherwise it will make them insensitive and merely a prey to sensationalism. At this age, it is not models and/or the data of specialist science they need, but the basic attitude of scientific work, which is: *thinking integrates the world of phenomena.*

Chemistry, a new subject introduced in Class 7, provides the right kinds of challenges and opportunities in the above sense. Here the young people get to know the world of substances and explore their characteristics. In addition, what they perceive can be used to form concepts, thus bringing them into the research process and helping them meet the world anew in a deeper way. Reality is not contained in an abstract concept but in thoughtful observation which does not look exclusively either at the one-sided concept or at the perception, but sees how the two are linked together.

Inorganic chemistry offers impressive possibilities for dramatic experiments that illustrate this. The main-lesson block often begins with fire and the process of combustion (an experience the youngsters are well acquainted with!), and proceeds via the burning of limestone to acids, alkalis and metals.

The historical and cultural aspects of the various technologies are always included in the lessons.

Chemistry in Class 8 turns to other questions. Organic processes in nature are more complicated and therefore much harder to understand. The human being, in whom all these processes take place, is the starting point and focus for these lessons. Understanding organic life processes, the creation and metamorphosis of substances, requires an active, imaginative kind of thinking to conceive of such processes. Concepts need to be formed that also relate to a sense of responsibility.

As with inorganic chemistry, physics in Class 7 has an equally 'dead' emphasis: mechanics. There are two aspects of this. On the one hand, the subject fits in well with the youngsters' search for practical ways of changing the world such as can be found and are applied in industry and transport. On the other hand, by practising and 'playing' with mechanical experiments they can become acquainted with the systematic work required by the scientific method while also enabling them to bring order into their own steps in thinking. Physics in Class 8 shows how mechanics extends into and helps to explain the other areas of physics (e.g. steam engine, Morse telegraphy, hydrostatics and hydraulics). Fixed concepts and reductionism are still avoided. But a beginning is made in using quantitative formulae based on the mechanics learnt in Class 7, such as the 'golden rule of mechanics', calculating the speed of sound, calculating pressure etc. Here we encounter an interesting paradox. As increasingly accurate observations are made with the help of measuring instruments – a process in which our direct experience withdraws from the phenomena – so, on the other hand, the human being becomes newly involved in a practical way by making apparatus, instruments and machines on the basis of the laws of physics. Decisive industrial changes take place as a result, which in turn lead to grave social consequences. As direct experience of nature fades, this is replaced by a working knowledge of the laws of physics, which forms the basis for an interventionist approach. This stage in consciousness reflects the profound shift in human consciousness from pre-industrial societies to the modern condition in which nature loses its identity as being and becomes an objective world described by the pronoun 'it' rather than 'thou'.

In Class 6, geography presented an overview of the globe as a whole. Now the focus is on individual parts of the world not yet dealt with in detail. The cultural aspects of unfamiliar regions provide a focus for understanding the relationship of human society to its geographical circumstances. The way individual cultures arise as the result of geographical context provides the pupils with examples of individuation at the cultural level as they themselves begin to become more aware of their own cultural identity. Directing the lessons towards cultural phenomena draws the youngsters' attention away from egotistical everyday concerns of gratifying needs towards more objective examples of lifestyles as exemplified by the cultural forms of other peoples, and especially non-European or Western orientated societies.

Biology is similar in this respect. Steiner suggested that Class 7 was the last chance to introduce the subjects of health and nutrition while the children are still relatively less self-preoccupied than they will be in the depths of puberty, and can experience the nature of the human being in a general way. These days, Class 7-age pupils are well into puberty and therefore it is a question whether the aspects of human biology usually dealt with in Class 7 shouldn't appear earlier in the curriculum. Nevertheless, if the topic *is* taken in Class 7, the teacher will have to accommodate the increased self-consciousness of the students.

Gardening has a role to play here in that it teaches about food plants and the worldwide origins of food resources. Class 8 then turns to the human form as such. In the anatomy main-lesson the skeleton is studied in detail, including the mechanics of bones and muscles, and comparisons are made with animal skeletons. Eye and ear are here seen as instruments serving the inner being of the individual.

The *discovery of the human being* is often preceded by history lessons in Class 7, when the (re)discovery by Europeans, of new continents, and the discovery by non-Europeans of the strange forces emanating from Europe, is a major topic. Another aspect of this whole theme, is the discovery of natural laws, and the discovery of laws in art. The beginnings of scientific thinking in the Renaissance, as well as the emergence of a new individual self-consciousness that began when long-held views of the world and of faith came under scrutiny, are clearly comparable to the developmental situation of youngsters as puberty begins.

By studying the rise of industry, the industrial revolution and the human being as the shaper of social order right up to the present time, the youngsters in Class 8 are led not out of but further *into* the real world. In studying cultural history they can experience how the world can be transformed by human beings; they can investigate the causes of events and thus more and more become citizens of the world.

The Renaissance discovery of the vanishing point in painting and architecture where everything meets or from which everything emanates is now the foundation for the themes in painting and drawing. Exercises in perspective and studies of works by the great masters Brunellesci, Massaccio, Piero della Francesca and non-vanishing point perspective (Van Eyck), lend more substance to art studies. Here the excitement of the discovery can be conveyed through biographical anecdote. The pupils are not yet mature enough to grasp the deeper levels of meaning that concerned the great artists of the Renaissance. This will be the theme of Upper School art studies. Having arrived at this structure in drawing they now have to begin imbuing it with new life. Once the elements of structure, perspective and composition have been introduced, colour can be reintroduced to express the feeling and mood element to painting.

English language studies in Class 7 could be a way of preparing for this. One subject, among many other parts of speech dealt with, is 'interjections' which are, after all, simply expressions of feelings and sensations given direct expression in language. During this period young people tend to become inarticulate in the presence of adults, yet they develop fluency in the rich vocabulary of teenage jargon. Both phenomena are aspects of the search for their own individual ways of expressing themselves and such stylistic exercises can be a great help.

Solo and chorus recitation of poetry and prose must be strongly cultivated. In Class 8, when the students are searching to find their own new language, a new beginning can be made in working with the various types of clause and with texts that characterise them. Lively interest can be generated by exercises in which sentence structures are sought to suit the different temperaments. As the pupils begin to notice the sanguine, melancholic, choleric and phlegmatic temperaments they begin to see each other in a new light, and often with considerable insight. The transition can then be made to stylistic studies and exercises, with particular attention to the special qualities of epic, lyric and dramatic poetry, whereby metaphor, simile etc. are given individual attention.

Drama is a most important theme of this biographical period. It should involve not only the reading or reciting of ballads but also a larger theatrical project, the Class 8 play. One of the important aspects of this is getting the youngsters working together in a social way on a work of art involving language.

Similar considerations apply to foreign language lessons. Exercises in writing reports and stories can relate to geography and social history i.e. themes of a universal nature. *"What I have said with regard to the characteristics of languages means that it is necessary – if we want to educate in a generally human but not specialised way – that we should take what comes out of the genius of a particular language regarding human nature and balance this by means of another language."* [38] The interest of the pupils can be focused on other peoples all over the world and this can help them develop an understanding of those who are different.

Once again astronomy can be related to geography and history. The pupils can be shown the Copernican view of the world and discuss how the view of the heavens changes in different parts of the world. The point of departure is practical, *perceived* astronomy, rather than theory. Practical navigation can be taught, thus linking the exploits of early voyages of discovery, with astronomy and orientation.

As with physics in Class 8, formulae now also begin to appear in mathematics. A start is made with algebra and equations, perhaps using interest percentages (Class 6) as a point of departure. Then the pupils have an analytical experience of perspective in mathematics when they learn about square roots. The realm of negative numbers is also entered for the first time. Learning how to gain an overview of things can also be schooled through practical business calculation e.g. in book-keeping, the basic principles of which can be introduced in Classes 6 and 7.

In geometry, theoretical proofs are practised in connection with the congruence of triangles using all kinds of definitions according to angles, triangles and quadrilaterals with inscribed or perimeter circles and also through the different proofs for the Theorem of Pythagoras (including the use of square roots) that links up with these. By repeating and constantly practising the proofs, the pupils can develop their capacity for forming judgments. Constructions in perspective provide the link with history and drawing, just as the construction of the Golden Mean in Class 8 allows for a link to be made with anatomy through anatomical proportions.

Forming exact judgments and concepts in geometry is less difficult than in music. The youngsters need to find their orientation in this realm that expresses soul qualities. As before, listening is every bit as important as solo playing and making music and singing with others. Like eurythmy, as we shall see, music at this age is important socially and therapeutically because it helps the youngsters form links with others and extricate themselves from the loneliness that is beginning to take a grip on them. Music lessons can introduce them to various composers and styles and also help them develop an understanding of composition.

Eurythmy is connected with this. Ballads and humorous pieces are worked on. Speech eurythmy also supports language studies by cultivating artistic interpretation, while tone eurythmy adds to and accompanies music studies. As mentioned above, doing eurythmy in a group allows for the practice and development of social skills. At a period when they can be shy, self conscious and awkward, the youngsters are helped by discovering that the formal principles of eurythmy can articulate their experience of dynamic space as well as providing an artistic medium for the expression of soul moods.

The Class 8 play has already been mentioned in connection with English studies. This is intended to be much more comprehensive than the short plays and scenes that have been worked on from Class 1 onwards in the main-lesson and foreign languages. This play for the first time allows the children to shape their emotions while still under the protective mask of a role in a play. This can be stimulating and motivating. In addition everything they have learned and worked on in the Lower School can be drawn on: making the scenery (painting and carpentry), sewing the costumes (handwork), making the posters (drawing), choreography (eurythmy, music).

In the description of handwork in Classes 1 to 3 we have already mentioned practical skill. Now we become increasingly concerned to combine this practical usefulness with a sense for the aesthetic, whilst relating natural materials to their environmental context. For example the youngsters might make shoes and then embellish them artistically to suit both purpose and wearer. Use of the sewing machine is practised so that in the coming years complicated pieces such as shirts, blouses, trousers, skirts and dresses can be made. Here design, function, material and technical skill are brought into a relationship with aesthetics and individual expression.

Just as handwork in Classes 7 and 8 gains an element of the artistic, so do crafts and woodwork. Useful objects of artistic design are made. The design takes account of both function and aesthetic appearance. Salad servers, candle holders, postcard stands etc. are made in woodwork. To make toys with moving parts you need a basic understanding of mechanics, enough not only to allow you to understand how something works but to be able to design it in the first place.

Two qualities are particularly important at this age, namely self-restraint and self-motivation. Things that prevent us from participating in the world, e.g. laziness, antipathy or fear, are tackled for the first time in subjects such as gardening. The weather itself provides a challenge because of its unreliability. Difficult procedures requiring patience and skill, such as transplanting, are learnt. If possible the whole gardening year should be experienced, from sowing, planting, cultivating (watering, hoeing, weeding) to harvesting, and then even selling the produce. A sense of responsibility is needed to sustain all this. The same goes for the care of shrubs and trees because in addition to immediate results it also requires foresight over many years.

History is mainly concerned with experiencing and understanding the past (although in Class 8 the future can also be allowed to appear). Gardening, on the other hand, is a responsibility directed to the future.

Gym and sport lessons provide the aspect of self-restraint and self-motivation that leads to clear experiences of self. Apparatus work and springing in all its many varieties, provide plenty of choice. Perseverance and stamina are schooled by more intensive running exercises. Ball games provide an important social balance to the more solitary disciplines. Once puberty begins a distinction is made between the sexes for the first time. Training is directed to developing strength for the boys and elasticity for the girls.

In Class 8 a year-long project is also undertaken by each pupil. Subjects and methods are many and varied. The aim is for the youngsters to produce and document work showing their own formulations and graphic solutions, their own craft skills or musical progress. The element of self-restraint and self-motivation can be particularly strong here. At a time when it is often difficult to 'reach' individual pupils, a project provides opportunities to enter into relationships with them based on an area of common interest. This enables teachers to continue an on-going relationship genuinely wanted by the pupils.

Summary:

The overriding theme is working with the world's laws by conversing with them and, in doing so, finding one's own voice. The students should experience how knowledge makes one capable of forming appropriate judgments and how forming judgments leads to new questions. The students should be led to bring together what they have learned into a meaningful world picture in which the human being as a striving ethical being has central significance. The students should also reach a degree of independent working that enables them to approach the Upper School equipped for a more subject specialist approach to learning which requires more initiative and independent working skills.

Even though at the founding of the original Waldorf school, the pupils left school after Class 8, Steiner's comment below is equally relevant when the students go on to the Upper School.

When you discharge a child from school you should have laid the foundations for him or her to be no longer tied to the body with every fibre of the soul; in thinking, feeling and will he must have become independent of the body. [39]

7.4   A Summary of the Upper School

Rather than provide developmental profiles for each Upper School class, we have described educational aims for each age group. This seemed more appropriate given the increasing individual differentiation that occurs during adolescence. Nevertheless one can identify an overall progression through the years of the Upper School that can be characterised as follows.

The Class 9-age student (15 years old) has reached a point in his or her development when the inner life of feeling in its search for independence can take extreme forms. Steiner once characterised the feeling life of the fifteen-year-old as akin to having been 'spat out' of the spiritual world. That means a radical distancing of the individual not only from the sense of being embedded in a secure world of certainties provided by family as much as by childhood innocence, but also from what that individual has learned. It requires the inner equivalent of re-learning how to walk, talk and think.

Thinking, feeling and willing as activities are often entirely at odds with each other. This can manifest in great clarity of intellectual argument and total inability to act out the consequences of those ideas; fierce assertion of emotional independence (don't tell me what to do, think or feel!) with an almost childlike dependency and need for emotional comfort.

On the other hand there is a strong will to engage in life, which needs equally strong ideals as orientation. The Class 9 age student seeks and welcomes clarity of explanation, sympathetic understanding from the adults around them and much open-hearted humour, the balm which smooths and makes bearable the inconsistencies of life. We can summarise the situation of the student on entry to the Upper School as follows:

- The awakening of a stringent logic and thinking potential that requires distance from one's own self and other people
- The search for balance between intellectuality and the realm of passion and urge-driven will.

- The experience of the emergence of a higher ideal humanity
- The search for a new harmony with the world, but one that should not be gained at the loss of the new-found and still tentative identity and personal freedom

The Class 10 age student (16 years old) often appears after the summer holidays as different in marked ways. The often tumultuous nature of Class 9 has given way to a desire to know outer facts, information and details, which requires of them a new intellectual focus. Previously students have mostly been satisfied to know how it is, now they wish to know *how we know* how it is. In other words they seek not only information but insight. Thus behind every question of *what*, is the question of *how*, of origins. How have things come to be as they are? Above all the students want to know how facts relate to *them* personally.

At this age young people experience their 'I' strongly in harsh judgments of sympathy and antipathy, especially the conventional world of parents, authorities, routines and rules. The facades of 'bourgeois' existence need to be torn down to expose what lies naked behind them. They can be rigorous in their pursuit of perceived injustice. Class 9 students are rarely quite so ready to fight and argue and yet the individual is never so prone to being hurt, as at this age. Dialogue with adults acquires a sharper, more existential tone. It is no longer merely an intellectual sport, as in Class 9. Now it is for real.

Class 10 students become in many ways the modern equivalent of medieval knights or warriors. They adopt many elaborate rituals in their behaviour, their clothing becomes their armour. Depending on fashion, this can be quite literal with the tendency to leather, chains, pins, studs, insignia, motor-cycle helmets, heavy boots, layers of clothing etc. These warriors are, however, not graced with the arts of chivalry. There is often a sense of imprisonment in their own inner lives, with a corresponding urge to break out. There is deep pain to endure and slow-healing wounds to bear. The clothing is not only protective armour, it is camouflage, disguise and mask. There is a heightened consciousness, a kind of double awareness that the adolescent is quite aware of what he does, how it appears and just how transparent the disguise is.

The sheer unbridgeable gulf between appearance and reality is often experienced as truly tragic. This age is highly prone to suicide and other lesser acts of self-destruction. They seek groups in which to hide among those who feel the same way, speak the same language, enjoy the same irony, who understand each other. If Class 9 was still lit by the remaining glow of the class teacher period, by Class 10 the light has entirely faded. This is one of the most decisive points in the whole maturation process. The individual has arrived and is in grave danger of diffusing. The temptation to flight in inner or outer 'emigration' is strong, to run away from the world of challenges, to hang onto childhood's certainties, to blot out the light of day.

Two powerful new forces, that of burgeoning sexuality and that of physical power, now further destabilise inner uncertainty. These tendencies have been there for a long time, for some individuals since Class 7. Yet in Class 10 most students have arrived at a certain low point in their overall development. Anthroposophical psychology recognises the significant 'Rubicon' experience of the child in his or her ninth year. This is taken account of in many ways through the curriculum. A further significant Rubicon challenge occurs in the sixteenth year, in Class 10. The students are confronted with a significant threshold experience in their inner development. Those who successfully negotiate the transition over this threshold, will have taken a major step in the individuation process. Those who don't, run the risk of falling prey to their own unredeemed soul forces. Much adult behaviour that we deem anti-social and immature, is a reflection of these unredeemed adolescent forces perpetuated into adult life in often pathological ways. In men this generally takes outwardly threatening forms, in expressions of power. In women, it often takes the form of dependency and self-denial, even self-destruction. The gender differences have many cross-overs.

The question of the 16 year-old is 'who am I?'; it will find an answer when the individual discovers that who I am is not solely determined by what I have inherited and what has happened to me in my life so far, but also by something that has to do with *me*? The Class 10 student can begin to explore new territory using the new powers of judgment that can be developed during this year.

Life begins at 17. This popular conception certainly highlights the fact that this age marks a significant new beginning. If the interest of the Class 9 student is strongly directed outwards into the world, if the interest of the Class 10 student is strongly focused internally, the Class 11 student's interest is a synthesis of both these directions, namely in insight. The young person at this age wishes to understand the inner principles that determine not only the human being's inner life and configurations but also those of the wider world. It is a question of finding the balance between inner and outer.

This balance is especially critical in social life. Social conscience awakens with the ability to empathise with the other person. What has previously been acutely experienced within one's own soul can be recognised in the other. Deeper dimensions to life now begin to reveal themselves. The young person has to find an inner orientation between appearance and reality, between what is said and what is meant. Above all the seventeen-year-old is called upon to find his or her own way, to make personal and binding decisions, to consider the full consequences of their actions. Polarities in life have to be resolved, have to find a higher synthesis to a new oneness. The choices to be made highlight that most characteristic experience of this age-doubt. Throughout the curriculum, the question of polarities requires an inner engagement from the student.

The student in Class 12 seeks an overview in which to reconcile two opposing forces that have become increasingly apparent through all he or she has learned, namely the tension between increased individualisation and ever growing global consciousness. These two trends will have become apparent through studies of science, the humanities and through practical experience. The curriculum has led the students to find inner and outer connections and correspondences between important phenomena in the world. Hopefully they have learned how to make an inner personal connection to that which they have learned. Now the question is turned round. The question is no longer how does the world affect *me* in my life, but how can I influence the world? This question needs to be asked in very concrete terms, in terms of economics, in social and personal life, in politics or in science. Am I a pawn or a King, a performer or a spectator? Where is my position in the world?

School has to become a place in which the student can find his or her own place in the world and actively cultivate it. The students should at last have the opportunity to define, create and live their own learning space, not alone but in partnership with fellow students and teachers. The emphasis should be on self-determination of objectives and pathways towards those objectives. This level of independence will be denied most individuals once they have left school for many years of further professional training or career-building. Perhaps some will never again have such freedom and at the same time such youthful geniality, untrammelled by life's responsibilities. It is a moment when students can give back to their education freely of themselves. It is fatal to the cultivation of true individuality, if this twelfth school year is determined by the wishes of teachers or parents, or indeed society at large in the form of examinations and the like.

Gaining an overview is a last chance to remain a generalist before plunging into the specialisation that profession and university life entails. A balance between independent working, choosing themes and projects which express a personal interest and seeking the linking, integrating overview between all fields of knowledge and experience is the challenge the 18 year-old demands. Recognising, even at this relatively young age, something of one's individual destiny is the corollary of recognising the global aspects of the destiny of humankind. Ultimately the Class 12 student wants a useful answer to the question, can the world be changed and am I worthy of being an instrument of change?

Learning to Form Judgments

The periods leading up to and following puberty (Steiner's own phrase *"Erdenreife"* was 'being ready for the earth') tend to make one want to look at puberty as a separate phase in itself. The nature of puberty has to be understood in the context of what goes before and comes after it. It makes itself known in advance both psychologically and physically, culminates in an obvious physiological process that is often felt to be quite dramatic, and then continues to have after-effects. These after-effects are not limited by the achievement of biological maturity (which has already passed its culmination as soon as the capacity to reproduce has been attained) but include the process of psychological maturation that goes hand in hand with it.

Steiner summarised this process as a 'new, third birth', the birth of the independent body of soul forces (the sentient body) in the individual. The first birth is the one we normally regard as such, the beginning of the path of life. The second is when the organic development reaches a culmination at the change of teeth, when the forces hitherto used to build the body become free to form and structure memory and imagination.

Prior to this 'third birth', feelings were the source of the child's inner life, but from now on they reach a new stage of independence. An individual's inner life confronts the outer world in a relationship that still has to find a form. Among other things, this relationship is created by the capacity to form judgments. The content of all lessons should respond to this need by challenging it and by providing a context in which the individual can develop his or her faculties. This means that the task of education is to provide learning opportunities in which objective laws that are accessible to thought can be experienced and made conscious. Real judgment can only be based on recognition of the true nature of phenomena.

This also provides a basis for doing things that are recognised to be necessary even if the personal part of one's feelings doesn't feel like it. This is where duty as a voluntary act can be discovered, together with responsibility for one's own actions. Adopting one's own standpoint becomes important, as does finding one's *own voice*, both of which lead to having one's own opinions. Once the first stages of this process have been achieved both physically and psychologically, and when the often tumultuous phase has died down, the young person achieves a new plateau of development.

By the end of the sixteenth year the crisis or transition of puberty can be regarded as completed. Bodily proportions reach a new harmony. There is a greater inclination for serious work. On the other hand there is also a danger of becoming eccentric: *"In all modesty, the young person assumes that he has a significant part to play in saving humanity, and plans his life accordingly."* [40] Teachers can help in such cases by setting an example of how judgments are formed. The youngsters must learn how to handle judgments in an appropriate way. It is clear that they are feeling and seeking for 'ideals', in their own selves as well as in others and in the world.

What they find in their search rarely comes up to expectation, and their comments are all too plain and often merciless. They can easily become sceptical. The science the teacher presents must be seen to have been successful in the steps it has taken towards knowledge. Pessimism about knowledge is not good for young people's psychological state at this age, though what they themselves say often expresses it. When they do this they are actually challenging the adult world to *"show me that this is not so"*. There is an entirely objective tragic element in young people of this age, for only rarely do they find others living in the way they seek to live, namely as self-determining adults.

School is no longer acceptable if it is felt to be running *alongside* rather than *within* real life. It must offer possibilities that lead to surefootedness in the here and now. The pupils will detect anything speculative or masquerading as reality. Their search for authenticity and truth is a more concrete version of their search for an unattainable ideal. It is the teachers' task to provide positive experiences in this search. If they fail, the young people will not find a foundation for their existence which can give them firmness and direction. They will remain empty, standing without a foothold in the stream of time. Adolescents who find only inadequate answers among their teachers and the adults around them may, later in life, struggle to overcome selfishness and insecurity. As adults themselves, they may be unable to find the altruism and confidence a healthy society needs.

Values: Meeting Real Needs

An education that takes its orientation from life questions of this kind can never be value-free. When the children were younger it was the task of the teacher to assess and choose what he or she told the children. Now the teacher must let the youngsters experience the teacher as a person with real questions. What encourages and develops the young people now are not results but rather the processes of the teachers' own self-education. Those teachers will be successful who can lay aside their own ingrained attitudes and remain 'life-long learners' themselves.

The third seven-year period does not end with Class 12 or even Class 13. The urge to enter professional or other specialist training makes itself felt. Aims become clearer. Faced with external influences such as the pressure to gain places in higher education or the possibility of unemployment, young people may become restless and gradually lose the will to learn. The challenges of public examinations can, in their one-sidedness, lame initiative and narrow the scope of interest.

The real needs of modern society for people of initiative, energy, flexibility, creativity and social competence, demand that Upper School students learn to learn, learn to work, learn to transfer skills from one realm to another, develop problem-solving abilities, be creative and above all have a fine sense of social responsibility.

For this reason many Steiner Waldorf schools have developed integrated Upper School programmes offering a variety of practical training in such fields as carpentry, environmental studies, electronics, metalwork, design and clothing, catering, child care and so on, alongside the usual range of subjects. There is an emphasis on project work and this is combined with a range of practical work experience opportunities. Such activities cultivate transferable skills in learning through making, team work and social competence. School in this sense becomes a real preparation for life if it provides opportunities for individuals to become free personalities capable of recognising and accepting the tasks life presents them with and whose soul faculties of thinking, feeling and willing are integrated by the activity of their 'I'.

In countries such as the UK, where the public examination system permeates the whole Upper School, or even into the Middle School, the question of life skills and developing real engagement and motivation is often subsumed by the narrowing effect of exams on the young person's horizon. Such schools work hard to find the right balance, not least in the consciousness of the students, who too often see the exams as the 'real' task. The challenge to awaken genuine ideals should not be underestimated. The real task of a Waldorf Upper School is to work with adolescents in such a way that they can ask: *what do I need to do to be useful in society?* rather than asking: *what do I need to do to get what I want?*

There are several aspects to this task. The young people must:

a) become familiar with the world and the tasks it sets them;
b) develop a range of skills that equip the individual to be creative and adaptable in fields beyond what they have specifically learned;
c) discover their own individuality;
d) develop powers of judgment and discernment;
e) develop a moral and ethical will based on insight.

Prepared in this way, young people will be able to contribute freely and responsibly as self-dependent individuals to the society and the times in which they find themselves, learning to take part in shaping the future.

Educational Competence

Steiner Waldorf education aims to combine schooling the intellect with caring for imaginative qualities and character building. Therefore artistic and practical activities are seen as being of equal value to the provision of knowledge. Each of these fields of experience should be integrated. Education is not solely a matter of intellectual training: it is a holistic process. Nor should education be restricted to specialist knowledge but should seek to engage the whole human being. Both pupils and teachers can regard themselves as 'successful' if they succeed in developing intellect, a rich emotional life and will in equal measure and if they bring about a feeling for freedom, equality and fraternity. People will then not reject the challenges life offers, nor will resignation be their reaction to crisis. Instead they will help to find meaning and seek and follow new ways. Shaping every lesson will be an 'art of education' which presupposes a creative teacher who is him or herself continuously in the process of developing. Education in this sense means teaching the right subject in the right way at the right time.

If the teachers succeed in working with and understanding the laws of human development, then they will become capable of 'reading' the human being. The various physiological and psychological phenomena that occur as a young person matures need to be linked with the overall human being. Comparison can be made to the plant whose totality can only be observed in the whole sequence of its life cycle. When a person has learnt to read the human being well enough to be able to base their educational actions on this insight, thus helping young people in the whole of their being, then he or she can be said to have gained educational competence. They can take on full responsibility for education in school. The curriculum is then no longer merely a syllabus to be ticked off item by item, for the curriculum then arises out of the conditions necessary for development at each specific stage.

7.5   Class 9
A survey of the horizontal curriculum for Class 9

In history attention returns to the period spanning the 15th to the 20th Centuries. The aim is to make the pupils acquainted with the leading ideas of this period. Great ideas and ideals bring about new developments (the French Revolution, the American Wars of Independence and Constitution, the Russian Revolution). Ideas can also be powerful instruments of evil, as the history of the Third Reich demonstrates. These exemplify the problems young people themselves have at the Class 9 stage: that the journey from ideal to realisation presupposes a perception of reality, that violence and failure can be a consequence of moral rigour and fanatical idealism.

The last 'blank spots' disappear from the European map of the world, and consciousness begins to encompass the whole globe. This history main-lesson is intended to awaken the youngsters' interest in the world. They also need to understand the historical forces that come to expression in the current global situation. At the start of a new millennium, the end of the Cold War and its proxy conflicts in Asia and Africa as well as the lingering forces of disintegration that followed the end of Colonialism have left a complex world, one in which the young person needs to find an orientation. The globalisation of both the world economy and communications systems is creating a new phase in world history, one for which the students have a keen interest. Their increasing familiarity with electronic media and in particular the internet needs to be put in a global context.

Important aspects of human invention and discovery are treated in physics, including the steam engine, locomotive, combustion engine, electric motor, light bulb, telephone, calculator, television, laser and computer (some of these may be dealt with in Class 8). The pupils in Class 9 come to grips with the rationally planned technology of the 19th and 20th Centuries. Many of these technologies have revolutionised people's mobility and ability to communicate. The relationship between the machines themselves and the kind of consciousness that accompanies their use is an important topic. The impact such inventions had on everyday life is important, as is their replacement through even more modern tools and systems. The post-industrial age is the world the students are growing into and this needs to be put into perspective.

It is also important for the pupils to get to know the individuals whose ideas and intentions led to specific inventions. Through such examples they can grasp technology as human thought which has become actual reality. A glance into the workshop of these thought processes and into the biography of the inventors provides the pupils with pictures that can rouse their enthusiasm while as yet avoiding the moral implications and cultural pessimism of today.

In mathematics, equations right up to probability calculations take centre stage. This provides good practice in formal, logical thinking. All kinds of quadratic equations and surface and volume calculations are done.

In geometry, Platonic solids with plane surfaces provide the opportunity to make inner pictures of processes before drawing them. The manner of depiction is chiefly that of diagonal section with vertical parallel projection which is easy to construct and easy to see spatially. Conic sections now also make their appearance. This is new as compared with Class 8. Ellipse, parabola and hyperbola are developed using dynamic exercises.

In biology, the subject begun in Class 8 in human biology continues: the human skeletal and muscular system and the sense organs i.e. those systems by means of which human beings experience themselves in physical existence. Carrying on from Class 8, the pupils can now be led much further into the shape and functions of the bones. Taking hold of these and overcoming gravity with them is what young people are unconsciously occupied with the whole time. The whole theme of uprightness has a central place at this age. This complements the experience of the sense organs. These enable the young person to reach out beyond his or her own body, which is often experienced as being 'too small'.

In geography in the Upper School an understanding of the earth as a whole entity begins in Class 9 with the study of the earth's mineral crust. The students' newly awakened but as yet disorderly personality forces and the growing capacity to form judgments are directed towards geological phenomena. A thorough understanding of the physical ground on which our existence is built with its tectonic and geomorphological processes can provide orientation and a sense that the structure of the landscape is the result of largely subterranean dynamic forces. The contrast between imperceptible yet inexorable processes of erosion and the dynamic of volcanic activity offer the students a picture of extreme forms of change. The levelling and up-building process of sedimentation offers a stabilising middle between these two poles. The extremes of forces and time scales are polarities which mirror the young person's way of experiencing the world.

In chemistry, the way substances come into being is studied: combustion processes, results of carbonisation, the decomposition of organic matter leading to the formation of humus, how fossil fuels are formed and metabolic processes in plants. Distillation allows the pupils to experience how substances evaporate and then become tangible once again, a process of clarification and purification like those they are experiencing inwardly at this time.

The study of art becomes a subject in its own right in the Upper School, and is very important for Class 9. It provides a balance for the inorganic, lifeless worlds of physics and chemistry with their strict laws, showing the pupils a different world, one in which human beings are free to create their own order. Getting to know great paintings and sculptures will awaken their enjoyment of art and teach them that it is a realm in which human beings can experience freedom. In European schools, the origins of the Western tradition are explored from Ancient Egypt, through Greece to Rome and Early Christian art leading to the Middle Ages and the dawn of the Italian Renaissance. The main theme is, art as a reflection of changing human consciousness.

Drawing is now exclusively chiaroscuro, black-and-white (possibly also lino cutting and printing), which mirrors the polarity in which Class 9 pupils find themselves. By dealing with this polarity consciously in shaping their work they experience what their soul now needs. Particularly important are the exploration of the transition from dark to light and the crucial transitional 'grey areas' of life.

English studies also involve two main elements. [41] One main-lesson period is concerned with the origins and history of drama and theatre. From sacred beginnings both tragedy and comedy have their spiritual aspects. The transition from sacred to secular and profane is an important one to experience at this age. Drama should have both a theoretical, historical aspect and of course be a practical skill to be learned, in drama workshops and plays. Shakespeare is naturally a high point of this study. Key elements in studying Shakespeare are on the one hand his theatre and the structure of his dramas but on the other the quality of the language. Shakespeare's leading characters provide studies in personality of the highest order. In wrestling with Shakespearean language the students discover the many levels of subtlety and meaning in the images and metaphors, which open them to the whole meta-level of language and human thought. In this they are able to make an inner connection to the spirit of language and thus consciously re-form a connection to spirituality which puberty has clouded or even separated them from entirely.

Humour is another theme. The subject of humour enables the pupils to stand back a little from their situation and see things from a variety of different perspectives. This involves an exploratory study of human nature and psychology. It also reduces to a bearable level the sharpness of criticism and self-knowledge. Laughter is an individual's way of beginning to cope with what happens to one. The varying emotions of empathy, compassion and weeping, laughing *at* and laughing *with*, can also be discussed from a social and psychological point of view. When these soul qualities are stimulated in an aesthetic way, Class 9 pupils can experience the all-pervading tension of polarities and the possibilities of resolution and redemption.

Finding their own voice requires practice, as do the practical skills of literacy. Book reports, study skills, essays, use of syntax and style all help the students master their written and oral skills and find a new conscious relationship to language. The process of distancing oneself from one's cultural environment also involves the mother tongue. This can lead to an 'in'-language or slang amongst young people in which expressions taken from other less-than-obvious lexical sources are often preferred. The shock effect of such language on adults is very much part of the process.

This tendency to become estranged from one's own inherited language can come as a bonus for foreign languages. The pupils get to know ways of thinking and expression that are not customary in their own language, and they enjoy being able to step back from things by this means. Texts for reading can be biographies of inventors, engineers, artists and other great personalities of the era with which the history lessons are concerned. In admiring individuals who have gone ahead of their fellow human beings along the path towards conquering the earth, the young people gain a degree of maturity in their own ideals and aims. Learning about the issues facing other cultures also helps broaden adolescents' perspectives. Indeed in our times the need to understand the other person, the foreigner, the refugee from another culture, gives the teaching of foreign languages a special significance. The entire cultural aspect of modern language teaching is very important at an age when youngsters are especially drawn into their own folk soul element, adopt more strongly their local regional accent, and begin to identify with the 'laddish' tendencies that come to expression in the adolescent culture that is often anchored in local prejudices, support of the local football team and so on.

Grammar is repeated systematically in a broad overview, and elements the pupils have been practising, open the way for new possibilities of comprehension. The path in foreign language learning has moved from immersion and imitation, through usage and learning by heart and has now led to the need to understand. Thus a systematic review of all aspects of grammar in Class 9 is very much from the aspect of consciously working with rules, structures, comparison of idiom and so on. This is the age when a grammar textbook becomes a useful tool in teaching. Earlier, such textbooks are more useful as points of reference and reminders of things already learned. Now the systematic, tabulated, abstract structure of a good textbook really comes into its own. As in the English lessons a balance of humour, biographies, everyday useful usage and exactness of expression is needed. It is crucial that language lessons remain at heart experiences of orality in language. Literature and grammar both serve the primary aim of providing resources to support the students speaking and communicating in the foreign language. This is a major challenge for teacher and student alike but one that is amply rewarding when successful, and tedious when not.

Music lessons take their departure from a similar viewpoint. By getting to know the biographies of great musicians the pupils begin to develop an interest in their immortal compositions. It is a good idea to place two great composers side by side e.g. Mozart and Beethoven, or Handel and Bach for Baroque music. Listening to the works of the great composers can lead to discovering the differences between the Baroque and Classical styles. In working through such compositions, either vocally or instrumentally, the pupils are guided to discover not only new depths of feeling but also the 'grammar of music's language', to hear and show how keys modulate, and thus to understand the metamorphosis from the Baroque to Classical style. The youngsters are willing to understand anything to do with metamorphosis, and if this is coupled with art, it can help them find clarity in their own 'rebuilding process'. From Class 9 onwards the pupils sing in the Upper School choir and/or play in the Upper School orchestra.

In eurythmy, through poems and musical compositions from the 20th Century and contemporary artists, Class 9 pupils are led into movement and choreography in a thoughtful and businesslike way. The students should become conscious of the formal elements in eurythmy, learn how to choreograph appropriate forms for the different styles of music or poetry, for the grammatical and linguistic elements, for the different keys and so on. There should also be the opportunity to experience other forms of dance, including both formal ballroom dancing, Latin styles, jive, line dance, folk and morris dancing as well as contemporary dance. In all this the youngsters must be fully aware of the artistic element, and a good leavening of humour should also be included. For eurythmy to really engage the students there must be regular opportunity to see professional performances as well as being motivated by regularly seeing Classes 11 and 12 students performing to a high standing. The students should be able to experience that other people take eurythmy seriously.

Gardening in Class 9 can either take the form of a long main-lesson or project block (work experience on the land, landscaping, laying paths and building flights of steps, putting up fencing etc.) or lead to a practical period of agricultural or forestry work. For two to three weeks the pupils live with farming families and share whatever work is going on in farmyard and field. Apart from many other new things, they experience nature as the element that shapes each day and the whole of life. The tasks depend on the locality and opportunities available to the school. The important element is the encounter with real physical hard work and the necessary practical wisdom of tools, the work and safety procedures and the teamwork that accompany such activities. The economics of farming are an important topic too, not least in revealing the true value of work and stewardship of the environment.

In carpentry and joinery, simple joints are studied and applied. In dressmaking, the pupils make their own patterns and then sew skirts, jackets, etc. Copper beating and basket making lead to similar objects by very different means of manufacture e.g. bowls or vases on the one hand and baskets of all sorts on the other. An inner space is created from the outside by hard work. In all these crafts, the student learns to experience the nature of the material, how it is won, processed and worked. The economic and ecological aspects of craftwork should always be integrated into the practical work and especially the link between landscape, raw material and work process. Above all, objects should be produced that meet a real need in the world and not merely be a demonstration of practice pieces. The same is true for information technology. All pupils should learn basic word processing and use this for practical purposes such as the presentation of work, designing and laying out magazine pages and so on.

Pupils who do not participate in the full academic programme for some reason are offered alternative lessons of a practical and social nature. Such students should be given the opportunity to develop a specialist interest with specific responsibilities within the school. This may include helping in the Kindergarten, kitchens, maintenance department, school theatre and so on. Whatever programme the school is able to offer, it is important that the students experience that their work is valued and that they are increasingly to take responsibility for it.

7.6   Educational Aims for Class 9
A survey of the horizontal curriculum for Class 9

By the end of Class 9 the students should begin to:

* show self-motivated interest in the world around them; acquire knowledge about what interests them through independent gathering of information and facts
* show structure in their thinking and be able to make logical, causal deductions; move from judgment based on feeling (Class 8) to judgment based on observation and understanding. Apply analytical processes to an overall nexus and discover the underlying principles
* know how to make the transition from idea to ideal, and from ideal to applied practice and move from discovery (Classes 7 and 8) to creation and invention. Engage their will in the realm of ideals
* appreciate technology as the 'fifth kingdom', the kingdom of culture, created by the human being; discover in technology the *thought become worldly reality*
* understand the transitions between polarities in many different realms of life and especially the arts
* understand that art and science reflect historical changes in cultural consciousness and that artists and scientists have world views that are expressed in their work
* learn to work and be able to learn through work. Have hands-on experience of as many areas of practical life as possible
* be able to work in a team and to solve problems together

A survey of the horizontal curriculum for Class 10

How does a Class 10 differ from a Class 9? Personalities become more individualised through the work. Steps need to be taken so that the pupils' own activity helps them find themselves. Clarity of thought and an increasing ability to form judgments should help pupils extricate themselves from the unstable nature of the forces of emotional sympathy and antipathy. Hence the effort to come to grips analytically with laws that can be understood through thought.

Steiner's curriculum suggestions for biology were: *"To make the human being as a single entity comprehensible ... The physical human being with his organs and organic functions in connection with soul and spirit."* [42] The point of departure is morphology, from which a physiological and psychosomatic consideration of the organs can follow step by step. This could include a comparison of the brain and nervous system with a study of the heart and circulation. The brain's relationship to perception, thought and memory provides a basis for discussing consciousness and moral aspects of conscience. The relationship of the heart and circulation system to emotional experience is important. In this way the young people come into contact with a part of themselves where there is interplay of those developmental processes to which they are so intensely exposed at this age.

In geography the holistic view now expands to include the earth's mantle of water and air and also the climatic zones and further spheres including the earth's core and the outer spheres, together with their varied interactions and movements. In this way we continue to build a foundation for an understanding of the biosphere and ecology. The aim is to enable the pupils to become more aware of the earth as a living organism that reacts with the utmost sensitivity to interference in its rhythms and cycles.

In gardening, cultivation and propagation now come to the fore. If gardening as such is given in Class 10, then the mysteries of grafting are taught. But just as in Class 9, where a practical period in agriculture can take the place of gardening, so can Class 10 have a practical forestry period. This period need not necessarily be regarded as an alternative; it can equally well be complementary to gardening, deepening understanding. It is also important at this age that the students have direct experience of work in a variety of professions. A period of practical work experience may replace the forestry practical.

The history main-lesson brings to the fore an aspect that is obviously linked to geography: human and cultural evolution governed by the earth and the landscape. This is an opportunity to explore human prehistory, from the emergence of modern *homo sapiens* and the Paleolithic Revolution around 40,000 years before the present. This can include a study of the high culture of Ice Age art, followed by the Mesolithic period of transition at the end of the last Ice Age. The development of agriculture and the founding of the first permanent settlements shows not only a major shift in the economy of prehistoric peoples but a fundamental shift in human consciousness. From there, the establishment of the urban civilisations, with their theocracies, temples, use of writing, bureaucracies, laws and hierarchical social structures, can be described. Significant developments in technology as well as the consequences of urbanisation, such as the transference of diseases from animals to humans can also be discussed. The main focus of these studies should be a comparison of the specific ways the various cultures reflected their natural geographical circumstances, and the ways in which complex human societies were structured. The links between human beings and the earth are experienced, as is the evolution of the human being who increasingly becomes an individual emerging from the group, be it clan, tribe or nation.

The English main-lesson has similar aspects to the history in handling the transition from myth to literature, from pre-literate cultural forms such as myth, saga, and religious ritual to the origins of literature with its shift from collective to individual experience. Another theme combines linguistics with poetic diction and aesthetics, in which both the origin and structure of language are explored.

The study of art has so far involved mainly the visual arts. Now poetry and language as an art, is added thus shifting the emphasis from art in space to art in time. The formal laws of poetry – rhythm, sound, and image – are investigated and practised in epic, lyric and dramatic examples (the 'poetry and metre' main-lesson). A second main-lesson can be devoted to a continuation of the study of painting with a discussion of art to the north of the Alps (from Dürer, Holbein, Grünewald, van Eyck to Rembrandt). Overall, formal composition and principles of shaping a picture come to the fore, to correspond with Class 10 pupils' need to grasp things with their understanding. In practical art, painting is reintroduced with colour exercises designed to develop a vocabulary of colour and then developed into motifs in which atmosphere and mood can be expressed. Print-making can also be fruitfully explored at this age. The logic involved in planning pictures or designs that may need to be drawn in mirror form, or in which a composite picture is built up using several plates or blocks, challenges the students' powers of thinking as well as the precision involved in the work. Print-making can be applied in a range of media.

Eurythmy supports poetry and the use of language through the use of suitable examples in which the group moves as a whole. The pupils should work out their own eurythmy forms.

In foreign languages humour also comes into its own. It is fun to get the point through a direct understanding of the language (without translation). A study of humorous texts, jokes and idiomatic expression can broaden the adolescents' social, psychological and cultural horizons. The pupils also begin to develop a feeling for style. Unabridged literature is increasingly used. The use of grammar as a tool can be appreciated through the pupils' enjoyment of clear thinking. Comparative studies of grammar using English and the foreign languages can heighten awareness of how the spirit of language expresses itself through the genius of the different folk souls. The history of the development of the various languages can enhance this insight into the changing consciousness which underlies language evolution. Being able to present arguments for and against various propositions in the foreign language calls for the ability to think in that language.

In music lessons the endeavour is to give the pupils a foundation on which they can develop a genuine appreciation of music. Examples are practised in choir work and a chamber orchestra. Harmony is explored through musical examples. Main-lessons in mathematics, physics, chemistry, geometry and surveying have similar points of departure. In physics the formative principle is particularly obvious. Nowhere else are the laws of nature so obvious or clearly followed as in classical mechanics. The pupils can proceed from experiment to observation and on to the laws, the formula and the calculation without loss of clarity. Clarity in observing, logic in drawing conclusions, the ability to relate cause to effect, and analytical thinking are all schooled.

One of the aims for Class 10 is to enter into practical life. The use of the right angle has wide-ranging application in Class 10. The relationship of the perpendicular to the horizontal provides a conceptual framework for many practical tasks involving both accurate observation and common sense judgment. In surveying, the right angle forms the framework for the theoretical calculations, as it does in technical drawing. In woodwork, as in most constructions, it provides the concepts of plumb, square and true. In dressmaking and tailoring all individual patterns relate to the rectangular shape of the woven cloth. Even in throwing a pot on a wheel, the process of centring the clay requires an awareness of the perpendicular in relation to the horizontal plane of the plate. In metalwork the forging of iron and the work at the anvil in transforming the metal through the rhythmical application of the hammer, into a range of shapes requires the exact application of force and knowledge of the material.

The surveying main-lesson provides a wonderful opportunity to come to grips with the earth – or a tiny part of it – by measuring and drawing it. After this one or two-week practical period, the pupils know this 'tiny part' like the back of their hand! Surveying requires three levels of measurement, common sense estimation, ground measurement using rods, chains and tape measures, and theoretical calculations based on the readings taken with theodolite and measures. All three systems require to be integrated in order to create a three-dimensional understanding that will be expressed in a series of section drawings. Having applied these technical skills to geography, they know exactly what is there and have also learnt how to work with accuracy. The main content of the first mathematics main-lesson in Class 10 is trigonometry, which is applied in surveying. The cosine also belongs to physics when calculations are needed.

Further work on mathematical laws is given by rhythmical calculations, raising to higher powers and logarithms. In Class 10 mathematics should be related to practical matters of everyday life. The realm of irrational numbers and incommensurability, from which the law of the Golden Mean can be derived, points to a different type of formative law applicable to the human being, and is more appropriate for Class 11.

In chemistry the pupils work on the polarities of acid and alkali and on the crystallisation of salts. This main-lesson is directly related to the geometry main-lesson in which the regular and semi-regular solids and their laws of symmetry are worked out and drawn.

In technology the transition from raw material to processed material to product is explored, for example in the path from fibre via thread to textile. This principle applies also to wood, where the whole timber cycle from tree planting and cultivation, to felling, sawing, drying, planing etc. comes to a culmination in joinery in Class 10. As in surveying and the other practical subjects, the objects the students make correct the pupils simply by being objective proof of what they have done. It is important that useful objects are made. In addition many other technical applications in practical life can be discussed e.g. the gears of a bicycle, how the toilet flush works, vehicle maintenance and information technology. Class 10 is the best point to explore the technology of recycling in which the cycle from raw material to finished product begins again.

Information technology is a part of technology that needs responsible discussion of how these things affect the human being. Understanding what information is, how it is (and has been) stored, and the social aspects of access belongs to this theme. A brief history of the recorded word and mathematical calculations is a part of this. The basic principles of how a computer works are described. On the basis of what they have learnt in physics and mathematics, it is useful for Class 10 pupils to work with the basic building blocks of circuits to produce adding machines in which the basic principle of computer hardware can be learned.

A practical period in first aid fits in with the pupils' need to be engaged in meaningful, practical activities. Inner confidence grows when you can react on the spur of the moment and know what is the right thing to do.

7.8   Educational Aims for Class 10

The students should begin to:
*   achieve objectivity and clarity in thinking; draw conclusions logically and causally; be able to form common sense judgments as well as formulating concepts
*   recognise natural laws using analytical thinking; apply conceptual tools to practical situations
*   understand how complex processes come about by studying their origins and basic principles
*   work with accuracy and apply what they have learned to respond to the practical needs of those around them

- take increasing responsibility for their own work and behaviour, and be able to make and follow through choices based on their own insight; form their opinions and be able to explain and justify them

7.9 Class 11
A survey of the horizontal curriculum for Class 11

An overview of the subjects suggested by the curriculum for Class 11 shows that the themes of going beyond the sense perceptible, finding the inner balance between polarities, 'processes' and 'renewal' are common to all the content given in the different subjects. If Class 9 was concerned with expanding horizons, Class 10 with seeing where things come from, Class 11 is about gaining insight.

Themes of this kind come into the mathematics lessons e.g. in analytical geometry, in the concepts of infinity and counter space and in the integration of geometry with algebra and arithmetic with geometry. The laws of Euclidean geometry are integrated into projective geometry. By considering the 'infinitely distant elements' (point at infinity, line at infinity, plane at infinity) the pupils learn to learn to think about infinity. In the study of vibrations, the content of Class 10's trigonometry is brought into movement, creating a base for understanding wave theory as the background to all varieties of wireless data transmission in the Class 11 physics block. Spherical trigonometry extends and enhances planar trigonometry. As with many subjects in Class 11, subjects experienced and worked on separately are combined: links begin to appear.

Similar aspects show up in biology where the study of cells and microscopy is the subject, as well as in the study of ecology. Here any insights into microscopically-small elements are always complemented by views of the macroscopically-large biosphere. The pupils probably already know this process of 'turning inside out' from their projective geometry work.

In chemistry the task is to provide a general overview by looking at the individual character of the elements in the way the chemical substances interact. The periodic system can also be dealt with in this connection. It is presented not as a pre-existing principle of order but as a particular conceptual model that opens the way to describing various laws and relationships.

Similar aspects can be found in physics. In Class 10 the observable forces of mechanics were the focus of study. In Class 11 we move on to electromagnetic fields, radiation and radioactivity and the theories on the nature of matter. Seen logically as separate systems these appear to be contradictory, yet which also point to the unimaginable realm of reality. Physics and chemistry can now be seen as a coherent unit.

The cycles and processes of progression and renewal are also themes in the history lessons, which are now concerned with the heritage from antiquity that contributed to the development and spread of Christianity and Islam. Questions about the meaning of life and of suffering as depicted, for example, in the Parzival epic can be found again not only in the cultural history of the Middle Ages (which is discussed in Class 11) but also in the pupils' own inner mood. The essential elements in this history main-lesson are antitheses as well as processes in the struggle to overcome them. One can see such polarities in the conflicts between Pope and Emperor, Church and State, Christianity and Islam, monarch and barons, peasant and lord, town and country etc.

Literature asks questions of the individual and society in ways that often challenge the existing, conventional world view. Great literature is always in some sense prophetic and original, though it rarely provides answers. Rather it stimulates the reader to go beyond himself or herself. It opens the soul to *extra-ordinary* experience. This is exactly what the young person in Class 11 needs.

The late medieval text of Wolfram von Eschenbach's *Parzifal* is a text, though only accessible through translation, which takes the reader on a journey through individual failure, pain and inflicted hurt, lost opportunity, guilt and disintegration, and leads to atonement and redemption. It is a unique story of a quest for selfhood which matches the adolescent's inner path. Precisely because it is formally based in an unfamiliar cultural context, the psychological archetypes portrayed stand out.

The themes alluded to in the Parzifal myth can be taken up in 19th and 20th Century literature. The questions of the imagination, the individual between nature and nurture, the source of the artistic and the sublime and the threat of materialism are themes which the Romantic period brought to expression. This period in art and literature strikes a chord in the souls of young people of Class 11-age. The biographies of Blake, Shelley, Coleridge, Clare, Hawthorne and Keats are of great interest in this respect.

In foreign languages great poets and playwrights also take the foreground. Themes from the English lessons can also be taken up in a suitable form, and perhaps the class will perform a play in one of the foreign languages.

There are two aspects to consider in the geography main-lesson in Class 11. On the one hand the pupils can now be led beyond the bounds of what they have so far been able to imagine. This can be served by going back over older traditions of cartography and letting them calculate and draw various projections of the globe. (Astronomy is sometimes given as a separate main-lesson. Again, this goes beyond the bounds of what can be imagined for the earth.) On the other hand, the youngsters in Class 11 begin to search for their own psychological and social position, their 'inner home'. This can be helped by a study of geography from the point of view of world economics. This makes them aware of yet another 'mantle' that humanity as a whole creates for itself. As cultural and economic creatures, human beings shape space and develop an ever increasing awareness of this space. Global economic relations and the principles underlying them can equally reveal blind, egotistical and exploitative forces as well as the concept of mutuality, ecological consciousness and co-operation.

Technology lessons have the theme of 'energy and matter'. The various means of energy production (solid fuel generators, nuclear generators, water and wind generators, solar energy) are thought through in detail and the consequences of irresponsible energy production discussed. The inalienable need for the world in which we live to continue, is nowhere more obvious than in the realm of energy production. Links with physics, chemistry and ecology are obvious. The 'matter' element of technology is taken up in the topics such as the study of paper manufacture and processing, including everything to do with the paper industry (including the media that use print) and also the recycling question.

The step from Class 10 to Class 11 in information technology comes in, going into processes that can no longer be detected with the senses. The relation between cause and effect that was discussed in Class 10 by following work processes step-by-step is now directed to situations that can only be understood in thought. Observations in electrostatics take place in a realm that is not sense-perceptible but has to be imagined. Semi-conductors and their technologies provide the background in physics and technology.

Art lessons also bring links into the foreground. Similarities and dissimilarities in the different arts lead to a confrontation between painting and sculpture on the one hand with music and poetry on the other. Opposite concepts such as Apollonian/Dionysian qualities or stylistic trends such as Impressionist/Expressionist become motifs for consideration of the underlying role of art in expressing the struggle for human consciousness and truth. This exploration can be made in an interdisciplinary way by relating developments in literature, the visual arts and music.

In sculpture and modelling as well as in eurythmy the students endeavour to express attitudes or moods of soul (question, answer, conversation, joy, sorrow, anxiety) in gestures of the human body. The body as the mirror of the soul, is discovered through gesture. The task is to try to discover the objective in the realm of the subjective.

In the eurythmy lessons these explorations involve practising examples of Apollonian and Dionysian moods in poetry and music, discussing stylistic characteristics and encouraging the pupils to form judgments. Poetry and music should combine to form a single element. The way children live in their own movement was lost at puberty. Now it can be won back at a new level and formed into gestures and movements that express each youngster's own identity.

A period of practical social work can form an important culmination for Class 11. For three weeks the pupils work in hospitals, clinics, homes or schools for the disabled. This opportunity enables them to experience others whose needs are greater than their own. It can also show them how they as individuals can bring a ray of light into the gloom of another person's life, though it is often the case that those receiving the care have in fact far more to offer. A new level of social perception can be developed. One of the most fundamental qualities learned through such work is tolerance, both of the weakness and failings of others but more importantly for one's own limitations. Long-term developmental possibilities can arise from such experiences.

7.10   Educational Aims for Class 11

By the end of Class 11 the students should begin to:
*   attain objectivity in their feelings and thus increasing capacity to form judgments of taste, style and social tact
*   bring mobility into their thinking, which goes beyond the logical causality of their thinking in Class 10 and can now synthesise and correlate different factors within a holistic view. This also means being able to think about infinite and non-sense-perceptible phenomena
*   have a self-directed sense of social responsibility
*   be able to correlate and integrate related phenomena in a more holistic understanding

7.11   Class 12
A survey of the horizontal curriculum for Class 12

The inner question of 18/19 year-olds differs from that of a 17 year-old. They want to know: *How can I, as an individual human being, make an impact on social, economic, technical or political affairs? What is my place in the world?*

The curriculum for Class 12, bringing together what has developed over the twelve years of school. It is intended to integrate, within an overall picture, the most important aspect of Steiner Waldorf education, the evolving nature of the human being and humanity's place in the world.

In biology all the knowledge and skills built up over the years are brought together in an overview. In this, biology has a special position in relation to the inorganic sciences. There are usually two biology main-lessons in this final year at school: botany of the higher plants, and zoology of the whole animal kingdom culminating in a view of the human being. On their journey through the Lower and Upper School the pupils have travelled a path that began with the familiar human being and went step by step into the kingdoms of nature as far as the mineral kingdom. In the later part of the Upper School the opposite path is travelled, from the simplest forms of life through the kingdoms of nature to the human being. This enables the idea of development as a motif for life to be discovered.

Geography also leads to a uniting overview. The pupils are on the brink of adult maturity and they naturally turn their attention to the current world situation and their personal future. They are ready to take another look at some of the questions of rights that have been touched on in earlier years, including those arising in the context of other subjects. The centrepiece of the lessons might be the cultural diversity of humanity, its races, cultures and socio-political realities. In this way the themes of Classes 7 and 8 are taken further, this time leading to an understanding of the cultural, spiritual forces that have shaped the earth . One could call this a 'cultural mantle' of the earth.

In a similar way the pupils in Class 12 should grasp the individual styles of speech and thought in the foreign languages they are learning, and get to know the important cultural impulses expressed in those languages, especially through original literature. This brings about a fundamental, qualitative understanding for the contribution each culture brings to world history, and in consequence also leads to a better understanding of the pupils' own culture and language.

One of the aims of the music lessons is to recognise, understand and describe the intrinsic language of 20th Century music. The pupils will need to form their own judgment as regards contemporary music. The range of different types of music in our time reflects the present situation of humanity, as expressed by many different individualities and cultural streams.

English lessons provide an opportunity to experience examples of contemporary literature in the English language and also translations of world literature. Central to this exploration is the aspect of how literature reflects changing individual and cultural consciousness. Classics of world literature can be taken which exemplify both the universal and the personal/cultural experience of our times.

Steiner's curriculum suggestions offer something for history that corresponds with the suggestions for geography. The pupils work towards achieving a qualitative understanding of the inner structure and periodic evolution of cultures. This asks questions such as: What characterised the Greco-Roman age? How did the Middle Ages differ from modern times? How are historical periods defined? Can one find the same stages of cultural evolution in geographical regions, such as the Far East in comparison to Europe? It is important in this main-lesson to show how historical events are an external aspect of internal processes of evolution.

This leads to an awareness of one's own point of view and also to the knowledge that by his or her own good or bad deeds, every individual makes history. In seeing how individuals can influence their own surroundings, one becomes aware of the individual responsibility. History teaching in Class 12, complemented by sociology, undergoes a change of viewpoint. Earlier in the school the structure has been chronological. Now different perspectives, processes and themes are studied that span large periods of time. This change of position enables the pupils to gain some understanding of the philosophy and methods of history as a science.

Social studies should now lead to political education in a way that is not merely theoretical. Given the general distrust young people have today in the world of politics, it is important to stress the necessity of awakening an active interest in political processes. One point of departure can be group work on various situations (e.g. a high court case, collective wage bargaining, putting a bill before parliament), and also excursions to visit political institutions and where possible have the opportunity to speak with politicians about their work and ideals. The material to be covered includes the development of the state, law and economy from the French Revolution up to the end of the 20th Century. One can study, for example, the development of citizens' rights and human rights. The East-West and the North-South conflicts are analysed. By taking examples and studying them in more depth, the pupils gain an overall picture of human civilisation and culture. (These studies can also take the form of specialist lessons beginning in Class 9, outside of the main-lesson structure.)

By introducing and discussing various models of chemical procedure, the chemistry main-lesson endeavours to lead on from the traditional analytical approach to a more process-oriented form of chemistry in which metamorphosis is central through, for example, phenomenological and qualitative study of the different kinds of protein. The pupils learn to observe and understand qualitative aspects alongside the measurable quantitative ones. Biochemistry is particularly important, and provides opportunity to present chemistry as something that can bring healing to humanity instead of poisoning the environment.

Technology can either continue on from the results of the chemistry lessons with an emphasis on chemical technology, or take further the computer technology begun in Class 11. For the former, one example would be the study of plastics, their manufacture and use in industry, or laboratory work on the problems of pollution, removal of waste, recycling of waste etc. If a practical period in industry is arranged in Class 12, it can be followed with discussions on health in the workplace. In connection with this, new technologies can be investigated and tested for efficiency. If the emphasis is on computer technology, the pupils write programs that must be usable in industrial situations. This allows them to experience how the human being is not the slave of the machine but the spirit who shapes it.

As with chemistry, physics is also treated phenomenologically. Having entered the non-sense-perceptible realms of physics in Class 11, the pupils in Class 12 now investigate new paths in the realm of optics. The applicability of quantum theory to the microcosm and of the theory of relativity to the macrocosm are combined in relation to human experience. Beginning with the sense of sight and by bringing thought to bear on the known facts concerning light, an attempt is made to find a relationship to the real nature of light. Parallel with this, art lessons can involve working through Goethe's *Theory of Colour* through painting. The question of one's standpoint becomes central. The questions that arise include the unique position of the human being in the world.

In both painting and modelling, art lessons also provide the opportunity for working with that part of the human body that most clearly expresses the individual: the head. Painting, modelling or sculpting in stone, the pupils give *their* head an unmistakable shape and facial expression. Such work can lead to questions such as: Is the human body an expression of soul and spirit?

A similar direction is followed in eurythmy. Here the task is to find a suitable form for the basic gesture in a piece of music or a poem, so that the depiction as a whole demonstrates the inner characteristics and quality of the work of art. In a eurythmy performance for the school community the young people are to show that they can express their own personality through movement and gesture.

In Class 11 in analytical geometry the path taken was from geometry as a depiction to geometry as an algebraic calculation. Now, in Class 12 mathematics, the class goes in the opposite direction. Through analysis the pupils begin with pure calculation and move towards an experience of integral and differential calculus. By learning the concept of 'differential quotient' the pupils come to understand a new dimension in mathematics. In addition to being able to apply this, the pupils should also understand and experience it. Only when this has happened can the drawing be added to the calculation. By deriving the form from the equation and the equation from the form we endeavour to generate an inner activity in the pupils as well as an understanding of what is qualitative in mathematics. This is essential for an understanding of applied physics. In this connection one can also show that equations of the same type can be applied in all kinds of different ways in applied physics: in optics, electricity, mechanics, space travel. By coming to understand the basics of integral calculus the pupils will recognise that in the realm of higher mathematics one mathematical process can correspond to an opposite one which opens up a yet further level of mathematical comprehensibility of the world.

Depending on what was done in Class 11, there can be a second projective geometry main-lesson, built either on perspective or on spherical geometry. If taken in this way, projective geometry would lead to an understanding of the application of perspective drawing in the architecture main-lesson and on the art trip. Spherical geometry can lead more towards astronomy or more towards the earth.

Another possibility for a second mathematics main-lesson would be to combine mathematics, botany, astronomy, embryology and geometry in an overall panorama, in a study of the principles of form. This depends very much on the general stage of maturity of the class.

During the industrial practical period in Class 12 the pupils are concerned with an entirely different concept of 'tolerance' from the one they met during their social practical period in Class 11. In industry the 'tolerance' met with might concern the exactitude of machine tooling in the production process of a metalworking industrial factory. During this practical period in industry (several weeks), the pupils have many different experiences to do with the work, with the people they are working with and, also, with themselves. The purpose of this practical period is to get to know economic and industrial life 'from the bottom up'. The pupils experience what it means to work with others towards a common industrial goal. They learn about the opportunities and problems of our modern world with its division of labour. They can observe how a mistake in one part of the process affects the whole production process. They may also have the opportunity to learn how to use an industrial machine accurately, how to check materials and carry out other controls. By their own experience they learn how much strength it takes to make a space between the polarities of work and leisure for conscious, creative mental work. This practical period thus fulfils many different educational tasks. An alternative to the industrial practical would be a work placement in a business or part of the service industry. The heart of such projects is to experience the moral aspect of work and serving the needs of others.

The Class 12 play demonstrates the responsibility of each for the whole and shows how efforts towards a common goal can bring about more than can be imagined by taking the sum of individual capacities. For the last time the class experiences its potential as a whole in putting on a big play, an opera, a musical, a cabaret etc. Speech, gestures, music, singing (possibly eurythmy), direction, scenery, lighting, making the programme and posters – all this has to be managed, in addition to putting on several performances, perhaps with double casting.

Some Steiner Waldorf schools round off the twelve years with major individual projects. Each pupil takes on a year-long project consisting of a practical/artistic theme and a theoretical theme (encompassing several subjects). This is worked on throughout the year, in addition to normal school work, with the help of a tutor or project supervisor. The practical results of these projects are displayed in an exhibition or performed during an afternoon or evening performance. The pupils speak in public to the theoretical parts and this is followed by a discussion. Giving these presentations in appropriate form is another aspect of Class 12's work.

In keeping with the element of Class 12 work that calls for a combination of many viewpoints and subjects, the main theme in art is architecture as the universal art, in which all the arts can work together to form a comprehensive work of art. An important theme in Class 12 is to philosophise about art and aesthetics. A history of philosophy and a comparative study of world religions can offer an overview of mankind's spiritual endeavours.

The work in Class 12, representing twelve years of Steiner Waldorf education, is intended to contribute to the aim of *getting to know the human being* in the sense formulated by Rudolf Steiner in 1920:
Knowing the world, the human being finds himself,
and knowing himself, he finds the world revealed to him.

7.12   Educational Aims for Class 12

By the end of Class 12 the students should be able to:
*   have an integrated view of the nature of the human being, human society and nature
*   articulate, explain and relate their own views on a wide range of topics which concern them
*   show a good degree of social competence

- show interest in questions of human destiny
- recognise and be able to characterise qualities through sensory observation and reviewing the facts
- move from the parts to a perception of what is whole in practical, social and conceptual contexts
- show the inner mobility of thought to move forwards and backwards within a process so as to be able to understand the whole and be able to articulate the idea behind the process
- begin to make connections and inner links between phenomena which express the activity of the underlying formative, creative principles in the world and thus reveal the interplay between spirit, visible form and matter
- understand the distinction between causal, analytical observations and teleological ones
- consider the relationship between law, necessity, freedom and responsibility
- think for themselves, and act out of their own insight whilst carrying responsibility for their actions

References

30 Smilansky, S., *Sociodramatic Play: Its relevance to behaviour and achievement in school, in children's play and learning.* Klugman and Smilansky, ed. New York Teachers' Press, 1990.

31 Steiner, R., *The Foundations of Human Experience*, Lecture 1, AP 1996.

32 Steiner, R., *Soul Economy and Waldorf Education*, Lecture of 1/1/1923, AP 1986.

33 Steiner, R., ibid, Lecture of 3/1/1922.

34 Steiner terms puberty *Erdenreife* which literally means 'ripe for the earth' or 'earth maturity'. This expression conveys the sense of a readiness to experience the full forces of earthly existence.

35 Steiner, R., *Soul Economy and Waldorf Education*, Lecture of 1/1922, AP 1986.

36 Steiner, R., Müller-Wiedemann, H., *Mitte der Kindheit*, Stuttgart, 1989, p119.

37 Steiner, R., *A Modern Art of Education*, Lecture of 15/8/1923, RSP 1981.

38 Steiner, R., *A Modern Art of Education*, Lecture of 15/8/1923, RSP 1981.

39 Steiner, R., *Practical Advice to Teachers*, RSP 1976.

40 Piaget, J., *Theories and Methods of Modern Education*, Frankfurt, 1974, p3.

41 The original German curriculum incorporates Steiner's suggestion that the period of German Classical Literature and in particular the biographies of Goethe and Schiller were appropriate for Class 9. Here the emphasis is on the friendship between these two outstanding personalities, a friendship that went beyond mere sympathy but had profounder sources. The key element was the mutual spiritual recognition which each found inspiring. There is no obvious parallel in English literature. The motif of a friendship which both inspires and yet leaves free is so crucial to this age, that other opportunities must be found within the curriculum to awaken this ideal.

42 Steiner, R., *Conferences with the Teachers of the Waldorf School in Stuttgart*, meeting of 17/6/1921, SSF 1986-1989.

8.0 THE VERTICAL CURRICULUM

Preface

It is necessary to re-state that Steiner Waldorf education lives in a process of constant renewal in terms of both content and method. Therefore every teacher is called upon to carry on educational research based on what he or she perceives to be either the developmental stage reached by the pupils in a particular class or changes in the world as time moves on. This was the sense in which Steiner gave his educational advice and curriculum suggestions to the teachers of the original Waldorf School in Stuttgart. These can be found in the lectures known as *The Foundations of Human Experience* (formerly *Study of Man*) and in the subsequent course of lectures *Practical Advice to Teachers*, as well as in *Discussions with Teachers and Three Lectures on the Curriculum.* The other main source for Steiner's indications on the teaching comes from the meetings he regularly held with the teachers and which are recorded in the *Conferences With Teachers.*[1]

He counted on the teachers' *educational imagination*, on their *responsibility towards the developing individualities of the pupils* and on their *unconditional commitment to whatever is educationally necessary.*

Certain pedagogical ways are followed by us at the Waldorf School, but we also have the greatest possible freedom ... Our whole curriculum is determined according to what is spiritually necessary, but on the other hand the teachers have the greatest possible freedom to do what they consider to be appropriate. [2]

An orientation in those 'pedagogical ways' that are determined 'according to what is spiritually necessary' can be discovered in *The Foundations of Human Experience* mentioned above which remains an inexhaustible source from which educational impulses can be drawn in teachers' meetings and in individual study. On the other hand they arise out of the way the teacher works on the subject matter of the lessons.

We must approach the curriculum in such a way that we find ourselves in the position of being able to recreate it within ourselves in any situation, so that we can look at children aged 7, 8, 9 or 10 and glean from them what we should do in each respective year. [3]

The following framework curriculum is intended in this sense. If it becomes nothing more than tradition to be followed to the letter, it will depart from what is meant by Steiner Waldorf education. On the other hand it is also important not to introduce changes in a subjective or arbitrary way, without prior thorough and responsible educational research. What is here presented as a range of possible teaching content is based on good practice that has proven itself and is founded on experience of children.

Checklists

Integrated within the sections covering English, Mathematics and Foreign Language teaching, guidelines are given for checklists to be used by teachers to monitor individual children's attainments. These lists describe what most children of normal ability range will be able to do, understand and repeat at the end of the designated school year. These attainments would constitute a minimum level. Similar checklists are being developed for other subjects. Such guidelines are for the teacher's own reference. They are not intended as criteria for implying any kind of success or failure but simply as an orientation for the teacher.

It is perfectly possible for each school and even each teacher to set their own guidelines for attainment if they can justify them. Those presented here can be used as a reference point. All experienced teachers know that individual children can be precocious or late starters. There are many cases of children who have appeared to develop intellectual, literacy or numerical skills slowly but have later distinguished themselves in these and others fields of ability. This point should always be borne in mind before judgments are made. The point about attainment guidelines is not to label this or that child as in some sense deficient but simply to have a benchmark to aim for and with which individual attainments at a given stage can be compared.

We make an important distinction between teaching content and minimum attainments. There are many experiences children should have because they help the child in his or her overall development. There are some things, however, that need to be mastered in order to be able to progress in a particular skill.

In some ways these minimum requirements are not age related; rather they belong to the internal logic of the subject. It is not easy to progress with arithmetic, for example, if the basic knowledge of number bonds and tables is missing or too fragmented to be of much use. If an individual, for whatever reason, has not mastered these basics, he or she will need learning support, remedial strategies or other aids in order to progress in being able to understand and use basic arithmetic. It is in this sense that the guidelines are given.

References
1   See the bibliography for the full references to these basic works.
2   Steiner, R., *A Modern Art of Education*, op. cit., August 1923, at an exhibition of work by the pupils.
3   Steiner, R., *Practical Advice to Teachers*, op. cit., lecture of 5/9/1919.

CURRICULUM NOTES BY RUDOLF STEINER

1. After puberty, it is essential that the practical subjects should become a part of the lessons. People must get to know the meaning of our modern technological age in school, not in the factory.

2. This needs to be counterbalanced by the aesthetic side of education. Impressions of beauty are the only thing that can unite human beings with their childhood and beyond this with eternity. Such impressions are needed to provide not only the courage to step beyond the limitations of knowledge but also to give a content to faith based on experience. Such impressions increase the value of work and justify leisure. Knowledge is something that can lead people towards the divine; will impulses are always only a germinating seed. Through beauty the picture becomes filled with all the magic of reality, yet it does not make demands in the way the will does.

3. Links with the spirit are severed if beauty is not there to maintain them. Beauty binds the 'I' to the body.

(From notes written down by Rudolf Steiner and quoted by J. Tautz in *Lehrerbewusstsein im 20. Jahrhundert*, Dornach 1995, p.116.)

ARITHMETIC AND MATHEMATICS

Classes 1 to 8

General aspects and aims

"Mathematics in the Waldorf School is divided into three stages. In the first stage, which covers the first five classes, mathematics is developed as an activity intimately connected to the life process of the child, and progresses from the internal towards the external. In the second stage, covering Classes 6 to 8, the main emphasis is on the practical ... The ninth year onwards is characterised by a transfer towards a rational point of view." Thus writes H. von Baravalle, the first mathematics teacher at the Waldorf School in Stuttgart, about the treatment of this subject, in his book *Mathematics Teaching and the Waldorf School Plan.*[1]

The first stage

Here two questions must be answered:
1. How should the first mathematical concepts be tackled?
2. What is the psychological basis on which to build them?

Question 1: Careful scrutiny shows that the teaching of arithmetical and geometric concepts is connected to the consciousness and activity of the child's movement organism. Counting is inner movement by which outer movement can be observed. E. Schuberth calls this *"the sensory content of mathematics teaching"*.[2] The results of Piaget's research on the development of intelligence in children also point in this direction: In the 'concrete operations stage' (12 or 13 years old), children still carry out movements when they want to connect one thing to another. Anyway, these movements are connected to the physical objects from which the children can as yet barely free themselves, if at all.

This leads on to Question 2: If the development of mathematical concepts occurs in the static, concrete phase, our purpose must not be to *"generalise and abstract"*, but to *"make concrete and look at individual cases"*.[3] This defines the means whereby it is possible to avoid confronting the children with abstract logical structures, but rather to immerse their whole capacity for experience in mathematics. We can now refer to form drawing where the consciousness necessary for using mathematics is nurtured and practised. This physical experience is a basis and assumption for a healthy immersion in the 'formal operations stage' (Piaget). The rule 'from hand, through heart to head' (which is meant by the child's above-mentioned 'whole capacity for experience') makes it possible for the children to bring their own capacities into play. *"It is evident that the best, most fruitful questions about concepts and explanations come from pupils who do not pose questions using a quick intellectuality, but a capacity for involved feeling, which allows clarity to come into thinking."*[4]

To this concrete approach in mathematics at primary school level we should add something further which does not depend on the element of movement. This is the quality, one might say the identity, of the individual numbers.

As the accent above is on a quantitative approach to numbers, as the result of a brief pause in movement or even based on the movement itself, we need to place our introduction to qualitative number concepts beside those of quantity. We approach these qualities when we examine many examples where the number in question is really active in the world, as for example the number 5 in the flowers of a rose. Here we use the child's desire to question what lies behind the world and human creations, that is, to seek what lies behind the phenomena. The nuclear scientist W. Heitler referred to this when he said in a lecture: *"One directs one's attention to qualitative phenomena, to characteristics which have something to do with the totality of the objects observed"*. Steiner recommended taking this as the starting point for an introduction to number concepts: *"We have gradually come to the point in the course of civilisation where we can work with numbers in a synthetic manner. We have a unity, a second unity, a third unity and we struggle while counting in an additive manner to join the one to the other, so that one lies beside the other when we count. One can become convinced that children do not bring an inner understanding towards this. Primitive human beings did not develop counting in this way. Counting began from unity. Two was not an external repetition of unity but it lay within unity. One gave us two, and two is contained in the one. One, divided, gave us three, and three is contained within one. If we wrote the number 1, translated into modern terms, one could not get away from the 1, for instance to 2. It was an inner organic picture where two came out of unity and this two was contained in the one, likewise three and so on. Unity encompassed everything and the numbers were organic divisions of unity".*[5]

This 'real' way of looking at numbers leads on to written numbers, to symbols. It is not a picture like that which should be used for introducing letters, but pictures of number qualities. The picture belongs to the being of the number, not to the outer symbolic form. At this point we indicate a further point of this 'quality-oriented' teaching: Today, especially, when we face the results of a quantitative world view in ecological catastrophe and destruction, it is increasingly important to make a beginning of this kind in teaching mathematics.

By beginning with the concrete qualities of number and by working with the properties of movement in counting and calculating, children develop a kind of intelligence which seeks and finds the way to reality.

This brings us to the *second stage*: the approach to mathematics teaching mentioned earlier. Here we must deal with the practical use of calculation.

If calculating has been practised thoroughly enough

during the first stage in the manner indicated, then applied calculation also gets a qualitative colouring. The forces of intelligence which are served by business mathematics as well as percentages and interest, are not 'value-free', but can retain a colouring for balanced testing and judging. The human significance of what is thought out, can and should be made clear. In this connection one should point to the suggestion by Steiner that elements of bookkeeping should also be taken up in mathematics lessons. To see what the general idea behind such an indication is, one should ask what skills may be developed through bookkeeping. There you will see how above all a moral method of trading can be decisively supported by these means.

All these themes can lead us on to other educational aims: inner mobility leads to imaginative ability in solving mathematical problems.

Through the experience of number qualities the children experience trust and security: Number, world and human being belong together.

The children can experience further security through the correctness of solutions to problems By this means they win some independence. *"For this reason mathematics is an activity suited to free children from the fetters of authority, even if, at first, they depend on the help of the teacher."* [6]

A final educational aim which should not be undervalued and which is connected with the latter: calculation is not possible without regular practice, which also makes it an excellent medium for schooling the will.

An explicit presentation of the *third stage* will be given under the heading 'General aspects and aims. Classes 9 to 12' and is therefore omitted here.

Geometry as part of mathematics teaching begins in Classes 5 and 6 and is taught in separate main-lessons. One of the principal intentions in this subject is to develop and nurture the ability to visualise space.

The controlled security of directed movement and the estimation of proportions and relationships, practised in freehand geometry, is well prepared for by form drawing in Classes 1 to 4.

The establishment of skills, knowledge and techniques partly in connection with subjects is taught with increasing complexity related to age.

- The pupil should gradually learn to discover, to grasp mentally and to apply geometrical properties, and the practical, drawn, solutions representing them.
- Work with geometric drawing instruments should lead to clear and exact construction.
- Patience, care and precision should be developed, as well as independent creative work through enjoyment of drawing.

Classes 1 to 3

Points of view and general themes:

The dynamics of will activity should be internalised by the experience of countability. Motivation should be awakened through pictorial description of number qualities. This dual aspect is important: on the one hand it educates the bodily senses through experience of movement, unfolding of movement possibilities (both coarse and fine), and co-ordination exercises. On the other hand internalising of the expressed activities in soul activity (i.e. calculation). Here the main medium for achieving this is the use of pictures. Through pictures children can grasp internally what is intended. Pure symbolic, logical presentation can never achieve this. (Nevertheless one should always be conscious that calculation is aiming at a pictureless world, in contrast to the introduction of letters of the alphabet.) In order to be able to handle quantitative numbers freely, an inner numerical space needs to be created, in which one learns to move, rhythmically at first, with varied number patterns. This is achieved, amongst other means, by a memory developed by learning the times-tables through rhythmic movement e.g. through clapping, passing bean bags or skipping. It appears important initially to approach actual calculation as concretely and visually as possible and to keep in mind the principle 'from the whole to the parts'. This means that the right connection between analytical and synthetic thinking is produced. Work with the temperaments should be formed in the sense given in the 4th discussion in *Discussions with Teachers.* [7] At the end of Class 3 the pupils should have a confident grasp and clear view of numbers up to 1020 at least. This does not mean just the quantity or extent but equally the quality of the numbers.

Content suggestions:

Class 1

In mathematics lessons the approach is analytical in the sense of the reference by Steiner given above. Starting with the number 1 as unity, numbers (symbols) from 1 to 10 should be produced in a qualitative manner (see 'Points of view and general themes' above), which are contained as manifold in unity. With written numbers one can begin with Roman numerals which are less abstract than the Arabic. [8] Alternatively, the Arabic numbers can be introduced in pictures as with the letters of the alphabet.

- Counting up to 110
- Learning up to the 7 times table by heart and through rhythmical practice
- Introducing the four rules using numbers up to 20 and also in written form (in notation the sum is written first 7 is 3 + 4)
- Number riddles
- First exercises in mental arithmetic

Class 2

- Further practice in mental arithmetic
- Extension of counting and practice of the four rules using numbers up to 100
- Practice in combined calculation

- Initial consideration of number connections 'Kingly' numbers and 'beggar' numbers (primes)
- Up to the 12 times table by heart
- Representation of tables in drawing
- Written analytically and synthetically practised calculations
- In the course of Class 2 calculations should be reversed (e.g. 3+4=7)

Class 3

- Mental arithmetic
- Sums using numbers up to 1020 or 1100
- Written addition and subtraction using several places (place value)
- Written multiplication using two place values
- Written division using units as divisor
- Up to 15 times tables 10 times table up to 900
- Square numbers by heart as a sequence
- Weights and measures (practical subject) and calculations with simple practical problems

Checklist for Classes 1 - 3 – Numeracy

NUMBER

Most children within the normal range of ability will be able to:

1   have working knowledge of four processes and their symbols + - x + (including processes in verbal and written sentence form)
1   appreciate number qualities 1-12
1   understand Roman numerals 1 - X and Arabic numerals 1-100
1   count from 1-100
1   know number bonds up to 10
1/2   understand difference between odd and even numbers
1-3   have work knowledge of the multiplication tables 1-12
1/3   apply simple mental arithmetic in narrative form using above listed skills
2   know number bonds up to 20
2/3   recognise, analyse and count to numbers up to 1,000
2/3   work with tables as division (24 shared between 6 is 4)
2/3   know patterns in multiplication tables 10, 9, 5, 4, 11
2/3   use place value to four places (ten, H, T and U)
2/3   carry numbers across columns e.g.

19	74
+2	x2

3   be able to recite tables 1 – 12 in chorus and individually

FORM DRAWING (see form drawing curriculum)

1/2   draw straight line, curves, linear forms, symmetry on vertical axis
1-3   draw common geometric forms freehand
3/4   draw symmetrical reflections: about horizontal and diagonal axis

MEASUREMENT

2/3   use money for simple bills and calculating change
3   tell time using hours, half hours, quarter hours on 12 hour clock
3   calculate simple practical sums e.g. how many milk bottles in a crate holding six by six, bricks in a wall, floor boards etc.
3   calculate simple sums in measurement of length, capacity and weight

Classes 4 and 5

Points of view and general themes:

Upon reaching their 9th year the children make a decisive change. Their close relationship to the world around them becomes different and more remote. The earlier harmony between outer and inner worlds is fundamentally broken.

This transformation in their soul is reflected in the mathematics curriculum when in Class 4 the children begin to work with broken numbers (fractions). By this means they meet something in the teaching content which they have also experienced in themselves.

It is not essential for the children to be able to manage fractions swiftly. It is much more important that they can experience these 'external' fractions very strongly. In connection with this, the historical development of fraction calculations in Egypt can give the teacher interesting and significant teaching ideas. In order to do general justice to the subject of fractions it is recommended to use the following three methods as an introduction: To proceed from the whole to the parts, from the parts to the whole, and to establish the principle of equivalence. After this the four rules are practised with fractions, the same with simplifying, expansion and division of the denominator into prime factors.

After this, decimal fractions follow as a practical application. Once the divisibility border is crossed the children can discover the practicality of calculations in Class 5.

The aim according to Steiner is as follows: In Class 5 we want to continue with fractions and decimals and to give the children everything which will allow them to calculate freely with whole and fractional numbers. [9]

In Class 4 form drawing is led into elementary geometry. Here one can begin again with the basic linear polarity of circle and straight line. In order that the pupils get as intensive an image as possible of these forms, it is recommended that they do not initially use compasses and ruler, but draw free-hand.

Although we deal with the most basic elements in the first geometry lessons, it is important to let the pupils feel something of that dimension which is connected with existential questions over and above the practical and utilitarian. This is made far easier if the beauty of form and strongly regulated connections of geometry are felt in addition to the working rules and methods.

In connection with stories from ancient Egypt

in the history lessons, the Pythagorean rope can be introduced as a first introduction to Pythagoras' Theorem.

Content suggestions:

Class 4

- Mental arithmetic
- Practice of written calculations using higher numbers
- Introduction to fractions: experience of a fraction as part of a whole. From part to whole, similar fractions and different fractions. Transfer of improper fractions into mixed numbers and the reverse
- Introduction to decimal fractions
- Revision: the four rules and written multiplication and division with several place values
- Freehand form drawing leads into geometrical drawing. Circle, square, triangle, isosceles and right angled triangle. Division of circle into 4, 5, 6, 8, 12 equal parts. This is done by organised guess work. Colouring and imagination will bring out different patterns

Class 5

- Constant practice in mental arithmetic
- Revision: The four rules with natural numbers
- Combinations of the four rules
- Calculations with fractions: Expansion and reduction of equivalents (division into prime factors)
- Illustration and comparison of fractions. Calculation with decimals. Consolidation of fractions methods
- Table of place values, rhythmically, through movement, and qualitatively introduced
- Introduction of the relationship of decimals to place values
- Measurements using decimals
- Recognition of connections between decimal numbers and decimal fractions

The main new task for Class 5 is learning to use a pair of compasses with accuracy, though some teachers prefer to wait until the beginning of Class 6. The forms previously drawn in Class 4 can now be accurately constructed. Children will naturally colour these flower-like forms, and thus make an obvious link with the botany main-lesson in Class 5.

A set square and ruler can also be used to draw accurate parallel lines.

- Starting with the construction of a circle, discovery of the main geometrical figures: triangle, hexagon, square, rhombus, parallelogram, octagon
- Division and joints on 24 point circle
- Construction of perpendicular bisector, angle bisection, perpendicular bisector, angle bisection, perpendiculars
- Construction of different triangles; equilateral, isosceles, scalene, right angled
- The various angles; acute, obtuse, reflex.
- Circles touching a triangle; inside (incircle) and outside (circumcircle)
- Pythagoras' Theorem; visually using knotted string. (Egyptians used this to construct their pyramids). Grains covering an area, theorem drawn using Roman tiles (Isosceles triangle)
- Tessellation (tiling) involving accurate construction of parallel lines
- Exact construction of pentagon/pentagram

Checklist for Class 4 - 5 – Numeracy

Most children within the normal range of ability will be able to:

NUMBER

4	carry out all four processes of number confidently
4	read and understand numbers up to six figures
4	know the multiplication tables up to 12 out of sequence
4	do long multiplication with numbers up to 122 as multiplier
4	find factors of a given number
4	identify prime numbers less than 100
4/5	answer more complex mental arithmetic questions involving a mix of processes (e.g. The 12.38 train to Reading takes 18 minutes but left 14 minutes late, when did it arrive? or I doubled a number and added 8 and got 32, what was the number?)
4/5	do long division including making use of remainder and estimating approximate answers.
4/5	find Lowest Common Multiple or Highest Common Factors
5	use all four processes with fractions including mixed numbers and improper fractions
5	understand how to use decimal notation, decimal fractions and interchange of decimal with common fractions
5	carry out four processes with decimals
5	use long division and multiplication using the decimal point
5	apply the Rule of Three (if, then, therefore) to practical problems

MEASUREMENT

4	record information such as height, weight, volume etc.
5	work with metric measurement including estimation
5	work with aspects of time including 24 hour clock
5/6	calculate average speeds

GEOMETRY

5	draw freehand archetypal geometric shapes: different kinds of triangle, rectangle, quadrilaterals, polygons and circles
5	divide circles into 17, 16 or 20 parts, deriving regular figures like pentagon and hexagon from them [10]

Classes 6 to 8

Points of view and general themes:

So far, concept-building about method given pictorially has been rooted in an approach to the child's soul. Now, after the 12th year, children can increasingly create order out of what has been gained with the strength of their ability to experience internal logic. This step is exemplified in *algebra*: It leads from the activity of calculating to observation of the processes and from there to the discovery of general relationships.

> *The purpose of an algebraic formula, of 'calculating with letters of the alphabet', is to express the formal, intelligible processes. This is a general step forward in the development of the child as only the method is formulated: By this means the transfer from an imagination-bound thinking to a conceptual thinking is facilitated ... The process: the delineation of a concrete problem (interest), the solution of the problem, the evidence of the validity of the solution method, and finally the applicability of the discovered rule. All this would be experienced by the children in many situations.* [11]

As the children approach puberty their feeling life expands in all ways. Mathematics can offer an important support in this stage of life. Their own subjective opinions and ideas are not required! Mathematics attracts their attention not only to the numerical material but especially to their own thinking. If the pupils manage to become confident and secure with mathematical laws, they learn self-confidence. When this is achieved the young people are on the way to the most important aim in mathematics teaching: that of gaining trust in thinking.

However, this thinking can now connect itself in a one-sided selfish way to its mentor, the human ego, but this leads to egoism. It is essential to link thinking to world interests in practical and necessary life situations. It is, however, important that the attempts to solve problems do not lead to resignation with the 'I can't do that' attitude, because mathematics lessons then achieve exactly what they should not. Instead of enjoyment and confidence, they create boredom and despair. There is hardly any other subject which is so equated to scholarly ability and intelligence as mathematics. To 'give up' here or to have problems means to give up generally, and simply to be 'stupid'.

For this reason, mixed ability classes make particular demands on the teacher as regards method or possibly even remedial measures. During the class-teacher stage, what the pupils have to do must be differentiated although all of them must deal with the basic mathematical questions. Work with practical problems offers a rich fund of activities for the pupils and can even be formed into a life skill, which might open various avenues to the real world of work. Working by means of mathematical exercises to make thinking energetic fosters an active connection to these areas. The practical activities bring the pupils towards life and reality and also to a description of basic connections.

Calculation is an education of the will in the area of thinking. For this reason practice lessons are added to the main-lessons from about Class 6 onwards.

The precision and beauty of geometrical figures are the teachers who will lead them to greater awareness. What has been experienced through amazement in geometry in Class 5 should be worked on in thinking in Classes 6, 7 and 8. Geometrical rules are sought and formulated. The pupils must also experience geometrical proofs adequately. It is important for them as they develop their individual forms of speech and expression that they can experience something like this, which is quite free of emotion and concerns itself purely with what ought to be. In Class 8 one can use the new subject of conic sections to approach the problem of infinity as one did before with parallels. Infinity is still not defined specifically.

Content suggestions:

Class 6

- Continuing with mental arithmetic
- Revision: calculation with natural numbers, positive fractions and decimals
- Unitary method, with direct and inverse proportion
- Percentages
- Application of percentages to business: interest, discount, exchange, profit and loss, VAT, general introduction to the use of formulae by means of simple interest
- Block graphs and pictograms

GEOMETRY

Class 6

- Geometrical proof of sums of angles of triangle: using cut outs, protractors
- Proof of above using calculations
- Accurate construction of angles using compasses, bisecting angles
- Construction of triangles from description
- Congruent triangles; the four principle cases for congruency
- Translations; movement properties of triangles and quadrilaterals; crown transformations, triangles in the same segment of a circle (colouring enhances this.) Thales' Theorem
- Leaf forms from; triangles, circle.
- Caustic curves, envelopes of a cardioid
- Congruent shapes, construction of similar angles Complementary, supplementary and other angles
- Construction of triangles, with altitudes, and angle and side bisectors

Class 7

- Continuing practise in mental arithmetic
- Revision: the four rules in natural and positive rational numbers
- Basic bookkeeping
- Introduction to negative integers (through debt calculation)
- The four rules with negative numbers

- Extension to cover all rationals
- The four rules with rationals and their connections.
- Introduction of brackets
- Recurring decimals, later on the value of π. Full understanding and comparison of decimal places and significant figures
- Compound interest
- Simple statistical data rendered in graphical form and deductions therefrom

ALGEBRA

- Simple equations, including brackets, fractions and negative numbers. Their practical application to solving problems
- Making and transforming formulae
- Powers and roots of numbers. The exact evaluation of square roots
- Ratio and proportion
- Calculation of the areas of figures bounded by straight lines and circular arcs
- Types of quadrilateral and their symmetries, leading to simple set theory

GEOMETRY

- Areas of geometrical shapes through construction and calculation
- Area of circle, and using this to calculate the value of π, by cutting the circle into pieces
- Pythagoras; theorem; area proof
- Shapes and stretches of simple shapes
- Tangents to circles
- Further transformations of pentagons. Construction of decagon and polygons
- Perspective drawing. (Can be linked with modern history main-lesson)

Class 8

REVISION

- Fractions
- Squares and roots
- Equations
- Practical problems

ALGEBRA

- The commutative, associative and distributive laws in algebra. The factors of the difference between the squares and the application of this to practical problems
- Volumes of rectangular blocks, pyramids, prisms, cylinders and cones. Density and weight of solid objects
- Simultaneous linear equations and problems
- The dissolution of complex brackets in algebraic expressions
- A brief look at balance sheets and mortgages
- Number systems. Binary arithmetic
- Further statistical work including mean, mode and median

- Graphs of more complicated curves. The solution of simultaneous equations by graphs

GEOMETRY

- Locus of line and plane
- Locus and conics defined geometrically
- Enlargements, rotation, reflection of shapes
- Angle properties of circle (angles in the same circle, intersecting chords)
- Construction of 5 regular Platonic solids. Orthogonal view of them
- Exact spatial perspective drawing including the golden section
- Discussion of general triangle sides and altitude formulae as part of the development of the investigation of Pythagoras' Theorem
- Optional: Internal and external angles of a polygon
- Similar figures especially triangles

Checklist for Classes 6 - 8 – Numeracy

Most children within the normal range of ability will be able to:

NUMBER

6	convert percentages to fractions and vice versa
6	estimate results by rounding off number prior to accurate calculation
6	business maths: balance sheets: profit and loss, discount, commission, VAT and book-keeping, bank accounts
6	work out averages including speed
6	read co-ordinates (e.g. for map reading)
6	use letters in formula
7	know powers of numbers
7	work out ratio and scale
7	use algebra as a general solution to specific problems
7	use negative and positive integers
7/8	know how to work with square roots
7/8	calculate compound interest, mortgage rates, income tax
6/7	make time and speed calculations
7/8	calculate mechanical advantage in simple machines e.g. pulleys, levers

DATA

6	present information via pictograms: use pie charts, bar charts, linear graphs (foreign currency exchange)
7	use algebraic graphs

GEOMETRY

6	make precise use of compasses, ruler, set squares to draw constructions of major geometric figures
6	make use of freehand perspective
6/7	use protractor
6/7	draw translations, reflections, rotations

6/7   know Pythagoras Theorem and its applications

7   use instruments to draw linear perspective

7   know properties of triangles, parallel lines and intersecting lines

7   know and apply formulae for area of regular geometric forms, including triangle, circle, parallelogram, derivation and use of

7/8   calculate areas of irregular forms

Classes 9 to 12

General aspects and aims:

The central point of mathematical activity is problem solving. The important question is how to solve problems, not what one gets as a answer. With this as the focus, school mathematics builds on both bases of mathematics: inspiration (induction) as a beginning and logical conclusion (deduction) at a later stage in the mathematical activity.

The most important aim will be to develop the ability of the pupils to think with a wide range of approaches until they get to the logical conclusion, and to give them confidence in themselves and in their thinking.

Another justified aim is to prepare the pupils to apply calculation methods to everyday life and also to give them the foundation for further education.

It is nevertheless valuable for the principal aim to give problems in many new contexts: It is more important than the division into subject areas, such as algebra, functions etc., to pose questions in various heuristic ways in order to 'unravel' a problem.

The pupils may rehearse their ability to guess, to test variations in an investigation and practise making theories. In order to find a clue for the solution one can simplify the problem; likewise, it helps to make analogies or to generalise the question in order to get an idea of the recurrent theme.

If there is a large proportion of creative problem solving, mathematics can have enormous value for the pupils' development in this period. They are given the opportunity to observe their thinking in a variety of ways: seeking points of departure, choosing examples or counter examples, systematically running an investigation and proving the results. They learn to analyse and to judge conditions.

The artistic educational quality of Steiner Waldorf education is especially evident in mathematics. One can create a fruitful dialogue with the pupils as well as between them. The curriculum indicates the aims and teaching content and curriculum questions, but how the lessons are formed is independent of the required knowledge of the pupils. In this regard it is an advantage if the teacher gradually forms a collection of problems tailored to a particular class.

It is important that pupils are allowed to make inner conquests of general value. They get most value from results which they guessed at first and were then able to prove.

As thinking is an expression of our ego activity, mathematics affords quite special opportunities for the pupils' inner development and self-knowledge.

In *geometry*, which can be taught as a separate subject within the framework of mathematics, the following applies in these classes:

- The pupils should practise methods of construction in 3D space.
- The pupils should learn to think in processes; they should break through to, and release, habits of thinking and habits of understanding, and thereby bring more openness and mobility into their thinking.
- The representation of spatial reality such as orthographic and other projections and perspective, are practised and investigated for their applications.

Class 9

Points of view and general themes:

With the introduction of combinations and especially when beginning with probability – subjects with which Class 9 often begins – the pupils can experience that the thinking which can reach out over what is given and can master these general cases offers them a practical tool for formal logical thinking so that even without special conditions prepared in the Lower School they can effect a 'new entry'. The study of equations, which is extended and deepened, offers a good field of work for their growing formal abilities through its transparent methods of solution. In addition, there are all kinds of series which lead the pupils into deeper study.

A further study of triangles with this new approach offers a medium for experience in simple proofs, whereby things already learnt already are brought into use (e.g. congruence rules from Class 8). The method is analytical, growing from the concrete to the general, from the geometrical construction to the proof. In geometry, work on the conic sections, which may be begun earlier and can be extended later on, offers a variety of construction methods, to create mobile ideas, which are also worked out by rigorous method. In the construction of one of the principal curves (ellipse, hyperbola, parabola), the subject of infinity which has been latent since Class 6, reappears more clearly. At the same time exercises should lead the pupils to a clear experience of the 3 dimensions. One can begin with the cube which visibly represents dimensionality. From this the most varied solids can be developed. Exercises are given to transform these in stages so that the pupils learn to picture them in a fluid way.

Oblique plan views are used to represent these.

The pupils should get to know the personalities whose thoughts they are using, through biographies or mathematicians (e.g. Pascal, Fermat).

Periodic excursions into irrationals and incommensurables with their polarities prepare for the unification of arithmetic and geometry in analytical geometry in Class 11.

At the appropriate moment the calculator can also be introduced.

The wealth of possible content does not permit a comprehensive tackling of subjects. The important thing for Class 9 is the 'how'. It depends on bringing to life concrete representative examples of general rules.

Content suggestions:

KNOWLEDGE AND SKILLS IN ELEMENTARY ALGEBRA

Revision of:
- Natural numbers, integers and rationals
- Divisibility rules, HCF and LCM
- Primes and the question of how many there are
- Calculation with four rules of polynomials and fractions
- Squares and roots
- Irrationals and the new subject of the domain of real numbers
- Direct and indirect proportion in connection with practical life (percentages and interest)

Algebra
- Linear equations in 2 and 3 unknowns
- Depending on the class ability: quadratic equations (can be done in Class 10)

Combinations:
- Permutations
- Variation
- Optional: basic elements of probability stemming from questions using combinations
- Elements of number theory (bases, particularly base 2 in consideration of computers)

Binomial theorem:
- Binomial coefficients
- Pascal's triangle
- Calculation with squares and roots, a look at the cube root
- Tricks for simplifying calculation without electronic aids based on the binomial theorem

Algorithmic calculations:
- Continued fractions and their use for simplifying fractions
- Converging fraction series for the golden section (see irrationals)
- Optional: the Euclidean algorithm for HCF and LCM with practical examples

Incommensurability in arithmetic and geometry:
- Extension of the number domain to include irrationals
- Extension of number series to include continued fraction approximations of roots
- Perhaps: root 1 to root 25 by continued fractions and their number series
- Squares and root 2
- Equilateral triangles and root 3
- Regular pentagon and root 5
- Derive the formula for pentagon sides and diagonals

Geometry
- Revision of work with angle types

- Alternate segment theorem
- Using the triangle to revise congruence; similarity, proportional division
- using parallels; the four main centres of a triangle and the Euler line
- The forms of Pythagoras' Theorem, extension of the theorem
- Revision and deepening of area calculation (triangle, right angle, square, rhombus, parallelogram, trapezium, deltoid, area transformation)
- Investigation of the circle (circumference, area, π).
- Volumes of solids (cube, cuboid, prism, pyramid, cylinder, cone, sphere)
- Conics approached from locus as well as other curves (Cassini, Descartes). (Could also be done in Class 10.)
- A variety of plane solids or bodies usually through a main-lesson on descriptive geometry
- Diagonals
- Platonic and Archimedean solids
- Training in symmetries based on the simple Platonic solids cube, octahedron, tetrahedron, dodecahedron, icosahedron, and their duals
- Training in visualisation of spaces by exercises in picturing to help drawing tasks, as well as separate description of spatial connections and construction methods
- Design of a simple alphabetic typeface
- Optional: The constant division of the golden section (application in architecture, nature and man) is also recommended for Class 10

Class 10

Points of view and general themes:

The pupils should be guided *"from knowledge to insight"* (R. Steiner). This means a completely new approach for the teaching method.

Trigonometry offers a wide field of activity for this. In the angle functions the pupils discover a completely new structure of relationships and also the practical use which can be got from this. The application of mathematical calculations should be experienced. This is possible through the parallel offered by physics (sine wave in statics, parabolas for projectiles), as well as the so-called 'surveying' project, which allows ideas to be shown in practice, where the pupils measure and draw a small ground area. Precision is learnt; the problems – not the teacher – correct the youngster.

Similarly, in another main-lesson the pupils learn the special meaning of the normal technical projections. The various possibilities for creating pictures can be seen as the start for this. In continuation of perspective, spatial projection and some elements of projective geometry are worked through in drawing.

For arithmetic a final area is logarithms as the summit and final stage of this development.

Calculators are now used more frequently.

In algebra, quadratic equations are now dealt with, if not done already, and the various solution methods and formulae are developed.

Mathematics in Class 10 should have a strongly practical character. One can therefore take up the bookkeeping begun in Class 7, and move on to double-entry bookkeeping. *"The pupils become more aware of commercial processes and the way businesses develop, which means that they can now reflect on these things. They will notice the aspect of interdependence, and the implications of social responsibility become evident."* [12]

Content suggestions:

As for Class 9, there is more material than can be dealt with here:

ALGEBRA

Quadratic equations
- The quadratic expansion
- Development and use of the general formula
- Development and proof of Vieta's root formula (principle points on a quadratic graph)
- Development of the general quadratic equation
- The significance of determinants
- Optional: linear and quadratic inequalities

Powers with whole and rational indices, logarithms
- Revision of methods with natural number indices
- Series with index of 2 or 3
- Extension of the index domain over rationals, integers and real numbers
- Development of logarithms and creation of a table base 2.3.10
- Calculation with logarithmic tables (briefly, for practice in use of tables)
- Commutativity, associativity, distributivity
- Rules of logarithms
- Solution of exponential equations
- Solution of logarithmic equations
- The logarithmic and exponential curves (first contact with functions)
- Optional: Logarithmic scales in science, Archimedean spirals, logarithmic spirals (morphological examples from nature, evolutes). The biography of Euler

Number series (or possibly in Class 11)
- First contact with series, especially monotones, e.g. arithmetic, geometric, exponential, the Lukas and Fibonacci series
- Application to calculation of interest and various means

PLANE TRIGONOMETRY (application in the surveying project)

- Revision of similar triangles and proportional division by parallels and its extension to the image through concentric similar shapes
- Angle measuring systems: degrees, gradients, radians
- Sine, cosine, tangent (cotangent)
- Solution of basic exercises in a right triangle and extension to include plane figures and solids
- Angle functions in circle of unity radius
- Use of angle functions in the general triangle by dividing into two right triangles
- Derivation of cosine rule (recognition of the special case of Pythagoras' Theorem)
- Use of these techniques for calculation in surveying
- Development of the sine rule
- Development of the trigonometrical area formula
- Graphical representation of angle functions

DESCRIPTIVE GEOMETRY

Description of plane solids by various means
- Representation of solids
- Exercises in interpenetration of solids
- Curvilinear solids
- Shadow construction
- The boundary case of an infinite point in shadow construction
- Transformation of a dodecahedron into an icosahedron; stages of interpenetration
- Screws, snails, spirals
- Technical drawing: designs and details of pupils' own carpentry

GEOMETRICAL WORK ON CIRCLE AND LINE

- Proof of the construction of the golden section
- Construction of the golden section
- Perhaps: the golden section in the human being (Dürer, Le Corbusier). See Class 9

ELEMENTS OF PROJECTIVE GEOMETRY

- The question of parallelism and the infinite point on a straight line.
  Optional: The circle as the curve of division; tackling problems of technology
- Periodic experience applied in mechanics in industry (e.g. linkages, drive machinery).
- Running a bank account book and diary
- Balance sheets and household budgeting
- Recording of a complete project
- Optional: Double-entry bookkeeping project

Class 11

Points of view and general themes:

The areas of geometry and algebra which were dealt with separately until now are brought together in analytical geometry. It will become clear 'to the pupils how geometrical forms have their counterpart in equations and how new geometrical forms can be defined by equations. Straight lines are dealt with as the track of a movement and functions elaborated. Vectors will also be formally established following their introduction in physics in Class 10. How far vectors are taken depends on the teacher's assessment of the maturity of the class.

The laws of Euclidean geometry are raised to a new

stage in projective geometry. Infinity should be grasped by working through the 'elements of infinity' (infinite point, line and plane). Through this the pupils acquire an extension of their thought space.

In a study of oscillation, trigonometry from Class 10 is brought into motion giving a basis for the wave theory background of radio communication (physics Class 11).

With spherical trigonometry the student can experience an enhancement of plane trigonometry. Like analytical geometry, this gives a connection between arithmetic and geometry. As in many areas, Class 11 sees how earlier separate areas of study come together: connections should be formed.

A new stage in thinking meets the pupils as they work with series towards the sum of an infinite series. In percentages, a new process is discovered as steps tend towards zero. Calculation of 'half lives' provides a link with atomic physics in Class 11, and this leads on to topical questions.

Again geometry should be explored in a separate main-lesson (timetable permitting) and the teacher can choose a selection of topics from the available range according to class ability.

Content suggestions:

SERIES AND SEQUENCES

- Introduction to finite and infinite arithmetic and geometric series and sequences (if not done in Class 10)
- Development of next term and sum of terms formula and applications in science and industry
- Perhaps: draw connections between part formula of higher order arithmetic series and binomial co-efficients
- Achieve a clear limiting value and find out sum
- Graphic examples of geometric series
- Development of the compound interest formula as a special case of geometric series: application to a variety of problems from nature and business (half lives, growth patterns, etc.)
- Discovery of e

FUNCTIONS (OR IN CLASS 12)

- Leibniz's idea of functions
- Domain and range
- Graphs of functions
- First inverse functions

ALGEBRA AND ANALYTICAL GEOMETRY

- Historical context
- Introduction to Cartesian and polar co-ordinates and their connection
- Point, distance and line in the above systems
- Linear equations in their various forms and their plane graphs using co-ordinates
- Application of calculation to geometrical problems (intersection of two lines, calculation of special points in a triangle)

- Introduction to vectors from physics I (if not done in Class 10)
- Discovery of the circle formula
- Investigation of positional relationship between circle and line (chord, tangent, external line; polar)
- Discovery of basis for the tangent equation and recognition of the significance of the determinant. By this means acquaintance with:
- Complex numbers as solutions to quadratic equations.
- Optional: Intersection angles of circle and line, separation into linear factors, discovery of formulae for ellipse, hyperbola, parabola, especially their tangents or asymptotes (can also be done in Class 12).

All solutions should be done both by calculation and graph!

OSCILLATIONS (mathematical basis for electricity main-lesson in Class 11)

- Revision of unity circle, gradients, radians
- Description of angle functions in Cartesian terms and also graphically
- Physical oscillations approached from mechanics point of view
- Perhaps: representation using polar co-ordinates, mathematical formulation of physical quantities (amplitude, frequency, wavelength, period, phase, frequency modulation, oscillation). Include the addition theorem, also algebraic formula of waves. Application: calculation and representation of 3-phase current.

Selected approach to projective geometry or spherical geometry depending the class's stage of maturity (possibly in Class 12)

PROJECTIVE GEOMETRY

- Infinite elements
- Concept of duality
- Desargues' Theorem
- Pascal's Theorem
- Basic harmonic figures, harmonic reflections

SPHERICAL GEOMETRY

- Pole and polar planes of the sphere, introduction to non-Euclidean geometry on a sphere
- The 'parallel axiom'
- Graphical representation of great circles and small circles on a sphere
- Spherical bi-angles
- Calculation of the surface area and volume of a sphere
- Construction of a spherical triangle by means of 3 defined dimensions (congruence rules); angle sum in a spherical triangle
- Construction of tangents in the triangle points on a sphere

MATHEMATICAL GEOGRAPHY

- Calculation of great circle angle, great circle distance and course angle
- Development of the sine rule of spherical geometry
- Optional: the cosine rule of spherical geometry
- Geographically derived measurements (metre, nautical mile, knot)
- Polar triangle

MATHEMATICAL ASTRONOMY

- Graphical representation of horizontal system and stellar position in space
- The equatorial system (RA declination)
- Perhaps: construction of a nautical sextant; the sun in the course of the year; calculation of time (local, time zone, sidereal; calculation of the calendar, the Platonic year, lunar and solar rhythms
- Algebra of switches; the concept of 'or' and 'and' can be shown with switches in parallel and series
- Set theory
- Mathematical logic

Optional: Boolean algebra (introduction of information technology (can be done in other classes).

Class 12

Points of view and general themes:

This class should take an important further step from what was achieved in Class 11. Just as Class 11 moved in analytical geometry from visual into algebraic, the reverse is done in Class 12. In calculus the pupils should move from the purely numerical into an experience of differentiation and integration. Limits of series should be grasped as the representatives of an endless process. The pupils should understand this new dimension of mathematics by working with the concept of the 'difference quotient': the quotients of two difference series which both tend towards zero produces something completely new. This should not be merely applied but should be grasped thoroughly and experienced. In calculus the equations should be made so translucent *"that one gets a feeling for what is what in equations"* [13]. Only then should the sensually visible graphical form of the calculation be shown. Find the form from the equation, recognise the form of the equation. In this way one nurtures inner activity in the pupils and also an understanding for the functional connections as well as the qualitative in mathematics, which is after all indispensable for a true understanding of current physics. In this connection it is also possible to show that functions of this type can be used decisively in applied physics; in optics, electricity, mechanics and motion. Quality and quantity part company.

While working through the basic rules of integrals, the pupils should recognise that there is also a mathematical method (differentiation), a polarity in higher mathematics which permits the mathematical grasp of the world to reach a new level.

Depending on what was done in Class 11,

projective geometry can be built up from the central projection (perspective), or spherical geometry worked through. Projective geometry can be worked through in such a way that it opens a link to understanding applications in bird's eye perspective, and perspective drawing in the architecture main-lesson on a possible art trip. Spherical geometry can be approached from a more representational or analytical angle, and tend more towards astronomy or to the earth (also in the context of descriptive geometry).

A further possibility for a second mathematics main-lesson consists of bringing together the sciences of mathematics, botany, astronomy, embryology and geometry in a great picture. Attempting this would, however, depend very much on the maturity of the class.

Content suggestions:

INFINITESIMALS

- Revision of function concepts, building on the number continuum
- (independence of real numbers)
- A look at the turn of the eighteenth century with the historical development of infinitesimal calculations through Newton and Leibniz
- Extension of the connections between function and graph by means of elementary functions

CALCULUS

- Development of difference quotients
- Discovery of differential quotients
- Working through the rules of differentiation of polynomials, reciprocal functions, root functions and angle functions
- Derivatives as increasing functions and their expression in the concepts of speed and acceleration
- Product, quotient and chain rules
- Optional: derivatives as inverse functions
- The connection between the initial function and its derivative shown graphically
- Discussion of curves for polynomials of order 2, 3, 4, and reciprocal functions
- Application in various areas of work including technology
- The function of e, natural logarithms (possible extension of current knowledge of these)
- Definition of function terms from characteristics of their graphs
- Maxima and minima with exercises from industry, optics (Fermat's principle)

INTEGRALS

- Derivatives and the return to the original function as opposite mathematical processes
- Development of integrals for polynomials
- Integrals functions as a function of the upper limit of a particular integral
- The concept of original functions and 'indefinite integrals'

- Flow fields
- Several integral rules (basic integrals)
- Principal rules of differential and integral calculation
- Areas bounded by curves in a plane and other applications
- Optional: solids of rotation

GEOMETRY (see also Class 11)

Projective and affine geometry, constructive and analytical

- Illustration of point and line
- Invariant elements
- Illustration of cones (analytical, only in elementary position relative to co-ordinates)
- Invariants
- Introduction to group theory elements as seen in the illustrations
- View of the development of mathematics based on the history of its important personalities (Felix Klein, David Hilbert, George Boole, Moritz Cantor et al)
- Optional: synthesis of mathematics, astronomy, botany, embryology, and geometry. Complex numbers. Probability and statistics (if not done in Class 9)
- Laplace and non-Laplace distribution
- Addition and multiplication rule
- Binomial distribution
- Hypothesis testing

References

1 Baravalle, H. von, *Methodische Gesichtspunkte für den Aufbau des Rechenunterrichts and Waldorfschul plan*, Stuttgart, 1984.
2 Schuberth, E., 'Wie Können Wir durch den Mathematikunterricht erzieherisch wirken?', in *Erziehungskunst* Book 4, 1976.
3 Ibid.
4 Ulin, B., *Finding the Path: Themes and Methods for the Teaching of Mathematics in a Waldorf School*, AWSNA, 1991.
5 Steiner, R., *Soul Economy and Waldorf Education*, op. cit., lecture of 31st December 1921.
6 Ulin, B., *Finding the Path*, op. cit.
7 Steiner, R., *Discussions with Teachers* op. cit., discussion of 25th August 1919.
8 Steiner, R., *The Kingdom of Childhood* op. cit., lecture of 16th August 1924.
9 Steiner, R., *Three Lectures on the Curriculum* op. cit., second lecture of 6th September 1919.
10 Some of these attainment targets differ, usually by a year from those in R. Jarman's recent book *Teaching Mathematics in Rudolf Steiner Schools for Classes I – VIII*, Hawthorn Press. The Curriculum Research Group see Jarman's summary as more appropriate for possible teaching content, whereas the checklists given here are intended to be a minimum attainment for most children within the normal ability range.
11 Schuberth, E., *Der Mathematikunterricht...* op. cit., p 159.
12 Brater, M., Munz, C., *Die Pädagogische Bedeutung der Buchführung*, op. cit., p199.
13 Steiner, R., *Conferences with Teachers*, op. cit., Vol 4, meeting of 30 March 1923.

ART STUDIES
Painting, drawing, form drawing
graphics, modelling and sculpture

Classes 1 to 12

Art exists for it own sake though its very character makes it fundamentally educative. As they learn to understand the physical world and its laws, human beings grow in capability. When they do art, on the other hand, they grow in creative freedom that is not aimed at any particular purpose. Art can of course have an illustrative function in support of other activities, or it may serve a dialectical purpose and both of these purposes have their place in the curriculum. However, art is essentially taught for its own sake. When practising artistic activities, children experience their own soul realm. This feeling of being caught up in the soul realm should take place in every lesson, and that is why art is never something that takes place separately from the lessons. Steiner formulated the educational task of art teaching as follows:

Children need art – both the fine arts and poetry and music. And there is a way of being actively engaged in both sorts that is suitable for children in their school years. If you are a teacher you should not talk too much about one or another art form being 'useful' for the training of certain human faculties. After all art exists for its own sake. Teachers should love art so much that they do not want this experience to be lost to children. They will then see how the children grow through their experiences in art. It is art that awakens their intelligence to full life.

A sense of duty develops if children can use their urge for action to gain control over matter in a free and artistic way. It is the teacher's artistic sensibility that brings soul into the school. They bring a happy mood into the children's seriousness and dignity into their joy. With our intellect we merely comprehend nature; it takes artistic feeling to experience it. If children are taught to comprehend things in a living way they become 'able' people, whereas children who engage in art learn to be creative people. In the first case they are merely applying their abilities; in the second case they grow through this very application. However clumsily a child models or paints, this activity awakens inner soul forces. When children engage in music or poetry they feel their inner nature uplifted to the ideal plane. They acquire a second level of humanity alongside the first.

None of this is achieved if art is taken as a separate, unrelated subject and not as an organic part of the whole of education. For all the child's education and instruction should form a whole. Knowledge, culture and training in practical skills

should all lead to a need for art, just as artistic sensitivity should reach into the realms of learning, observation and the acquisition of skills. [1]

Painting – Classes 1 to 12

General aspects and aims for Classes 1 to 8

From Class 1 to Class 8 painting is integrated into the main-lesson and is thus the domain of the class teacher. We distinguish between painting or drawing as depiction or illustration (using wax blocks, wax or oil chalks and later coloured pencils, in main-lesson books for example) and painting with watercolour paints. The former accompanies all subjects and is a regular part of classroom working in support of the themes of the lessons. Painting with watercolours, on the other hand, usually takes place once a week during a main-lesson.

Painting with watercolours provides the class teacher with a further opportunity for getting to know the children's soul constitution in even more detail. Different temperaments and constitutions reveal themselves through what and how the children paint.

Steiner based his indications for a painting curriculum on Goethe's *Theory of Colour* and this approach forms an important part of Steiner Waldorf initial teacher training[2]. The children should experience the objective, psychological (sometimes referred to as moral) impression that is called into being when they perceive a colour. In their fluid, transparent nature, watercolour paints are an excellent medium for this. An additional possibility for making these discoveries is provided by painting straight on to damp paper, i.e. wet-on-wet. In this medium, the colours can more freely move and blend. The following general guidelines may be of help:

1. In painting lessons, an artistic approach should be practised at all levels. The techniques of painting with watercolours, from wet-on-wet to veil painting, must be practised thoroughly so that they can be handled to a high standard.

2. The purely artistic work with the paint itself should not be overlaid or detracted from by expecting the children to create a 'picture' of something specific. We begin to paint with children in a way that is very similar to abstract painting. Painting like this 'out of the colour' must be done in a manner that is psychologically concrete for the children. The tasks that are set should relate the affective qualities of the colours themselves to definite psychological qualities, such as moods which could be described, for example as quiet and retiring, strong and bold, cold and hard, warm and expansive. The outer form is an expression of an inner experience. The teacher prepares these experiences by telling 'painting stories' that bring the colours to life before they are used.
   You must let the forms arise out of the colours. You can talk with the children in the world of colours. Think how stimulating it would be if you could reach a level of understanding with the

children at which you could say: Look at this coquettish mauve with this cheeky bit of red peeping over its shoulder; and all of it is standing there against the background of a humble blue. You must make it quite objective – this is what works in a way that shapes the soul – so that the colours themselves also do something. Once you think out of the colours you can work with each other in fifty different ways. You must get the children to live within the colour by saying something like: What if the red looks out through the blue! This must be created by the children. [3]

When the children have explored and experienced the colours in this way sufficiently intensely and for a long enough time, we can move on to finding shapes out of the colours, shapes of minerals (mountains, stones), the atmosphere (clouds, sunsets, sky moods), plants and animals, whereby the awareness of the primary qualities of the colours themselves continue to be constantly strengthened. The external form must arise out of the inner experience of the colour. The temptation to be led astray by the wish to produce something aesthetic and illustrative should not be underestimated! It is not that this natural wish on the part of the children should be resisted but rather that *they* be challenged to be true to the nature of the colours.

In Classes 7 and 8 the wet-on-wet technique is joined by an entirely different element. This is veil painting. The way of working is much more differentiated and requires patience and observation. The method requires a palette on which colours can be mixed, time to observe how the picture is developing, and a well-practised technique of applying the paint.

With wet-on-wet the process is strongly sympathetic in that the child is drawn into the inner activity and dialogue of the colours as it happens. They can go with the experience as it unfolds. The process is more important than the outcome. Looking at the paintings the next day is more like an 'antipathetic' process in that the children can stand back and see what happened, can see the outcome. With veil painting the sympathetic and the antipathetic come together, and this 'breathing process' is led not by the teacher but by the pupil.

"Art is a daughter of freedom", said Schiller in his *Letters on the Aesthetic Education of Man*. The pupils should experience this in painting lessons by creating for themselves the conditions freedom needs.

Figurative painting or drawing accompanies all subjects, usually in the form of a picture drawn by the teacher on the blackboard. The starting point for figurative drawing is always the coloured surface and not the outline. Outlines and contours arise in nature for the most part where surfaces of different colours meet. Illustrations in main-lesson books, pictures relating to nature studies or later on geography, and also accurate and aesthetically pleasing depictions of experiments in physics and chemistry, all require continuous practice and further development of drawing techniques to meet the needs of the subject.

Class 1

Points of view and general themes:

Painting lessons in Class 1 contribute to a schooling of the senses that nourishes the soul of the child. When a colour is perceived by the senses, a non-sensory element is also at work, so the perception of colour leads on beyond these limits and into a world of objective, moral qualities. In Class 1 the aim is to get to know and characterise the 'movements of soul' awakened by colours. The children get to know these movements of soul through the act of painting; they learn to characterise them when the pictures are discussed after the painting day: *"The children gain flexible inner images, flexible feelings and flexible actions of will from these experiences of colour. Everything in their soul becomes more flexible..."* [4] It is important to create a quiet, unhurried mood in the painting lessons. The children also need time to establish all the practical work habits to do with preparing for the painting lesson and clearing up afterwards.

Colour stories introduce the exercises and personify the colours in their character and interactions. *"Yellow is a bright cheerful character who spreads out into the world; everywhere he goes he brightens things up. One day he comes across blue, who is sitting there quietly..."*. Perhaps most effectively such colour stories can accompany the actual painting process so that dialogue between the colours can occur. It also provides an imaginative way of offering the children technical guidance while they are painting; to a child who is hesitant with the yellow encouraging words can be offered along the lines of *"yellows want to shine right across the paper, right up to the edge and beyond"*, or to a child who is more in a hurry, *"blue is very strong but it doesn't want to be too strong and take the shine off yellow."* Such images can be a help to children, not to mention the colours themselves. Colour pictures can be used in age-appropriate ways throughout the Lower School as an imaginative yet objective approach.

Whether the teacher paints with the children or demonstrates beforehand, or indeed does not paint at all but merely describes the process in words, is a matter of pedagogical judgment. All three options will be appropriate in different situations. With simple colour exercises the teacher can stick a piece of soaked paper onto the blackboard and paint in front of them. If the painting doesn't take too long, it will hold long enough before drying and peeling off. This has the advantage of visibility. Its main advantage is to demonstrate the use of the brush, which children can learn far better through imitation than by following verbal instructions.

Once a range of basic colour exercises have introduced the colours and the techniques of painting, paintings can be done which relate to the narrative content of the lessons, fairy tales, legends, fables and myths. This goes for all classes from Class 1 upwards. Initially it is more a question of reflecting the mood of a story, a dark forest, the golden colour of Rapunzel's hair, the prince's cloak, but gradually the paintings can become more figurative, showing plant or animal forms and later human figures. Always one strives to let the figures arise out of the colour itself, rather than being illustrative or defined by outlines. No attempt is made until Class 4 or 5 to impose any form of perspective, except in the most elementary way, with trees growing upward out of the earth, etc. though the children should be free to portray the images however they feel them to be. The watercolours lend themselves to nature moods though no attempt should be made to impose any form of naturalism. The colours should be appropriate to the mood in a way more akin to expressionist paintings, say in the landscape and plant paintings of Nolde, or even the more formalist abstraction of Klee's watercolours. This progression goes for the first four classes and will not be repeated in the succeeding descriptions.

Content suggestions:

- Start with the polarities yellow/blue and get to know the colour 'tones' that have much or little tension (yellow/green)
- Paint with the primary colours yellow, red and blue
- The colour surfaces are chosen freely by the children after the teacher has told them a 'colour story'
- Extend the palette by adding the three mixed colours
- Thoroughly ground in the technique of wet-on-wet painting including the necessary preparation (wetting the paper and fixing it to the board)
- Paint on coloured paper, or first paint a wash in one colour and, when the paper has absorbed it fully, apply a second colour
- Fairy tale moods

Class 2

Points of view and general themes:

In keeping with the theme for Class 2 (see 'Horizontal Curriculum'), the children can practise balancing what is missing, creating symmetry, or duality. The aim is to activate the souls of the children in this direction. It is important that the teacher should not let the 'colour stories' become subjective or arbitrary but that he should be guided by the colours themselves. This is the only way the children can learn to participate in the life of the colour harmonies.

Content suggestions:

- Exercises that aim to let the children experience colour harmonies that are:
  - **characteristic** (red and yellow, yellow and blue, blue and red, orange and green, green and violet, violet and orange)
  - **complementary** (red and green, yellow and violet, orange and blue)
  - **characterless** (yellow and orange, orange and red, red and violet, violet and blue, yellow and green, blue and green)

- Exchange exercises: for example the middle colour is changed into its complementary colour while the surrounding colours remain. Then the surrounding colours are changed while the middle colour remains. This is done with the children's actual pictures, i.e. the individual picture is the object of the exercise. This can be done in a sequence of exercises

Class 3

Points of view and general themes:

The emphasis in Class 3 is on the 'grand act of creation' of the world (Genesis) and the small-scale shaping of the world through farming and house building. Painting lessons can take up this theme. The children investigate not only the creation of a picture by means of colours, but also how the mixed colours themselves come into being.

Content suggestions:

- How the primary colours yellow, blue and red arise out of light and dark
- Intensification to the plus and minus sides of the colour circle
- How the mixed colours of green, orange and violet arise
- The seven days of creation as a painting exercise in colour, starting from the creation of the light, the polarity of light and dark, the creation of above and below, the earth and the waters, proceeding to the plants and animals. Finally a human figure, becoming two can emerge as a whole form out of the colours

Class 4

Points of view and general themes:

Up to the beginning of Class 4 the children have been painting with watercolours to make colour harmonies and 'colour stories' in a free way. Now, by being linked with animal studies or the stories of the main-lesson (Norse mythology, for example), the exercises are now introduced in a way that enables the colours to come together in shapes that depict the essence of the subject figuratively. Painting in 'blobs of colour' requires strong concentration from the children. Form must be found from colour, and colour from the theme of the day.

Content suggestions:

- Let animal forms arise out of colours
- Painting linked to nature studies, trees, simple landscapes with hills and mountains and sky, patterns of fields in a range of browns, greens and yellow, simple generalised shapes of buildings such as a castle or large church, a farm house or barn
- Figurative themes related to the story part of the main-lesson (Norse mythology), e.g. Nifelheim, the

World Ash Tree, the Dark Kingdom of Hel, Ragnarok, Viking ships with sails, etc.
- Painting on coloured paper creates new and wider possibilities for creating colour harmonies and colour moods

Class 5

Points of view and general themes:

The ever-changing colour processes in nature reveal the forces at work in the plant: sun forces and earth forces, light and darkness. An initial painting exercise can be linked to these polar opposite effects. [5]

As mentioned above, painting can echo or take up the themes of the main-lessons. Let it be said once more that it is not a question of painting illustrations but of letting the colours of nature find their own forms. In this way the painting lessons can provide a qualitative deepening of themes that come up in the main-lesson. At the same time themes from plant studies can provide an opportunity to take what has been seen and heard into their painting lessons as well.

Content suggestions:

- Develop plant moods from green and yellow
- Contrast 'rose red' and 'lily white' with the pink-white of water lilies. Find the qualitative difference between 'moss green' and 'birch green'
- From now on the children can begin to work with more subtle differentiations and nuances of colour
- Rather than observing the wonderful coincidences of a watercolour picture when the results of the lesson are observed and discussed, we now look more at the way the children have consciously sought to discover and consciously create colour differences
- Maps can be painted showing the qualitative differences between coastline and ocean, river forms, mountains and plains etc.
- Images from mythology can be taken

Class 6

Points of view and general themes:

As with other subjects, painting too needs to take into account the children's twelfth year and the various characteristic psychological developments it brings. Steiner's curriculum suggestions regarding art point to 'projection and shadows'. The pupils should gain a clear idea of how shadows come about and they should make appropriate observations of this. There are various ways of approaching chiaroscuro and the study of shadows. Here are two:
1. One possibility is to leave colour on one side and work solely with charcoal or chalk. This would mean that from Class 6 onwards painting is replaced by drawing (see 'Drawing in Class 6')
2. Another possibility is to keep on with painting and tackle the questions by means of painting exercises

Content suggestions (for painting):

- Obtain grey and black from the three primary colours and the mixed colours. This is a long process in painting that needs building up in stages
- The grey or black of shadows obtained through using colours can be tried out in themes from plant studies (trees) or mineralogy. If the shadow aspect has been studied through tree studies in drawing, these can be transformed into colour
- Paint themes from the main-lessons such as geology or history

Class 7

Points of view and general themes:

A new technique, veil painting, requires the pupils to practise patience (waiting until the paper, or a layer of paint, has dried) and endurance; they cannot simply set to and get on with it. The colours, too, do not provide the elementary satisfaction of the Early Years period, for they have to be applied very delicately and are very pale. This technique provides many new possibilities for achieving differentiations and depths of colour. The theme of 'perspective' in drawing lessons is taken up through painting in this way.

Painting can also be expanded in another way in connection with geography. If 'Asia' is on the programme in Class 7, then the pupils can practise painting with ink. Chinese brushwork requires so much concentration and self-control that it is therapeutic not only for individual children but also for the sloppiness of the teenage years in general. As regards self-discipline, it could be a good predecessor for veil painting.

Content suggestions:

- Veil painting with watercolour paints
- Practise with a single colour initially
- Conscious application of perspective by means of colour
- Observe what a colour requires of one in a painterly composition
- Ink drawing and painting in connection with geography lessons
- Work with ink brush and pen
- Proper preparation of the paper
- Inner preparation of the painter for work with the brush

Class 8

Points of view and general themes:

Veil painting continues and the technique is perfected. The children might try to carry out the same task once in wet-on-wet and once by the veil technique. The aim of such exercises is to develop the pupils' ability to judge and to strengthen their understanding of painting as an art. What does it mean to work *with* the colours in a particular technique and on a particular theme, or *against* them and thus also against the theme. In this way necessity, opposition and freedom can be practised artistically.

These exercises, that go hand-in-hand with the students' search for themselves, can be strengthened even further in a way suggested by Steiner:

If I were teaching 13 to 14-year-olds who had never done any painting before, I would then get them to look at Dürer's Melancolia. *I would show them the wonderful distribution of light and shadow: the light by the window, the way the light is distributed on the polyhedron and the sphere. In fact, making* Melancolia *one's starting point is really a very good idea indeed! Get them to metamorphose the black and white into imaginative colourings.* [6]

Such exercises can reveal the possibilities and appropriate ways of painting. They provide not only a continuation but also for the moment a conclusion of what we began in Class 1 as a path of painting, aiming at discovering the inner qualities of colours, and their moral effect.

Content suggestions:

- Continue with veil painting. Nature studies emerge entirely from colours, using various techniques
- Metamorphosis exercises going from wet-on-wet to veiling and vice versa
- Transformation of chiaroscuro, or black-and-white compositions into colourful imaginations, e.g. Dürer's *Melancolia*, or *St. Jerome in his Study* (also in Class 9, if painting lessons are given)
- Similar exercises could be done with Franz Marc's pencil sketches alternating with his colourful animal studies

General aspects and aims for Classes 9 to 12

The psychological changes in puberty described below in connection with drawing in Classes 9 to 11 can be observed and described with much greater differentiation in Class 10 as psychological processes. The youngsters are endeavouring to emerge from their isolation. They are searching for friendships and want to enter into relationships with other human beings. In the process, sympathies and antipathies are often vehement and radical, so the teacher is faced with a wide range of tasks: the tendency to see everything in black and white needs to acquire other, richer nuances of colouring. The youngsters' newly-awakened interest in other human beings and their environment needs to be intensified and supported, otherwise there is a danger of this deteriorating into too great an interest in one's own personal affairs and feelings. The young people seek help from the subjects they are taught as well as from their teachers in maintaining this 'forward direction'. They want to experience enthusiasm and develop the will to change as they seek for their own orientation.

Occupying themselves with living, changing colours is thus not only appropriate but also necessary for the psychological situation in which 16 to 17-year-olds find themselves.

With chiaroscuro or black-and-white drawing there is often only a single correct way that obliges you to use a particular artistic solution. With colours the situation is entirely different. The inexhaustible profusion of colour variations has a liberating effect and also helps the soul find orientation. Finding such orientation on the basis of new discoveries in the act of painting can help activate the young person's will. Drawing can lead to an experience of 'reaching a conclusion', a 'death process' or a 'passion mood'. But with painting all is redemption, release, renewal and 'resurrection'; this remains unspoken in the lessons but can be felt deeply and existentially. The purpose and importance of art as such is not something that stops at the school gates. It is relevant equally for art teacher and for the pupils working with art:

What is important in art can be clearly stated: It is not its purpose to embody something supersensible but to transform what exists and is perceptible. Reality is not intended to sink to the level of a means of expression. No. Reality must remain as it is in all its independence. But it must be given a new form, a form in which it satisfies us ... This is not "the idea in the form of a sense-perceptible manifestation"; it is "a sense-perceptible manifestation in the form of an idea". [7]

What would the consequence be if young people were not enabled to experience these picture-forming powers of resurrection? There would be deep and all-embracing resignation and helplessness that would seek release in disorientation or else in aggression and destructive violence. In this context art lessons, and among these painting in particular, have an essentially social component that has existential implications for individuals in society.

The image-less legacy of the Old Testament, "Thou shalt not make graven images", has come down to us from ancient times. Human beings now need to turn back from such purely abstract laws and enter once more, now purposefully, into an ability of the soul to make pictures. Only through pictures, through imaginations, will social life be able to establish itself in the right way. [8]

In the present chapter the following subject/class grouping is taken as the basis:

Class 9:	—	Drawing	—
Class 10:	Painting	Drawing	Modelling/sculpture
Class 11:	Painting	Drawing	Modelling/sculpture
Class 12:	Painting	—	Modelling/sculpture

Summary of general aims:

- Awaken from black/white to the experience of colours
- Experience painting as an expression of subtle psychological feelings about the world and human beings
- Discover painting as an aid to achieving a more subtle and varied view of the world
- Discover in painting how to ask after the purpose and meaning of art

- Call up, cultivate and practise image-creating powers to make them available in achieving 'realistic imaginations' and 'future-oriented, concrete imaginations'

Points of view and general themes for Classes 10 to 12:

The time has come to experience the difference between watercolour and oil painting techniques (the possibilities of creating and mixing colours, and the various brush techniques).

The pupils should learn independently to assess these techniques as to their suitability for the purpose in hand.

Painting experiences from the Lower School are refreshed. Colours are now more consciously used because their nature and expressive possibilities have been understood. The students should learn to search for appropriate expressions of specific experiences by means of colour and form. They should acquire a feeling for the expressive content of the colours. Individuals should gradually discover a personal style based on an objective understanding of the techniques learned.

Reflection is for the most part done during art lessons, while the pupils' work is discussed during painting lessons. The purpose is to help recognise the connection between content and form, the effect of the means used, the 'readability' of a statement, and the power of its message.

Content suggestions for Classes 10 to 12:

Increasingly the pupils themselves should choose the problems they want to work on and the medium they want to use. The teacher's role is to help them overcome difficulties in decision-making. The advice will refer to themes, techniques, design and how to organise the work. The pupils should also be given the opportunity to embark on larger-scale projects and work on these in the way they think best. The project selected should be used to increase concentration and depth rather than be a superficial occupation involving all kinds of different partial tasks.
- Basic exercises for coming to grips with the individual nature of colours.
- Contrast colour harmonies (warm/cold, major/minor etc.), also chords with three colours
- More wide-ranging exercises based on Goethe's colour theory. Application of Goethe's theory of harmony and disharmony
- Contrasting themes shaped entirely out of colour experiences
- Nature and landscape moods; metamorphosis of black/white (etchings by, for example, Dürer, Rembrandt, Munch, et al) into colour imaginations
- The development of colour imaginations for a motif as a basis for unfolding a free painterly imagination
- Tree and flower studies (e.g. trees in sunshine, storm, and rain etc.)

- Translation of specific moods into colour and form: joy/sorrow, adagio/allegro *et al*
- The human head and face in various forms
- Free imitation of historical art schools, e.g. Impressionists, Expressionists, Modernists, Cubists, Surrealists etc.

Materials and techniques

- Oil paints, oil brushes on prepared paper or canvas
- Observing brush techniques and the structure that results in painting with oils
- Unconstrained painting using the veil technique or other liquid paints
- Watercolour painting
- Exploration of other appropriate painting materials

Form Drawing, Drawing and Graphics – Classes 1 to 11

General aspects and aims for Classes 1 to 8

Drawing lessons are very different from painting lessons. A form that has been drawn is always a result, something that has come to rest or, put more bluntly, something 'dead', i.e. at the end of a process. The drawing lessons are, however, not primarily concerned with the result but with the process, the skill involved and the feelings that arise while the activity is going on. These feelings are connected with the form; they are triggered by the form and shaped by it. As with painting, this is the moral realm of forms.

The children are initially not expected to draw some external object; they are to experience a quality of movement. This kind of drawing (which leads to freehand geometry in Class 5) is called *form drawing* in Steiner Waldorf schools.

In the early years of school the children are shown how to draw simple forms and form transformations and experience their qualities. This helps to develop a lively inward ability to comprehend forms. From this the children and later the young people learn to understand the form gestures that come towards them in things created by nature as well as by human beings.

This is important for their further development. When young people experience the form gestures of what they meet in nature (in landscapes, plants, animals etc.), in art, and in other artifacts made by human beings, they gain a rich and realistic relationship with the world. Ordinary looking, not filled with powers capable of creating shapes, can only comprehend what has been finalised, what has become petrified in its final form, what is dead. Such looking confines human awareness to what is dead in the world. Looking that is creative leads the human being beyond the surface of what has become and takes him down into the inner life of things. [9]

Kandinsky, an experienced artist who nevertheless continued to make his researches with regard to the line, formulated the above thus: *"If a line drawn in a picture is freed from having to denote something specific and can therefore function as something specific itself, then its inner sound is not weakened by any subsidiary role, so it can exert its full strength."* [10]

So initially the purpose of form drawing is to awaken the children's sense of form. This is needed and used when they learn to write and read. So form drawing is a preparation for techniques that belong to our civilisation.

If children have learnt to orientate by means of movement in the classroom as well as on paper, this can help later with spatial problems that might arise for those who are dyslexic. Such children derive a good deal of help from the therapeutic possibilities of form drawing.

Steiner had this therapeutic aspect in mind as well when he encouraged the teachers to find and develop forms that would have a helping, liberating effect in cases where a child is completely dominated by a particular temperament. Awareness of space is called up and stimulated by shapes that are a part of the spatial experience, such as symmetry, movement and counter-movement, repetition, enhancement. For children who have something extremely one-sided in their nature, an important aim is to learn to orientate and move properly in space. In fact, however, today's civilisation contains so much that is destabilising and disorientating that form drawing as a school subject has a generally therapeutic function to fulfil for all children.

A branch of form drawing developed in work with special needs children is called *dynamic drawing*. This also seeks to release health-giving powers by utilising the enlivening, awakening element of searching for primeval forms and form gestures.

Teachers and therapists need to be clear about the psychological effects of the different shapes and forms, i.e. they must develop the ability to know which forms work more on the will, which work more on the feeling life and which have an effect on the capacity to make mental images.

When geometry begins in Class 5, form drawing is absorbed into geometric drawing. By Class 6 the children have reached 'the age of causality', which calls for real accuracy in their drawing. At the same time they also embark on a new kind of artistic drawing, namely drawing with charcoal. This is initially more akin to painting, and its content is chiefly the contrasts of chiaroscuro. In keeping with the children's psychological situation, this drawing leads on entirely logically to projection and shadows. Before these are constructed geometrically in the older classes, 'feeling shadows' and 'looking for shadows' is handled entirely artistically. Having passed through perspective drawing in Class 7, drawing lessons in Class 8 end with studies on light and shade in connection with perspective. These studies can either involve drawing geometrical solids arranged like a kind of still life, or the children can copy woodcuts or etchings by the old masters, who also practised these themes, using them to develop their techniques. Exercises and encouragement of this kind lead on to the lessons in the Upper School.

Class 1

Points of view and general themes:

Straight lines and curves are the starting points for form drawing. This begins with the discovery that the line is a path along which one can move. The children should experience the characteristic difference between straight lines and curves through drawing them, after having explored their character through whole bodily movement in space. The definite direction of the straight line requires concentration and the will to be guided by thinking. The dynamic, meandering curved line with no specific direction leaves room for individual variations; the will is guided by feeling. Once the children have become confident in line drawing, symmetrical form and form completion are the main elements in Class 1.

Form drawing forms a preparation for the introduction of writing.

Content suggestions:

A form drawing main-lesson often precedes the introduction of writing. [11] Straight and curved lines are practised in alternation, in different sizes and in a variety of forms. By this means these basic forms, needed during Class 1, are developed.

- Exercises with vertical, horizontal and diagonal lines, with angles (acute and obtuse), star shapes, triangles, squares and other regular-sided shapes
- Exercises with convex and concave curves, waves, circles, ellipses, spirals, lemniscates and so on
- Continuous patterns and sequences as a preparation for cursive writing

Class 2

Points of view and general themes:

Form drawing – as a branch of 'pictorial learning' (Steiner) – aims to cultivate inner perception in a way that will enable thinking to develop without slipping into an intellectual mode. One way of practising this inner perception is to give the children one half of a symmetrical form and let them find and complete the corresponding half themselves. To do this they have to be inwardly active, and must feel that the pattern they have been given is something 'unfinished'. So the aim is to complete, to make perfect in their imagination (and of course also on paper) something that is as yet incomplete or imperfect.

Content suggestions:

- Exercises around a vertical central axis (which can also be there only in the imagination) mirroring curved and straight and curved forms. Symmetry and reflections
- Then a similar exercise with a horizontal axis; form transformations: making straight-lined forms into curved ones, or vice versa, also with mixtures
- Exercises around a diagonal axis; later also using

two perpendicular axes (either vertical/horizontal, or two diagonals)
- Borders around pages of written work or illustrations
- Running and rhythmical forms

Class 3

Points of view and general themes:

Having practised the axial symmetries, the children can now work on free 'asymmetrical' symmetries. This helps them develop a sense of style, for now they have to discover appropriate corresponding shapes in a free way. These exercises are also suitable for cultivating a capacity to imagine spaces inwardly. This helps prepare qualitatively for geometrical drawing. The sense of form is developed through more complex symmetries and cross-over patterns. These elements are fundamental to design, balance and coherence of shapes and to a sense of contrasting form. The patterns learned can be applied to illustrating (e.g. letting for title pages) and to handwork (e.g. embroidery).

Content suggestions:

- More complex running forms and rhythmic patterns
- Spirals and forms which overlap, coil and intertwine
- Mirrored forms and reflections in vertical and horizontal format
- Forms based on triangles, squares, pentagons etc.
- Four-fold symmetries i.e. forms combining horizontal, vertical and diametrical symmetries
- A corresponding outer form must be sought for an inner form, and vice versa. Variations: if the inner form is angular, find a 'curved answer', and vice versa
- Practising differentiations in this way inside a circle, whereby the shape of the circle must be included as a part of the exercise
- Practising 'balanced' forms

Class 4

Points of view and general themes:

Spatial imagination continues to be practised and taken further, leading to a summary at a higher level of what has been practised so far. A lot of consciousness is needed when lines cross each other at different angles. This promotes concentration.

Content suggestions:

- The story material in Class 4 (Norse mythology) provides material for form drawing in the shape of intertwining ornamental motifs (engravings on brooches and bracelets; decorations on weapons, helmets, the prows of ships; Celtic, Carolingian and Langobardic intertwining, boarder and knotwork motifs). A new feature at cross-over points is to make them look plaited by showing where the strands go under and over each other. In connection with this, nautical knots can also be practised and then drawn

Class 5

Points of view and general themes:

In Class 5, form drawing leads to elementary geometrical drawing. Once again the starting point can be the polarities of straight line and curve. To enable the pupils to gain an intense experience of these, it is good to begin with free-hand drawings without compasses or ruler.

Although we are still only at the very beginning of geometry, it is important to give the pupils a sense of the dimension of geometry that goes beyond practical applications and leads to the solution of the ultimate riddles of the world and life. This is easiest done by letting them appreciate not only the laws that govern geometry but also the beauty of its forms and their strictly regulated mutual dependence. [12]

Content suggestions:

See the geometry suggestions for Class 5 in the chapter on 'Arithmetic and Mathematics'.

Class 6

Points of view and general themes:

Having reached their twelfth year and begun the growth spurt including that of muscles and sinews that accompanies puberty, the children now gain a new relationship with gravity. This leads to a new field in drawing. In Class 4 the intertwining ornamentation already called for an awareness of space in drawing. This is now expanded to include flat surfaces in *chiaroscuro*. We now embark on the conflict between light and darkness, dissolution and densification, height and depth, lightness and heaviness. This world of contrasts is a more existential experience than that of linear forms. However, the children's work with light and dark is not done in an abstract way. In *projection and shadow studies* it links up with a scientific subject, i.e. physics. The pupils must gain an exact understanding of how the lit surfaces of a solid relate to its shadow. It is the shadows that feel their way out into space and allow the solid body to appear on the flat paper. The question of cause and effect that comes to the fore at this age and even becomes a problem needing attention, is thus also central in drawing lessons.

Content suggestions:

- Free drawing exercises with charcoal, shaping a surface with light and dark using various shading techniques
- Sphere, cylinder, cone and cube are drawn as spatial solids. Various sources of light and the way these change the shadows are taken into account. Shadows falling on the wall, on the floor and across angled surfaces. A combination of solids casting

shadows (shadow still life), whereby shadows also falls on to other solids

Class 7

Points of view and general themes:

Light and shadow exercises are continued in Class 7. Perspective drawing now means that these can be constructed more accurately. Perspective and exercises involving the vanishing point are what the pupils need at this age, in an inward sense. They are looking for their own, unmistakable standpoint. How often do they love to flee into their own inner vanishing point! There is something mysterious about this point: on the one hand it is the most minute, most intimate thing imaginable, and on the other it contains a new beginning and infinite possibilities within it. These drawing lessons aim to research this point in ever new ways, while of course also introducing the laws of graphic, spatial construction.

Content suggestions:

- Projection and shadow studies: interpenetration of solids (a cylindrical or edged rod piercing a sphere, a cone piercing a cube, a cube piercing a sphere, and so on). Special attention is paid to the surfaces of intersection and to the shadows cast on to varying backgrounds (plane, angled, concave or convex surfaces).
- Perspective: central perspective, bird's (vertical) or frog's (horizontal) eye view, drawings with more than one vanishing point. The distribution of light and shadow must always be observed
- Studies involving actual objects such as a building or an interior space

Class 8

Points of view and general themes:

Class 4 saw a summary and integration of all that had been learnt in form drawing. In Class 8 the second phase of drawing lessons culminates and is brought together in geometry, projection studies and perspective: *'Combining technique with beauty'* (Steiner) signifies a 'redemption' of geometrical and perspective laws through art. The functional aspect is evaluated aesthetically and depicted accordingly. For 14 to 15-year-olds it is difficult to form aesthetic judgments because of the labile nature of their subjective feelings. Something is accepted as valid only if it is right and true. So in drawing, too, it is important to apply the laws of graphics correctly, not only in free compositions but also in studies of the old masters like Dürer or Leonardo. These themes continue in the Upper School, when the techniques are perfected, e.g. in etching.

Content suggestions:

- Time can be spent on preparatory studies for copying Dürer's *Melancolia*. Details of the picture

are worked on freely, such as the sphere, the polyhedron, the tools and instruments. The garments are also studied, as are nature (day, night, land, sea, sky, earth), architecture and animals etc.
- The beginnings of the laws of proportion. The golden mean as a secret of composition. Finally Dürer's etching is copied
- In connection with nature studies, Rembrandt's etchings of trees and landscapes can be studied and copied

General aspects and aims for Classes 9 to 11

In the Upper School, painting and drawing are given their own timetabled lessons, usually in rotating blocks parallel to other arts and crafts. They are now also taught by specialist teachers, rather than the class teacher.

In the Lower School, artistic activity was embedded within other subjects, and similarly individual pupils were more a part of the class community as a whole so that the element of individual giftedness was less of an issue. For Class 9 pupils this can become somewhat critical, for now they are not only thrown back more on to their own resources, but they also have to experience that the imaginative powers of childhood have decreased. Having earlier been full of ideas and originality, they now find that they increasingly need a 'key' with which to regain access to those faculties. Thus it is not possible simply to continue with what was done in the Lower School.

The students in the Upper School now need to develop an awareness of the complementary roles of arts and crafts, the cultivation of the aesthetic for its own sake as an expression of inner feelings and the transformation of materials to produce artifacts which meet real and practical requirements in the world. The integration of these two aspects is important since art is based on the practical mastery of materials and techniques and making artifacts without concern for the aesthetic element is mere functionalism. The third element in this integration is that of schooling accurate observation. This is particularly important as a basis for balanced judgment.

When inherited capacities (childhood imagination and creativity) begin to fade, space for something new becomes available. Art lessons should take this into account and make use of it. If this is done, the youngsters feel the wind of change that they are seeking psychologically, and then art lessons can gain a contemporary, modern, existential significance for them.

One example of how these three elements can be integrated is in black and white shaded drawing which depends upon accurate observation as well as an understanding of the laws governing light and shadow. The techniques to be mastered have a strong element of craftsman-like skill and the medium itself gives full expression to the psychological qualities of light and dark and their infinite transitions.

Another example is the designing and painting of posters. Here the pupils can experiment with modes of expression using colour and form in response to a practical need. They school their sense of how image and text work together and should become confident at selecting the most sparing and therefore effective means. Posters for events in the life of the school (plays, summer festivals, bazaars, etc.) are designed and made. Many techniques can be learned and employed, such as collages, printing using stencils, monotype, coloured linocuts, offset lithography, silk screen and so on, depending on the art department's resources. Computer graphics also have a role to play, though it makes sense to have explored the medium using manual techniques first.

The following courses can be offered from Class 9 upwards with a progression over several blocks through Classes 9-12. Once the students have had basic instruction in the various techniques in Classes 9 and 10, they can apply these skills to project work throughout the Upper School.

Black and White Shaded Drawing (Classes 9/10)

Points of view and general themes:

The main aim is the schooling of the perception of artistic and natural forms by bringing will activity into sense perception as well as developing a sense for the artistic possibilities of light and dark.

The pupils should be able to apply techniques and their own artistic experience independently in artistic processes. They should be able to carry out independently the making of a pre-sketch, sketch and the finished drawing as a process.

Content suggestions:

- Abstract basic exercises to learn about the expressive possibilities of light and dark
- Create a balanced surface in all exercises
- Movement directions (e.g. rising/falling), movement and counter-movement (e.g. raying outwards/pushing inwards)
- Where to place the emphasis in the distribution of the components on the surface
- Different ways of shaping surfaces either with continuous, soft transitions of light into dark grey or with clear, clean borders through edges (without outlines); the result should be a rich spectrum of light, silvery greys via many intermediate stages to dark grey; hatching, diagonal shading etc.
- The pupils should recognise the various shading techniques in the graphic work of masters (such as Dürer, Rembrandt or Blake) so as to be able to use them later on themselves

The pupils should gain basic insights into spatial relationships and be able to make these visible in three-dimensional sketches and models.

Tasks that arise out of the above exercises:
- Exercises for studying basic shapes: sphere, cube, pyramid, cylinder, polyhedrons, pentagon, dodecahedron etc.

- Elements of flat and curved surfaces should be studied and drawn in light and dark
- Drawing of shadows from solids
- Freely combining various solids to form compositions
- Organic and cubic shapes, various light effects in landscape moods
- Drawing from nature during excursions. Utilising the sketches in free compositions
- Depiction of a simple interior space with a light source and corresponding shadows. Or drawing of the human skull
- Building up a drawing from small elements using the shading technique that makes it possible to observe a slow process of development; building up a drawing from superimposed surfaces using the broad side of the chalk. Use of black chalk or charcoal
- Poster design

Printing (Classes 9/10, though more usually 10)

Points of view and general themes:

- Using a variety of media to introduce printing on paper or fabrics such as lino-cut, woodcut, block printing, etching, copper plate
- Getting to know the strong tensions between black and white in a print
- Experiencing the possibilities this technique offers for expressing emotions
- Limitations of where this can be applied (e.g. in illustrations)

Content suggestions:

- Exercises in making lino-cuts: relationship between the intended picture and the way the means are used (material and non-material such as rhythm, contrast, proportion)
- Function of the hand drawing e.g. as pre-sketch, sketch, study, or as an independent means of artistic expression
- Aspects of style and important masters of (examples from various periods)
- Origin and development of graphic printing as a medium for reproduction and as an artistic medium.
- Use of the tools, techniques and materials of the media practised
- Exercises in etching: from sketch to finished print of a landscape, beginning with a mood and leading to a figurative landscape
- Copperplate etching, use of etching needle and etching press
- Handling etching inks
- Use computer graphics for layout purposes in connection with tasks such as producing theatre programmes, student magazines, presentation of project work
- Design posters

Clay Modelling / Sculpture

General aspects and aims for Classes 4 to 8

Points of view and general themes:

Wherever appropriate during Classes 1 to 3 the class teacher will let the children model with clay, wax or plasticine. From their ninth year on, modelling can begin as a complement to form drawing. The starting point might be elementary experiences of the sphere and the pyramid. Modelling is developed from the interplay of the hands, which together form an inner space. It is not a matter of adding bits of clay or plasticine here and there but of working with the whole lump, a given amount that can be changed and shaped. Pressure and counter-pressure shape the form of the surfaces. In drawing, corrections are made by 'the will working through the eye' (Steiner); in modelling it is the hand that feels the surfaces, thus becoming a kind of organ of perception and formation. Modelling can add depth to form drawing and also to other main-lesson subjects from which it derives inspiration.

In modelling the underlying principle is that of the metamorphosis of form. That which is given, the material, is transformed through the activity of the soul in a process that reflects the inner metamorphosis that comes to expression through child development. In modelling we are working particularly with the formative forces at work within the nature of the developing child. In the process of modelling itself, the senses of form, movement and touch are especially active. In looking at the work, either in progress or at the completion of a project, the child's powers of 'seeing' are activated in a particularly intensive way.

Seeing in this sense means not merely literally using the eyes, though this is in itself no easy achievement, given the tendency to 'see' what we want to see rather than what is there. When observing form we perceive the form *activity* that the clay actually expresses. This includes its inner movement (frozen in the outer shape) such as direction, expansion or contraction, but also balance, symmetry, sense of gravity or levity and sense of life or lifelessness. The children learn to understand the vocabulary of form and how to read it. This also requires a verbal vocabulary to describe it, and developing this is also part of the task.

When the children are fully engaged in the task of modelling, they are usually quiet, concentrated, breathing deeply and unaware of their surroundings. This mood is sometimes difficult to achieve. Creating the right mood is important if the children are to connect to their own formative forces. If they are unable to do so, this manifests in lack of concentration, superficial forms and a tendency to fragment the piece. Respect for the material itself helps, which comes from exploring its properties. The lesson may begin with simple exercises to familiarise the children once more with the clay or modelling material. Equally important, however is a clear picture of the task in hand. Rather than show the children pictures of what they are to model, giving a verbal description or even asking the children to act out the mood or form they are to model is a great help. This need not take long but is a major help in engaging their self-activity. When working figuratively or abstractly, it is important that the children have a strong feeling for what the form is going to express.

Objectively describing what has been modelled is an equally important part of the lessons. The children need a certain distance from their own work, perhaps even waiting until the next lesson. Their judgment of form needs to be carefully schooled through accurate observation and description, which encourages them to 'slip into' the form and describe what is 'happening'; is it sleeping or resting? Is it slowly swelling? Is it reaching out in a certain direction? Is it striving upwards but leaving most of its volume behind? Is it withdrawing? Is it just a hollow shell with no more activity within, shaped not by inner activity but outer forces, like erosion? Such conversations can be held with children using age-appropriate terminology quite soon in modelling lessons, once the children have good experience of the main elements of form. Especially important is an awareness of the relationship of forms to their surroundings and particularly the way forms respond to each other. This can be done quite simply by placing two forms in different relationships to each other and asking the children to describe what they are saying to each other.

Content suggestions:

Class 4
- Simple solids such as sphere, pyramid, cube, modelled with hollow of the hands
- In support of the animal main-lesson, beginning with a sphere, make animal forms (sleeping cat, resting deer, cow lying down, etc.)

Class 5
- In the plant main-lesson, beginning with a sphere or egg-shape, make buds, fruits and other plant forms. These need not be naturalistic; the important thing is to sense a growth movement that forms the unformed material
- Human figures can be made, at first standing then sitting. Figures that work with the whole form as an entity, with arms and legs unarticulated (e.g. wrapped in a cloak, crib figures etc.) are easier for the children before dealing with the static problems of legs. Later the arms can move away from the body and the legs can take up a stance

Class 6
- In connection with the geography main-lesson, mould the shapes of various types of mountain: granite, chalk and sharp-contoured shapes that resemble crystal forms. Caves and waterfalls with boulders can be modelled
- Work with figures can proceed to include groups, mother and child, farmer and horse, figures wrestling etc. Keep the detail of faces, hands, feet, clothing etc. to a minimum

Class 7
- In connection with projection and shadow studies, or with geometry, solids such as the cone, the cube, the pentagon, dodecahedron, etc. can be modelled. The latter in particular can be obtained from the sphere by using the flat of both hands
- Starting from the sphere or a geometrical form, a sequence of form transformations can be undertaken
- In figurative forms, explore gesture and movement, starting from figures turning, bending, pointing, reaching, again leaving facial expression minimal

Class 8
Studies linked to the temperaments can be taken up in modelling:
- Studies of earthy dryness (melancholic), fiery flames (choleric), watery softness (phlegmatic), and airy evaporation (sanguine). These can be done abstractly and figuratively
- Studies in dramatic gesture; adult protecting child, dancing, sleeping, lovers embracing, using whole body language gestures which have first to be acted out before being modelled

General aspects and aims for Classes 9 to 12

Once again the important thing is to develop the manual dexterity needed to work appropriately with various materials, but also to become submerged in artistic activity that is free of any specific 'purpose'. The creative process as such is experienced consciously. The youngsters are offered a realm in which step by step they can experience the intrinsic laws of art and at the same time the freedom of their own expression. Modelling lessons can help mould and differentiate the pupils' life of feeling while at the same time stimulating their enjoyment of being creative.

Modelling proceeds through wood and stone carving to sculpture proper.

Classes 9 or 10

Points of view and general themes:

The pupils should once again re-experience the basic elements of modelling, volume, surface, transitions between planes, line or edge and point. The main aims are:
- Recognising and being able to describe the different qualities of modelled shapes
- Becoming conscious through observation of the movement of surfaces.
- Experiencing shapes from inside and from outside This is a new realm of experience for the pupils They must learn to distinguish between organic and inorganic shapes
- Becoming competent in the manual skills and techniques involved

Content suggestions:

Experiment with the basic elements of modelling using clay to make reliefs, e.g.:
- Compositions arising out of a flat surface
- Compositions arising from concave and convex surfaces
- Curved and angular shapes
- Compositions from surfaces that turn in on themselves
- Endeavours to find a holistic composition within a specified form language

The pupils learn to experience the reality of the space around them. Possibly a negative cast of the relief is made in plaster of Paris, and then a new positive cast is made from this negative.
- Make masks from a clay base, from the relief form to a complete three-dimensional figure
- Sphere (a form at rest within itself)
- Model a complete figure that not only looks satisfactory from every angle but also constitutes a plastic whole. As with the relief, the starting point as a rule is a basic geometrical form. These basic forms can be developed into animal figures. Perhaps suitable motifs from history of art lessons are taken up

Techniques:

- Working with clay, either a single lump or using the building up technique used in ceramics (e.g. coil technique)
- The technique of applying plaster of Paris
- Taking a cast in plaster of Paris
- Casting with lead, silicon or synthetic resin
- Various techniques of mask making including paper and fabric
- Woodcarving. Following clay model, repeat the form by carving in wood. Relief forms are a suitable starting point. Geometric and organic forms are possible
- Stone carving can be introduced using a soft stone such as chalk or tuff

Class 11

Points of view and general themes:

Once the basic elements of modelling have been practised in Class 10, Class 11 can move on to studying the movement of form on the one hand and the psychological expressiveness of form on the other. Stone and woodcarving lead on to monumental sculpture.

Content suggestions:

The modelled *form as an expression of movement*:
- Form movement as a shift of mass
- Transition from static geometric forms to dynamic movement
- The surface turned in on itself as an expression of movement

- A series of shapes showing stages of a movement, e.g. a falling drop, a growth form, etc.)
- Form transformations: variation/metamorphosis (also possible in Class 12)
- Transformation of an organic movement into an artistic form

The modelled *form as a expression of soul*:
- Suitable modelled expressions are sought for various soul gestures
- Contrasting feelings (e.g. sorrow/joy) are depicted
- Conversation between two forms
- Abstract forms can be taken further to become concrete and figurative
- Model the human head in three dimensions (e.g. working from inside a hollow form to create the form from within)

The expressiveness of the human form can be studied. Suitable ideas are brought in from art history (medieval sculpture, e.g. the portal figures in Chartres, Expressionist sculptures, e.g. Barlach, Kollwitz, abstract sculptures, e.g. Arp, Bill, Moore). Exercises may include:
- Facial proportions as bearers of expression
- One-sidedness of specific features, e.g. grimace, caricature, animal-like face
- Character studies based on the head
- Physiognomy as a mirror of human moods
- Self-portraits
- Contrast opposite types of head and face: man/woman, old/young, beautiful/ugly, laughing/crying, etc.

Techniques:

- Initial designs are usually worked on through sketching, then usually worked in clay; later other materials are used
- Plaster of Paris techniques
- Woodcarving
- Working with other materials (depending on what the school can offer)

Class 12

Points of view and general themes:

The pupils should achieve some degree of maturity and independence in their work with modelling and carving; they should develop the ability to work freely with the forms they have discovered.
- Transformation of naturalistic forms into an artistic whole; simplification; stylisation
- Combining separate form elements in a whole work, e.g. incorporating copper and wood, glass and wood or metal, stone and metal (in jewellery and brooches)
- Making use of all experience gained; first attempt at using sculptural techniques on a larger work
- Working out individual possibilities of expression

Content suggestions:

Sculpture or modelling as an expression of spiritual intent

The theme for the year could be: sculpture as an expression of spiritual intention. The important thing is that the students choose a motif or theme that expressed their own artistic aspirations. They should undertake a major artistic project for the year, working through an entire process from initial sketches and studies, through models in wax or clay to a finished exhibited piece in a material, or combination of materials, of their choice. Such a piece should be accompanied by a description of the theme, the process and reflections on the outcome.

Techniques:

- Modelling in clay
- Woodcarving
- Stone sculpture

If possible, depending on what the school can offer, other sculptural techniques can be used, e.g. casting in bronze.

References:
1 From notes of a lecture given at a conference on art and education at the Waldorf School, March 1923. This translation is taken from, Jüneman, M. and Weitmann, F., *Drawing and Painting in Rudolf Steiner Schools*, Hawthorn Press, 1994.
2 An introduction to this theory can be found in the book by Jüneman and Weitman quoted above. This book gives a most comprehensive account of the practice and theory of painting and drawing in Steiner Waldorf education.
3 Steiner, R., *Conferences with the Teachers*, op. cit., meeting of 15th November 1920.
4 Steiner, R., *The Child's Changing Consciousness*, op. cit., lecture of 19th April 1924.
5 Jüneman and Weitmann, op. cit., p46.
6 Steiner, R., *Conferences with the Teachers*, op. cit., meeting of 5th February 1924.
7 Translated from *Methodische Grundlagen zur Anthrosopie* (GA 30, Dornach 1989, Introduction).
8 Jüneman and Weitmann, op. cit.
9 Kranich, E-M., *Formenzeichnung*, Stuttgart 1985, p30.
10 Kandinsky, V., *Der Blaue Reiter*, Munich, 1979.
11 It is very difficult to describe form drawings in words and considerations of (a different kind of) space prevent the reproduction of drawn examples. The reader is advised to refer to the illustrated booklet, *Formdrawing*, by Arne Breidvik, SSF Resource Books, reprint 1999.
12 Bühler, E., *Formenzeichnung. Die entwicklung des Formensinns in der Erziehung*, Stuttgart 1985, p158.

General aspects and aims

The prevailing paradigm of contemporary chemistry is the atomic theory and any chemistry book for children will show models of atoms and molecules in the first pages.

The transformation of matter into the modern materials we take for granted in our daily lives is founded on this theory, which has guided human thinking for two hundred years to the discovery of atomic energy. Despite its material success, the atomic theory remains a theory and certainly the version that appears in young children's books, in school textbooks and in the popular scientific media has been superseded by a sub-atomic world view where so-called particle behaviour is subject to laws that contradict those of our macroscopic world. Should young children be so thoroughly saturated in a particle model of matter which, for all its powers, is simply not accurate? At what age can they appreciate the difference between model and reality? Does the simplistic representation of the atomic theory meet young children's educational needs?

An assumption lies within modern chemistry that the laws derived from the inanimate mineral world can completely explain the living world. Nevertheless, there is a large and increasing number of scientists who question the materialistic and reductionist assumptions on which this view is founded and whose research is directed by a different perspective. Are we equipping our children for the future fruitfully by maintaining that an organism can be explained by viewing it in terms of atoms and molecules?

Against these considerations, the Waldorf/Steiner chemistry curriculum is informed by the same developmental picture as the rest of the curriculum. The time to bring a consideration of the atomic theory is in Class 11, for example, with the topics of genetic theory, evolutionary theory and Darwinism. At the other end of the curriculum, the fairy tales of Class 1 contain the imaginative pictures that will support the kind of paradoxical thinking demanded by an appreciation of quantum theory in Class 12. In Class 7, the emphasis on observation rather than theory, is paralleled in physics and life sciences.

Points of view and general themes:

Kindergarten to Class 6

In popular understanding, the word 'chemistry' implies crystals, powders and liquids in bottles. If the study of chemistry is not to isolate children from the living world, then it must be deeply integrated into the life science curriculum from the beginning and not used during this phase of childhood to train them into current materialistic/reductionist explanations. All the considerations given to the place of the life sciences therefore apply to the chemistry curriculum. The whole curriculum, from Kindergarten onwards, supports the approach to chemistry that will come to focus in Class 7.

In Class 6, within the geology main-lesson, limestone, silica, chalk and coal illustrate the way in which what is dead and mineral can arise from life. Living organisms shed enough materials in growing and dying that they can be responsible for substantial geological strata. It is only relatively recently that science has acknowledged the living origins of such deposits and it is an important counterbalance to the prevailing view that a dead mineral world is the foundation of life (evolved from a 'primeval soup'), to see that dead matter can arise *from* life through excretion and death.

Class 7

Now chemistry becomes a subject in its own right. The approach should be phenomenological, with the emphasis on accurate description and the children's own experiences, rather than those mediated entirely by measurement. It is also important to maintain the widest possible connections with world processes, in nature and in the human being. The study of combustion, for example, will include observations of the burning qualities of different materials, descriptions of the power of a forest fire, the nature of biological respiration and the ritual/sacrificial use of fire in different cultures and legends.

The imaginative and pictorial faculties engaged here provide a deeper basis for a conceptual understanding of the roles of oxygen, carbon dioxide and energy as well as the role of the plant world over the whole earth.

Biographies of scientists such as Priestley and Lavoisier show how science is set in an historical context and how determined and creative individuals pursued their fascination with the phenomena.

The technical applications (welding, smelting, fire extinguishers) then take their place within much wider moral, social and environmental perspectives.

Possible lesson content:

COMBUSTION:
- The burning of all kinds of dead material (e.g. straw, cotton, pine needles, spores, alcohol, gas)
- The role of air in fire – forest, bush and oil fires, firestorms and chimney effects
- The generation of oxygen from pondweed and mineral sources
- The combustion of sulphur, carbon and phosphorus (volcanoes, charcoal burning and fireflies)
- The role of oxygen and carbon dioxide in human, animal and plant
- Smoke and ash, acid and base
- Indicators, using red cabbage, beetroot, litmus
- The chemistry of the candle

SALTS:

- Limestone and marble, origins and chemistry. Natural formations, caves and cliffs, flora of chalk soils
- The lime kiln and the lime cycle (limestone-quick-lime-slaked lime-chalk). Cement and mortar
- The reaction of concentrated hydrochloric acid and solid sodium hydroxide to illustrate the power of the acid/base polarity in forming salts. Practical applications (e.g. toothpaste, the farmer's use of lime)

METALS:

- The chemistry and the cultural/historical/technical significance of those metals that can be obtained from the earth, naturally or by reduction of the ore with charcoal (e.g. iron, copper, lead, mercury, tin, silver, gold)
- Smelting of iron – historical links with charcoal burning

Class 8

Points of view and general themes:

The thinking ability at this age is ready for more conceptualisation and children are increasingly interested in technical applications. The choice of plant and food chemistry for Class 8 introduces quite complex chemistry, while maintaining the wider picture of the plant world, human diet, agriculture and food technology as well as relationships with other main-lessons. Simple experiments which involve measurement and testing are more appropriate now.

The general theme is how metabolism and the food chain involve a direct relationship with nature and the seasons, although the ripening process can be halted (e.g. pickling), slowed (e.g. storage), or accelerated (e.g. cheese). Food production also involves separating out and purifying what was in the natural environment. The food products may still retain some of their connection with these origins until they finally become isolated into chemical substances (e.g. starch powder, vitamins). The need for cooking rather than eating food raw needs to be examined along with the highly processed food habits of the Western world. Issues of health and diet arise.

Possible lesson content:

- The process that changes grain to flour, various cereals and milling techniques
- The properties of dough, the role of gluten
- Breadmaking (practical). Sourdough and yeast breads
- Extraction of starch from flour, potatoes or rice. The qualities of starch, testing with iodine
- Glucose as the primary product of the plant/sun relationship. Other sugars in nature. Testing for sugar (Benedict's or Fehling's solutions)
- Sources of sugar (historical and cultural). The effect of sugars on the teeth and the diet. Blood sugar and diabetes
- Glucose extraction from sugar beet and its manufacture from acid and starch

- Fermentation (practical) and decay
- Germination of seeds – starch/glucose
- The roles of starch, protein and yeast in bread-making
- Protein in milk, eggs, fish, beans, meat, feathers and fur
- The qualities of fats and oils, their relationship to water and fire. Their origins in plant and animal
- Milk – raw, pasteurised, "long life"
- Cheese and yoghurt (practical)
- Soap manufacture
- Cellulose in plant and insect. Its role in human diet Paper manufacture and recycling (practical)
- Leather and tanning
- Biographies (e.g. Pasteur, Lavoisier, Priestley)

Classes 9 to 12

General aspects and aims
(see also Life Sciences and Physics)

Following a developmental theme, adolescents in Class 9 are in a process in which the forces of their childhood which leant on the adult world now thrust them towards stark questions of identity. The accompanying emotional upheavals are sometimes cause, sometimes effect, but they are the horse which the rider must learn to master and take responsibility for. Through Class 10 the rider gathers the thinking powers that make some sense of the conflicts that meet him inwardly and outwardly until the qualities of the steed are more familiar and the explorations have more self-discipline. The potential for thinking to guide and to achieve, dawns in Class 11, while in Class 12 the individual takes stock of the past and lays plans for the future.

The chemistry curriculum accompanies this development. In Class 9, the substances formed in the living plant and the substances created in its decay are followed up in technological processes – for example, through the oil industry. For the pupils in Class 10, the conceptual clarity required to study and analyse mineral substances, meets their new thinking ability, while in Class 11 they are ready to compare contrasting models of how matter is currently understood and to see how the atomic model has arisen historically. In Class 12, the environmental and social issues that have accompanied all these studies are examined in their relationship to the human being and the whole earth. At the same time unusual substances and reactions highlight some of the lesser known features of matter, in mineral substance and in the living world.

Class 9

Points of view and general themes:

On the basis of the work done in Class 8, a more comprehensive and detailed study of the plant world brings Class 9 to focus on the principles of plant chemistry and the manufacturing and technical processes that have arisen from it.

Although much of the work would conventionally be called 'organic chemistry', the approach is to follow the transformations of substance (e.g. sugar-ethanol-ethanoic acid-ester) within the plant rather than examine substance in isolation as would be the case with a systematic study of an homologous series. Likewise, the use of formulae and equations is an unnecessary abstraction. Where pupils in a particular class show real interest, then it would be much better to use structural formula.

Many of the technical processes may have been examined in Class 8 (e.g. paper, ethanol), but these should be extended to highlight the principles (e.g. cellophane, esters). There needs to be a focus on the oil refinery and its attendant processes as the basis for Western material progress (from fuels to medicines, plastics and pesticides).

The theme of plant decay and decomposition to coal and oil, followed by analysis into individual molecules, needs to continue down to elements such as nitrogen, phosphorus, chlorine and hydrogen, as well as sulphur and carbon with their allotropic properties.

Class 9 needs to engage in individual practical work to test themselves with the hazards of apparatus and chemicals. Young people of this age should be encouraged to explore, to trust their senses and their thinking (though safety and health considerations are, of course, vital). Although they need to structure their observations, ideas and records, following a rigid scientific procedure with controlled experiments, testable hypotheses and exact measurements should not be allowed to dominate the mood of an investigation. The key elements of the scientific process of investigation can be distilled from the reflections that creative and enthusiastic teaching can demand from them. The more disciplined scientific training in method and thinking needed for Classes 11 and 12 is built up through Class 10.

Possible lesson content:

- Photosynthesis and respiration as processes of oxidation and reduction
- The chemistry of sugars, starch, cellulose, alcohols, acids and esters both within the plant and in technological applications (e.g. cellulose, soap, artificial flavours. Explosives: sugar, starch, guncotton)
- Enzymes. Fermentation. Aerobic and anaerobic respiration
- Alcohol abuse. Addiction
- Carbon and nitrogen cycles
- The chemistry of oxygen and carbon dioxide. Air pollution. Ozone
- Destructive distillation of wood and coal
- Factional distillation of oil
- Exploration and drilling for oil, refining and catalytic cracking, products of oil refining
- The chemistry of hydrocarbons and its everyday application (e.g. plastics, refrigerants)
- The chemistry of hydrogen
- The ecological and environmental consequences of the use of hydrocarbon derivatives (e.g. carbon dioxide, pesticides)

- Our personal, local and global responsibility for their use. Alternatives. Recycling
- The chemistry of non-metals (e.g. sulphur, chlorine)
- Biographies (e.g. Alfred Nobel and those not told in Class 8)

Class 10

Points of view and general themes:

Class 10 have gained sufficient control over their thinking to grasp concepts and work with them in following processes and in practical work to follow procedures. They seek clarity and are ready to take on the discipline of measurement through precision instruments – weighing and volumetric calculations. By way of contrast, projective geometry brings another kind of precision and quite a different perspective on crystalline form.

The mineral world provides rich opportunities to focus Class 10 on these considerations. Acid-base polarity in the forming of salts leads to practical work whose principles can be followed in living organisms as well as in the human being. The reduction of ores and the chemistry of metals leads to the Reactivity Series and the Periodic Table, laying the basis for the atomic theory in Class 11.

Possible lesson content:

- Mineral forms – geology and geography – geometry and symmetry
- The origin and history of common salt
- Crystallising, dissolving and melting
- The biological significance of solutions (e.g. osmosis, plasmolysis)
- The thermal decomposition of salts (e.g. calcium carbonate)
- The formation of salts from acid and base (the lime cycle, cement)
- Acid-base polarity in the living world (e.g. breathing, the digestive system). Indicators and titration. Insoluble salts
- Analytic chemistry: tests for acid radicals and metal ions
- Electrolysis of a molten salt (e.g. lead bromide)
- Industrial applications (e.g. electroplating) and historical discoveries (e.g. sodium, aluminium etc.)
- Chemistry and technology of metals, particularly those discovered by electrolysis
- The Reactivity Series

Class 11

Points of view and general themes:

At this age, the pupils' thinking ability can firmly grasp the clarity of a model while holding a perspective which can challenge it as well as consider other possibilities.

Quantitative chemical laws should be introduced and the historical discoveries which led to the Periodic Table. This should be presented as only *one* way in which a coherent picture of the chemical elements can be summarised.

This is the age at which the atomic theory can be taught in detail. Although only a small number in the class are likely to be considering chemistry as a science to specialise in, when the approach is historical with attention to biographies and to the moral, social and environmental implications of nuclear weapons and nuclear power, the whole class can be engaged.

By way of contrast, homeopathic effects could be considered. Homeopathy offers a good example of an effect that cannot be explained through the dominant model. The calculation to find out at what dilution atomic theory would find no molecules at all, could be an exercise for the pupils. There is also much recent research to show that water and chemicals are involved in intimate electromagnetic relationships with living tissues. Such research from scientific periodicals shows that the models of science are always under review and that quite different models from the atomic model, with its implicit materialism, may arise during their adult lives. Such models need not be alternative but rather complementary, illustrating the reality that we can arrive at different interpretations of 'the facts' when we look from different points of view. Even 'the facts' may be different.

Such discussion would be harder in Class 10 and probably impossible without vehement polarisation and adversarial argument in Class 9!

The mood should always be entirely positive towards a science that is ready to develop new ideas, remaining open-minded towards all phenomena and grounded in clear thinking and exact observation. It is unfortunate that science is usually presented as synonymous with technology and that its current ideas, from 'big bang' to Darwinian evolution, are to be believed as if they are absolute truth. This is not a healthy point of view for the future of science.

Possible lesson content:

- Establishing the concepts of element, compound, mixture and the basic laws of chemical combinations
- An historical and practical approach to:
  - Laws of conservation of mass, constant and multiple proportions.
  - Relative atomic mass, the use of formulae and equations.
  - Gas laws.
  - Avogadro's number.
  - The Periodic Table

- Radioactivity, the atomic theory and the Manhattan Project (along with the Physics main-lesson).
- The moral, social economic and environmental effects of nuclear power.
- Homeopathic and/or other models of the interaction of matter and life.
- Biographies (e.g. Dalton, Lavoisier, Mendeleev, Curie, Bohr, Rutherford, Oppenheimer).

Class 12

Points of view and general themes:

As in other areas, Class 12 needs the opportunity to have an overview of the subject. Such an approach would survey the origins and historical development of contemporary atomic theory already worked with in Class 1, look at the global effect of chemical technology (economic, social, environmental) and consider the effects of a range of chemical substances on the human organism.

The exploration of unusual chemical reactions gives a practical side to studies at this level and keeps alive the sense of the unknown in such phenomena.

Possible lesson content:

- Greek ideas of the atom and the elements and those represented by Dalton, Bohr and modern Quantum physics
- The impact of petroleum products on 20th Century, building on Class 9 and looking to the future of transport and renewable energy sources
- Enzymes, hormones and other biosecretions and their relationship to bodily processes
- Poisons – curare, mushrooms, cyanide
- Addictive substances and their relationship to consciousness
- Impact of chemicals on the environment (e.g. nitrates, hormones, pesticides)
- Carbon as the physical/chemical vehicle of life. (Concepts such as allotropy, an homologous series, polymerisation, the benzene ring)
- Unusual reactions e.g.:
  - Belousov-Zhabotinsky (BZ) reaction (spatial forms from a chemical reaction)
  - Nitrogen iodide (unusual explosive)
  - Phosgene (luminous spontaneous combustion)
  - Iodine 'clock' (time reaction)
  - Sequence reactions (colour changes and gaseous emissions)

Introduction to the Practical Curriculum

"The more we take into account... that intellect develops from the movements of the limbs, from dexterity and skills, the better it will be".[1] This motto stands above not only the craft curriculum, but the curriculum generally. Learning through doing and learning through making are twin aspects of the same fundamental attitude to education that permeates the Waldorf Curriculum. Thinking and understanding arise out of activity and movement, indeed living thinking is internalised movement. In view of the fact that modern life has deprived children of so many opportunities to imitate and practise meaningful movement through the activities of the hands, education has to compensate if children are to develop in a healthy way. Practical work harmonises the child's soul faculties and thinking, feeling and willing, just as stories work down into the life processes and bodily rhythms in an equally harmonising way.

Obviously the craft and handwork curriculum has a crucial role to play in this experience of learning through doing. The Crafts Council is well aware of this vast constituency of makers which it serves and represents. But, in addition, it saw an urgent need to examine the central learning role played by making – not only in learning the skills to overcome the well-documented famine of competent makers, but also in learning life skills – in schools, higher education and through adult life. It realised that the contribution was only incompletely recognised – and its potential even more rarely appreciated.

As a recent report by the Crafts Council concludes: *"Making is a creative process that develops skills and competence by engaging with ideas and materials. Knowledge and understanding acquired through 'learning by doing' allows young people to enjoy a sense of achievement which will sustain a life-long interest in the made world.*

Creative and practical skills, developed in education, can provide valuable experiences which will support the national economy and improve the quality of everyday life." [2]

This however is an area of the Waldorf Curriculum that has remained limited, conservative and traditional in its approach. Innovation has been limited especially in the UK. The crafts have been preserved in a niche which appears to many students as increasingly isolated from their interest in modern technology.

In many European countries (with the resources to support it) the craft curriculum has been extended to include full apprenticeship programmes in a range of subjects. Many schools [3] have moved practical subjects and the crafts lower down into the school, so that children in puberty, from the age of 12 and 13 onwards, can begin their 'earth maturing' their engagement with the world of matter, materials, practical human needs and the development of skills at an age when they really need it. There is no doubt that this trend was anticipated and encouraged by Steiner himself. The famous comment in lecture 7 of the Torquay Course, about the wish to include a shoemaker on the staff, comes to mind: *"Nevertheless we do try to make children into practical workers."* In the Oxford course, Steiner also indicated that practical work presently being done at the Waldorf school in Classes 5 or 6, should in future be done by pupils in Class 3.

These innovations are important as they mark real attempts to meet the developing needs of today's children. Naturally a 16 year-old will be more competent than a 13 year-old, so many craft teachers prefer to teach older pupils. But perhaps the 13 year-old has a greater need for the experience. Nor is it a question of either/or, both need it. Unless pupils have practised a craft to a certain level of competence over several years, the creativity and self-directed activity we strive for will hardly be achieved. If we want the students to make real things that serve real needs in the world, they will need to have the time in the timetable to do so. Merely sampling a range of crafts is a form of consumerism!

Furthermore, practical activities need to be integrated into the whole curriculum and not compartmentalised into specialist lessons. That means, each craft or handwork activity needs to be experienced within a context, related to the rest of life. This also has to occur in age-appropriate ways. That means progressing from play to work, from picture to ideal, from archetypal gesture, through craft to technology. Of course, the various hand skills need to be taught in regular lessons and blocks, the challenge is how those activities can integrate with the rest of the curriculum and how they can make the transition into modern technology and work with synthetic materials.

The increase in learning and behavioural difficulties among children has many causes but can certainly be seen as a symptom of a lack of integration, perhaps even a disintegration of the soul forces of thinking and willing. What comes from the head cannot be carried out by the hand, and what the limbs learn through meaningful activity, does not translate into conceptualisation and understanding. Learning through doing is a mode of learning that 'ascends' from the limbs to the head. Reflection and analysis of what the hands have made, brings consciousness into the intelligence of the limbs.

Mediating between these two realms is the affective realm of feeling. On the one hand, sentient experience of the materials and processes provides a rich basis for a differentiated life of feeling. On the other, the aesthetic-artistic experience transforms those feelings into the basis for sound judgment. This is a rhythmic process of exchange.

From Handwork to Technology

HANDWORK, BASKETMAKING, DRESSMAKING, SPINNING, BATIK, WEAVING, CARDBOARD WORK AND BOOKBINDING

Classes 1 to 12

General aspects and aims for Classes 1 to 8

Handwork lessons are more than a means of promoting dexterity and skill. Through rhythmically repeated movements and exercises while working on tasks suited to the age of the children, the hands – expressing the middle realm of the human being – help to bring about both a strengthening of the will and of the capacity for logical thinking; the transition between these is the cultivation of the feeling life. J. Piaget stated that schooling intricate manual skills was essential for the development of intelligence. He said that the mental operations we carry out only function properly – i.e. bring about real thoughts rather than combinations of words – when they are prepared by physical actions. According to him, mental operations of logic (amongst which are: reaching conclusions, forming judgments, and comprehension) are nothing other than the result of taking actions into the mind and co-ordinating them there. This approach has been borne out by research done by Prof. Matti Bergstrom of Helsinki University. [4] Everyday language still uses physical expressions to describe mental operations, e.g. 'to grasp something', 'to take up the thread', 'to get one's thoughts tangled up'. Mention should be made at this point of the difference between an intellectual education as opposed to a training of the intelligence.

The intellect focuses on grasping facts. Acting in accordance with indications or outside guidance is intellectual action. The intellect seeks to conform with what already exists or is known.

Intelligence, by contrast, is not directed to finished things. It understands what is in movement or still in a state of becoming. In keeping with this, intelligence is formed through 'activity', through movement and manual dexterity.

> *If we do knitting in the right way with children, making objects that are useful ... we are often working on their minds more strongly than we do when we teach them things that are assumed to belong to mental training.*
>
> *As I said yesterday, the whole human being, not only the head, is a logician; when you remember this you will learn to appreciate properly the importance of exercises in manual dexterity. It was not merely a fad when the matter came up about boys, too, learning knitting and similar skills. When the hands work in this way, capacities are built up that considerably increase the ability to form judgments. This ability is least promoted by teaching children to perform exercises in logic.*

In handwork and crafts, the formative qualities of above/below, heavy/light, light/dark, inside/outside form the basis of the work for children of all ages. All the tasks are performed by both boys and girls. They are not done for their own sake but in order to develop the capacities of the children. They should always have a practical purpose and awaken a social awareness for the work of other people.

Respect for the source of the material and the final handling of worn, used and spent artefacts are, in addition, the first stages towards individual responsibility for the environment and resourcefulness. This means that the preliminary skills for craftwork are best integrated throughout the curriculum.

It is precisely in the encounter with the material world that we can appropriately meet a world of 'process'. In our overly sanitised society children need to play with and explore basic materials and processes; likewise adolescents need an appropriate challenge, one that will help to equip them with essential skills to manage the practical affairs of life and to develop a moral sense of responsibility for the environment; both the natural and human.

A curriculum of activities in association with main-lessons as well as the formal handwork for children within the Lower School as well as pupils in the Upper School, can be developed where a school consciously opens up to the potential of its environment. Many of the necessary materials can be responsibly obtained from their primary source within the school grounds or nearby locality.

Although many of the crafts have their formal lessons, the crafts are integrated throughout the curriculum. The children encounter a material such as wool, in the Kindergarten, where they learn its tactile, scented qualities. They collect it from fences and hedges, use it to make gnomes and stuffed cushions. In the Lower School they learn to learn and learn about sheep farming. They may experiment with plant dyes in the Middle School. In history and geography lessons they learn the economic aspects of the wool industry. By the time they start weaving and textile technology in the Upper School, they already have a very broad understanding of wool, its qualities and origins. This example can be extended to wood and timber, plant fibre, clay, metal and other natural materials.

Quite apart from the formal handwork curriculum, the children in the Lower School should have many opportunities to work with their hands in many different lessons, using whatever materials are to hand, especially natural materials such as wood, plant fibre, leaves, bark, clay, water, material, paper, curd and so on.

Craft work is not as specifically related to age groups after the age of 12 or 13 as other subjects, though the way it is taught is. There is great variation in schools as to when the various crafts are introduced. The important issues are as follows:

- There is a progression from materials taken from the animal kingdom, through the plant kingdom to the mineral kingdom
- Learning the sequence from naturally occurring objects and materials to processed material (e.g. planed wooden planks, or paper)
- The progression from using the hands to handtools to machines
- Teaching the subject in age-appropriate ways

HANDWORK

Class 1

Points of view and general themes:

The task in Class 1 is to make the transition from play to work in a playful and artistic way. The children initially learn by imitating the teacher. Boys and girls learn to knit on two needles. On the one hand, knitting trains awareness and dexterity of both hands and, on the other, it awakens and promotes the children's mental powers through the transformation by which a one-dimensional element, the thread becomes a two-dimensional fabric which has a three-dimensional function. The children should begin to develop a sense for practical design and for suitable colours and simple shapes.

Content suggestions:

• Teasing wool into thread by hand
• Felting wool
• Making knitting needles using dowelling rods, sanding and waxing
• Knitting using plain and edge stitches: gnomes, balls, recorder bags, small dolls and animals, potholders etc. often starting with white cotton before moving on to wool, in primary colours
• Embroidering woollen objects with silk thread using straight and diagonal lines
• Cords for handles or skipping ropes, using cotton or parcel string, and the handles made of wood
• Willow whistle made out of a green stick
• Subsidiary work: form drawing, designing small knitted objects, tearing tissue paper for making transparencies, etc. often in connection with the seasons, festivals and main-lessons, making a wooden drop spindle, free form nest basket using grasses etc.

Class 2

Points of view and general themes:

Once both hands have practised knitting plain and purl sufficiently, crocheting can begin. The emphasis in the activity is on the dominant hand and even the dominant side of the body. Alternating between chain stitch and doubles can have a harmonising effect on the individual child's temperament.

Content suggestions:

• Finger knitting, French knitting, making and using a knitting nancy
• Knitting: purl
• Crocheting using chain stitch and doubles to make: nets for balls, bags for recorders, small bags etc. Also crocheting round potholders
• Plaiting threads to make bands and cords
• Start dolls which can be made with a simple flat construction
• Clothes for dolls can be knitted or felted

• Stitching of seams with overstitch or running stitch
• Subsidiary work: as in Class 1, including as preparation for house building, felting pieces to make tent structures

Class 3

Points of view and general themes:

The first garments are made to be worn. Beginning with the head, caps are knitted or crocheted. The techniques learnt can be used elsewhere. There is plenty of room for the children's imagination in making glove puppets. Form drawing is practised thoroughly from Class 1 to Class 3 in order to further the children's formative capacities.

Content suggestions:

• Knitting/crocheting hats, jumpers, scarves
• Knitting or crocheting, glove puppets
• Embroidering with silk to enhance the shape and reflect the use of the object
• Consolidate basic stitches and stitching
• Practising the techniques learnt
• Subsidiary work: build Classes 1 and 2. Rural crafts including wattle and daub, hurdle making, clay oven etc.

Class 4

Points of view and general themes:

There is a particular exercise that is very helpful at this stage of the children's development: cross-stitch. With its symmetry, and supported by colour and form, cross-stitch helps children to gain confidence and inner firmness in this initial phase of their becoming independent. An understanding of a meaningful design to suit the purpose of the object begins to awaken.

The crossing work is enhanced by plaiting and braiding techniques.

Content suggestions:

• Use of scissors, needles, pins and thimbles
• Cross-stitch, sewing by hand
• To their own design the children can make embroidered and sewn pincushions or book covers, recorder bags, shoulder bags etc.
• More complex plaits, cords and strong ropes
• Felt animals stuff with wool
• Construct a simple pit forge, burning charcoal, to make a simple poker

Class 5

Points of view and general themes:

At this age the children have a new need for harmony; they seem to rest within themselves. A new technique to learn, that fits in with this, is round knitting on five needles. Over the next two years it is the turn of hands and feet to receive garments, and the children make their own designs called for by the use of the object.

Content suggestions:

- Knitting on five needles: socks, mittens, gloves
- Use felting technique to make garments
- Consolidation of stitching skills
- Whittling wood

Class 6

Points of view and general themes:

To suit the psychological stage the children have reached leading up to puberty, it can be helpful to make three-dimensional objects either based on the human or animal form, or garments for people: soft dolls or animals (to their own design and pattern). The important aspects are the processes of turning inside out (which corresponds to the children's first attempts to show their inner being externally), of stuffing and shaping.

The increase in size and heaviness of the children directs their attention to their feet. So now they can make slippers, designing the colouring to suit the function.

Content suggestions:

- Human or animal forms in a pattern design, sewing the parts together
- Making slippers with a felted upper on leather sole (see woodwork curriculum)
- Macramé, fishing nets, shopping nets, friendship bands
- Tie-dyeing

Class 7

Points of view and general themes:

As the children approach physical maturity an awareness of body shape can be channelled into clothing; shorts, blouses, smocks, waistcoats can be made. Pupils should design their own garments. Knowledge of the materials is broadened and recorded.

Content suggestions:

- Leatherwork, belts, pouches
- Slippers, sandals or moccasins including working out the shape of shoes and making the pattern
- Various methods can be used, using materials such as cloth, leather or plaited threads, etc.
- If possible, a shoemaker can be asked to help, and a visit to a shoemaker's workshop arranged
- Hand-sewing simple garments, shirts, waistcoats, bags, rucksacks etc.
- Hand-looms can be made and simple weaving techniques learned
- Using green wood and scrap wood, constructing a shaving horse and pole lathe (related to mechanics main-lesson)

Class 8

Points of view and general themes:

With puberty or 'earth maturity' the pupils gain an inwardly experienced understanding of cause and effect, and the need to understand how mechanical things work. So now they can begin to used the treadle sewing machine. To use this properly they need to understand its structure and function. Using this machine gives ample opportunity to practise the co-ordination of foot rhythm (will), hand skill (feeling), and attentiveness (thinking). Knowledge of the materials is deepened and formal records are kept (folder, notes in a project book etc.), with an emphasis on the different qualities and use of the various materials to enhance awareness to differentiation. Care and maintenance of materials is also important e.g. washing, ironing, dry cleaning, differences between natural and synthetics (related to hygiene and nutrition main-lessons).

Content suggestions:

- Using the sewing machine to do double seams, oversewing, hemming
- Machine sewing household linen, aprons, gym shorts, pyjamas, boy's shirts
- Costumes for plays
- Constructing a clay bread oven
- Cooking and bread making
- Building a Cretan windmill with cloth sail.
- Building a coracle, tepee etc.

General aspects and aims for Classes 9 to 11

Handwork lessons in the Upper School build on what the pupils have learnt during the Lower School, especially as regards handling textiles. In basketmaking and dressmaking they practise two skills that increasingly call on them to make their own designs but also to be more and more accurate, learning how to make the transition from soft, pliable stuffs to hard, spiky canes. They are helped in three ways:
- Their manual movements must be appropriate and skilful
- Imagination and individual taste are developed as they design the object to be made
- Finally, every work sequence must be properly thought through. Mobility in thinking and the ability to make a mental picture of something are practised, and can be checked and corrected when the result becomes reality. The students should learn to evaluate what they have made in terms of appropriate use of material and technique, form and function and aesthetics

It is important that the pupils learn the origin and production processes of the materials they use, where possible learning the skills involved.

The crafts practised are those that use wool, thread, material, cane or paper (cardboard). Even the simplest objects made are intended for daily use. The link between the object being made and ordinary human life should be obvious as the children work. The lessons should provide insights into the properties of the materials used and the techniques needed, into the connections between function, material and form, and into the links between human being, machine, production, commerce and industry, and the environment.

Working practically and theoretically with the different materials will help the youngsters to school their faculties of thinking technically and to become more aware of life processes in nature; it will help them learn to invent, plan and organise processes and to develop an appropriately critical attitude as consumers. Such work will also play a part in developing their personality, in furthering their technical education and deciding what profession or occupation to aim for later on.

Learning through doing and learning from having done is essentially a moral process, in that the will to do better is motivated and this motivation is not egotistical but objective. The pupil feels the need to make a better basket, better in the sense that it serves a real need and in that form relates harmoniously to material and function.

From Class 9 onwards, craft studies usually take the form of blocks of lessons. They vary depending on the location and preferences of the school.

The aim of all the subjects is:

- Accuracy in planning, carrying out and checking the work
- Meeting a real need

Two main directions are followed:

- Design should be functional and pleasing to the senses
- The technical workmanship should involve the most economical procedures using the most appropriate materials

Class 9

BASKETMAKING

Points of view and general themes:

Traditional basketmaking is also taught in Class 8. The basic skills can be learned in Class 8. In Class 9 the emphasis is on design, different materials and individual creativity. In keeping with the youngsters' stage of development (their growth is for the most part complete), they now need some inner firmness (upright posture and steadiness). Shaping a basket in the right height and breadth can help with this. The sense of touch is also experienced.

In Class 8 willow cultivation and processing is done in preparation for basket making.

Content suggestions:

- Getting to know the origin and preparation of the materials and use of tools
- Making some of the basic parts:

- Weaving the base, the uprights and the final border, following the specific instructions of the teacher
- Free construction of a basket in which the types of weaving are chosen by the youngsters to suit the purpose and the aesthetic design
- Exercises in imagining the finished work:
  - Making sketches of the planned work.
  - Describing a piece of work when finished.
  - Writing a self-evaluation of the process and finished product.

Class 10

DRESSMAKING

Points of view and general themes:

The pupils experience the need to make accurate calculations and to work with accuracy. They recognise certain laws of number and measure and develop an understanding for the work and skill of others (e.g. those who have hitherto made their clothes for them). Differentiating between made-to-measure and off-the-peg garments. If possible, a visit to a factory should be made. Dressmaking is fruitfully related to costumes and drama productions.

Content suggestions:

- Measuring for a garment (getting to know their own proportions)
- Drawing the pattern; altering the pattern
- Selecting the material: quality, weave, structure
- Cutting out, marking, tacking, trying on, sewing
- Finishing: fastenings, seams, trimmings, neck openings
- Getting to know the electric sewing machine
- Buttonholing by hand or with the machine

Appropriate design:

- Fitting, colour, colour gradations
- Sewing one or more garments

TEXTILE TECHNOLOGY

Points of view and general themes:

It would be good for the pupils to get to know all the phases humanity has gone through in textile making, from ancient times right up to industrialisation. In the Lower School the children have learned drop spinning and basic thread work. In spinning, the important aspect is the co-ordination of hand and foot, so this needs much practice.

Content suggestions:

- Preparation of material (wool or silk) from cleaning to dyeing
- Study of materials
- Individual design

Spinning fibres with spindle or spinning wheel:
* Getting the spinning wheel ready
* Spinning yarn for weaving
* Getting to know the characteristics of various wools and silks
* Various kinds of design
* Deciding yarn thickness to suit the job in hand

The development of the spinning wheel up to the spinning machine. Visits to museums or a spinning factory.

BATIK
(painting on silk or other forms of textile design)

Points of view and general themes:

Free artistic work always taking into account the ultimate purpose. It is important to have a comprehensive, exact and qualitative picture of the person or environment for whom a piece of work is intended, e.g. temperament, age, style. Pattern, colour, shape, technique are chosen accordingly.

Content suggestions:

* Preparing the material
* Selecting the colours
* Planning and describing the work phases
* Various techniques
* Design
* Producing the squares, scarves, cushions, tablecloths, curtains or garments, etc.

Classes 11 and 12

WEAVING

Points of view and general themes:

Weaving combines handwork and technology, so the youngsters should be given some insight into the historical development of weaving. Depending on the capacity of the pupils, the spread of techniques should be as broad as possible, from delicate squares or scarves via larger garments (also cushion covers, tablecloths, mats etc.) to the design of rough linen work. (Weaving is also possible in Class 10 – see Technology if the emphasis is on 'Bookbinding and Cardboard Work'.)

Content suggestions:

Elements of weaving:
* How warp and weft work together
* The basic techniques of weaving
* Getting to know different types of loom
* Designing a piece of weaving

Calculating:
* Length of the warp
* Number of threads in the warp
* The amount of yarn that will be needed
Working at the loom:
* Setting up the warp

* Setting the frames
* Using two or four shaft looms
* Making a woven piece of work
Possible: Visit to a handweaving shop.

CARDBOARD WORK AND BOOKBINDING

Points of view and general themes:

Following the making of paper in Classes 7, 8 or 9 and practical tasks cutting and stapling sheets and card to make exercise books, the students move on to bookbinding itself in Classes 11 or 12. In Class 10 printing is often introduced, including the use of hand-made paper. Getting to know the new materials and noticing their characteristics requires attentive senses and sure judgement (characteristics such as: tone, colour, texture, smell, elasticity, firmness). The precise technique of bookbinding, with its strict sequence of moves, schools disciplined thought and action. It is possible to consider every step of a sequence forwards and backwards, checking and improving. The next step cannot take place before the previous one has been done properly. The work itself shows the pupils the sequence of tasks that have to be carried out.

Content suggestions:

Cardboard work:
* Handling the materials: paper, cardboard, textiles, leather (as a covering), adhesives. (In Class 10 the students can bind main-lesson books using heat binding techniques and pre-cutting paper and card with the guillotine)
* Carrying out the different tasks introduces the pupils to the various tools, apparatuses and machines (presses, cutters)
* Partly copying and partly designing their own work, the pupils make: picture frames, blotters, folders, little boxes, photo albums

Bookbinding:
'From the flat board to the finished book' (ideally with gilt edges):
* Folding proof-sheets or writing paper
* Sewing for paper binding
* Hardcover binding
* Half leather, patent leather or parchment bindings

The content of the book decides what bindings, binding materials and cover designs are used. Various materials are studied.

JOINERY, CARPENTRY, METALWORK AND CERAMICS, WOODWORK

Points of view and general themes:

In Classes 1 – 3 the children are handling natural wooden twigs and branches which they find. These can be combined to make simple creative toys, or arrangements on the nature table, or to make furniture for dolls or gnomes. Introduction to basic tools suitable for children of this age, e.g. knife for handcarving, saw, drill and bit, hammer, rasp etc.

Content suggestions:

Classes 4 and 5

- Using bark and twigs (with suggestive shapes) make twig figures, fabulous animals, gnomes, sheep with shepherd, bark boats and so on
- Making simple utensils such as stirrer, whisk, small spoon, paper knife etc.
- Simple log constructions e.g. climbing frames, flower bed borders, edges etc.

From Class 5
- Begin studying trees and different timbers
- Use of hand axe to make tent pegs etc.
- Use of adze to shape timber, make dugouts
- Splitting and chopping to make firewood and kindling
- Make hollowed out bird boxes out of large logs

Class 6

Points of view and general themes:

In the craft lessons we take up something the children learnt earlier; what has been prepared beforehand now works on into the future. Thus craft work refers back to the very first lesson in school when straight and curved lines were drawn. Both are present in the background of the articles made by the children. For example a wooden spoon has a straight handle and a rounded (and concave/convex) bowl. The children work inwards from the outside; filing and chiselling always mean you have to work inwards towards the shape. Long movements (e.g. planing, sawing, cutting) relate to the straight line. Short movements (e.g. chiselling or carving by hand) relate to the curve.

Content suggestions:

Useful objects and toys are made.
- Making objects in daily use such as cooking spoons, palette scrapers, stirrers, flour shovels, darning eggs, mallets, wood hammers, garden dibbers etc.
- Toys, e.g. hopping bunnies, waddling ducks, pecking birds, bears on a seesaw etc. Making toys requires that the characteristic movement has to be understood, and also calls for skill and an understanding of mechanics. This can begin very simply, e.g. seesaw or eccentric wheels etc. In Class 7 such effects can be improved on, with the children giving free reign to their imagination
- Safe handling of tools and appropriate treatment of materials is aimed for (e.g. correct cutting methods)

Class 7

Points of view and general themes:

Physics in Class 7 brings a first introduction to mechanics. The children now want to apply what they have learnt. For example the pendulum, the crank, the lever, the seesaw etc. used in making moving toys can now be applied to cranes, mills, propellers etc. With animal toys, more care will be taken to make them move in a realistic way. Some carpentry is also now introduced, e.g. use of the mortice chisel, bowsaw etc. Making usable items featuring a hollow (e.g. a bowl) is an important aspect at this age. In addition to the confident use of the necessary tools, the youngsters also learn to shape the inner and outer form properly.

Content suggestions:

- The class might undertake a larger communal project for the Kindergarten or a bazaar, such as a farm with barn and animals, or a village with houses, towers, a well
- Carving bowls
- The toys can look much more effective if they are well painted
- Nutcrackers, boxes with lids, pen holders etc. can follow next
- Greenwood work

Class 8

Points of view, general themes and content suggestions:

The pupils learn to plan the best sequence of operations in the production of an item, e.g.:
- Greenwood turning on a pole lathe
- Making a besom
- Making a picture frame
- Making gardening implements etc., making and putting handles on tools

More can be expected of them with regard to both manual skill and design.
- Combining good design with a good fit and accurate work

Proper carpentry work can begin even before the technology subjects of the Upper School, e.g. planing.
- Simple carpentry projects i.e. shelving, storage boxes

Larger projects can be undertaken, possible as communal tasks, e.g.
- Large seesaw, go-carts, skate-board ramps

Another possibility is:
- Making proper nesting boxes for birds, or feeding tables for birds

Let the pupils choose:
- Combining wood with metal (e.g. wooden plinth for copper bowl)

General aspects and aims for Classes 9 to 11

Craft lessons in the Upper School build on the skills

learnt in the Lower School. Now the motto is: 'Every lesson must be a lesson for life'. The tasks set should not only continue to promote the pupils' development but also be meaningful for society at large. Steiner was insistent that crafts and technology should be based on meeting real needs in the world and *not* an artificial process of preparing exercise pieces. He also expected all teaching to be a preparation for life. Steiner did not make many specific suggestions regarding craft work in the Upper School, but he did emphasise in connection with technological studies that many practical tasks should not be tackled too late in life, i.e. they should be practised between the ages of 15 and 18.

In the Lower School, craft lessons served to help the children grow into the world. Now the time has come for them to learn how to meet the challenges of the world. In this they are educated not only by the teacher, who functions like a master craftsman with his apprentices, but also by the materials, the tools and the tasks they are set.

Wood is now not so much something that stimulates the imagination but rather a material challenging one's technical skills. It is something that is alive and has grown, and it poses technical problems. The pupils find themselves caught between their own wishes as to what they want to make and the specific characteristics and limitations presented by the wood. Bringing these two into harmony is helped by the classical methods of joinery. Through good design and accuracy in working the pupils learn both how wood functions and the techniques needed to work with it.

CARPENTRY AND JOINERY

Class 9

Points of view and general themes:

By making bookshelves, boxes with lids, step-ups, tool boxes, etc., the pupils practise work that requires accurate measurement. They check the quality of their own work. The finality of procedures involving the disposal of wood shavings is an important educational experience. Regular practice of specific procedures (e.g. planing, sawing) strengthens the will.

Content suggestions:

- Study and care of tools
- Knowledge of the different woods, their characteristics and uses
- Gaining confidence in sawing, planing, chiselling for the simpler joints
- Accuracy in surface treatment and the final finish are essential
- Application of these skills to useful tasks
- Forestry work
- Rustic garden furniture
- Discussion of environmental aspects of processing wood.
- Recording of information about techniques and materials

Classes 10 and 11

Points of view, general themes, and content suggestions:

- Expanding and deepening skills in the techniques learnt now calls for greater precision through practising and becoming independent in sorting out how to tackle a task
- Accurate preparation of wood
- Joints such as tongue and groove, dovetailing, etc. are applied; these require accurate working. Handheld electric tools are introduced and their proper use learnt
- Making simple pieces of furniture involves artistic aspects as well as constructive ideas. The latter should be split into separate stages that combine together to create a finished piece
- Putting together separately constructed parts, e.g. fitting a door into a frame
- Carving of printing blocks
- Technical drawing in relation to woodwork projects
- Recording skills and techniques learned

Class 12

Points of view, general themes, and content suggestions:

If there are opportunities to continue joinery into Class 12 (as Steiner suggested), the pupils should design their own furniture to be realised via technical drawings and sketches of details. Artistic design, form and function come together and static requirements are met in aesthetically pleasing ways. The pupils can also make accurate cost estimates.

Depending on the teacher's competence, other tasks can of course be brought into woodwork lessons in the Upper School, e.g. making boats or musical instruments.

METALWORK

Classes 9 to 12

General aspects and aims

Steiner made no suggestion about metalwork. Inflation was rampant in the days when he was working with the teachers of the first Waldorf School (1923) and there would have been no question of introducing this subject. Had there been an opportunity, he would surely have seized it, for he spoke often about metals and on one occasion mused that at least once in a lifetime everyone should experience fiery, molten metal.

The following suggestions are based on experiences gained over the last 50 years. These are so positive that metalwork has meanwhile become an essential ingredient for Upper School pupils at Steiner Waldorf schools.

All ancient civilisations developed hand-in-hand with the expansion and refinement of obtaining and processing metals. Unlike wood, clay or stone, ores have to undergo a process of transformation before the metal becomes usable. By carrying out the tasks of shaping, heating, smelting, pouring and smithing the youngsters experience those historical processes of development. Pliable copper elicits their own powers of form which have also been brought to bear in other artistic lessons. Iron awakens or promotes the virtues of courage, alertness, and quick, sure seizing of opportunities. Rhythmical hammering is in itself a healing activity.

COPPER BEATING

Class 9
(often started in Class 8 and continued in Class 9)

Points of view, general themes, and content suggestions:

A first metalwork block acquaints the pupils with natural origins and the basic properties of copper, e.g. its divisibility and elasticity. They can then be more aware of what they are doing when shaping it, and they also experience how constant hammering makes it harder, while heating makes it softer and more pliable. Most of the tasks are rhythmical, and this promotes perseverance and concentration. (Rhythm takes the place of strength.)

The techniques learnt are marking out, cutting, hollowing, planishing, riveting and soldering, both soft and hard and the objects made are bracelets, bowls, boxes, candlesticks, bookends, oil lamps etc.

Class 10

Points of view, general themes, and content suggestions:

A second block takes all the techniques further. The skill of raising the copper in cylindrical, tumbler shapes is added. This makes it possible to manufacture beakers, vases, jugs, watering cans, baking tins, bells, etc. This technique requires much concentration and accurate hammering. Soon the pupils want to carry out their own designs. So they should also learn annealing, hard-soldering, bending and shaping around a form and tin-plating.

Knowledge of how to handle brass, pewter or even aluminium and stainless steel extends the possibilities both of experiencing the metals and of making objects. Closed vessels are preferred, which corresponds to the wish to turn inwards that is typical of youngsters at this age. The students can also learn the techniques of working with copper pipes in plumbing (and could also make copper rods for use in eurythmy).

IRON (WROUGHT IRON)

Classes 9 to 11

Points of view, general themes, and content suggestions:

Whether one introduces copper or iron first is a

question of pedagogical research and experience. Some teachers see the application of will needed in hammering iron as an ideal introduction to metalwork these days. Copperwork demands greater delicacy of touch and rhythm and should perhaps follow iron. On the other hand iron may simply require more applied will and strength than Class 9 students have available. Copper is shaped cold (having been annealed). Iron has to be heated. The pupils immediately learn the difference between working with cold or red-hot iron. They experience how the glowing iron responds to the hammer's beat.

The firm stance at the anvil, the proper handling of the various hammers and tongs, the courageous blow accurately aimed, the alertness and quick reactions needed at forge and anvil, all these are profound experiences and important education tools. Basic techniques such as pointing up, stretching, splitting, bending and compressing, after much practice, can be used to make nails, fire-tongs, spits, candlesticks, fire-pokers, decorative hooks and a variety of tools such as knife and chisel, drawknives (for greenwood turning) etc.

Some procedures need two pairs of hands. This brings in the element of collaboration. More responsibility and care are also needed, as working in pairs is more dangerous.

Old tools can be repaired and restored, new handles made and toolkits made up for use in the Third World.

The pupils will also hear about mining and smelting as well as the industrial production of steel, steel alloys and stainless steel.

METAL CASTING

Classes 10 to 11

Points of view, general themes and content suggestions:

Beautiful and important experiences are provided by casting, which some schools are able to include in their syllabus. It is a profound experience for young people to watch the metal melt in the crucible, and then receive an entirely new form, made by themselves, when they pour it into the mould. Care in shaping the mould is essential for a successful operation. Failures, which are inevitable, have more educational value than anything the teacher can say. The huge delight at success is infectious.

First of all easily melted metals (lead, tin, zinc) are melted in the ladle and poured in a mould. More complicated shape can be attained in moulds and two-part sand moulds. Lost wax casting can be the crowning experience. Then brass and bronze are melted in the furnace. These materials can be won through recycling household scrap. Medals, small figures and all sorts of useful objects, even a small bell, can be produced. Later silver and gold can be used for jewellery making.

All this gives a very practical experience of the link between technology (perhaps visiting a foundry) and art history (bronze sculptures).

MASK MAKING

Points of view and general themes:

Mask-making using a range of media provide adolescents with many opportunities for exploration of the human psyche, in association with drama, literature etc.

Content suggestion:

Class 9

- Face casting using clay and plaster.
- Transformation of facial gestures to express a wide range of ages, psychological types. In Class 9 this should be more exploratory.

Class 10

- Masks are made more objectively as stage props to represent and express particular characters
- Use of metals and moulds
- Use of wood and leather

Classes 11 and 12

These skills are developed further. Use of masks in other cultures is studied.

PUPPETRY

Puppetry can be offered as a subject in its own right, or may be offered as an option to students from Classes 9-12. With increasing differentiation in the Upper School, students may drop one or other subject, a second foreign language for example, and concentrate on craft work. Puppetry is a very suitable alternative.

General aspects and aims

Puppetry is an artistic craft. The first task is to create the puppet. Glove puppets are the simplest, needing only a properly formed head and a dress. Shadow puppets, marionettes and rod puppets pose all kinds of technical problems requiring knowledge of mechanical and optical laws.

So one of the aims of these lessons is to apply artistically what has been learnt in mechanics, optics and technology. Marionettes do not necessarily need strings and frame-jointed limbs. 'Soft' marionettes, i.e. stuffed dolls without legs and with lead-weighted arms, can be manipulated without a cross-frame. For performances to Kindergarten children this kind of marionette is preferable.

For proper performances the handler remains invisible (except in the Kindergarten, where he or she can be seen by the children). The handler is simply an 'intermediary'. The puppet is the main actor. The glove puppet, the marionette or the shadow puppet 'tells' the puppeteer what to do. The pupils have to learn how to manipulate the different puppets. This is the second aim.

The third aim is social and educational. By remaining invisible through having to stand behind, above or below the puppet, the puppeteer has to make a sacrifice. For some pupils, having to stay out of the limelight is a sacrifice, while for others it is their great chance to perform something through the puppet which they have perhaps not been able to bring themselves to do on the stage. All the handlers are dependent on active help from their co-puppeteers. Handling technically complicated puppets often needs two or more helpers who have to work 'hand-in-hand'. In puppet theatre performances, the interplay between scenery makers, lighters, musicians, speakers and handlers is often more intensive, because it is more intimate and requires a greater degree of mutual empathy and care than real theatre.

Perhaps the most important *aim of these lessons* is learning to *respect what is small*.

Sometimes there are opportunities to take a travelling puppet show on the road. This enables the pupils to make a gift to the various homes, special schools or hospitals where they have perhaps been working in their practical social work period. Their social commitment thus gains an extra dimension.

Spanning the four classes of the Upper School, a puppetry course can be designed to take account of the pupils' on-going development.

Class 9 – The Marionette

Points of view and general themes:

More than with any other puppets, manipulating a marionette calls for real artistic ability. The pupils can experience how constant practice rewards them with the ability to breathe life into dead material.

Content suggestions:

- Getting to know the mechanical laws and analysing the movements of the marionette
- Constructing the various joints
- Moulding heads, hands and feet
- Constructing the cross-frame
- Dressing the marionettes
- Manipulating the marionettes
- Making the scenery and working on the text
- Combined effect of language, light, music and movement of the marionettes

Class 10 – Shadow Puppets

Points of view and general themes:

Mechanical and optical laws govern the construction of the puppet and the scenery. The shadow picture should be as clear, sharp and precise as possible. Together with the skill of moving the puppets, another important aspect is combining various elements to create a 'shadow picture' for the scenery.

Content suggestions:

- Looking for and adapting an appropriate text

- Designing the shadow picture in painting and drawing
- Experiments with coloured and simple shadows
- Construction of the shadow puppets
- Manipulating the puppets
- Designing the scenery and working on the text
- Combined effect of language, light, music and movement of the marionettes

Class 11 – Glove Puppets

Points of view and general themes:

Marionette players stand above their puppets; shadow puppet players stand behind theirs. Glove puppet players go down below them. Glove puppets can be especially expressive because of the way they are manipulated from within. Puppeteers need enthusiasm, discipline and also humour if the movements are to be artistic and not merely grotesque.

Content suggestions:

- The history of puppetry
- The glove puppet as the archetypal form of artistic puppetry
- Modelling or carving heads and hands
- Improvisation exercises
- Handling the puppets
- Making the scenery and working on the text
- Combined effect of language, light, music and movement of the marionettes

Class 12

Points of view and general themes:

There are various ways of bringing the puppetry course to an end:
a) The experiences gained can provide a basis for putting on a performance (fairy tale, novella, drama, opera).
b) If the piece to be performed portrays different levels of experience (this world and the next; daytime/night-time consciousness; archetypal figures, elementals etc.) various types of puppet can be combined.
c) Special puppets can be developed for special purposes (e.g. performing in homes for people with sensory disabilities).

Content suggestions:

What is done will arise out of the above possibilities. What has been learnt will then be combined or deepened accordingly. If there is enough time, larger performances can be prepared [e.g. *The Magic Flute, Dr Faustus, A Christmas Carol* (Dickens), *Momo and the Grey Gentlemen* (M. Ende) etc.]

References:
1   Steiner, R., Basel Course 1920.
2   Eggleston, John (ed.) *Learning Through Doing: A national enquiry into the value of creative practical education in Britain*, 1999, p5.
3   See report by Rawson, M., *Learning to Work, Working to Learn*, SWSF, 1997.
4   Quoted in Mitchell, D., and Livingston, P., *Will-developed Intelligence*, AWSNA, 1999, p9.

General aspects and aims for Classes 1 to 12

Language is our most important means of mutual understanding and is therefore the primary medium of education. It is also a highly significant formative influence in the child's psychological and spiritual development and its cultivation is central to the educational tasks of Steiner Waldorf education. It is the aim of the curriculum to cultivate language skills and awareness in *all* subjects and teaching settings. Clearly the teaching of the mother tongue has a pivotal role within the whole education.

THE SPOKEN AND WRITTEN WORD

Language has two primary forms within education, the spoken word and the realm of orality and all forms of literacy. It is the task of English lessons to cultivate both. Literacy fits like a glove on the hand of orality. In the pre-school years the emphasis is on language acquisition and is essentially concerned with oral language. With the introduction of writing and reading, a new form of linguistic consciousness emerges. Vital though this is to the developing human being, it needs to be based on spoken language and so the cultivation of oral skills always underpins literacy.

In terms of the emerging child's consciousness, the transition from orality to literacy reflects the historical and cultural transition from pre-literate to literate traditions. Through literacy and the written word, consciousness is significantly re-structured and this factor is important to understand from the point of view of methodology. One can compare the fundamental differences between the pre-literate and literate mind as follows:

Oral consciousness is mythic, whereas literacy tends to a rational and historical sensibility. Situational thinking, exemplified by the riddle, the fable, the parable or the metaphor compares with logical thinking, definitions, categories or syllogisms. Oral thinking involves concrete mental images, as opposed to abstractions. Oral language characterises; literate language structures and defines. Pre-literate thinking is often expressed in the form of collective, communal, contextual memories linked to ritual and situation, whereas literate memory is individual and internalised. Epic, myth, poetry and performed drama are forms of expression which draw strongly on the oral tradition whilst prose belongs to a literate tradition. The oral mind tends to have an experience of self through the context, whilst literature lends itself to self-experience. We can also see this in the distinction between shame and guilt; shame is in the eyes of others; guilt is internal within the soul.

This broad-brush comparison paints two opposing forms of consciousness. Historically, literacy proceeds out of oral traditions and largely replaces them. Yet both qualities are needed to complement each other in the school learning context. As Norman Skillen put it:

School is the product and traditional servant of literacy. Its whole ethos – from its typical architecture to its organisational structure and patterns of required behaviour (sitting still, keeping quiet etc.) – is determined by literacy. But if orality is not given its rightful place, the school will not be a wholesome environment for children and literacy will ultimately suffer. [1]

The task is therefore to cultivate a transformed orality, which, as Skillen concluded in the article quoted above, *"is none other than the power of imagination itself."* Imagination and analytical thinking are two poles of experience that need to be integrated. The cultivation of both the oral and the literate forms of language support this process. Imaginative, holistic thinking are called upon when the child is challenged to participate, to do, to engage in complex situations. Analytical thinking requires that the individual stand back from a situation. Whenever the pupils are engaged in experiential learning, whenever they are challenged to enter the unknown, the realm of the intuitive – be it in mathematics, drama, the arts, crafts or eurythmy, transformed orality will be at work. It is one of the primary tasks of teaching English language and literature to establish a strong culture of orality upon which an equally strong culture of literacy depends.

THE NATURE OF LANGUAGE

In the three archetypal stages of early child development, gaining uprightness, learning to speak and the development of thinking, language has a mediating role. From a certain perspective speech is internalised movement and thinking is internalised speech. There is a clear progression from movement and gesture to speech and from speech to thinking. In this inner metamorphosis of movement, language works as a formative force in the developing child's being.

The relationship between movement and gesture, speech and thinking is a key to all aspects of language teaching. At all levels of linguistic experience, from the formation of the sounds, the letters of the alphabet, the rhythm of sentence structure, we find the metamorphosis of movement and gesture into structured form. Movement and gesture translate into figures of speech, metaphor and mobility of thinking. The task of language teaching in the Lower and Middle School is to expand the child's repertoire of linguistic experience through usage. Making this conscious is essentially a task of the Upper School where the stages of this metamorphosis can themselves be explored.

An example of how this might be done would be an exercise such as taking a soliloquy by Macbeth, and analysing the movement of thoughts throughout the passage, observing the rhythms of the syntax, unwrapping the imagery of the analogies and finding the levels of meaning, feeling the effect of the sounds Shakespeare uses in a given phrase and ultimately expressing the whole as movement and gesture on the stage without words.

All these qualities of language are cultivated in the Lower and Middle School. Only after the age of fourteen does it become necessary to make the processes more reflective through analysis. Mediating between these two processes, experiencing and analysing language, is performance, whether through recitation or acting.

LANGUAGE AS A FORMATIVE PROCESS

Initially speech itself structures both the physical organs used in speaking and listening as well as the neural structures that perceive, organise and understand words and sentence structures. This occurs as the child acquires her native language. Subsequently language becomes a medium for the child's soul life. On the one hand, language works to enable the child to express herself and relate to the world, whilst on the other hand it works through its syntax to order and structure thinking, to categorise and conceptualise and thus to enable the child to find meaning. These two elements flow together in narrative structure which enables the child progressively to order her experiences and thus find meaning. Language is our primary mode of representation and is the main medium through which we construct our picture of the world and especially the relationships within it.

Language has a twofold origin. As an expression of thoughts, feelings and intentions, it arises out of the soul as a stream wishing to grasp and communicate with the world. Its other origin gives expression to the universal spirit of language, the Logos, which comes to individualised expression and underlies the structures of the world's various languages. The universal aspect of language enables the human being to gain access to thoughts that can be thought in any language and thus opens the mind to universal concepts. In the process of individuation, language facilitates the progression from an identity based on the family and cultural group the child is born into, through one in which the individual can express his or her own thoughts by finding their own voice, leading ultimately to access to a universal and objective reality. The mother tongue provides the crucial link between these stages.

The close bond between spoken language and the cultural and geographical context within which the child grows up also needs to be nurtured through schooling, particularly before puberty. Local dialect, regional accents and the whole vernacular tradition of nursery rhymes, skipping chants and so on, are important for the child's feeling of belonging to a particular place. This oral element is supplemented by the rich vocabulary of local place names, legends and folklore that are usually authentic to the local linguistic culture. With puberty, children descend more deeply into the physical qualities of their environment and to counter this, language needs to expand beyond the vernacular and seek more universal qualities in the realm of ideas. It is at this stage that young people lose their intuitive connection to the spirit of language and must regain this through conscious work.

As Steiner put it:

The speech absorbed by the child through imitation bears the same relationship to the whole human being as do the milk teeth. What human beings possess by way of language ability by the time they have reached puberty...is something they have achieved, anew, for a second time, just as the principle of obtaining teeth has had to be worked at for a second time. [2]

During the pre-school years the archetypal qualities intrinsic to the actual sounds of spoken language work formatively on the child. In the period between 7 and 14, the child lives linguistically much more in the emotional content of the words, in the moods and feelings they evoke. Words express something of the inner nature of what they describe, albeit clothed in cultural and personal associations After puberty the individual not only has to find his or her own voice (both literally and metaphorically) but has to find access to universal concepts and ideals through language.

In summary we can say that language works formatively at a physiological level in the speech organs and neural apparatus. This process needs time and appropriate models to imitate. At the psychological level language provides a medium for communication. Its syntactical elements help structure thinking and mental representation. The *being* of language reveals something of the inner nature of the world it describes and allows the individual access to universal concepts.

When literacy is introduced, the child's will forces are directed into the cognitive activities associated with mental picturing, representation and memory. To translate the movements of lines in two dimensions on paper into an inner voice which speaks, requires both directed will and imagination. If literacy is to be a living activity leading to living thinking, the imaginative forces of transformed orality must permeate it. The cultivation of orality after the transition to literacy is crucial. It essentially occurs through practising speech, listening, recitation, gesture, drama, debate, discussion – all of which require an inner dynamic and movement. But transformed orality is also cultivated whenever the imagination is engaged consciously and given form and structure. The livelier the interplay of linguistic exchange, the more spacious the 'field' in which language can grow, inviting the individual to move about in it.

The following curriculum suggestions for Classes 1 to 8 will be dealt with under the headings Speaking and Listening, Grammar, Writing and Reading, Narrative Content and Reading Material.

Checklists for literacy skills in Classes 1-3 are given on p. 113, 4-5 on p. 116 and 6, 7 and 8 on pp. 119-120.

Class 1

SPEAKING AND LISTENING

These aspects are emphasised from the children's very first day at school. Following the recitation of a morning verse in chorus the 'rhythmical part' of the main-lesson begins. Here recitation of poems alternates with short musical exercises (singing, playing the lyre or recorders). The transition from Kindergarten child to schoolchild is marked by the way the children can now recite not only nursery rhymes but also longer seasonal poems. Songs and ring games are also included. The main elements of this pattern are maintained for several weeks before any change is introduced. [3]

Stories are told by the teacher from traditional sources including folk tales and nature stories which the children subsequently recall and retell in their own words and may be enacted. Telling fairy tales requires a specific approach. A simple sentence construction and avoidance of dramatic language used by the storyteller helps prevent subjective feelings from coming into play and bringing the fairy tale down into the realm of the child's direct everyday experience, where it loses its validity. Folk tale figures are not to be taken literally but archetypally.

The value of genuine fairy tales for a healthy psychological development of children would require a separate chapter in its own right. What concerns us here is the role of language. Experience has shown that if the class teacher works on story telling with sufficient seriousness, the children's imaginations will be stimulated by the archetypal images rather than the stereotypes suggested by film, cartoon and comic book. These associations soon disappear and the children are ready to listen. They sense that the different language of the fairy tale and the way it is told is something new into which they can grow. They enjoy learning whole sentences and passages word for word by heart.

Teachers consciously prepare such stories by learning the content by heart and choosing language that is clear, artistic, rich in expressive vocabulary and which enhances the meaning of the story. In listening, the children acquire a sense for narrative structure and sense of style. They are able to extend their active vocabulary, learn idioms and phrases through emulation and experience wide variety in the means and form of expression. When the natural rhythms and intonations of the language are consciously used, the children acquire a certainty of feeling for basic punctuation and sentence structure. This provides a basis for the subsequent grasp of the use of commas and full stops. A sense for the different articulation of questions, statements, commands and exclamations is acquired aurally, as well as the distinction between words describing activities, things and attributes. They can also experience the linguistic expression of emotional qualities such as surprise, curiosity, denial, willing affirmation, enthusiasm and so on.

The directness of the oral approach to storytelling (as opposed to reading) stimulates the child's engagement, interest and imagination. This provides an empathetic basis for future reading and appreciation of literature, which depends on the readers' ability to recreate the content of the text in their own imagination in a fluid and uninhibited way. This approach is continued throughout the following years with age-appropriate developments.

Initially, literature in written textual form is in many respects a kind of foreign language for children. This is even more the case for non-literary texts. Being able to feel at home in this strange land requires the child to leave the stepping stones of the individual words and swim in the meaning of the sentence. Beyond that the reader must be able to enter into the imagination

of the writer. This faculty is greatly assisted by listening to and emulating quality oral language that stimulates an interest in story and ideas generally and awakens an interest in literature.

The 'story part' of the main-lesson is also an artistic cultivation of language. In a lecture to teachers in Basle Steiner stated that all lessons to do with language should be built up artistically. *"Children bring their instinct for language to school with them. But it will probably be up to us to shape their feeling for style by the time they reach their ninth year."* [4]

Steiner Waldorf education attempts to cultivate and encourage the significance of oral linguistic abilities whilst cultivating literacy. Speaking and listening play a key role in the Steiner Waldorf approach throughout the curriculum. Poetry and verses are recited throughout the curriculum and this begins on day one in Class 1.

To be able to shape and carry through the 'rhythmical part' of the main-lesson which includes the learning and recitation of poetry, the teachers will have had to strengthen their own relationship to lyrical expression as well as practise a suitable way of speaking. Steiner Waldorf teacher training includes schooling in 'speech formation'. Some schools also have a trained speech teacher who can assist the class teachers in their preparation. When, for example a poem is introduced to the class for the first time it is very important that it should be spoken by heart. The teacher must have familiarised herself with all the nuances of sound, rhythm and other aspects that are special to the poem. Then, by first reciting it to them and then gradually getting them to join in, she will teach them the poem, i.e. will commit it to their memory in an artistic way.

The 'rhythmical part' also includes speech exercises (e.g. tongue twisters) both for the whole class and for individual children, especially when their pronunciation needs to be cultivated and kept under observation. Orientation (e.g. Simon says) and coordination exercises also have their place in the 'rhythmical part'. Here the children learn to follow verbal instructions.

The first exercises in repeating what they have heard begin now. The teacher will only tell the next part of the story once the children have repeated what they have heard on the previous day. Initially the children who volunteer have a turn, but eventually every child should be able to stand up in front of the class and retell a part of the story, if necessary with inconspicuous help from the teacher.

GRAMMAR
Grammar is not yet taught at this stage. It is up to the teacher to emphasise sentence structure, be aware of how the sentences are formed and draw attention to striking words or syntax in the text used. Careful cultivation of clear speaking and well-structured sentences creates an 'aural' awareness of language structure.

WRITING AND READING
The children gradually learn to write throughout the first school year. Reading follows writing on the principle of 'first do then understand'. *"In seeing to it that*

the child speaks well we are laying the foundation for correct writing. Running parallel with this telling and retelling of stories we introduce the child to a kind of language of pictorial forms." [5] Before the letters are introduced, the children practise form drawing, using sequences of straight and curved lines within a horizontal framework. Out of this follows the introduction of the capital letters through the media of movement, gesture, speech, picture, name and symbol. Consonants are evolved out of pictograms, vowels out of interjections and expressions of feeling.

Writing is a highly complex activity and time taken to establish the skills involved is time well spent. The psychologist F. Kainz described the process as follows:

Learning to write during childhood is an intensive process lasting several years that has the effect of retraining the effectiveness of specific neuronal systems. Writing is difficult because it is served by a number of complicated movements. But complicated movements ... can only be carried out successfully if they have been thoroughly practised. This practice is an optical-motor achievement of procedural memory based on a physical substrate. We may imagine that the functional fine tuning brought about by practice leads to most delicate changes in the movement centres of the central nervous system. [6]

The process proceeds from pictorial representation of the letters to formal writing. This includes exploration of the relationship of sound and symbol through the use of emergent writing.

The shapes of the consonants as capital letters are presented to the children embedded in an artistic drawing made by the teacher with an accompanying story that emphasises the character of the letter. The letter F, for example, may be evolved from a drawing of a fish, and W, perhaps from the shape of the waves. The letter is separated from the pictogram and drawn and practised in its own right. We begin with upper case, then introduce lower case later on in the year, spending more time on it because lower case can be more difficult as letters are sometimes only distinguished by their orientation: d/b/p/q, m/w, h/y, u/n, etc. It is important to make sure that the letters are written correctly, anticlockwise, from the top downwards, etc.

A common mistake is to teach every letter of the alphabet with a story and a picture. The alphabet will take all year that way! Once you feel the children have understood the concept – experience (story), picture, letter – then ¡you can teach the remainder of the alphabet more economically.

This approach is used for the consonants. The special nature of the vowels is shown by the way they can appear as interjections expressing emotions. Wonderment can sound like 'ah!', surprise like 'oh!'. Experiences like this at the level of feeling, embedded in a short description and expressed in a picture, pave the way for the discovery of the letters for the vowels. Experiences in eurythmy lessons can be very helpful here. The English vowels and diphthongs are introduced as strong, mutable elements that bond words together.

In English, however, we don't call the letter 'A' *ah*. It rarely makes that sound unless it is accompanied by an 'r' (as in c*ar*t). Although it is important to get the feeling, musical, cosmic quality of the vowels across to the children, it is also much more helpful to concentrate on the short vowel sounds (*a* in *a*pple, *i* in *I*ndian, *e* in *e*lephant, *o* in *o*range, *u* in *u*mbrella). This gives them the tools to read and write simple words.

There should be a clear distinction between the *names (and long vowel sounds)*, for example 'A' for '*Angel*', 'E' for '*Eagle*', 'I' for '*Icicle*', 'O' for '*Opal*', 'U' for '*Unicorn*'.

In this way the routes that lead to the different letters are enriched and enlivened in a variety of ways. If the synthetic method has been applied for a while, then – once the children have learned a number of letters – a new letter can be derived by an analytical process. This has an enlivening effect. Alternating between synthesis and analysis in this way amounts to more than merely a helpful way of teaching. Steiner advised that both methods are as important for children as waking and sleeping, breathing in and breathing out. [7]

In the early lessons, exercises that serve a conscious command of right and left are also essential. Steiner called this '... *letting the children use their own body to become skilful in developing pictorial thinking.*' [8] For example one can say to the children; with your right hand quickly touch your left knee, your right ear, etc. In form drawing, mirror images (right/left, above/below) also help orientation in the dimensions of space.

The children learn to read by reading what they have written or what the teacher has written on the board. The first words that the children read and write in school should be of significant content and already be familiar to the children. Sentences of meaningful rather than banal content should be chosen such as, "The sun gives light to the world."

Several methods of teaching reading are integrated. These include the whole word or analytic method, the phonetic method and the spelling method. Steiner described this integrated reading method as follows:

If the letter forms have been gained through painting-drawing, and if one has gone on to a kind of phonetic (and) or whole word method, which is now appropriate because it leads the child to an appreciation of wholeness, and prevents it from becoming too fixed in details – if all this has been done, there is yet something else... It is this: the single sound by itself, the separate M or P, this too represents a reality. And it is important to see that when a sound is part of a word, it has already entered the external world, already passed into the material and physical world. What we have in our soul are the sounds as such, and these largely depend on the nature of our (humanity's) soul (condition). [9]

Steiner gave a detailed analysis of the qualities that each of the various reading methods involves in the lecture quoted above. Their transformation and integration through what he called a *"certain pedagogical skill and artistry, which will avoid a too one-sided drill in pronouncing the letters in the conventional way,"* is the crux of the matter. *"Instead, the child will gain some experience of how the letters came about and this is something which can live within its formative forces, something which is real for the child."* If the children are taught in this way, and assuming as Steiner did in 1923 that the children start at the age of seven, *"they will be able to read in due course – perhaps a few months after their ninth year. It does not really matter if they cannot read earlier, because they have learnt it in a natural and wholesome way. Depending on the various children's response, this stage may be reached a little earlier."* [10]

To many contemporary educationalists this may seem very late to have learned to read. What is not clear is whether Steiner meant independent reading ability or at what level. But assuming he meant that children should be able to read text with familiar vocabulary on their own, it is still quite late by conventional standards. One must however see this late start as a conscious extension of orality. Learning in the first three classes does not depend upon literacy skills but on the skills of orality, thus considerable learning in a wide range of topics and areas of experience occurs. Rather than literacy leading the learning process, it complements and supports it.

The fact is, the moment children learn to read is very individual regardless of the methods used. Generally the child will read when she is ready. The systematic and careful introduction of literacy skills benefits all children, but especially those with learning differences. For those who apparently acquire the skill easily the time ad care taken at least enhances their sense that writing and especially reading are something special.

In fact in most Waldorf classes most children can read and understand what they have written by the end of Class 1. Steiner advised that *"if we proceed rationally in these matters we shall bring it about in the first year that the child can put on paper, in a simple way, anything he may wish to or words that are spoken to him, and he will be able to read simple things."* [11] By the end of Class 2 they can read and understand printed letters and can use cursive script. Nevertheless, reading and writing are not used as means of access to information or as learning tools. These are skills which are acquired which take their context from the overall context of the lessons. This is a fundamental distinction from learning to read and write *in order to* learn.

Class 2 (age 6-7)

SPEAKING AND LISTENING
In addition to reciting in chorus, more and more of the children practise speaking poems solo in front of the class. Short poems are enacted or are accompanied by gesture. Those with a strong rhythm and much repetition are especially suitable, such as *The Key of the Kingdom* and *This is the House that Jack Built.* To fit in with the story material of this class, fables can be recited (alternating chorus and solo recitation) or perhaps acted. The children are encouraged to retell the stories they have heard and the experiences they have had. Speech and articulation exercises such as tongue-twisters are practised and the different qualities of oral expressions are explored which emphasise certain elements e.g. speaking in a fiery or watery way, stressing verbs of action, being aware of descriptive elements and names, in short experiencing the qualities of word types and moods.

Fables, legends, folklore and nature stories concerned mainly with animals and the local environment are the story material for Class 2. In their content these reveal a broad scale of human activity and relate to the natural world. Animal and other fables are about one-sided aspects of moral qualities (greed, cunning, envy etc.). Legends, and in particular the lives of the Saints look at the other side of human nature, the part where the hero as holy man or woman brings harmony to one-sidedness and by turning towards God gains the strength to serve his or her fellow human beings. There are many examples from a wide range of cultures with the Celtic tradition offering many appropriate stories. The fables of Aesop, Leonardo da Vinci, Lafontaine, Lessing, as well as the animal stories of the Native American traditions also provide important examples. As far as the language is concerned, such legends enable the children to hear and speak in a way that differs greatly from the fairy tale style. The brevity and simplicity of the language of fables initially astonishes the children ('Is that the end already?'). But then they notice they are left with more to think about. The story should be told and retold and listened to several times before a conversation several days later brings this to their attention. The relatively dry tone of the fables is abundantly compensated for in the warm style with which the life and deeds of saints can be told.

GRAMMAR
The children should be made aware in an imaginative way of the character of activity words (verbs), naming words (nouns) and describing words (adjectives and adverbs). *"This should be combined in a simple and obvious way with a talk about the formation of sentences."* [12] Punctuation is taught on the basis of the spoken rhythms which indicate when the sentence starts, finishes or pauses.

WRITING
The transition to lower case cursive script is prepared by suitable form drawing exercises, especially running and rhythmical forms. Lower case letters followed by cursive script are introduced with appropriate writing materials. This usually means changing from wax stick crayons in Class 1 to coloured graphite pencils in Class 2. Care and attention is paid to developing a fluid style of handwriting. The children's effort to orientate themselves on the page supports their endeavours to make the page beautiful and gives them an aesthetic interest in their writing. Steiner considered this important since this activity involves the writer more intensely in her work. [13]

The content of written work is related to the main-lesson themes and the children's own experiences. As a general guideline, about a third of writing is composed by the children, the other two thirds comprising texts prepared by the teacher and copied from the board and texts dictated by the teacher. Steiner suggested that the children in Class 2 should be able to write down, *"little descriptions of everything they are told and later what they have learnt about animals, plants, meadows and woods."* [14]

In Class 2 the children should be taught a good beautiful, flowing, cursive script, and their pencil hold and posture regularly checked. The letter formation too should be checked time and time again. The children use fat, soft pencils 2B, 3B or equivalent, which will encourage flow.

Free Writing

Compared to mainstream schools, very little free writing is done by the children in Steiner Waldorf schools. Instead, the children write about the stories they have been having in their main-lesson. By the middle of Class 2, most of the children will be getting keen on writing. A good way to support this is by encouraging them to write letters (at home or in the writing lesson) to the class teacher and to each other. This way the children are using writing as an archetypal form of communication – spelling the words as they think they sound – and the teacher can pick out some of the spelling mistakes and use them as part of the literacy programme. The letters also have to be read, providing valueable reading practise.

One suggestion is to make a letterbox for the classroom. All the letters can be posted in the letterbox and someone's job is to be the postman. The postman sorts out the letters in alphabetical order and delivers them to the appropriate address (desks: i.e. 3rd desk from the front, near the window). The less able spellers can draw pictures for the words they cannot spell. *Note:* This activity can be delayed to Class 3.

READING

The children continue practising reading with texts they have written themselves or provided by the teacher. A differentiated approach is used including whole class reading, child to adult, child to child and solo reading. There is regular practice in the recognition of auditory, visual and kinaesthetic patterns through teacher-led exercises. Spelling is based on a whole language approach reinforced by contextual, phonic and kinesthetic methods.

In Class 2 the emphasis is on phonics – how spoken sounds are encoded by written letters and letter groups.

Class teachers must have a thorough knowledge of phonics, but need to be flexible about which facts to teach – and to whom. To insist pedantically on teaching every detail to the whole class is a waste of time, since many children will not need it. Other children will need all the detailed teaching and practice they can get.

Phonics:

Consonant digraphs:	ng	ch	wh	ck	qu
Vowel digraphs:	oo	ee			
Vowels + r:	ar	er	or		
2 – letter cons. blends:	tr	gr	gl	cl	st etc.
Diphthong:	oi	oy			
Doubled consonants:	e.g. – fu *nn* y	Da *dd* y			

Soft c rule: c followed by c, i or y says 'ss'
'Magic' *e* and its effects on the preceding vowel (making it say its name).

Practise listening for a given sound and locating it at the beginning, middle or end of a word.

Word building: Making plurals by adding *s* or (after s, x, ss, zz, ch, sh) *es*.

Adding *-ing* (when it does not involve changing the root word).

Adding *-ly*

Various activities: games can be used to practise identifying and locating:
* the first sound – or digraph – in a word
* the last sound – or digraph – in a word
* the vowel within a word

Other games include:

Rhyming games

Alphabet games (incl. alphabetical order)

Learn to spell some essential irregularly spelled words such as: 'was', 'are', 'have', 'said', 'they'.

Spelling bees; words chosen by the class teacher to conform to patterns already covered.

Substituting letters to make new words.

As the second stage in the teaching of reading, many teachers make a reading book for their class. This is best done in the teacher's own handwriting – the children are used to this – it can then be reproduced on a photocopier or risograph. The children can make their own covers and add drawings to go with each story, thus individualising the book.

The book should include stories the children are familiar with such as fables, saint stories, poems, tongue twisters etc. It is important to use reading patterns that have been taught (and learnt!) – ideally getting progressively more difficult. Simple word games are also a good idea. These can go alongside the reading text, for example on the left page and then if the class is asked to read silently the faster readers can then start on the word games. For children who have a difficulty with reading it is a good idea to put one simple summarising sentence on the left hand page for them to read – after the teacher or other better reader has read the right hand page. This is a form of shared reading, which is known to be one of the most effective ways of building the bridge between being *read to* and reading yourself. (Often parents are willing to help with the reading lesson. Please prepare them before hand so they understand about short vowel / long vowel sounds; particular techniques you have used; which children need special encouragement, etc.)

By now the children are *almost* ready for printed books. First however, they need an introduction to printed letters – the 'g' in particular, but also 'a' and 'I' – and the general layout of books: chapters, introduction, index, etc.

At this stage the hardest task for the teacher is to find and choose a good class reader and good reading schemes for individual reading.

High standards of artistic presentation, topic, story quality and age appropriateness are important criteria in the choice of reader. On top of that it is important to find books that are not too difficult and are graded so that the language used is very simple – using mainly phonic words – and gradually gets harder introducing more and more spelling patterns. Some existing Waldorf readers are too difficult and can seriously affect the confidence of less able children. There may be a social reason for a class reader – the children hopefully learn to be patient, help each other, etc. – but it is worth asking oneself what good it does for a group of children with extraordinary different reading abilities and reading styles to read the same book out loud.

Reading in Classes 1/2 – summary

1. Teach reading via writing – reading (familiar text) from the board and main-lesson books
2. Teacher makes class reader in her or his own handwriting
3. Introduction to printed letters (g, a, l!)
4. Individual reading schemes and class reader if necessary.

Once the children can read, class teachers make every effort to cultivate the habit, by establishing class libraries, by recommending a particular book, by maintaining contact with local public libraries, by presenting the problem at parent evenings, by talking about it with parents.

Children with learning differences

By the end of Class 2, the class teacher should know which children have specific learning differences in literacy, such as forms of dyslexia. Children who appear to be making slow progress or are presenting specific problems may just be slow or late developers. However, by the end of Class 2 it is prudent to have looked at all other possible reasons for the learning difference, such as evidence of physical disability in vision or hearing or fine motor co-ordination. If there is a learning support specialist in the school, it is wise to have the whole class screened. If not, observe and contemplate each child individually and make a list of strengths and weaknesses. The following checklist may be helpful:
- poor balance
- poor co-ordination
- clumsiness
- jerky movements
- difficulty in throwing / catching ball (with one hand)
- mixed dominance
- can't stand / sit straight
- poor pencil hold
- poor letter formation
- unable to write in a straight line on lined (or marked out) paper
- does not place the descending 'tails' of letters below the line
- does not place the ascending 'tails' of letters above the line
- mixes capitals and lower case letters
- reverses / inverts letters and / or numbers (b/d/p/q, u/n, s, 2, 3, 5, 7, 6, 9)
- puts too many (or not enough) legs on the letters n, m

- is bright, but has real difficulty with writing / spelling / reading (or one of them)
- unclear speech
- does not know the days / weeks / months
- has a poor memory
- does not learn what has been taught
- cannot tie her / his shoe laces
- messy appearance, shirt hanging out, laces undone etc.
- is intuitive
- is imaginative
- looks young (baby face)
- has parents or siblings with SpLD

If three of these points are identified, the child may have a special learning difference (SpLD), and may not learn by the same methods as many of the rest of the class. The teacher needs to find out the way the child learns. **Advice can be given by the Steiner Waldorf Dyslexia Association based at Michael Hall School, Sussex, UK.**

It is in any case important to test all the children's dominance, co-ordination, balance, penhold, posture, etc.; as well as letter reversals; and if they have retained what they have been taught (see above), before the end of class two in order to design a literacy programme for Class 3.

Class 3 (age 8-9)

SPEAKING AND LISTENING

The children take an important step in their development during Class 3. This will become very obvious to the teacher once a good number of them have completed their ninth year and entered their tenth. Steiner pointed to the importance of this step on many occasions: *"Now the child begins to differentiate more and more between himself and his environment."* [15]

Near the beginning of the main-lesson simple nature poems now fit in well with the children's feeling for life. The children enjoy reciting descriptive poetry, especially if rhythm and rhyme run smoothly from line to line. They can also cope with longer poems, and humorous ones can be included. Texts composed by the teacher, perhaps in rhymed verse form, can arise out of the practical subjects of this year, house-building; preparing mortar; craft work; farming. Small plays can also be performed which take up some of these themes. [16]

The stories of the Old Testament provide the material for the narrative content of the main-lesson. The creation of the world and of the human being, to whom God gave the earth as a place to work, are subjects that turn the children's attention to created nature. It is up to the teacher to decide what further material following on from the loss of paradise is appropriate, also with regard to the great figures of the Old Testament: Noah, Abraham, Moses etc. It is essential to retain the lofty distance of the Old Testament stories by means of the powerful language in which they are couched, for that is where they will retain their reality. In this way the children will encounter another new style of language.

There is no real consensus about what stories might

replace those of the Old Testament in cultures where these may be deemed inappropriate. Certainly they would have to include the themes of divine creation, a single Godfather as figure of authority, the giver of law, the Fall and loss of innocence, the need for law to structure human society and the concept of obedience.

Retelling orally parts of the content of stories and experiences in and out of school is a consistent part of each day's work and remains so throughout the school in age-appropriate ways which develop narrative skills.

GRAMMAR

Steiner brought entirely new impulses to the subject of grammar, hoping again and again to see them put into practice. Teachers still stuck in the old ways of looking at grammar found it quite difficult to adapt, as is shown in the final teachers' meeting at which Steiner was able to be present. His dissatisfaction after listening in to lessons meant that Steiner Waldorf education received a legacy of particularly valuable suggestions. One of these is recorded in the meeting of 6th February 1923, when Steiner explained the main reason for wanting a 'living grammar'. The children should learn to link a feeling with everything they name; they *'should get a feeling for what the perfect tense means, or the present tense'*. To achieve this one must understand the distinct character of the main parts of speech and realise that we teach grammar not to correct wrong usage, but to awaken the children to the living structure of language. Steiner gave the following example of how grammar should be introduced.

We make the children aware of the difference between a statement, a question, and a feeling sentence, if we let the children speak these sentences or sentence part (i.e. clause) in such a way that the feeling sentence is spoken with a different emphasis than a statement, if we show the children how a statement is spoken in a neutral, disinterested way and a feeling sentence... with a nuance of feeling, if we work towards this artistic element in language, and only then, taking this artistic element as our starting point, develop the grammar and syntax. [17]

This theme keeps reappearing in many variations right up to Class 8 and beyond: develop the whole world of grammatical forms out of the artistic element, with the help of feeling. [18]

By comparing the feeling sentence with the other two types of sentence, the knowledge gained by the children arises entirely from the artistic element: intonation, emphasis, melody all point to the grammatical form.

In a second grammar main-lesson the children are introduced to the three main grammatical elements: noun (naming word), adjective (describing word), verb (doing word). The children should now become aware of their different character. What is new is the task Steiner set in the way the class teacher should prepare for this main-lesson:

In what is expressed by nouns we are made aware of our independence as individual human beings. We separate ourselves off from the world outside when we learn to name things by nouns ...

When we describe something with an adjective an entirely different element comes into play. By saying: The chair is blue – I am expressing something that links me with the chair. The characteristic I perceive unites me with the chair ... When I use a verb: The man is writing – I not only unite with the entity about whom I am using the verb, but I also do with my ego the activity he is doing with his physical body. [19]

This is an unusual approach to the task of learning about parts of speech. Steiner justified it by saying: *"Now that you know about this ... you will speak about nouns, adjectives and verbs with an entirely different inner emphasis than you would if you knew nothing about it."* [20]

The reason is as follows: instead of working towards confining things to a system (that of types of word) you turn your attention to the human being. You ask: What is it that language does in the human being by offering her three main types of word? How do grammatical structures help her to become aware of her position in relation to the outside world? The teacher needs to grasp the distinct fundamental relationship to the world that a noun or a verb expresses. This task that Steiner gave the teachers is, of course, only for them and not for the children. They only experience the entirely different emphasis. The teacher creates a space for the children in which they can experience that in their language, in what they say, there are naming words, describing words and doing words and that each type expresses a different activity.

In Class 3 noun, verb, adjective and adverb are characterised. Basic sentence structure is analysed and the correct use of full stops, commas, capital letters and question marks is taught.

WRITING

With the introduction of cursive script, the children's writing begins to become more individual. Great emphasis, however, is placed on neat, well formed and above all, legible writing. The children learn to become aware of the three zones of writing, the parts of the letters that site on, above or below the line (even where no line literally exists). It is also important at this stage for the teacher to draw the child's attention to the position and activity of the hand. At the same time the child has the task of making sure that what is written looks beautiful. Steiner called this *"drawing writing"* in which the writer *"pays close attention to his writing"* and *"develops a somewhat aesthetic relationship with it"*. [21] When they have had sufficient practice the children are taught how to use a school fountain pen. This provides a further opportunity to have another good look at the children's posture while writing, and improving this if necessary. The reason for writing beautifully is to express respect for the person who will be expected to read it by presenting him or her with clear, well formed letters and word-shapes.

The children are encouraged to write longer, more complex compositions based on main-lesson themes and their own experience. Writing also includes instruction and practice in formal letters (thank you letters, requests and inquiries) and diaries as well as simple descriptions of nature moods. Out of the emergent writing of the children the teacher takes up issues of grammar and correct usage, sentence structure, punctuation, spelling etc., and provides instruction and guidance as opportunity presents itself.

The children are encouraged to read aloud and clear speaking is important for good spelling. *"The two skills complement one another ... By getting into the habit of listening properly you become inclined to remember the word-shape on the basis of the inner picture."* [22]

Spelling is systematically practised through guided word recognition, word families, similarities and letter combinations, e.g. ee, oo, ou, gh, th, st, sh.

READING

Reading progresses to the differentiation of reading material and reading for different purposes i.e. to understand instructions and tasks, to find information or read timetables. Children are encouraged to use reference material and regular reading lessons are introduced. Reading aloud is practised with an awareness of content and punctuation. A wide range of printed texts is made available. As in Class 2, a range of reading techniques is used including whole class reading, group reading, and individual reading, paired reading (child to child, child to adult). Graded reading schemes may be used in Classes 2 and 3 but the emphasis is on 'real' books and quality literature. In terms of text understanding the approach is essentially hermeneutic and contextual.

Checklists for literacy skills in Classes 1-3

Most children of normal ability range will be able to:

WRITING AND READING
1 recognise sounds, shapes and names of all vowels and consonants in capital letters and most of the lower case letters
1 know alphabetical order of letters
1 distinguish vowels from consonants
1 copy sentences accurately
1 write their own first name
1 spell a very few familiar words, such as 'the', 'in', 'to', 'and', and 'so'
1 know that writing is written-down speaking
1 know that some letters represent more than one sound
1 know that every word has at least one vowel
1 know that writing moves from left to right and from top to bottom
1 read and understand what they have written in the classroom
1/2 be acquainted with digraphs 'th', 'ch' and 'sh'
1/2 make plurals by adding s or es

2 recognise, write and read printed letters and cursive script
2 be able to read and spell simple consonant digraphs, vowel digraphs and 2-letter consonant blends

2 be able to read and spell using the soft c rule and magic e rule
2 add –ing or -ly
2 spell using 3-letter blends
2 read, write and spell correctly days of week, months, numbers and other familiar topics and words such as was, were, are, said, their/there, have
2/3 write short descriptions or accounts of recent events or stories
2/3 can read and spell letter combinations in common words
  • sh, th, ch, wh, ph, gh
  • ee, oo, ei, ea, ai
  • ow, ew, aw
  • y as vowel and consonant
2/3 read with developing enthusiasm

3 use the soft g rule
3 spell vowel and vowel/consonant digraphs
3 spell simple compound words
3 recognise common homophones
3 write thank-you letters
3 write in well-formed cursive script
3 read aloud texts containing mainly familiar words in context
3 read simple books aloud and silently.

GRAMMAR
2/3 know by hearing when a sentence starts and stops
2/3 know how to use capital letters, full stop, recognise questions

3 recognise and characterise verb, noun, adjective and adverb e.g. an adjective describes a noun, an adverb tells us how we do something

SPEAKING AND LISTENING
1 recite in chorus
1 speak short verses alone
1 listen to the teacher and other children
1 follow verbal instructions given by teachers in all subjects
1 speak simple speech exercises and tongue twisters in chorus
1 speak multiplication tables in chorus
1 recall main points of story told by the teacher
1 share news with the class

3 recite poem alone
3 recall more complex events and stories
3 give an explanation of what they are doing to an inquirer
3 perform in short plays

Classes 4 to 8

During the first three classes literacy skills have tended to be wholly integrated. From Class 4 onwards there is an increasing differentiation of skills practice. As more time tends to be devoted to literacy skills, it is important to maintain the cultivation of spoken language through recitation and speech exercises, reporting and describing, discussing and listening.

Class 4

SPEAKING AND LISTENING

During Class 3 the children gradually became more detached from their wish to imagine their surroundings through imaginative stories told by their class teacher. Now, in Class 4, they turn much more directly towards nature and the world as it appears to external perception. As well as reciting seasonal nature poems, they now also enjoy poems that tell of human beings who are 'street-wise' or even 'wise' in the loftier sense. [23] Poems relating to the main-lesson topics, such as the study of animals, local geography and history are chosen for recitation.

The main subject for the narrative content of the main-lesson is legends, tales and songs from the Icelandic epic *The Edda*. Speaking and stepping the rhythms of alliterative poetry gives the children the experience that speech carried on the breath can be filled by the rhythm of a slower or faster heartbeat, depending on the content. In speaking alliterative poetry, the will element in speech is strengthened, an experience which enables the children to bring their feeling life into strong connection with their breath and pulse, which has the effect of centring them. The artistic element of the poetic imagery prevents this from being a merely physical activity. Being centred, the children can stand more firmly in life and orientate themselves in relation to their environment.

NARRATIVE CONTENT AND READING MATERIAL

Apart from these smaller selections from *The Edda*, the legends of the Norse gods and heroes provide the main story content in Class 4. After the creation story of the Old Testament, the children now enjoy the great creation images from the Norse Myths. Their initial question: 'Which is true?' is easy to answer. Both are true. Although a high mountain looks different depending on whether you approach it from the South, North, East or West, it remains the same mountain. Considerations like this lay the foundations for a willingness to look at things from several angles.

Should Norse Myths be told in all Waldorf schools, or just those within the Northern European cultural orbit? The consensus appears to be yes, but... The myths of the Norse Gods do appear to have a universality to them whilst the legends of the Heroes are much more related to the specific folk soul and culture. Perhaps tales of 'local heroes' would be more appropriate here. In the UK, the story of *Beowolf* can be told or read in translation, as can the stories contained in *Harald's Saga*, which recalls the life of Harald Hardrada, a key figure in the events of 1066. The historical background of the Vikings can also be a theme appropriate in this class.

GRAMMAR

Among the many comments he made about how the learning child relates to grammar, Steiner also pointed to a link between grammar and the ego or 'I'. In a talk on language given shortly before the Waldorf School opened in Stuttgart, he said: *"By entering consciously into the structure of language one learns a great deal from the genius of language,"* and this, he said, was *"of the greatest importance"*. A little further he then added: *"We owe to language in particular much of what we have in our ego, through which we feel we are a personality."*

When appropriate methods were used in the classroom, he continued, the children's ego-feeling is awakened in the right way. *"If it is wrongly awakened it actually fans the flames of egoism, but if you awaken it in the right way it fans the flames of the will ... for selflessness and for living together with the surrounding world."* [24]

Five years later, in a teachers' meeting on 19th June 1924 he spoke of this again: *"Working on language in connection with grammar is related to ego-development ... Not that you should ask how to develop the ego from grammar; it is the grammar itself that does that."* [25] When the children *"consciously live their way into the structure of language"* they become aware of the great link that embraces all human beings who share their language with them.

The basic structure of grammar is of course common to all languages. Universal Grammar, or generative grammar is, according to modern linguistic theory since Chomsky, innate and facilitates language acquisition. Raised to consciousness, grammar gives the child an archetypal experience of relationships in the world, as they are expressed by the different parts of speech.

The theme for Class 4 is tenses: *"It is just this time that one endeavours to call up in the children a clear idea of the tenses and all that comes to expression by changing the form of the verb... A child must clearly feel that she cannot say 'the man ran' when she means 'the man has run'; ... that she acquires a feeling for when to say 'the man stood' and when to say' the man has stood'... Forming language plastically is what we should practise in the mother tongue when the child is about ten years old, a feeling for the plastic formative quality of language."* [26]

In English the children need to become aware of the qualities of the main tenses, past, present and how the future is formed. The forms of modal verbs and auxiliaries, *to do, to be, to have, can, may*, etc., can be learned in connection with the tenses as well as question forms and negatives.

In answer to a question about how to treat the perfect tense in German, Steiner said: *"I would pull out all the stops in discussing with the children the parallel between the past and the perfect. What is a perfect human being, a perfect table? I would bring out the connection between what is perfect and finished and the perfect tense."* [27]

In English it is clear that we must find equivalent phenomena. The distinctions between the simple past tense and present perfect or past perfect would be examples. The formation of all the tenses, past, present and future should be taught, including the use of simple and continuous forms.

Prepositions are words indicating direction. Spatial

relationship and locality are also themes that belong in Class 4. Initially the literal spatial relationships indicated by *in, on, at, above, beyond*, etc., can be explored. These need to be physically experienced in space and can be pictorially represented e.g. through a picture of workers in a house, on the roof, at the corner, going into the cellar etc. Other grammatical topics which can be taken include the use of adverbial phrases of time, place and manner; sentence structure and the identification of the main clause. In punctuation the use of question and exclamation marks can be taught as well as the use of the comma.

WRITING AND READING
Essay writing still chiefly involves recounting accurately in writing what has been heard verbally. Formal letters are also practised, e.g. writing to a farmer, a baker, a jeweller about a possible visit to their business premises by the class. The children also learn to write with a fountain pen, perhaps having first made and used a goose feather quill.

In spelling the children should be learning groups of related words and learning common but difficult words such as *beautiful, experience, create*. They should also be taught to guess the pronunciation and spelling of unfamiliar words. The children are shown how to use a dictionary.

The children write accounts of the stories and experiences they have had in school and in daily life. They write descriptions of animals, scenes from history, their impressions of local landscapes, journeys they have made and so on. Specialised vocabulary and terminology may be provided by the teacher on the board. They may also copy important texts such as sayings and quotations, poems and the texts of songs. Dictation in a range of modes remains an important tool for listening, spelling and word recognition.

Class readers may be used but these are supplemented by access to a wide range of literature in the classroom and in the library.

Class 5 (age 10-11)

SPEAKING AND LISTENING
Most children enter their eleventh year while they are in Class 5. This can mean a final blossoming of child-like gracefulness and musical mobility before rather more coarse tendencies set in during the time leading up to puberty. The relaxed openness of Class 5 pupils allows the teacher to offer them all kinds of variety in terms of texts for recitation. In addition, their first history main-lesson suggests excerpts from early oriental cultures, such as the Bhagavadgita, the Mahabharata, the Vedas, or Sumerian, Akkadian and Egyptian hymns and prayers.

Such literature coming from so far away both in time and place astonishes the pupils and helps prepare them to be open to other cultures and also respect and appreciate them.

Poems continue to be recited and where appropriate verses in hexameter form can be taken. Prose texts from the Gospels can also be learned by heart and recited. Another field of oral work is word pictures, in which children describe a plant or the mood of a particular landscape.

NARRATIVE CONTENT AND READING MATERIAL
Stories and reading material are taken from ancient eastern cultures (Hindu legends of Krishna and Arjuna, the Sumerian legends of Gilgamesh, Egyptian and Greek mythology) up to the time of classical Antiquity, as well as stories from the Celtic tradition. There can be alternation between the teacher telling a story and the class reading in chorus, or exercises in reading aloud and listening. Steiner also suggested describing scenes from history a year before history lessons proper begin. It is up to the teacher to make a selection.

GRAMMAR
There is plenty to work with here in Class 5. Both now and in the near future it is important not to make grammar too technical and full of rules. The emphasis is on usage and the qualities that each grammatical form express. One should first explore the phenomenon before labelling it. Having introduced a terminology, it is important, though, that it is consistent and mutually agreed with the foreign language teachers. Successful foreign language teaching depends to a large extent on the grasp of grammatical phenomena that the children acquire through understanding their own native tongue. Many colleagues prefer the normal grammatical terms to avoid confusion and to make life easier for the teachers of foreign languages. In fact it is very useful if the class teachers first consult with the foreign language teachers on what aspects of grammar need to be emphasised as a support for the foreign languages.

The active and passive voices can now be considered. Attention is paid to the new role played by the subject, which retains its subject-character in an entirely new situation. That the passive voice is willing to leave the doer unnamed is only touched on, without any discussion at this stage.

Another important grammatical phenomenon that belongs in Class 5 is direct speech. When children report what others have said they usually use a lively mix of direct and indirect speech. They should now become aware of what this entails: *"At this time, try to get the children to report freely in direct speech not only on what they have seen and heard but also on what they have heard and read. Let them report as they would if what they say were within quotation marks. Try to let the children practise distinguishing between telling their own opinion and reporting the opinion of someone else. Then do the same in writing; let the children make a clear distinction between what they themselves think or have seen and what they have heard another person say. In connection with this you can also try to perfect the use of the punctuation this entails."* [28]

The children must differentiate between their own opinion and the opinion of others. They must pay attention to repeating exactly what the other person has said. Using direct speech correctly provides a foundation for the coming year, when the indirect speech will be studied.

The qualitative difference between the simple and

progressive forms should be clearly distinguished with many oral examples e.g. *I drink milk but I am not drinking at the moment.* Negatives and questions forms are also important to discuss and explore. Functional words such as pronouns, conjunctions and the comparison of adverbs and adjectives (a pupil once asked 'isn't there anything better than *best*?') can be discussed. It is always important to draw attention to the qualities that sentences have by including conjunctions or pronouns (do we know who *he* is in the sentence, *he is not here*?) Sentence structure can be ordered around subject and predicate, direct and indirect object (*who did what to whom and how*?). The concept of subject, predicate, direct and indirect object and adverbial phrase can be introduced.

Prepositions can also be introduced which have a temporal quality (*in 5 minutes, at 2.23 a.m., around 7, within the hour, up to midnight* etc.). In punctuation, the use of commas (again!), quotation marks, colons, semi-colons, hyphens and brackets should be introduced (or revised).

WRITING AND READING
Essay writing in Steiner Waldorf schools in Classes 5 to 8 contains aspects that differ from what is done in other schools. The main-lessons in these classes (e.g. botany, geometry, geography, acoustics etc.) provide material that requires clear description (e.g. of experiments) and characterisation. Events such as class outings provide the opportunity for requesting information and making arrangements that can be encompassed in examples of business letters. The aim of all this is to learn how to state intentions and wishes succinctly and with clarity, to strengthen willingness and ability to listen accurately to what is said, and to school alert powers of observation. This helps the children develop the will to make reports that accord with the facts and are not embroidered with arbitrary imaginative detail.

> *You will cultivate the children's idealism in a far better way if you do not approach it in too brutally direct a manner ... If during this period (13th to 15th year) you introduce the children to what is done in real life they will retain their healthy relationship to the idealistic needs of their soul. This will only be extinguished if these needs are senselessly drawn on while the children are still too young.* [29]

This is what Steiner said in connection with writing essays at this age. Descriptive essays on experiences the youngsters have had and subjects that call on their imagination do not come into play until the Upper School when their capacity to form judgments is developing.

Checklists for literacy skills in Classes 4 – 5

Most children of normal ability range will be able to:

SPEAKING AND LISTENING
4   Perform in a play and speak several lines individually, increasing in length by the end of Class

5 and be able to perform on stage before the school community.

WRITING AND READING
4   know how to use a dictionary
4   write with an ink pen
4   write an accurate account of events or stories heard in class
4   write a formal letter
4   know irregular plurals
4   know more irregular families of spellings
4   know remaining vowel and vowel/consonant digraphs
4   make a reasonable guess at unknown words in a text
4/5 read confidently and independently

5   read aloud fluently with awareness of punctuation including direct speech
5   take down a dictation on a known subject with reasonable accuracy
5   use a dictionary to find unfamiliar words for both spelling and meaning
5   use of common suffixes and prefixes

GRAMMAR
4   use the comma and exclamation and question marks

5   use quotation marks in direct speech, colon and semi-colon, and appropriate use of paragraphs
5   know use and character of all major parts of speech: nouns, verbs, adjectives, adverbs, prepositions (time and space) the articles, conjunctions, interjections
5   use simple and continuous verb forms in all tenses, including present perfect and forms of the future, in questions and negatives and active and passive moods

Class 6

SPEAKING AND LISTENING
'A good strong diet' is needed in Class 6. Ballads, in particular, are likely to satisfy with their dramatic effects. Examples include: *Horatius* (from the *Lays of Ancient Rome*) by Thomas Macaulay, *The Pied Piper of Hamelin* by Robert Browning, *Meg Merrilies* by John Keats, *Sir Patrick Spens*, *John Barleycorn* by Robert Burns, *The Rider at the Gate* by John Masefield, *Schaffhausen* by Brien Masters, *Via Dolorosa* by Brien Masters.

In addition to these, it is good to go on letting the children recite nature poems in keeping with the seasons, traditional and modern ones e.g. *When Icicles Hang by the Wall*, *Love's Labour Lost*, Shakespeare, *The Scarecrow* by Walter de la Mare, *The Snow Storm* by Ralph Waldo Emerson, *Michaelmas Song* by A. C. Harwood, *Spring the Travelling Man* by Winifred Letts, *Winter* by Christina Rossetti, *Sea Fever* by John Masefield and countless others. (The examples given here are only intended to exemplify the range.)

Public speaking and elementary rhetoric can be

taught through the presentation of short talks as well as through preparing and delivering exhortations, commands, directives (the pupils are studying Rome!). Steiner was keen that the pupils should experience the power of language to express beauty as well as power.

NARRATIVE CONTENT AND READING MATERIAL
According to Karl Stockmeyer's record of what Steiner had to say about this, it would be good to tell scenes from more recent history. In practice most class teachers tell stories from Roman and Medieval history. Longer prose works are suitable for reading.

GRAMMAR
In the original curriculum, Steiner laid great stress on the subjunctive mood (Konjunctiv in German), especially in connection with indirect speech, for which the foundations have been laid with direct speech in Class 5. However, Steiner's real interest in connection with the subjunctive becomes obvious in an example he gave:

> We now endeavour to give the children a strong stylistic sense of what the subjunctive mood is. As far as possible we should demonstrate this by means of examples to help them distinguish between what can be directly stated and what has to be expressed by means of the subjunctive. A strong feeling for the inner mobility of language must become a part of the children's sense of language. [30]

The original example given in the passage above had the distinction between the statements, *I'll see to it that my sister learns to walk* (i.e. I'll personally ensure it happens) and *I'm concerned that my little sister learns to walk* (i.e. I expect someone else to see to it). (Ich sorge dafur, dass mein Schwesterchen laufen lerne or Ich sorge dafur, dass mein Schwesterchen laufen lernt). The distinction is not as apparent translated into English. However when we report what someone else has said and cast doubt on the statement, or distance ourselves from it, there is an equivalent shift of focus and identification with the deed. *'I will come'* becomes in indirect speech: *'he said he would come'*. This can also imply: *'he said he would come but I don't believe he will'*.

The third sentence depends on different spoken emphasis (on *said* rather than *would*). This subtle distancing can be experienced by the pupils once they have mastered the technicalities of indirect speech and reporting verbs (such as: *she offered the opinion that; he countered with; they denied strongly; we asserted our rights; he went on to say; she added* etc.). The subjunctive as such, is better dealt with in Class 7 or 8.

In Class 6 one can discuss transitive and intransitive verbs as well as infinite forms. Present perfect can be introduced as an experience or state which began in the past and continues in the present, lasting, with all probability into the foreseeable future e.g. *I have lived in York for seven years (and do not have plans to move away)*.

The difference in meaning between the modal verbs *can, may, should, must, have to, would, ought, should* be (may/can be) explored. This provides excellent opportunity for indirect moral education in relation to

necessity, possibility, duty and lawfulness, capacity, desire and wish.

Sentence parsing can be taught in Class 6. The students enjoy this analytical activity, drawing up columns of categories. Relative clauses can be identified as well as adverbial phrases of tune, place, manner, reason etc.

It is also useful (and welcome) at this age to teach abbreviations of all kinds as well as the common symbols used in business letters and on keyboards.

ESSAY WRITING
Here what was begun in Class 5 continues. There is now more stress on accurately describing experiments whilst at the same time imaginatively and dramatically retelling scenes from history. The children also write descriptions in connection with nature studies and geography. Spelling continues to be practised.

Class 7

SPEAKING AND LISTENING
In keeping with the pupils' awakening sense of their own personality, it is now important in the lessons that the teacher should begin to reveal something of his or her own personal relationship to lyric poetry, including modern lyric poetry. If some of the pupils are also beginning to have preferences for good poems and poets, these are also included in the lessons as recitation material.

NARRATIVE CONTENT AND READING MATERIAL
Texts are chosen which widen the children's horizons with regard to other peoples and cultures. The history main-lessons provide an orientation for text material, especially stories related to the Age of Discovery and the Renaissance. The pupils are encouraged to read around the subjects that relate to the main-lesson and to do some independent research into topics that support the classroom work. They are also encouraged to read widely, both non-fiction and works of literature. Short book summaries which the pupils either give as verbal or written reports help stimulate interest and prompt others in the class to extend their reading.

GRAMMAR
By and large there is considerable flexibility within the curriculum for Classes 7 and 8. Many of the topics here described can be done in either class. As usual in his *Three Lectures on the Curriculum*, Steiner is direct and specific with his advice for this class. *"One must try to develop in the child, in sentence building, a truly plastic capacity for giving expression to wish, wonder and surprise. The child should form sentences which really do bear an inner relationship to the form of the feeling itself."* [31] However, Steiner advised against *"mistreating poems or other literature"* for this purpose. The children are asked to express 'a wish' or 'something they admire' and then try to formulate this in suitable sentences, *"Then, by comparing the sentence expressing a wish with one expressing wonder, one brings to light the inner formative power in the language and develops it further."* [32]

Grammatically you first draw attention to the difference between a purely indicative statement *'I want ...'* and a subjunctive one *'If only I had ...'*, *'If only I could ...'*, *'If only I were able ...'*, *'If only it would ...'*. You look at how you can intensify the indicative statement by means of adverbs: *'I so very much want ...'*. The interesting auxiliary verbs *'to be able to'*, *'to have to'*, *'to want to'* etc. are brought to the fore. In expressions of astonishment or admiration the contrast between a statement-clause and a feeling-clause initially worked with in the first grammar main-lesson in Class 3 now reappears, but at a much higher level.

There is an educational concern that can be recognised in all this. To wish, to be astonished, to admire – these are expressions of feelings familiar to pupils in Class 7. When such feelings are raised into consciousness in the apparently neutral realm of language, they begin to realise how close wishing is to immoderate or unrealistic desire, or how astonishment and admiration could turn into fascination or being 'carried away'. The full palette of moods and their combinations can be explored in their linguistic expression; wonder and devotion; astonishment with a hint of fear or with scepticism; shock leading to fear or shock leading to humour; urges and desires as opposed to longing; encouragement with a hint of challenge; denial as renunciation or sacrifice or denial as self-defence; resignation with acceptance, or resignation with regret or even ill will. There are many such examples of soul moods which can be explored thus helping the young adolescents to begin to map out the contours of their inner life and given their feelings words.

Understanding sentence structure is important for the same reasons as those just described. The conventions of word order can be almost endlessly modified to imply subtly different meanings. [33] The meta-level of meaning is deeply interesting to pupils at this age. That is to say, they are interested in individualising what they say, finding their own voice and style and also being able to hide behind the mask of language so as not to reveal their own inner feelings.

One can show that in its moods (imperative, indicative, and subjunctive) the sentence expresses the standpoint of bodily-sense immediacy, of balanced inner action, and of ideal, spiritual possibility and potential.

Another aspect of this exploration of the use of language is to explore the realm of metaphor and imagery in which pictures are used to represent other implicit experiences. The progression from concrete experience of words in relation to concepts in the Lower School is transformed into metaphorical meaning. The poetic expression *the moon was a ghostly galleon,* can assume little metaphorical significance if the listener has not first learned to associate concrete images with each of these words, *moon, ghostly, galleon.* The same is true of poetic usage that relies more on the sense impressions of the sound of the words, such as *where the wind's like a whetted knife.* The pupils first have to have been immersed in the aural experience of the pure sounds, especially in eurythmy before the full force of the poetry can be experienced. Expressionist images such as Ted Hughes' line: *"The wind flung a magpie away and a black-backed gull bent like an iron bar*

slowly" rely for their effectiveness on direct sensory experience of wind, magpies and seagulls as well as the metaphorical power of word sounds and images.

In Classes 7 and 8 such aspects of poetry can be brought to expression through speaking and listening. It is not necessary yet to analyse form and function and aesthetic principles. That should come in the Upper School. At this stage language as a phenomenon needs to be experienced. The other side of this is practising the craft of writing. That means getting punctuation right. It means finding the right formal techniques for different purposes, be they letters to the bank manager, accurate eye-witness accounts of real events, factual summaries, commentaries, notes and so on.

ESSAY WRITING

There will be little change as far as essay writing is concerned, but a new aspect can be introduced. In answer to a question in one of his meetings with teachers, Steiner suggested on the spur of the moment: *"Essays on subjects such as 'the steam engine, a witness to human strength', immediately followed by 'the steam engine, a witness to human weakness'. Give them subjects like this in quick succession."* [34]

Though we would not necessarily take this suggestion literally, the implication is clear. The point is to look at issues of historical or social relevance from contrasting angles, and perhaps even weigh one against the other. The pupils need to work on how to observe existing facts and consider what can be said that directly relates to these. Both in writing and orally the children need to give accurate descriptions of processes, events and other observations. The children should be given guidance on essay writing style. *"Use their mistakes to show them what is correct, also stylistically."* [35] was Steiner's advice.

Class 8

SPEAKING AND LISTENING

On the whole what was suitable for Class 7 continues to be in order for Class 8. The content is best prepared in advance or brought in 'incidentally' while the poem is being learnt, so that the recitation can be effective through the poem's overall artistic form rather than weighed down by questions of meaning. Themes should relate to the other main-lessons such as modern history and should contain a strong biographical and emotional content. Examples include *Survivors,* by Alan Ross, *Ghosts, Fire, Water,* by James Kirkup, *Bayonet Charge,* by Ted Hughes, *I, Too Sing America,* by Langston Hughes.

NARRATIVE CONTENT AND READING MATERIAL

This follows the point mentioned above, biographies, historical texts and novels portraying aspects of modern history.

Steiner repeatedly emphasised the suitability of certain works for 13 to 14-year-olds by Schiller, Herder or Goethe. Of course only brief extracts were suggested. In English one might draw on quality literature from the 19th Century, Dickens, Melville, Hardy, or passages from non-fiction works such as Darwin's

Voyage of the Beagle, Thoreau's *The Natural Man*, extracts from *Chief Seattle's Speech*, the opening lines of Jefferson's *Declaration of Independence*, passages from Tom Pain's *Rights of Man*, or Martin Luther King's speeches. When the pupils are carefully introduced to the language of those times without any pressure or hurry, they feel they are being taken seriously. They sense that their thoughts can gain wider dimensions on the basis of these unaccustomed modes of expression and that new fields are becoming accessible to them. They can then approach other prose literature more critically with the powers and skills they have thus developed. The pupils are encouraged to research their own individual interests and this can become a project for the whole year, culminating in a written and verbal presentation.

Class 8 can also now make its first acquaintance with a major drama production. They will of course have performed plays as a class throughout the class teacher period. The difference in Class 8 is the level of 'professionalism' that should be striven for. The way must be paved with a lot of preparation if this is to be a full theatrical experience. It is important for the teacher to first tell the story of the action before getting the children to take different parts and reading the scenes. If a piece of classical drama is chosen, the unaccustomed style of the language will be more easily assimilated in the overall story and the characters are already living in the pupils' imaginations. It is still possible at this age for the class teacher to write or adapt their own play, with parts and themes tailored to the class' needs and abilities. Though perhaps lacking in high literary merit such ventures have the major advantage of being suited to a particular group of pupils. In terms of casting, it is also still appropriate to cast pupils in roles through which they will have a positive challenge to develop aspects of their personality. Giving the leading roles to those most theatrically gifted may lead to a more polished performance but may miss many opportunities for pedagogical development. In the Upper School it is more appropriate to cast plays according to ability in the service of the play. In the Middle School the play serves the cast as a social community.

GRAMMAR

Sentence structure can be analysed from the perspective of style and sample sentences can be written in different styles to emphasise various elements or create a range of moods e.g. epic, descriptive, lyric, dramatic, questioning, commanding, legal, nonsense, satirical, obscure. Meter, rhythm and rhyme can be studied and applied to the pupil's own poetic efforts.

Conditional sentences and if clauses can be introduced to describe chance situations, expectations, possibilities, theoretical or impossible situations or putting oneself in another person's situation. All of which help the self-preoccupied adolescent to see other perspectives, empathise or even speculate about others. The work in Class 7 on figures of speech such as metaphor, analogy, simile, proverb can be continued and discussed in connection with style. Each of these forms expresses a complex situation in the form of a picture.

Qualities familiar in one area of life can shed light on other, apparently unrelated, areas. Apart from deepening a sense for language quality and extending vocabulary at a time when young people are losing their connection to the language, of their environment, such figures of speech open up the meta-levels of ideals and ideas as realities. Of course the abuse of words equally belongs here in the discussion of cliché, jargon, euphemism, slang and swear words. At this age one can discuss the brutal, sexist and racist attitudes that common swear words imply.

Idiomatic speech forms can be studied, using extracts from literature to exemplify them. The richness of phrasal verbs, in particular can be explored (*turn in, turn up, turn on, turn out, turn down* etc.).

There is another very attractive aspect of language and literature that is also connected with 'interest in other people', one that has not been touched on by many other education writers. Steiner pointed to this in 1922 when he suggested that one might enter into the *"characteristic, moral images in the style. This can take you a long way. For example look at a reading passage from the point of view of the temperaments. I do not mean the content, but the style. You can speak of a melancholic style or a choleric style. Take no notice of the content or even the poetic content and look solely at sentence structure."* [36]

This poses a double task for the teacher. First you have to awaken the pupils' sense for the four temperaments by means of simple descriptions or examples. Then it is a matter of finding reading material in which one or other of the temperaments really does show up in the sentence structure. These are to be found, though not easily (Edward Lear's *Limericks* provide some examples). By questioning and testing what are the style elements that make a text phlegmatic, choleric, sanguine or melancholic, the pupils are led to yet another angle from which to look at sentence structure. In our experience this is a relatively unresearched field.

SPEAKING AND LISTENING

The pupils can now be encouraged to research topics and give short talks to the class. The teacher can advise them about sources and literature. Among many other possibilities, the discussions on the temperaments can provide stimulating ideas for essays. Such discussions can take the form of formal debates where a topic is chosen and individuals argue for or against a given position. Such topics should have a close relation to reality, yet leave the pupils open to argue a case they do not necessarily support. This is an aspect of advocacy that has important moral and social functions. The ability to represent someone else's situation or view to the best of your ability is an important skill. Drama exercises are also fertile ground at this age for practising self-expression.

Checklists for literacy skills in Classes 6, 7 & 8

READING

6   read books in a range of styles and give a verbal summary of the main content

7	give a written summary of a book, highlighting main characters or events in the narrative
7	use books as reference resource for independent study
7	use a thesaurus and etymological dictionary
7	use a bilingual dictionary in French and German (if learned as foreign language)

WRITING

6	write a formal business letter or inquiry for information
7	write in different styles including: an account of a scientific experiment, a personal diary, a description evoking a specific mood (early morning in winter, anger or frustration, curiosity about some unresolved situation), a formal letter (e.g. complaint), adventure story, short poem
7	make notes summarising a spoken presentation, following a recall session
7	write an essay on a theme discussion in lesson summarising the main points or highlighting a chosen aspect

GRAMMAR

6	understand the main parts of a sentence: subject, predicate, object, indirect object and adverbial phrase
6	understand different meanings of modal verbs: can, may, should, ought, would
7	use of reported speech
7	use of the conditional forms and If clauses
7/8	be familiar with use and meaning of the following figures of speech: simile, metaphor, image, analogy, proverb, aphorism, euphemism
8	use of subordinate clause, relative clauses
8	be aware of poetic style e.g. characterise lyric, epic, dramatic poetry
9	be aware of the distinction between formal language, idiom, slang, obscenity, jargon

SPEAKING AND LISTENING

6	be able to recite a poem alone
6	give a short talk using notes
7	be able to give a short talk on a prepared topic freely using notes only as a prompt
8	be able to perform in a full length play
8	be able to debate a chosen theme

Classes 9 to 12

General aspects and aims for Classes 9 to 12

There are usually two English language main-lessons in each year from Class 9 to Class 12.

The content of the main-lessons as stated here is not binding. What is more important than sticking to traditionally successful main-lessons would be a clear study of the children in a particular class, on which a choice of new content would be based. The content here suggested has been tried and tested over many years, so any new content would need to be subjected to equally thorough-going investigation.

The few literary suggestions made should be taken as examples only. We have intentionally refrained from setting up a list of recommended literature in order to avoid any mis-understanding that might assume there to be a sanctioned reading plan. There cannot be and must not be an approach to literature to which teachers are expected to adhere. Apart from which, such an approach would anyway need to be varied to suit different cultural contexts. The examples given are based on the Upper School curriculum used in the UK.

Class 9

Points of view and general themes:

When the youngsters enter the Upper School their eight-year orientation towards the personality of their class teacher ends. His or her place is now taken by the specialist teachers whose subjects, material and methods are inter-related and suit the specific age (15) of the youngsters. Teaching is increasingly addressed to the awakening powers of thought and judgment, which call for a stronger training of the intellect and logic. More consciously than hitherto the pupils experience disappointments in relation to the trust they have had up to now in beauty, truth and goodness. They grow irritated with the world around them. In adults as well as themselves they notice a discrepancy between what they say and what they do. Since inwardly they are oriented towards ideals while they search for the truth, they tend to react radically to any inadequacy. On the other hand they are extremely sensitive to any slight, real or imaginary. They suffer as a result of their own inadequacy. While still strangers to themselves they wrestle with questions of sexuality, first love and the violent forces of sympathy and antipathy.

The educational task arising from all this is to strengthen the youngsters in the moral demands they make on the world while at the same time helping them come to terms with reality. English literature main-lessons in Class 9 deal with material, themes and topics that strengthen their youthful powers while at the same time making it possible to talk about these things. The existing and seemingly unbridgeable contrasts in the human world, which can be resolved in both tragical and comical ways, are presented as the task the suffering individual will have to face up to. By working consciously with language in both writing and reading the youngsters are given some means of bringing order into their impulsive, subjective feelings while also being led out of their inner world to the objective world around them. As well as working with themes in literature, the pupils are also given the opportunity to further develop their language skills both verbally and in written form.

Content suggestions:

FIRST MAIN-LESSON:
The history of drama from its ancient ritual origins to the development of modern theatre is studied. The main emphasis in early theatre is on Classical Greek drama, including the social, religious aspects and a description of the development of the Greek theatre. Usually at least one full play is studied such as Sophocles' *Antigone*. Medieval drama and in particular the Mystery and Morality plays are discussed including the historical background, the change from sacred to profane contexts through moving performance out of the church into the churchyard and from there onto the streets on pageant carts and the role of the Guilds in taking responsibility for the various scenes. Extracts in original language and modern translation can be taken from Cycles such as the York, Wakefield or Coventry to exemplify the typical range of style, from the highly stylised ritual of the Creation, through the slapstick comedy of Noah, through the pathos of the nativity to the social satire of the Shepherds (particularly Mac the Shepherd in the Wakefield cycle). A highlight of this main-lesson is the flowering of Elizabethan theatre and the life of William Shakespeare. A Shakespeare play would be studied, and scenes from other plays taken as examples. The main-lesson can conclude with a modern play. Obviously actual performance and visiting the theatre is an important complement to such a theme.

SECOND MAIN-LESSON:
Their radical views make Class 9 pupils inclined to regard their own standpoint as absolute, which narrows their horizon and perspective. Humorous works can have a loosening, releasing, distancing effect. Laughter is one of the essential psychological activities of the human being, leading to a sense of inner freedom. Examples from epic, dramatic and lyrical works provide an opportunity to discuss humour (comedies, novellas, anecdotes, jokes etc.). The (often painful) biography of a humorist can be introduced. The aim is not so much to work towards an 'aesthetic of the comical' as to show how the experience of humour can be another dimension in building one's personality and strength of character. Humour often approaches the tragic and closeness of comedy and tragedy should be explored. Sympathy, empathy and weeping are the polar opposites of laughter, to be regarded as reactions to initially alarming events. In working on the aesthetic aspects of both laughter and tears, comedy and tragedy, Class 9 pupils experience in both main-lesson periods how phenomena in the world are held in the field of tension that unites these two extremes. This gives them opportunities to modify their own absolutist views and make them more realistic.

ESSAYS AND LANGUAGE:
In addition to working with the content of literary works, the pupils of Class 9 also continue to study and cultivate their own use of language. Grammar is revised and firmed up, where possible in combination with foreign language studies. Spelling and punctuation are schooled, together with the different types of expression made possible by word usage and syntax. Subjective descriptive essays as well as objective reports and general essays are practised in equal amounts (compiling tables of contents, making précis of texts and conversations in class, reports, descriptions of pictures and experiments, re-telling something read aloud, descriptions of mood). Literary passages can be rewritten. Stylistic skills are developed in texts the pupils produce themselves.

Oral work includes conversations on a particular theme, dialogue, discourse taking into account the correctness of arguments and logical conclusions, and pupils' solo talks.

There are plenty of classical and humorous pieces that are suitable for recitation and fit in both with the content of the two main-lessons and with the inner situation of the pupils at this stage in their development.

Class 10

Points of view and general themes:

The pupils of Class 10 (age 16) begin to put aside the tumultuous and 'naïve' externalisations of Class 9. The difference between girls and boys becomes more apparent. They are extricating themselves from the group without yet being quite capable of standing alone. Class 9 pupils like to engage in quick-witted repartee. Class 10 pupils prefer to explain their views so that the reactions they get gives them a sense of their independence in which they find a degree of orientation. On the one hand, they are excessively concerned with their appearance while, on the other, they want to be accepted for what they are underneath this façade. On the whole Class 10 pupils emancipate themselves from their parents to a considerable degree. They experience independence, but also its price: loneliness. Language enters a crisis phase. The pupils are often *no longer* and at the same time *not yet* capable of expressing their inner experiences in a suitable way.

Content suggestions:

FIRST MAIN-LESSON:
The original curriculum foresaw working with Norse mythology through excerpts from *The Edda*, the *Volsunga Saga*, the *Iceland Saga*, the *Hildebrandslied* among other examples which can give the youngsters images that help them replace old blood ties with their own responsibility for themselves. The *Nibelungenlied* is treated in its entirety, with parts being read and others told by the teacher. In working with this the pupils discover, among other things, how a mythological picture-consciousness is transformed into literary pictures and then epic poetry. In addition they learn about the transition from being restricted within the Germanic tribe to a more Christian, ethical consciousness. In English, texts such as *Beowulf, The Seafarer, Tristan and Isolde* may be read. Medieval legends such as *Sir Gawain and the Green Knight, Piers the Ploughman* and tales from Chaucer are taken. The overriding theme, beyond the actual content of these

texts, is the transition from myth to literature. Some teachers study ancient mythologies such as the *Epic of Gilgamesh*, the *Old Testament*, the *Iliad* or *Odyssey* or Ovid's *Metamorphoses*. It is also possible to look at modern literature which has taken mythological themes or forms.

SECOND MAIN-LESSON:
One of the two Class 10 mother tongue main-lessons can offer Nibelungen motifs through other, including modern, works of literature.

The art of poetry main-lesson, which is a part of aesthetic studies, completes (see Study of Art/Aesthetics section) the Class 10 main-lesson programme.

By writing their own lyrical or other poems and working more independently with different forms of poetry the pupils are helped to make the transition from expressing themselves to encountering themselves, since the lyrical form makes it easier to describe one's own inner moods.

ESSAYS AND LANGUAGE:
In working with dialectical themes the pupils can practise discussing and representing opposing points of view. This can be done in writing as well as orally. Writing literary descriptions of characters in novels is also something dialectical, but bound to an existing text.

Class 11

Points of view and general themes:

The pupils of Class 11 have reached an age where they are interested in understanding more subtle psychological processes than the predominantly black and white, polarised perspective of Classes 9 and 10. Their social awareness increases as they stop merely condemning what is going on in the world and instead begin to think they might be able to contribute to changing things. Their own experiences are now increasingly included in the basis on which they make judgments. On the whole the irritations of post-puberty come to an end and they reach a new stage in finding themselves. They begin to take an interest in their own biography and are now more concerned with the path to be followed in developing their individuality than they are with the goal at the end of it. If Class 10 was more concerned with origins and causes, in Class 11 the students begin to experience boundaries and start to ask whether there is something higher from which they can take their orientation, some kind of 'lodestar', some meaning. During this phase the pupils search for their own task within the overall reality of society.

English lessons aim to meet this need for a more exact and differentiated perception of the different levels of language and seek to help the students grasp these in a more individual way. The lessons focus on a more intensive confrontation with the human being's inner world and the process by which he or she finds ego-awareness. The pupils become aware of their responsibility towards other individuals.

Content suggestions:

FIRST MAIN-LESSON:
Wolfram von Eschenbach's *Parzival* provides the focus for one of the two main-lessons. This most important work of medieval literature deals with the evolution of consciousness and is thus highly suitable for Class 11. There are several important aspects: the encounter with the medieval courtly world, the limitations (and possibilities) of a society that is guided by external principles; the Gawain sub-plot which reveals a whole cosmos of human abysses and tasks in connection with the relationship between 'you and me'; the *Parzival* story itself which concentrates on inwardness and the individual's path through the stages of failure, guilt, atonement and grace. The *Parzival* story has a suitable form for an educational context because it combines history with the general and the individual, and the developmental process is more easily seen than in a modern novel. The medieval world picture was strictly formed and inward-looking. In the story the search for self ends in an idealised way with Parzival's integration into the world. In addition, the story contains many archetypes of psychological development encountered by Western humanity.

This courtly work offers many opportunities for essays, exercises on language and structure, historical studies and questions of literary form.

SECOND MAIN-LESSON:
The second (or alternative) main-lesson could focus on *Parzival* motifs in the literature of the 19th and/or 20th Century. There are many archetypal themes that keep reappearing in literature where they are given new treatment and lead to different answers (the process of becoming an individual, the search for God, being hurt and inflicting pain, 'you and me', the quality of love, guilt and atonement, responsibility for the consequences of one's actions, tolerance). It is up to the teacher to decide whether to focus more on literary history or whether to make a more systematic study of themes in selected modern works.

It is quite common for English teachers to focus on the Romantic Period of English literature (often with reference to other European literature e.g. the German 'Sturm und Drang' period) against the background of social, artistic, political and philosophical trends. This includes the role of Imagination in artistic perception and creativity as well as the role of the Romantic Hero. This usually involves study of the lives and works of Blake, Wordsworth, Coleridge, Byron, Shelley, Keats and Clare.

ESSAYS AND LANGUAGE:
These build on the foundations already laid: description, dialectic essays, analysis of poetic and other texts, style exercises, etc.

Class 12

Points of view and general themes:

The pupils are about 18 years-old in Class 12.

Having passed through the stages of readiness for school followed by biological maturity, they now become socially mature. When they were little they let the adults lead them step-by-step into their 'inherited' world and integrate them into the values of their parents' social milieu. Later they rebelled against this, but now they are consciously seeking a society and a world that is worthy of the human being which they want to have a share in building. This step can be experienced either as a major step forward and great opportunity or as a profound existential crisis. What does it mean to live in today's world? Am I ready for it? To what do I want to direct my energies? Many questions arise concerning their hopes and fears about profession, partnership, lifestyle and aims in life. Behind these there is another, more profound, perhaps hidden questioning: What are the limits of human knowledge? What is the foundation of moral action? What is evil? What is the meaning of human life?

English lessons must take account of the impulses that arise out of all this. Modern problems are reflected on through the mirror of world literature. An overview of literature is given.

Content suggestions:

FIRST MAIN-LESSON:
One of the two main-lessons in the original German curriculum (not necessarily the first) is devoted to Goethe's drama for humanity *Faust*. More than almost any other work of German literature it characterises the modern human being's search for knowledge. All kinds of themes open up as the text is studied. Discussions arise in class about the question of scientific research and its moral and ethical limitations, about evil, about freedom and responsibility, about love, egoism, guilt, transcendency. Other works can be taken (and usually are in English speaking countries). These include major novels by:

I. Allende, *The House of Spirits*, K. Atkinson, *Scenes Behind the Museum*, S. Bellow, *The Rainman*, A. Camus, *The Outsider*, J. Conrad, *Lord Jim*, L. de Berniers, *Captain Corelli's Mandolin*, C. Dickens, *Hard Times*, F. M. Dostoievski, *Crime and Punishment*, R. Ford, *Wildlife*, E. Hemingway, *The Old Man and the Sea*, H. Hesse, *Magister Ludi/Glass Bead Game*, A. Huxley, *Brave New World*, Joyce, *The Dubliners*, F. Kafka, *The Trial*, N. Kazantzakis, *Christ Recrucified*, H. Melville, *Moby Dick*, A. Solzhenitsyn, *Cancer Ward*, L. Tolstoy, *Resurrection, Anna Karenina*, L. van der Post, *The Seed and the Sower*, T. Wilder, *The Bridge of San Louis Rey, The Eighth Day*.

Drama: J. Anhouilh, *Antigone*, S. Beckett, *Waiting for Godot*, A. Chekhov, *The Cherry Orchard*, Ch. Fry, *The Sleep of Prisoners*, J. Giraudoux, *Intermezzo*, H. Ibsen, *Brand, Peer Gynt*, A. Miller, *The Crucible*, J. B. Priestley, *An Inspector Calls*, T. Stoppard, *Rosenkranz and Guildernstern are Dead*.

SECOND MAIN-LESSON:
If one main-lesson is devoted entirely to a single work, the other can serve to give a survey either over English or else even world literature. Several great works can be presented individually or by comparing them with one another. It would seem sensible to concentrate mainly on modern works, but let us not forget older works that might provide something of *'what human beings need for life'* (R. Steiner). Literature (drama, epic, lyric) consists of creations by individual human beings, or even humanity as a whole, representing steps in human consciousness. Through literature these steps can be perceived by the readers and listeners. People's aesthetic judgment has changed over the centuries, so pupils would be well advised to keep an open mind as to modern literary endeavours. Rather than give the pupils a finalised view of poetry or literature, one should strengthen their sensitivity to different literary qualities. By allowing them to reflect and take their own measure of great works they will have been given an appropriate foundation for doing this.

ESSAYS AND LANGUAGE:
The pupils can be helped to improve their understanding of the written language by a number of exercises in text analysis through which they can learn to recognise historical characteristics and types of work. They can comment on and discuss these verbally and in essays written to set questions. The thoughts, language and imagination they put forward are suited to the subject in hand. If necessary, any exercises practised in Classes 9 to 11 can be continued.

The Class 12 Play

The high point in Class 12 is the public performance of a self-chosen, carefully discussed and artistically-produced play. The pupils take part in all the practical aspects of the production: making posters, costumes and scenery, preparing the music, and doing the stage directing and production themselves, quite apart from acting in it. It is impossible to overemphasise the importance of acting for each pupil's own biography as well as for the social community of the class. The drama gives the pupils an experience of the power of speech/language. Through wrestling with questions of rhetoric they gain a sense of how people can be influenced. This helps them be more aware of being manipulated, and it also gives them worthwhile yardsticks against which to measure and assess artistic productions of all kinds.

References
1 Skillen, N., "The Uses of Orality", in *Steiner Education* Vol. 32, No. 2, SSF, 1998.
2 Steiner, R., *The Renewal of Education*, lecture of 20th April 1920, SSF, 1981.
3 More detailed advice on the cultivation of oral skills and the introduction of writing and reading can be found in Avison, K., *A Handbook for Class Teachers*, SSF, 1995, and Rawson and Masters, *Towards Creative Teaching*, SSF, 1997.
4 Steiner, R., *The Renewal of Education*, op. cit. Lecture of 4th May 1920.
5 Steiner, R., *Three Lectures on the Curriculum*. Lecture of 6th September 1919, SSF, 1991.

6   Kainz, F., *The Psychology of Language*, Vol. 4. Stuttgart 1967, p52.

7   See Steiner, R., *The Renewal of Education*, op. cit. Lecture of 5th May 1920.

8   See Steiner, R., *The Kingdom of Childhood*, lecture 15th August 1924, RSP, 1982, also *The Renewal of Education*, op. cit. Lecture of 28th August 1920.

9   Steiner, R., *The Child's Changing Consciousness and Waldorf Education*. Lecture of 18th April 1923, AP, 1996.

10 The statements come from the lecture cited above, p94, AP, 1996.

11 Steiner, R., *Three Lectures on the Curriculum*. Lecture of 6th September 1919. SSF, 1991.

12 Ibid.

13 Steiner, R., *Waldorf Education for Adolescents*. Lecture of 15th June 1921. SSF, 1993.

14 Ibid.

15 Steiner, R., *The Child's Changing Consciousness*, op. cit. Lectures of 17th and 18th April 1923.

16 Rather than clutter the text with references to available reference material, a comprehensive bibliography for each subject is given at the end of the book.

17 Steiner, R., *The Renewal of Education*, op. cit. Lecture of 4th May 1920.

18 One of the best examples of this approach is described by Michael Rose in "Towards a Living Grammar" in *Paideia*, No. 17, September 1998, SSF. A series of articles in *Paideia*, No. 14, may also be of interest.

19 Steiner, R., *Practical Advice to Teachers*, op. cit. Lecture of 25th August 1919.

20 Ibid.

21 Steiner, R., *Waldorf Education for Adolescents*, op. cit. Lecture of 15th June 1921.

22 Steiner, R., *Practical Advice to Teachers*, op. cit. Lecture of 26th August 1919.

23 See Bibliography for anthologies of suitable poetry.

24 Steiner, R., *Practical Advice to Teachers*, op. cit. Lecture of 25th August 1919.

25 Steiner, R., *Conferences*, op. cit. 19th June 1924.

26 Steiner, R., *Three Lectures on the Curriculum*, op. cit.

27 Steiner, R., *Conferences*, op. cit., 12th June 1920.

28 Steiner, R., *Three Lectures on the Curriculum*, op. cit. Lecture of 6th September 1919.

29 Steiner, R., *Practical Advice to Teachers*, op. cit. Lecture of 26th August 1919.

30 Steiner, R., *Three Lectures on the Curriculum*, op. cit. Lecture of 6th September 1919.

31 Steiner, R., *Three Lectures on the Curriculum*, op. cit. Lecture 6th September 1919.

32 Ibid.

33 See Rawson and Masters, *Towards Creative Teaching*, op. cit., pp117-124, for examples of what is described here.

34 Steiner, R., *Conferences*, op. cit., 28th April 1922.

35 Ibid., 25th May 1923.

36 Steiner, R., Excerpts from *Two Education Lectures* from the German GA 302, typescript Z 418 in Rudolf Steiner House Library, London, lecture of 22nd June 1922.

EURYTHMY

Classes 1 to 12

General aspects and aims for Classes 1 to 8

When the original Waldorf School was founded, Steiner included eurythmy among the core subjects from the beginning. As an entirely new subject and one which is exclusively taught in Steiner Waldorf schools, eurythmy has a unique position within the curriculum. Applied appropriately at different ages and in different phases of development, it is an important aid to human development. Eurythmy is an art of movement that engages the whole human being, integrating bodily movement with movements that arise within soul, thus creating a harmonious relationship between the soul-spiritual element and the body.

In contrast with gymnastics, which has different aims with regard to taking hold of the body and making it fit, lithe, harmonious and free, the important thing about eurythmy is that it is essentially an artistic process. Gymnastics has to do with the whole human being coming into a relationship with the physical laws which govern space, those of levity and gravity and the balance the human being achieves between these two polarities. Eurythmy also works with the polarities of levity and gravity, not physically but essentially through the inner experience of the soul, with what can be called *ensouled* movement and is therefore more akin to dance than gymnastics.

What makes eurythmy an art is essentially twofold; the fact that on the one hand, the soul has to play a part in how the movements are carried out, and on the other hand the fact that the movements are based on objective laws as experienced through the soul. The aesthetic aspect arises through the artistic judgment that is exercised in interpreting the nature of the content chosen to be performed in eurythmy, usually poetry or music. The artist chooses from the range of musical, stylistic, linguistic elements and moods and choreographs and performs an interpretation. To say that the soul plays a part means that the feeling life is stimulated and out of this inner movement, outer movement arises. As an art, eurythmy also strives to be true to the objective qualities inherent in speech or music that it gives expression to. Though eurythmy is a performing art, it also has important educational and therapeutic aspects because practising its elements cultivates an integration and harmonisation of the movement organisation with the affective aesthetic realm of the soul. Eurythmy is also increasingly making an important contribution to adult education and can even be found in the work place, where enlightened employers recognise its valuable contribution to social processes and personal development. Eurythmy is a key element in initial teacher training within the Waldorf schools movement and continues as a regular part of on-going teacher development.

What is shaped emerges from movement and movement comes to rest in what is shaped. The human body is shaped by and through movement and it serves to reveal the ego or 'I' as a speaking being. In speaking and listening the movement organisation is actively stimulated, both as producer and receiver of the sound impulses. In speech, movement is focused and condensed to the point where it becomes acoustic energy that becomes audibly manifest in spoken sounds. Informing the shape, structure and content of what is spoken is the soul with its thoughts, feelings and intentions. In eurythmy, the inner movement that gives rise to speech is transformed and externalised in the form of outer movement. The body becomes an instrument to make this movement visible.

When human beings hear the spoken word, their movement organisation is activated and they begin to move in their soul; when they themselves speak their inner being becomes active in movement. Steiner was able to perceive these inner movement intentions that arise in the speaking and listening human being. Out of this he drew a language of gestures made by the whole human being, a 'visible speech'. It springs from a seed within the human being, and it shapes and educates the body as a means of expression, an instrument of expression. In the young child and probably in earlier times of human evolution, speech, song and human movements were once an all-embracing unity. Both during the course of individual development and through human evolution, these elements separate out. It is the task of eurythmy to reintegrate these elements into a new higher synthesis.

Eurythmy is the articulation in movement and gesture (incorporating other elements such as colour through costume and lighting) of the stream of movement, raised to conscious form through the soul. It is a language of movement with its own alphabet comprising archetypal gestures representing the spoken sounds, both vowels and consonants, as well as the tones of the musical scales and the intervals. It possesses its own lexis, comprising complex gestures expressing concepts such as soul moods, colours or the distinctive qualities of thinking, feeling or willing. Furthermore eurythmy has a formal syntax in the form of the elements of its choreography, movements in space which both integrate the elements of individual tones or sounds, the lexical elements into coherent phrases, sentences or melodies. These syntactical elements can also be used to express the equivalent of grammatical forms such as question, statement, command or determining qualities such as major or minor keys in music.

Each vowel gesture expresses the sound and colouring of a specific quality of soul (astonishment, marveling, asserting oneself, fear, joy etc.). Each consonant movement shows a specific force that differentiates and shapes. Human beings, especially children, when they are open to their experiences, enter into the varying movements of enlivening formative forces. In the swishing wind, for example, they may experience the sound represented by the letter 'S', in the movement of waves in water 'W', or in the growth and unfolding movements of plants 'L'. Every sound of speech expresses itself in a characteristic archetypal form and specific movement.

The rhythmical movement of speech is another element that shows in the metre of a verse (e.g. hexameter), the rise and fall, the repetition of sounds (rhyme). The rhythm of speech movements lives in the dynamic of the breath. Breathing is contracting and expanding, damming up and releasing.

The human physical form musical laws and relationships within the proportions of the skeleton. Being able to hear the formative elements in music, Steiner taught how the notes and intervals could be expressed in gestures, thus making music manifest as 'visible singing' through bodily gestures, and especially through the arms, filled with the soul element. The inner feeling, for example, produced on hearing the interval of the fourth can be translated into a gesture formed by the hands and arms. This is not merely a subjective response but is intrinsic to the physical organism. The artistic element arises in the inner experience that accompanies the process and in the application of the gesture to a specific moment in a piece of music. Naturally eurythmy does not translate every element in a poem or piece of music but selects what expresses the chosen interpretation, just as a painter chooses a spectrum of colours from the entire palette to express certain qualities or moods of her subject.

Eurythmy is taught in groups, though as a therapy it is usually taught in one to one situations. It requires its own specialised spaces, ideally incorporating a sprung wooden floor. The architecture of the space must provide enough room for group movement yet offer a containing environment, free of external distractions (such as large picture windows) Such rooms require a colour scheme which does not distract but creates a quiet concentrated mood. Eurythmy lessons are usually accompanied by a pianist, though in the younger classes, other instruments are often used as well. The children require appropriate footwear, usually a form of gymnastic shoe which gives a firm grip yet is flexible enough to allow good sensitivity of the floor by the foot. As a performance art, eurythmy makes use of silk gowns which both allow a freedom of movement and which reveal the subtleties of movement, especially in the loose veil which covers the arms. Since the emphasis for the viewer is to be the whole movement itself, facial expression and the physicality of the body itself play a subsidiary role. In school the children only wear costume for performance and eurythmy lessons are usually conducted in normal clothing with eurythmy shoes.

Educational aims

The aims of eurythmy within the curriculum could be said to be entirely pedagogical. Knowledge of eurythmy is neither required by society in any formal sense, nor has anyone ever had to do an examination in the subject! Nevertheless the aims of eurythmy lie at the heart of the Waldorf curriculum. Steiner Waldorf education without eurythmy would not justify the name.

As a new art form, however, and one that is at present only taught in Waldorf schools it is often little understood by the wider school community. An important part of the work of eurythmy teachers is working to increase this understanding through lay courses in the school communities and through talks and demonstrations. Its value is being increasingly acknowledged, not least given the general dramatic increase of pressures on the developing human being. The contribution of eurythmy to harmonising developmental processes, of integrating the spheres of thinking, feeling and willing and of cultivating an aesthetic sense cannot and should not be underestimated.

Given the vital contribution that eurythmy can make to child development, considerable effort is made by those responsible for its development to train more people, more effectively to teach eurythmy. There are still too few teachers qualified and able to work with this art form in schools. As such its further development has a high priority within the community of Steiner Waldorf schools worldwide.

- Eurythmy aims to harmonise the child's soul-spiritual nature with the bodily organisation by making the body a more flexible and responsive instrument to the soul's intentions.
- Practising the elements of eurythmical movement helps the children become more graceful in their movements, more coordinated, more alert and more at ease with themselves. Eurthymy also reveals blockages and hindrances within the movement organisation. What the children reveal in their movements can, to the practised eye of the teacher, contribute to an overall picture of their potential and what must be overcome to release it.
- Through learning the gestural vocabulary of sounds and musical tones in eurythmy, the children form an inner connection to the qualities inherent in the elements of language and music, a process which both engages the whole human being whilst supporting the development of linguistic and musical literacy.
- The artistic work done through the choreography of poetry, prose text, narrative and instrumental music deepen the children's aesthetic appreciation of literature and music experientially, a method which complements other approaches within the curriculum.
- Working with geometrical forms and their transitions in three dimensional space help the children have a more comprehensive experience of the principles of geometrical form and cultivate an inner sense of orientation.
- When working in groups the children have to concentrate on their own movement while developing the social capacity to sense the movements of the group as a whole. When both these are successful,

they enjoy their participation in this mutual flow of movement. Being able to move in a harmonious and coordinated way together with others requires not only peripheral perception but also a willingness to allow the others to have their own space. The mutuality of social processes is a quality which eurythmy cultivates at many levels.

- Experiencing eurythmy performances by other pupils or adult professional groups can work at a non-intellectual level that only an integrated artistic medium can engage. Eurythmy is not read but experienced in a holistic way, given openness on the part of the viewer. Children of all ages can enter into this realm of experience through good eurythmy performances, which reach beyond the stage and meet an uninhibited response in the audience through a rich tapestry of sense experiences. They can receive vivid living pictures which the soul can digest. Like all good art, eurythmy provides subtle yet powerful nourishment for the soul life.

Since eurythmy is only taught by teachers who have undergone a four or five year basic training in eurythmy, followed by a specific training in pedagogical eurythmy, it is not necessary in what follows to describe these in detail. To explain everything comprehensively to the non-eurythmist would require an entire book! The indications given here should make sense to trained eurythmists, who know, for example, what is meant by *walking a harmonious eight frontally*. For the general reader, the introduction has attempted to briefly explain what the educational task of eurythmy is. The curriculum that follows is merely a summary of possible activities. Using fairytale images, the eurythmy can involve many sound gestures in various moods. Elemental beings, elves, gnomes and so on are figures that can be introduced through narrative. The texts can include nursery rhymes and verses. Pentatonic music on the lyre or flute can accompany the eurythmy. Contraction and expansion movements in and around the circle provide the main form gesture.

Copper rod exercises can be used from Class 1 onwards to enhance and amplify the child's inner experience of his or her bodily and spatial movement and orientation. These exercises are designed with the therapeutic aim of enabling the child to gain inner confidence through centring the child in his or her equilibrium. In some cases, such as exercises involving dropping or throwing and catch, there is an awakening effect which strengthens the child's courage. There are many social aspects in group exercises.

It is very much up to the individual teacher's judgment when and how to introduce these exercises.

Kindergarten

Fairy-tale mood provides the background for the lessons. The transition to Class 1 is marked by the introduction of geometrical form and structure based on the straight line and curve.

Class 1

Points of view and general themes:

Spatial forms and arm movements are developed out of and in accordance with the children's imaginative experience. The circle of children is experienced as the 'sun', or as the 'castle garden'; the straight line is the 'golden bridge' or the 'magic ladder', and so on. The archetypal form of the circle is the starting point for eurythmy lessons and all movements start from the circle and return to it. The content of the lesson is woven into a narrative whole, the different elements flowing one into the other. In an ideal situation, the lessons flows as one integrated movement, articulated by a strong clear overall picture.

Content suggestions:

- Walking straight and curved lines, spirals, lemniscates or figure of eight patterns (without the children crossing between each other)
- Arm gestures for vowels and consonants are embedded in narrative and thus imitated unconsciously; this strengthens the natural movements and ability to imitate
- Short melodies in the pentatonic mode, the interval movement for the fifth, accompany the stories
- Various rhythms of walking, running, hopping, jumping, stamping and so on
- Fine motor skills are schooled by means of dexterity exercises, as is the distinction between right and left, forward and back

Class 2

Points of view and general themes:

The wholeness symbolised by the circle form now becomes polarised, through a dialogue of opposites. Following the main-lesson pattern, short animal stories now provide one point of departure, with different types of stepping being practised and perfected. More difficult tasks can be undertaken, e.g. the children walking forms round each other. The mood of the fifth remains the foundation in music eurythmy. This accompanies the lessons rather than being depicted in all its elements.

Content suggestions:

- Continuation of material begun in Class 1
- Circle and straight line continue; two circles now come into being. The forms are practised starting and returning to the same point, or starting, going round and returning to the same point
- Exercises in opposite pairs, e.g. educational exercises such as 'I and you', 'We', or mirror forms (children opposite each other)
- The same in music. Short dances in two circles with opposite pairs
- Dexterity exercises continue
- The seasonal round is accompanied with poems

Class 3

Points of view and general themes:

Forms and gestures of eurythmy are now shaped to accompany the psychological development of the children who experience a stronger differentiation between themselves and their surroundings in their ninth year. The children learn to become more independent in the space around them. However, to prevent the children separating too much, a prime exercise is contracion and expansion, which cushions the fall. More complex forms, including the spiral, triangles and squares are moved. Rhythms become more distinct both in spoken and musical work. There is a greater distinction between the elements of language, movement and exercises. Towards the end of the year (or in Class 4) the major and minor thirds come more to the fore in preparation for the first excursion into musical work. The sounds of speech are now recognised as such and separated off from overall word pictures. Thus the children can now learn the individual vowel and consonant forms. These processes will continue in Class 4, or can even be put off until then.

Content suggestions:

The subject of crafts and craftspeople links with the main-lesson themes:
* Rhythmical stepping movement to poems and music
* These can also feature geometrical shapes such as triangle and square in a playful way
* Different movements to specific motifs, e.g. the four elements, earth, water, air and fire
* Recognising question and answer in music and speech (question and answer spiral)
* The children are now expected to recognise some of the speech gestures
* Vowels are practised
* Continuation of dexterity and concentration exercises
* Experiencing the major and minor third (though this may be deferred until Class 4)

Class 4

Points of view and general themes:

Once the children have crossed the threshold to the middle of childhood we need to develop and practise new psychological forces of imagination and morality with them. Side by side with their mother-tongue lessons, their homogeneous experience of language now gains elements of differentiation as grammatical components make their appearance, in eurythmy too. In this way the children take in grammar not only through their understanding but also through feelings and will. Movement in a centrally oriented circle is now often exchanged for movement facing forwards, which gives a different sense of space. As independence develops, this is accompanied by all kinds of dexterity and concentration exercises and interval exercises (major,

minor, thirds). In eurythmy, action precedes understanding, so any comprehension of active and passive in grammar lessons and of major and minor in music lessons will only be brought in during Class 5. Music eurythmy proper can now begin as the children experience 'the human being as an instrument'.

Content suggestions:

* Grammatical elements of language are depicted in spatial forms (nouns, verbs, active/passive)
* Mirror forms continued, rod exercises requiring quickness and dexterity
* Concentration exercises
* Alliteration in poetic diction is explored through movement and rhythm
* Major and minor thirds
* Learning to hear, move and recognise the beat and movement of the pitch
* Listening exercises with intervals
* The first gestures for specific notes, the C-major scale

By the end of this year the children should be centred in the six directions in space (right-left through major-minor, up-down hrough the pitch and forwards and backwards through the rhythm).

Class 5

Points of view and general themes:

Work with grammatical forms continues. Special emphasis is now on shaping the gesture of a sound or word. The beauty, rhythm and form of language can be practised, experienced and understood. The geometry of the human form is consciously discovered and experienced in the five-pointed star, which has also been walked in previous classes. The children walk this form to experience it spatially. As a link with history lessons, texts from ancient cultures are used. The mood of the ancient culture epoch is taken up and explored through its characteristic form of movement and gesture. Poetry from foreign language lessons can also be done in eurythmy for the first time. Two-part melodies are practised in music eurythmy. Concentration and dexterity exercises (e.g. rapid orientation in space through varied form elements) are enlivening and stimulating.

Content suggestions:

* More complex forms (various lemniscates, star forms), culminating in Dionysian forms e.g. I, you, he/she/it forms
* Further grammatical forms
* Forms practised with frontal orientation
* Texts from ancient cultures. The character of the different cultural epochs explored through music, gesture and movement
* Foreign languages in speech eurythmy
* Continuation of concentration and dexterity exercises
* Various major scales

- Two-part melodies and rounds
- Stepping all rhythms – especially the Greek rhythms
- Specific pedagogical exercises given by Steiner e.g. Peace and Energy Dance or Dance of the Planets

Class 6

Points of view and general themes:

Parallel with geometry lessons, various geometrical form metamorphoses and shifts are practised spatially (triangle, square). These exercises support the children's growing capacity for orientation and abstraction. At this age the unity of movement that has been taken for granted hitherto gradually becomes unbalanced. Rhythm and symmetry exercises and musical interval exercises can be a help in recreating co-ordination. The use of exercises using a copper rod, help the children to form a coherent inner image of their own spatial dimensions, which helps not only in co-ordination but in integrating their movement organisation at a time when rapid physical change and growth may lead to a loss of their sense of their physical boundaries. The dramatic element now enters speech eurythmy, and this can be used to enrich and deepen the children's life of soul. The octave is expressed as a general movement impulse in walking, jumping and speech gestures, as well as music. All the exercises must involve the co-ordination of sequences of movement and attention to accuracy. The Roman theme of strucure and law, which characterises the Class 6 curriculum, is reflected in eurythmy by a strong emphasis in all grammar forms.

From Class 6 onwards the social aspects of eurythmy need to be consciously cultivated.

Content suggestions:

- Elements of grammatical form, rod exercises
- Metamorphosis of geometrical forms. practised with frontal orientation
- Practising the musical scales in eurythmy gesture
- Interval gestures, especially the octave, with the corresponding spatial forms, in stepping, jumping etc.
- The children are encouraged to find their own transitions from one gesture to the next.
- Listening exercises e.g. identifying major and minor; intervals
- The complete grammar forms
- Difficult concentration exercises e.g. involving sequences of stepping and clapping

Class 7

Points of view and general themes:

As in their English language lessons, the children can now also experience in eurythmy the more subtle shades of linguistic expression e.g. conditional clauses and various exercises in soul moods such as sadness, joy, seriousness, and above all happiness. More complicated form transformations in geometry give an experience of structure from outside. Exercises for upright posture

become more conscious; these continue in various forms up to Class 12.

Content suggestions:

- Elements of grammatical form are expanded through dramatic gestures
- Foot position, head position, yes and no; in preparation for the soul gestures in Class 8
- Complicated versions of shifts in pentagon, hexagon, heptagon, octagon
- Concentration, foot and rod exercises
- Major and minor scales
- Interval forms
- Humorous pieces
- Phrasing of music/poetry
- Beat/rhythms
- Pedagogical exercises e.g. Look into yourself, look into the world

Class 8

Points of view and general themes:

All the modes of expressing spatial and soul elements are combined in longer dramatic poems. The fundamental laws of eurythmy movements are taken to a point from which it will be possible to continue building in a new way in the Upper School. Ballads and humorous pieces with their strongly contrasting soul moods and polarities correspond with the pupil's inner situation at this time. Here the soul gestures are needed to characterise the 'plot' of the ballad. Also, the children are well into the throes of puberty, with new experiences for the soul. They are becoming independent from their parents, having their own feelings and are often chaotic. The soul gestures show the reality of these movements and moods of soul. We all feel laughter, knowledge, but also despair or greed! In music eurythmy they can work on forms for larger groups; this cultivates social awareness. The tension in the interchange between major and minor is compatible with this phase in their lives.

Content suggestions:

- Soul gestures performed with the arms
- Ballads, humorous pieces, music using the interval forms
- Dionysian forms of thinking, feeling and willing
- Intensive work on major and minor
- Geometrical transformations, rod exercises
- Concentration exercises in many variations
- Pedagogical exercises e.g. The outer has succeeded...

Classes 9 to 12

General aspects and aims

There should be an obvious change in method at the beginning of the Upper School. The exercises practised and increasingly brought to awareness hitherto are now taken up and shaped anew through knowledge. Texts and musical pieces are freely choreographed or worked on by applying the laws that apply to the movements. The aim is twofold. On the one hand movement is to be schooled and expression-through-movement practised; on the other hand the young people are to learn to carry out and experience eurythmy as an 'expressionistic' art. Both viewpoints are intimately related.

In the educational exercises there is a transition from concentration exercises to more dynamic movement. Moving in space must be transformed from strictly geometrical forms to ones that are more free and artistic. Rather than copying what the teacher does, the pupils will increasingly be expected to apply their own inner motivation and ability to create forms. They should learn to make use of the different elements in an alert and independent manner. For Class 9 the approach must be for the students to observe: what do we have to express ourselves, and what do we experience from our environment. This includes the relationship of our physical body to the space around us. Contrast is the key to Class 9. As in Bothmer Gymnastics, we can build up a consciousness for the laws of space, weight and levity, light and darkness, contraction and expansion, joy and sadness and so on. The lessons themselves should be structured through the use of strong contrasts, e.g. use of major and minor keys, harmony and dissonance.

Class 9

Points of view and general themes:

- Dynamic of speech, music, movement in space; getting to know polarities
- Various poems and poets
- Perceiving and consciously utilising the structure and geometry of one's own body
- Independent execution and formation of gestures
- New element: shaping harmonies
- Minor/major dissonants

Content suggestions:

- The pupils are led to make make their own forms and share in making communal forms (choreography)
- Re-working basic elements
- Intensive work on threefold walking, making it flow and carry over
- Free rhythms, light/dark, loud/soft, etc.
- In tone eurythmy the students work simultaneously with the different voices in music
- Chords
- Strong melodic movements
- Beat, rhythm
- The morning verse can be taken in eurythmy
- Recapitulation of all the pedagogical exercises done in the Lower School but with greater consciousness

Class 10

Points of view and general themes:

- Understanding and including the contrasts of human being and world, individual form and circle
- Increasing external and internal agility
- Make the link with main-lesson subjects: poetry, history (ancient cultures)
- Learning to express soul experiences through gestures
- Dynamic is complemented by the psychological activities of 'thinking, feeling, will' and their corresponding expressions
- From dance to festive movement
- Musical dynamic; continuation and differentiation of what was learnt in Class 9

Content suggestions:

- Exercises in polarities
- Threefold walking
- Dramatic gestures
- Selecting and consciously practising basic forms for new themes
- Forms for pronouns, for epic, lyric and dramatic poetry. Verse forms, rhyme forms.
- Work on longer musical works
- Classical forms (e.g. rondo)
- Group forms to be worked on together
- Rod exercises can be done with a more aesthetic element

Class 11

Points of view and general themes:

Independence in shaping movements: individual form/environment.
- Moving freely and shaping the 'invisible' space behind, which can only be filled by applying one's consciousness
- Stylistic work
- Musical expression of bathos/pathos in eurythmy
- Linking up with main-lesson themes: in art history, especially 'Apollonian/Dionysian'; and in connection with art lessons: gestures and forms of colour moods
- Polarities
- Astronomy: planetary movements
- Solo work
- More difficult musical interpretation

Content suggestions:

- Planetary movements; poems in various styles
- Colour movements
- Silent forms
- The language of gesture
- Practise the qualities of notes and intervals building on the basic elements learnt
- Foot and head positions in relation to grammar and the soul moods

• Pedagogical exercise – I think speech

Class 12

Points of view and general themes:

Overview of all expression possibilities offered by eurythmy.
• The pupils themselves work out group forms, lighting, costumes (the complete work of art)
• Control over one's own body as an instrument of the soul
• Differentiating between movement, attitude and gesture

Content suggestions:

• Exercises in all styles
• Examples of work with modern poetry and music
• Eurythmy as an expression of the relationship between human being and world
• Understanding eurythmy as a modern art
• Eurythmy as a synthesis of impressionism and expressionism
• The Zodiac and Planetary movement
• The Twelve Moods by Rudolf Steiner

Classes 1 to 12

General aspects and aims for Classes 1 to 12

The aim of foreign language teaching in Steiner Waldorf schools is to encourage a positive attitude towards people of other cultures and languages, as well as fostering human understanding generally through establishing the ability to empathise with another person's perspective and way of seeing the world. Learning foreign languages offers the individual other perspectives on his or her own language, culture, attitudes and mentality, thus helping the pupil see the world in a more differentiated way.

The aims therefore of learning foreign languages are composite. On the one hand, the practical, utilitarian goal of being able to understand another language through listening and reading and being able to express oneself with a good degree of fluency in speaking and writing. On the other hand, to introduce the students to the character, customs and traditions, literature, culture, geography, history typical of the peoples who speak the given language. The third, pedagogical aim of foreign language teaching is to assist the overall development of the child through the subject specific qualities, as well as giving the individual insight into different ways of viewing the world, thus broadening the pupil's own perspective.

Learning foreign languages orally strengthens the pupil's ability to listen to another person, to follow and grasp the other person's spoken and unspoken intentions, since it enhances sensitivity to language at all levels and not merely the semantic level. This encourages greater powers of understanding, forming balanced judgments and empathy, all qualities needed in complex social situations. Being competent in at least two other languages supports the ability of flexible, mobile thinking, since the different languages allow access to different realms of experience and this in turn stimulates greater interest in the world and other people.

Language is threefold in its basic nature. It facilitates self-expression, communication and provides a framework for dialogue, speaking and listening. Secondly, language is a means of structuring and representing concepts and thoughts. This enables the child to map his or her experiences. The universal principles of syntactical relationships enable the translation of meaning from one individual to another but also from one language to another. Every language can be translated into every other. Thirdly, language is revelatory by nature. In contrast to materialistic conceptions of language, Steiner Waldorf takes the view that language, in its phonic, lexical and syntactical elements gives expression to something of the essence of what it describes. This is why language is such a powerful formative force. Gaining insight into the syntactical and grammatical structures common to all languages provides a good basis for the subsequent study of language and linguistics.

Teaching methods

Initial contact with the foreign language in school is a broad experiential and contextual one, which becomes increasingly more conscious through analysis. There is an intrinsic progression from oral to literate language and the oral element remains paramount. In building literacy on orality, there is a strong emphasis on the gesture and situation. Language holds a middle position between movement which is internalised to become speech and speech which is further internalised in thinking.

Given that a large percentage of communicated meaning in normal conversation is non-semantic, there is a strong emphasis on gesture, pantomime, body language and the entire non-verbal realm of orality remains important throughout the curriculum.[1]

Working intensively with language harmonises and extends the child's affective responses to the world. Not only do the pupils become more articulate; they have more to say. Thus the process of foreign learning languages can serve to meet the developmental needs of the child as well as enabling them to develop abilities which serve their own individuation process whilst developing social competence.

In working with the nature of language itself, and assuming that the teaching method respects the inner principles of language and language acquisition, the child engages his or her own being with the being of language itself.

During the first three years of instruction the child is immersed in the orality of the language within the context of the lessons, most, if not all of which are conducted entirely in the foreign language. The children are introduced to a range of activities, verbal exchanges (greetings, question and answers to everyday situations), verses, poems, counting rhymes, skipping chants, songs and games designed to engage them and carry them in the stream of the language without the need for translation or explanation.

Once a repertoire has been built up within the first 3 to 4 lessons, new material is continuously introduced whilst existing material is regularly repeated and extended through variation. As well as oral work, the children enact situations in a lively way.

It is not necessary for the children to have an intellectual grasp of all they hear and repeat. During this time they are able to develop a sensitivity to the basic intonation patterns of the foreign language in a way that will be much more difficult after the age of 10 or 11, when the plasticity of the speech apparatus and its neural counterparts are that much more formed and therefore less malleable. This is an important factor in Steiner Waldorf language teaching methodology.

Teaching is entirely through the spoken word, in commands (do this, do that), question and answer exchanges, singing and reciting by heart (i.e. without visible text), and this is often accompanied by gesture, pantomime and the use of pictures. Whole exchanges of dialogue can be learned by heart and an extensive range of vocabulary and grammatical structures are acquired in situ, as it were, rather than in an abstract or schematic way. In fact during the first three years the children are systematically introduced to and exercise unconsciously all the major elements of grammar as well as building up a wide vocabulary of common words. Just as the movement curriculum supports the child enter into the stream of movement from the periphery, so too in language lessons the children are helped to engage in the stream of language, which forms their language organs (perceptual and speech producing organs), builds up active situational vocabulary in memory, forms habitual structures of expressions, idioms, intonations. In short the child is helped to step into the stream of language. At a later stage this stream, as in the movement curriculum is reflected back in awakened consciousness and ability.

By the end of Class 3 the children's vocabulary should include: parts of the body, articles of clothing, phrases describing the activities associated with daily domestic and school life, the objects visible in the classroom and home, the colours, the times of the day, the days of the week, months, seasons, typical weather conditions, common forms of transport, familiar professions and what they do, common phenomena in nature – plants, animals etc., being able to ask and answer simple questions using the vocabulary listed above. They will also have regularly used the main forms of the verbs, tenses, be familiar with personal pronouns, directional prepositions, some adjectives and adverbs and the common question words.

Assessment at this level is a matter of the teacher noting the apparent potential of the individuals in the class in terms of memory, pronunciation and courage to speak, and discussing these with the class teacher and parents.

From Classes 4 or 5 a more conscious learning of language coincides with the new developmental stage the children are now entering. They continue to practise what they have learned but begin also writing and reading, as well as being made aware of the structure and spelling of the language. Drawing on what the children have learned by heart and ear in the first three school years, the children start by writing what they already know and understand. Once the phonetic values and letters have been established the children can move onto unfamiliar texts.

The methods of book writing and use of materials follow the patterns established by the class teacher. In fact close collaboration is essential for all stages of foreign language learning, in terms of classroom management skills and habits, but especially in the teaching of grammar. The foreign language teacher must build on grammatical concepts established in the mother tongue by the class teacher. Topics being discussed in main-lesson, such as farming or arithmetic can reappear in the foreign language lessons, once the basic skills have been established in the main-lesson.

In terms of teaching economy, it can make sense wherever possible to delegate specific topics from the main-lesson to one or other subject lesson. Relevant aspects of geography and history, for example, can be taken by the foreign language teacher. However the main area of collaboration lies in the class teacher creating work habits and behaviour standards with the class that are resilient enough to encompass the foreign language lessons. Given the high risk factors, especially at self conscious ages, for pupils in expressing themselves in a foreign language, not to mention the sheer amount of things that have, ultimately to be painstakingly learned, the task of foreign language teaching depends on good co-operation.

The words of any language carry with them something of the outlook of the people who speak that language. Thus there is always an untranslatable content differentiating words in one language from those used in other languages for the same thing or concept. For this reason direct translation is avoided as far as possible. Therefore gesture, pictures, movement, direct situational experience or word-games are relied on to facilitate comprehension. Great imagination is required on the part of the teacher to awaken appropriate inner pictures in the child's mind that associate sounds, words and content. However, the effort is amply rewarded by a much stronger affective response by the pupil, which by and large leads to long term memory, rather than short term or 'list-orientated' vocabulary. Words on their own are relatively useless. They must be bedded into useful grammatical structures, i.e. whole sentences that can be varied.

The topics chosen by the teacher and the pace at which they are covered depends on the teacher's assessment of the capacities of a given class, but are likely to include simple conversations about school and home, family, the weather etc. There will also be question and answer sessions involving a knowledge of numbers, the time, the season, the times of the day, the content of the reading material, or recent events of interest to the class. Activities will usually include the recitation of poetry and speech exercises, singing, discussion of grammar points such as singular or plural, verb forms (which may be recited and learned by rote), the conjugation of verbs in various tenses, aspects of history, geography or culture.

Throughout the Middle School, the children continue their oral work, which always remains at the heart of the teaching. This often takes the form of acting out short plays or scenes. Reading material is introduced once the children are familiar with the letters and can read familiar sentences, usually in Class 5 and form a focus for vocabulary work. The children also build up their own reference book with systematic lists of vocabulary, often grouped by theme, grammar rules and tables showing declensions. This is preferred to the use of a set grammar book as it gives the teacher greater flexibility in the sequence of themes introduced and the act of formulating a rule they themselves have worked out is an important aid to memory. One can also limit the amount of grammar to what it is strictly necessary to know. Grammar is very much reduced to a 'need to know' basis in the Middle School.

The children often have a separate book to record all the poems, verses, songs and exercises they have learned (invaluable if there is an unexpected change of teacher). They also have exercise books in which written work is practised either in class or as homework. No text books are used to teach from, though dictionaries are introduced at the end of Classes 6 or 7, when they children are familiar with their use.

Block teaching

It is essential to have 3 weekly lessons in each language throughout the school, if high standards of language ability are expected. In the Upper School this may increase to 4.

Block teaching has been introduced in some schools (usually not before Class 5). This means that a class has a block of 3-4 weeks during which all language lessons in the weekly timetable (should be 6) are given over to one language. The idea is to build on continuity, then allow one language to lie fallow for a period. The advantages and disadvantages are disputed by adherents and proponents, with no clear outcome. What is clear is that the benefit depends on the quality of the teaching. A good teacher can get a long way with some 18-24 consecutive lessons, but probably would also do so with the normal arrangements. The practical disadvantages of longer absences of teacher or pupil because of illness can cause havoc with continuity, as can changes of teachers. New teachers may be challenged to master a Middle School class if they have to teach them every day. Blocks suit project work but not regularity of learning.

Pre-conditions for good languge learning

Language learning benefits from group sizes in which each pupil can feel actively involved and challenged at his or her own level. It also benefits from imaginative and artistic teaching. Teachers of foreign languages in Steiner Waldorf schools, not only require to be fluent in the language, love to speak it and read its poetry and literature but also show a deep interest in the cultures that speak the language. On top of this they must be conversant with the anthroposophical understanding of the nature of language, the nature of child development and be well skilled in speaking, gesture, drama and mime. Without this background, the method here suggested will be very difficult to achieve. This is said out of a deep sense of responsibility to the children but also to many inexperienced teachers who are asked to teach in ways they neither understand nor have been trained for.

Summary of the main focus throughout the classes

Classes 1-3: building a basis of the language, establishing a love of language, basic vocabulary, all grammatical structures unconsciously practised, communication.

Classes 4-6: raising everything learned to consciousness, writing down what has been orally learned in Classes 1-3, extending what has been established.

Classes 7-9: learning new, self-directed learning methods, joy reading literature, awaken an awareness for comparative language studies. Discovering the lands, history and cultures of German-speaking peoples.

Classes 10-12: work with the spirit of the language and the folksoul of the German speaking peoples.

GERMAN

Class 1

The teaching method

The children usually take everything in a mood of wonder and empathy. There is a strong tendency for the whole class to repeat everything chorally as one, though this should not prevent individuals from speaking alone. By the end of the year each child should have mastered everything that has been learned as a class. There must be considerable repetition and all that is learned is done so thoroughly.

Lesson content

- Narrative songs (e.g. Dornröschen/Hänschen klein)
- Verses and songs involving actions (e.g. Zeigt her eure Füsse)
- Finger games
- Acting upon simple commands (steh auf, komm mal her)
- Counting (cardinal numbers)
- Naming parts of the body, daily activities (eating, washing, dressing), colours
- Emphasis on the appropriate use of prepositions in context
- Phrases for use in simple conversations (e.g. Wie heisst du? – Ich heisse..., Wo wohnst du? – Ich wohne in)
- Games repeating individual structures or items of vocabulary (e.g. Hast du...? / Ist es...?)
- Listening to stories and learning them

Attainment targets

By the end of Class 1, the children's active vocabulary should include:
- The main colours
- The main items in the classroom
- Parts of the body
- Days of the week and seasons
- Numbers up to 20

They should also be able to respond to simple commands and basic questions.

Class 2

The teaching method

A strong element of dualism is necessary during this year, in ja/nein, in question and answer, in ich/ du. The children have a stronger need to communicate than in Class 1. They respond best to authentic situations, such as having native speaking guests, making real recipes etc. The teaching should have a strong rhythmical element in both the lesson structure and the nature of the activities, with strong contrasts between quietly becoming conscious (sounds, exact pronunciation etc.) and lively involvement. There should be a dynamic balance between being loud and quiet, speaking and listening. There also needs to many variations around common themes (e.g. an ever increasing range of possible answers to a give question, wie kommst du zur Schule?)

Lesson content

*   Activities from Class 1 to be continued and enlarged upon (e.g. poems/folk songs/items in the classroom/commands etc.);
*   Recitation of cardinal and ordinal numbers;
*   Months of the year and when children's birthdays fall;
*   Vocabulary of nature (mountain, river, tree, flower, moon etc.);
*   Articles of clothing (e.g. Hampelmann-Lied);
*   Daily routine activities (e.g. Ich ziehe mich an/ wasche mich);
*   Listening to simple stories; acting out of stories etc.;
*   Talking about themselves e.g. birthday, age, family (e.g. Ich habe einen Bruder etc.)
*   The forms of 'sein' and 'haben' in sentence forms (e.g. 'Ich bin der Konig, Du bist die Königin, er ist der Prinz' etc.).

Attainment targets

By the end of Class 2, most children should;
*   Know the months
*   Know a range of natural features (mountain, sun, moon, tree etc.)
*   Know cardinal numbers up to 100, ordinal numbers up to 10
*   Respond to simple questions about themselves, e.g.: Wie alt bist du? Wann hast du Geburtstag? Wo wohnst du? Hast du einen Bruder / eine Schwester?
*   Wie heisst dein Bruder / deine Schwester / deine Mutter / dein Vater?
*   Apply simple structures (e.g. Ist es...?/Hast du...?/ Ich möchte...)
*   Follow a simple story
*   Point out/name different items in their environment
*   Know a number of songs, verses and rhymes by heart

Class 3

The teaching method

Wit, in both senses of the word, is the keynote for this year. The children have a much stronger feeling for language, for nuances both of pronunciation and meaning. They require longer, more varied texts to learn. They enjoy acting out humorous scenes and short plays which involve individuals learning and carry roles alone. This year also sees intensive preparation for the coming year and the introduction of literacy. Texts are learned that are later written, key elements of grammar are rehearsed orally (use of articles, verb endings and personal pronouns, singular-plural forms, even the kinds of words, once these have been learned in English grammar). Speech exercises, tongue-twisters, riddles and beautiful poems are the daily diet in recitation.

Lesson content

*   Conversational work to be continued
*   Topics include; numbers, colours, places (town, village, city, country), forms of transport, clothes, time (clock), more complex commands, items of food, sayings and simple stories
*   Acting out and learning individual parts of a dramatised story
*   Picture 'dictations'
*   Verb forms and tenses in sentence structures (e.g. Der Bauer mäht das Korn, die Maurer bauen ein Haus, du backst uns Brot)
*   Verses practising grammatical forms (e.g. tenses)
*   Learn use of the main prepositions
*   Learn use of question words
*   Learn personal pronouns in context

Attainment targets

More consciousness should be brought to the use of the language. Children should:
*   Be familiar with basic items of food, clothing, furniture
*   Be familiar with forms of transport, places and directions
*   Be familiar with times of the day (morning, evening etc.) clock times (hours, quarter hours, minutes)
*   Be aware of the different genders
*   Take a more active part orally (e.g. supply the next step of a story which the teacher is re-telling)
*   Apply structures practised more freely
*   Recognise the most common question words, wer, wie, was, wann, wo
*   Use the main spatial prepositions in context: in dem Raum, auf dem Tisch etc.
*   Recognise the main personal pronouns (ich, du, er...)
*   Recognise possessive adjectives (mein, dein...)

Class 4

The teaching method

At around the age of ten children gain a new level of self-consciousness. They need to individualise much that had been collectively learned. Writing is introduced as a conscious and more individual noting down of what has been accumulated in the collective memory. Furthermore, at this age they require a strong sense or order in their surroundings and in their work. A systematic structure to lessons, good planning (especially close co-operation between class teacher, eurythmy teacher and language teachers is essential) and individual attention is necessary at this age, not least because the introduction of literacy highlights weaknesses that some pupils have that have not been so apparent before.

Using material learned by heart in the first three classes, writing in the foreign language is introduced. The children learn to recognise vocabulary they already know. Before printed reading material is introduced, they read what they themselves have written. Care is taken in the introduction of the letters to distinguish between the German sound represented by the letter, its German name and its English name. It is better to take time to clarify all these things at this stage than have to continuously correct in the years to come. Both writing and reading require much practice. While imitation and repetition continue to play an important role, the children should begin to recognise characteristic spelling forms, inflections (word endings, plural forms etc.).

Vocabulary lists can consist of word families (key words relevant to a particular theme such as parts of the body, the classroom, seasons, colours, simple commands and question forms). These lists need only be in the foreign language and they can be illustrated where appropriate. It is not necessary at this stage for the pupils to write word for word translations. Wherever possible, nouns should be learned in sentences with appropriate verb forms and simple adjectives. After writing whole sentences, it may be useful to underline nouns and verbs with a distinctive colour. The writing of such vocabulary is the end of a long process of oral learning.

One effective way of practising vocabulary is to summarise simple stories using familiar words. The children may copy down two or three sentences giving the basic outline of the story. The text should include as much repetition as possible.

Other than copying such material from the blackboard, written exercises can include simple dictations (two sentences can be learned by heart and written down). The children should initially have access to the original text when writing a dictation, only when vocabulary has been thoroughly learned, is it appropriate to require 'blind' dictations.

In Class 4 elementary sentence structure is learned, nouns and simple verb forms are practised. Example sentences are drawn from the familiar range of classroom dialogue. Singing recitation, simple dialogue and word games continue to be a basic part of the lessons. Great care must be taken that the children really understand the grammatical forms being referred to. They should formulate the essential (i.e. pragmatic rules as opposed to those usually found in grammar books) rules themselves. Discussions about German grammar should be conducted in English.

Oral work should continue in a lively way with speech exercises, verses, poems and songs, as well as question and answer sessions, increasingly involving the children among each other in groups. Everything that the children now speak should be understood. To facilitate this a kind of consecutive translating can be practised, which means generally formulating the content. The children can be asked to 'translate' what other children have said in this manner. This does not mean literal word for word translations, but putting the gist of what has been said into one's own words.

In Class 4, the children are usually introduced to exercise book work based closely on the forms used for main-lesson work. These handwritten books form the equivalent of a text book. Initially one main-lesson book should suffice for simple writing exercises. Later it is useful to have a book for poems and songs, a book for vocabulary and grammar. The children should be encouraged to see written work as the equivalent of etudes in music, an essential craft leading to an art.

Situational games, little plays, guessing games and so on still form an important part of the lesson.

Lesson content

- The children write down and read verses, poems or songs learned in the previous years
- The alphabet is practised as well as spelling and short dictations
- The first introduction of grammar includes: present tense forms of common verbs with personal pronouns (other tenses can be read in context of texts), parts of speech, nouns with article, plural forms and common adjectives, prepositions in, an, aus, auf, über, unter, vor, hinter, zwischen, simple sentence structures (subject and object), use of singular and plural nouns with singular and plural verb endings (Das Kind singt ein Lied; Die Kinder singen schöne Lieder)
- Question words are continued
- Texts are written describing animals, the weather, household items etc.
- The children continue to learn and recite seasonal and nature poems

Attainment targets

By the end of the year the children should:
- Know the German alphabet
- Be able to spell out their name and some common words
- Read practised words and sentences accurately
- Be able to give simple descriptions
- Recognise nouns, verbs and adjectives
- Know the verb forms in the present tense
- Know the gender of some common nouns
- Know the plural forms of some common nouns
- Be able to construct simple sentences of their own

Class 5

The teaching method

At this age (age 11) the children should have a strongly rhythmical memory. They can and should learn much at this age. It is also an age in which the beauty of language can be cultivated. Their enjoyment of the language is essential and to build on this the children's own creative imagination should be called into play whenever possible, even in thinking up suitable homework tasks. Lessons should never be tedious and to avoid this they should have a brisk and varied pace. Children enjoy reciting quite long poems and can sing complex rounds. Building on the simple structures learned in Class 4, the children strengthen their grasp of grammar. Vocabulary should now be consciously learned and practised. A first reader can be introduced. The first endeavours at creative writing can be attempted, including poems on given themes, such as nature moods or animals.

The oral work includes question and answer dialogue, speech exercises and many varied poems, all recited by heart (and learned by repetition). Apart from its intrinsic value, the reciting of poetry is a good way of cultivating clear pronunciation and sentence melody, as well as reinforcing idiomatic vocabulary. The content of such poems (seasonal, narrative etc.) need not be explained in detail; an imaginative though simplified introduction can suffice.

With increasing diversity of vocabulary, the children should be encouraged to use the words they know in imaginative ways, for example by writing short stories. To awaken an interest in the words themselves, the children should hear and read vivid and characteristic descriptions of people, places and situations.

Vocabulary arising out of the reader is introduced before the new part of the text. Other topical themes will also have to be introduced as the need arises. Simple comprehension questions to the reading text or to other topics should be practised first orally with the whole class, then individuals are called upon. Only then should the questions be put in written form. Such questions and their variations can form the content for homework exercises, dictations etc.

Once new grammatical structures have been introduced (in English), practised and understood, a simple statement of the essential rules should be written (ideally in the pupils' own formulations) (in English) in a book specially kept for the purpose. These rules are best kept separate from whatever other exercise books are used. A self-made grammar book can be started in Class 5 and used through to Class 8. From now on, grammar should be raised to greater consciousness by using a comparative method, which compares German to English.

A love of reading should be encouraged.

Plays, as ever, are the best way of engaging a class's interest.

Lesson content

- Songs/poetry, plays, stories
- Practice reading using a class reader
- Answering simple questions on a story both in speaking and writing,
- Practise orally strong verbs
- Grammar: work with verb tenses, cases (Accusative/Dative), prepositions, basic adverbs and adverbials of time, manner, place, sentence structure (e.g. with modal verbs/subordinate clauses)
- Systematic build up of reader and theme related vocabulary, vocabulary tests, regular dictation

Attainment targets

By the end of the year the children should:
- Be able to respond to simple questions to a text
- Be able to retell small portions of a story freely
- Be able to use and identify present, past and future tense of the verbs learned
- Be aware of the different sentence structure in English and German
- Know the position of the adverbs

Class 6

The teaching method

Class 6 marks the threshold to puberty. The young person's intellectual faculties need to be awakened to the conceptual structures of language and to a systematic overview of what they have learned and have yet to learn. They need to be able discuss how much they need to learn, how much can be learned in a month, in a term and this has to be regularly reviewed as they also need tangible evidence of progress. What have we learned? And what did we not manage to learn and what were the reasons? Where this does not occur effectively, the children respond with bad behaviour, express doubts about their ability to learn – or the teacher's ability to teach! They need to learn how to learn vocabulary in a more conscious way.

At this age the pupils can usefully learn the conjugation of verbs, declension of nouns, adjectives, the use of terms such as nominative, dative etc. In other words, order and structure and visible planning are important in Class 6!

Dramatic, heroic poetry and much humour are the essential ingredients in speech work. Short, dramatic scenes can be acted out. In oral work one can weave in as many idiomatic phrases and everyday conversational vocabulary as possible.

The geography and characteristic episodes, historical and mythical personalities form a main theme in Classes 6, 7 and 8.

Once a reasonable basis of grammar and vocabulary has been achieved, the pupils can be encouraged to express themselves more freely in German. Letters, simple descriptions, diaries, summaries of stories can form the material for written exercises.

At this age the teacher must reckon with considerable differences of ability within one class. Exercises should be differentiated to suit the range of learning needs. This does not necessitate dividing up a class. Obviously children benefit from relatively small group sizes of around 15. Classes can be divided into equal groups or according to the ability to work in a group. Dividing them at this age into language ability groups is counter-productive at this stage. However, children entering the school at this stage with no previous knowledge of the language should be taught separately until it is realistic for them to join the class.

Lesson content

- Songs/poetry (of a dramatic nature)
- Improvising or learning short dialogues of a dramatic or humorous nature
- Reading of stories, a balance between a class reader and allowing individual reading to take place is necessary – class reading at this age will have to be short. (Reading always benefits from the challenge of a specific task given to the class, something to discover in the text, even to observe how often a particular word appears)
- Questions/answers both of a conversational nature and on stories
- Grammar: comparison of adjectives, uses and forms of the genitive and dative; attributive adjectives of weak and strong declension, use and forms of passive/active voice, word order in main clauses and compound sentences, rules for gender of nouns
- Keeping a grammar book up-to-date for reference
- Maintaining a vocabulary list with genders and plurals; revision of grammar covered so far
- Geography: the geography of Germany, Switzerland or Austria can be done in Class 6 (e.g. in the form of an imaginary journey), combining descriptions of the main geographical features of the various regions (e.g. Alps, Vor-alps, Schwarzwald, Bavaria, Rhine Valley, North German Plane, Thuringia, North Sea and Baltic coast etc.) their economies and cities, something of the local traditions, dialect, folklore, culture, recipes etc.

Attainment targets

By the end of the year, children should:
- Be able to speak more freely about themselves and their environment
- Be able to speak more freely on what they have read in class
- Recognise and give examples (e.g. from a text) for the areas of grammar covered so far
- Understand the grammatical terminology involved
- Have a good imaginative picture of several regions of a German speaking country

Classes 7 and 8

The teaching method

The method for Classes 7 and 8 follow closely on that described for Class 6. Lively, varied lessons (i.e. never stay too long on one activity, especially grammar), with plenty to learn, regular tests and dictations, group work, involvement of the students in the lesson planning and structuring. Book work should be maintained at a high standard. Where this breaks down, it may be necessary to work more closely with the class teacher and parents to gain extra time to rewrite shoddy books. Everything the pupils do must make sense to them. There is a strong emphasis on

cultural, geographical, historical and topical themes. These may form the subject of reading literature and in Class 8 individual work projects (e.g. biographies etc.). Idiomatic and colloquial language is also important and regular space should be given in the lessons for practising conversation. Class exchanges and penfriends should be encouraged.

Essentially the grammar themes listed for Classes 6 to 8 overlap and may be taken in almost any order that practically suggests itself, with the more complex phenomena such as the Conjunctive, reflexive verbs, separable and inseparable verbs etc., left until Class 8.

The pupils should be introduced to two-language dictionaries and should begin to do simple summaries in translation of short, prepared passages.

Lesson content

- Biographies (related to main-lesson programme: scientists, explorers etc.)
- historical and cultural topics, modern life etc.
- Extracts from literary works
- Continuation of the geographical theme begun in Class 6 looking at those regions not yet covered
- Vocabulary work, idioms, colloquial speech, polite and impolite forms, slang, words with various specific meanings e.g. da, denn, doch, irgend, ja, noch, schon, wie, translation of certain English words with multiple uses (about, after, any, ask, be, before, call, catch, change, enjoy, even, feel, finish, get, go, just, know, late, leave, lie, like, look, lose, marry, now, number, only, order, put, remember, so, take, that, then, time, very, work)
- Grammar: direct and indirect speech, revisions of all cases, the use of and translation of the gerund, prepositions (in das < > in dem) and the cases they take, simple subordinate sentence structure, comparison of adjectives and adverbs continued, pronouns; possessive pronouns, reflexive pronouns, reciprocal pronouns – *wir lieben uns, wir schreiben einander, sie reden miteinander* etc.; welche: *was für ein, wer, was*; demonstrative pronouns – *der, die, das – ich bin mir dessen bewusst, derselbe, derjenige, selbst, selber, eine, keine, jemand, niemand, jeder, alle, etwas, nichts*; the remaining tenses of the verbs; the subjunctive mood, the subjunctive mood in conditional sentences, verbs governing the dative, accusative and dative, the genitive, translation of English verbal ing-forms. The use of punctuation and especially the comma.

Attainment targets

By the end of the Class 8, the pupils should:
- Understand the use of the cases
- Know all the tenses
- Know which case accompanies which preposition
- Be able to compose short pieces of writing of their own with reasonable accuracy
- Have acquired a firm grasp of sentence structure
- Be able to express themselves clearly in simple

sentences in a range of everyday situations (age, where they live, shopping, social exchange, asking their way etc.)

The Upper School

The teaching method

Rudolf Steiner gave no specific recommendations for teaching methods for foreign languages in the Upper School, except that the teachers should regularly change their methods around in order to avoid routines setting in, which are deadly for the lessons. The main points of view may be summarised as follows:
- Pupils and teachers should share an interest in the themes that are studied, which implies collaboration in their selection
- Enthusiasm is the main factor in language teaching, as a counter to scepticism
- Presence of mind and openness to the world need to be practised, in order to be alert to the latent questions that live in the souls of the students

Class 9

A new phase of teaching begins in Class 9, which could be described as a dialectical phase, in which the question is asked, what can language do? Two primary factors influence what can be done in this class. Firstly, due to a significant change in how the individual relates to his or her memories – a symptom of puberty – young people not only become self-conscious in their speaking but often claim to have forgotten or never learned large areas of vocabulary and grammar. The second factor, also age-related is an unwillingness to concentrate for long.

However, an alert intellect is what they usually bring with them and this suggests the solution. Class 9 age students need to systematically re-learn all the main elements of grammar, and re-build their active vocabularies. It is usually the case that they have not in fact forgotten everything, but the need to understand it anew makes it seem like it. Here grammar books can for the first time be really helpful in offering, abstract summaries, tables of declensions and lists that appeal to the more intellectual aspect of their thinking. Many students positively welcome the opportunity to write out the main rules and lists once more as an aid to their memory. Basically everything needs to be gone over again and this may take into Class 10, though the aims is to get through it quickly, as their interest and motivation will be hard to maintain. There is much opportunity for using the more able pupils to present aspects of grammar that they have grasped, to the rest of the class.

On the other hand their attention span prefers short, powerful texts, short scenes of a dramatic or humorous nature, dialogues. This is a good time to perform a German play with a class or group, with as much involvement of the students as possible in choosing, rehearing and producing the play. If a whole play is too much, short scenes can be taken. Texts for reading can

also include newspaper extracts. Whatever is chosen, the students must find it stimulating, relevant and something they can form an opinion about.

Conversation should be cultivated as a key element in all lessons. If there is a very wide ability range in the class and this inhibits speaking, this should be openly discussed with the class and socially creative solutions be collectively found that result in groups of students speaking German to each other. Every opportunity should be taken to encourage foreign visits, exchanges, contact with young German speakers and so on. Likewise topical current affairs issues should be discussed. Humour remains all important in Class 9, along with the feeling, we are learning how to learn!

Class 10

The over-riding theme for this class is the language itself, its origin, its elements and how it works as it does. This includes the history and development of the language, etymology, comparison with other European languages, and especially the relationship to English. Extracts from literature of several periods can be taken as examples of their period. The same can be done with poetry. In both cases, that of studying the literature and history of the language, the students should be encouraged to form a characterisation of the qualities of the German language itself. Some linguistic theory may be taken to add a theoretical dimension to the discussions.

Examples of literature from which extracts may be taken include: *Altes Testament* (übersetzung von J. Zenk); Luther's *Bibel, Neues Testament, Das Nibelungenlied*; Schiller, *Der Verbrecher aus verlorener Ehre*; Goethe's *Die Leiden des jungen Werthers* or *Die Wahlverwandtschaften*; Nietzsche's *Die Geburt der Tragödie*; Kleist's *Das Erdbeben in Chili, Zwieg, Ungeduld des Herzens*; etc.

In discussions the students are often drawn out of themselves when debating the rights and wrongs of a matter they themselves feel strongly about. Topics can be chosen in consultation with them and vocabulary prepared. Homework should consist of preparation for a set-piece debate. The rules of debate must allow for moments in which each side can gather their arguments (and vocabulary) once more or take stylistic advice from the teacher as impartial adviser. Topics can be prepared as projects by individuals and presented to the class.

Class 10 can prepare a full German play involving as many of the group as wish to take part.

Class 11

Here the beauty of the language and its greatest proponents must stand in the foreground. The works of great poets of various periods should be studied and recited individually and in chorus. The students' ability to form aesthetic judgments should be exercised to the full with the analysis of classic and modern literary texts. These are often best approached through themes rather than merely through the content alone.

The power and subtlety of spoken language should

be a main focus of practice and study, especially in its three primary elements of grammatically – speaking correctly, rhetoric – beautiful speaking and dialectic – to speak persuasively powerfully. Individual students can choose a theme or an individual poet and work on several pieces, coming to a presentation and performance. Class 11 can also sees the performance of a major piece of drama in German.

Topical texts and themes are taken for discussion.

Class 12

There can be an overview of the transition to modern literature using extracts or by taking one major work. The choice is vast and depends upon the knowledge of the teacher and the interests of the students, but should at least consider the following possibilities: Böll, *Die verlorene Ehre der Katherine Blum*; Borchert, *Die Hundelblume*; Feuchtwanger, *Jud Süss*; Frisch, *Stiller*; Fontane, *Effi Briest*, Grass, *Die Blechtrommel*; Handke, *Die Lehre der Sainte Victoire*; Hesse, *Das Glassperlenspiel*; Jean Paul, *Der Titan*; Kafka, *Erzählungen*; Lenz, *Verlassene Zimmer*; Rilke, *Die Aufzeichnungen des Malte Laurids Brigge*; Strauss, *Die Widmung*; Walser, *Ein fliehendes Pferd*; Wolf, *Christa*; Kindheitsmuster.

The three inner aspects of language as a unity, freedom in creativity, equality in communication forms and fraternity in meeting the being of the other. Comparative linguistic studies can be helpful, as well as studies of speech act theory. Recommended study material are Heinz Zimmermann's two books, *Grammatik* and *Sprechen, Zuhören in Erkenntnis –und Entscheidungsprozessen*.

In both Classes 11 and 12 there is an emphasis on the Spirit of the German Language and the Germanic folksoul. This should be approach through the language and literature in particular.

FRENCH

Aims and teaching methods are those stated for foreign languages above.

Classes 1 to 4

The same basic method and content are used as those described for German. In Classes 3 4 the French alphabet, writing and reading are introduced, as in German. In Class 4 the first play with individual parts can be performed

Content suggestions:

Class 1

- Narrative songs e.g. *Il était un petit homme, J'aime la galette, Pirouette cacahuète*
- Verses and songs involving actions, e.g. *Savez-vous planter les choux, Pomme de rainette, toc-hoc-hoc, Monseur Pouce es-tu là?, Sur le pont d'Avignon*

- Finger games (*Voici ma main...*)
- Commands (*Lève-toi, Ouvre la porte, Viens ici...*)
- Phrases in conversation (*Comment t'appelles-tu? – Je m'appelle...; Quel âge as-tu? J'ai ... ans; Où habites-tu?*
- Games with questions: *Qu'est-ce que c'est? – C'est...; Qui a ...? J'ai...; Est-ce que c'est toi?*

Situational vocabulary e.g.
- Activities: simple miming of daily activities, counting, guessing games
- Colours, parts of the body, family members, animals, nature, days of the week, seasons

Class 2

Activities continued:
- simple stories with strong repetition; counting; guessing games; picture dictations
- poems which make good plays (e.g. *L'histoire de la galette, Le chat et les souris*)
- Questions: *Où habites-tu?; Comment s'appelle ta maman, ton papa, etc.; Est-ce que tu as des frères et soeurs?; Comment s'appelle ton frère, ta soeur?*
- Simple structures of negatives: *Est-ce que c'est ça? Non, c'est n'est pas ça; Est-ce que c'est toi? Non, ce n'est pas moi*
- Songs: *Promenons-nous dans les bois*; *Jean petit qui danse*; *Derrière chez mois*
- Learning and acting out fables

Class 3

Conversation can include the time and weather, and the date.
- *Quel temps fait-il? Il fait beau...* etc.; *Quel jour sommes-nous aujourd'hui?*
- Acting out plays about the market using songs and stall-holder cries
- Verb forms: *être* and *avoir* in sentences – *je suis un garçon, une fille...; j'ai un chat; il a un poisson rouge*, etc.
- Notice words with 'le' or 'la'
- Use and recognition of question words and expressions: *où, quand, quel, qui, combien; est-ce que / que'est-ce que*
- Prepositions in sentences: *il est devant la table; nous sommes à côté de...*
- Personal pronouns: *je, tu...*
- Possessive adjectives: *mon, ma, mes; ton, tu, tes*, etc.

Class 4

Writing and reading are introduced using material the children already know by heart. Simple punctuation is introduced. Nouns and articles, adjectives, adverbs and whole verb structures are identified.
- Recitation of verses and poems
- Songs
- Conversation topics, as in Classes 1, 2 and 3, with more emphasis on description of animals, the weather and local surroundings

- Vocabulary for everyday situations is practised
- Writing down verses and short familiar texts
- Practise of recognition and articulation of phonetic elements distinct to French
- Verb forms in present tense learned by heart, written down
- Short dictations of learned text, verb forms
- Initial spelling exercises
- Use of the articles, practise gender and plural of familiar nouns
- Simple oral and later verbal descriptions e.g. of animals, the weather
- Word games e.g. le loto, magie noire

Class 5

Stories, conversations and dialogues in keeping with the pupils' immediate surroundings.
- Stories, school, home, family, body, clothes, meals, course of day and year, telling the time, date, directions in space
- Introduction to France
- Songs, verses, easy poems
- First letters to penfriends

Suggested readers: e.g. D. Fink *La Claire Fontaine, Vols. I & II*, Pädagogische Forschungsstelle. A. Denjean *La Tarasque à Tarasacon*, Pädagogische Forschungsstelle.

Depending on the stage the class has reached, grammar now involves practising the following and subsequently explaining the rules in English (mother tongue), after which they are written down:
- Definite and indefinite article
- Agreement between subject and verb
- The apostrophe
- Present and future of: aller, venir, faire, prendre, mettre, avoir/être
- Verbs ending in er and ir (e.g. finir)
- Questions with 'Est-ce que'; interrogatives: qui, que, quand, comment, ou, pourquoi
- Negative: 'ne ... pas'
- Adjectives describing nouns and agreement with the nouns, i.e. including the feminine form of adjectives ending in e
- Prepositions, but in a context
- Pronouns in the nominative
- Modal verbs: vouloir, pouvoir, devoir (present tense in Class 5; future in Class 6
- Comparisons of adjectives: plus – le plus; moins – le moins

Class 6

Reading of descriptions or dialogues in subjects such as:
- Living in town and country, holidays, household
- Shopping, seasons and festivals, weather, illnesses, sport and games
- Poems, songs, anecdotes, stories and fairy tales (e.g. *Les contes de Perrault* or *Contes basques*
- *Poésies, textes et chansons pour les langues*

moyennes des écoles Waldorf, Pädagogische Forschungsstelle, Stuttgart 1986)
- Geography of France: cotrasting regions, culture, customs and food and wine
- Suggested readers: D. Fink *La Claire Fontaine, Vols. I & II*; A. Denjean *A travers la France par le légendaire de ses provinces*. Also: reading an easy book.

Grammar

- Past: passé composé, passé simple, imparfait
- Irregular verbs: savoir, voir, dormir, etc. and repetition of verbs learnt in Classes 4 and 5
- Negative 'ne ... rien', 'ne ... personne'
- Nouns and adjectives with plural ending x instead of s
- Regular comparison of adjectives
- Demonstrative and passive pronouns
- 'Tout', 'tous', 'toutes'
- Relative clause with qui and que
- Clauses introduced with: parceque, puisque, comme (causal); quand, pendant que (temporal), avant que, après que; pour que, bien que

Class 7

Suggested subjects for reading and speaking:
- Leisure pursuits, stories from French history and legend. The history of Paris up to the present
- The people and countryside of France, poems and songs
- Dramatic scenes
- Possibly a longer, exciting story, e.g. Daudet *Lettres de mon moulin, Tartarin de Tarascon*; Lamorisse *Crin Blanc*, or *Le voyage en ballon*, or *Le ballon rouge*; Denjean *Jacquelin*.

In grammar the following are practised:
- Pronouns le, la, les, en, lui, leur, y/en
- The partitive: pas de, beaucoup de, etc.
- Pluperfect
- Irregular comparison of adjectives
- More irregular verbs
- Indirect speech in the present tense

Class 8

Lively descriptions of life in France:
- Professional life, history, travel stories
- Dramatic scenes, poems, songs
- A longer story or one-act play, or scenes from a longer play; Molière's comedies; Malot *Sans Famille*; Daudet *Le petit chose*; Dumas, selections from *Les trois mousquetaires*, or *Fabliaux du moyen-age*; Hugo *Fantine*, or *Gavroche*; Verne *Le tour du monde en 80 jours*.

Grammar

- 'Subjonctif'
- Irregular 'subjonctif': pouvoir, faire, aller, vouloir etc.

- Indirect speech in the past tense
- Agreement of the participle with 'avoir' and 'être'
- Use of the 'conditionnel'
- Subordinate clauses: pour que, quoique, sans que
- Reflexive verbs, including imperative and negative
- Impersonal phrases and passive constructions
- The passive mode

Classes 9 to 12

General aspects and aims

In Classes 9 to 12 the pupils consolidate what they have learnt in comprehension, speaking, reading and writing and begin to apply it in all realms of daily life and in connection with media, literature and other complex themes such as youth culture, professions, etc. Since one of the important aspects of learning foreign languages is to gain a feeling for the speakers of that language, the lessons will also include the more receptive, artistic aspect that works more on the feeling life, and is just as important as active practice which makes a stronger call on the will. The pupils need to increase the accessibility of the language and their fluency in it. Vocabulary and phrases are expanded to comprise the pupils' wider horizon, and exercises in pronunciation and spelling continue as before. Grammar is deepened and widened during Classes 9 to 12. Special attention is paid to the tenses in subordinate clauses, agreement of the tenses and the proper use of prepositions.

Class 9

Points of view and general themes:

Conversation and reading themes are now expanded to include descriptions from the lives of great individuals (inventors and discoverers, social reformers).
- Stories or dramatic scenes
- Poems and songs
- Retelling, speech exercises, making up stories to pictures.
- Conversation in everyday situations

Content suggestions:

Literature/reading:

Biographies, e.g.
- Henri Dunant (founder of the Red Cross)
- Napoléon, Robespierre, Jeanne d'Arc
- Albert Schweitzer
- Joffo: *Le sac de billes*

Romans policiers, e.g.
- Simenon: *L'Affaire Saint-Fiacre*, or *Le témoignage de l'enfant de choeur*

Discoverers, e.g.
- Champollion, Marie Curie

Novellas, e.g.:
- Malot: *Sans famille* (also in Class 8)
- Hugo: *Gavroche*, or *Cosette*

Recitation:
Ballads and poems, e.g.:
- Hugo: *La retraite de Russie, Ceux qui vivent, Paris, O soldats de l'An Deux, Le mendiant, Entrevue au crépuscule*
- Verlaine: *Chanson d'automne, Il pleure*
- After Claudel: *Jeanne au bucher*
- Baudelaire: *L'Albatros*, etc.

France and its history:
- Bretagne, Provence, Paris, Alsace
- The French Revolution, e.g. theatrical depiction by Mnouchkine or summaries of original texts
- The Jews in France (1940)

Practising the language:

Comprehension:
- Oral and written retelling of what the pupils have read (letters, short dialogues)
- Recounting a sequence of events
- How to use a dictionary
- Work with intonation and vocabulary continues

Grammar:
- Practising the 'conditionnel', the 'gérondif', reflexive verbs
- Exercises on 'passé simple', 'passée composé', 'imparfait'
- des 'participe passé'
- Exercises on 'partitif'
- Forms like 'pour que' or 'pour'
- Infinitive clauses
- Relative clauses: 'qui', 'que', and also 'lequel' etc.
- Pronouns, also with 'passé composé' in the negative.
- Negative in several clauses: ne - ni - ni; ne - pas - ni
- Temporal expressions
- The derived adverb and how to use it
- Difference in meaning between adjective and derived adverb

Exercises / written work:
- Comprehension – oral and written
- Oral retelling of material read, written précis
- Answering questions on the content of a text
- Free essays on themes from the reading material

Class 10

Points of view and general themes:

Beginning of a systematic overview of French literature: popular songs, newspapers and magazines. Students can prepare short talks on such topics.

Content suggestions:

Literature / reading:

Novellas, short stories, e.g.:
- Rochefort *Les petits enfants du siècle*
- Daudet: L*es compères battus, La farce du Cuvier, Les lettres de mon moulin*
- St Exupéry: *Le petit prince, Gargantua*
- Corneille: *Le Cid*
- Hugo: *Jean Valjean*
- Mérimee: *Carmen*
- Branche: *Mort et élévation*
- Biographies of authors and poets: Ronsard, Daudet, Baudelaire, St Exupéry, Prévert in the form of talks

Recitation:
- Ronsard: *Mignonne allons voir*
- Baudelaire: *L'étranger, Initiation au voyage*
- St Exupéry: extracts from *Le petit prince*
- Prévert: *Jour de fête, Déjeuner du matin*
- Eluard: *La bonne justice*

France and its history:
- France in the Middle Ages
- Origins of the French language
- Le Canada, la Tunisie, le Maroc

Exercises:
- Retelling from varying perspectives
- Formulating agreement and disagreement
- Short talks
- Comprehension exercises
- Letters

Grammar:
- Indirect speech in the past
- Agreement of tenses
- Consolidating 'subjonctif' and 'conditionnel'
- All subordinate clauses
- How French relates to Latin and English
- Emphasis on parts of a sentence, e.g.: ce n'est pas moi qui

Exercises / written work:
Verbal and written exercises on vocabulary and the content of texts in the form of essays, reports and retellings.
- Talks on a biography or a country

Class 11

Points of view and general themes:

- Texts from the 17th, 18th, 19th and 20th Centuries
- Exercises on style
- Selected scenes or a whole play are performed
- Selected passages from newspapers and journals
- Encouragement to go on pupil exchanges or visit France

Content suggestions:

Literature / reading:

Selections from:
- Molière *L'Avare, Le médecin malgré lui, Le bourgeois gentilhomme*
- Maeterlinck: *Les aveugles*
- Camus: *L'étranger, Le malentendu, L'hôte, Les justes*
- Voltaire and Rousseau
- Bosco: *L'enfant et la rivière*
- Taine: *Voyage en Italie, Les origines de la France contemporaine*
- Balzac: *Un épisode sous la terreur* etc.

Recitation:
- Vian: *Chant pour la vie*
- Rimbaud: *Le dormeur du val*
- Selections from Molière
- Hugo: *Sur une barricade*, etc.

France and its history:
- The Enlightenment
- Napoléon III and the Commune
- Minorities in France: the Bretons, the Basques, Occitanean culture; l'Algérie

Practising the language:
Essays.
Short talks on topical subjects such as:
- 'Moslems in France', or 'Life in the Banlieue'
- Conversations in class with pupils taking different parts
- Attempts to write poetry
- Work on stylistic nuances

Comprehension exercises:
- Comparing the vernacular with literary language

Grammar (including revision):
- Other ways of expressing the conditional
- The adjective and its comparison
- Use of the free pronoun 'soi'
- Uses and forms of pronouns
- Revision of the 'passif'
- Forms and use of 'futur antérieur'

Exercises / written work:
The pupils should be quite independent in writing their own essays, reports, retellings, letters.

Class 12

Points of view and general themes:

People of the 20th Century
- Contemporary literature
- France's important contributions to world literature and history

Content suggestions:

Literature/reading:
Texts from literature describing social conditions (Balzac, Zola or similar).

Texts by authors writing about the meaning of life, e.g.:
- Sartre: *Les mouches, La putain respectueuse*
- Beckett: *En attendant Godot*
- Ionesco: *Les chaises, La cantatrice chauve, La leçon, Le Rhinocéros, Le piéton de l'air*
- Camus: *La peste*
- Mauriac, Gide, Lusseyran: *Et la lumière fut, La pollution du Moi*

Recitation:
- Apollinaire: *Le pont Mirabeau*
- Aragon: *Rien n'est jamais acquis*
- Sartre: Extracts from *Les mouches*
- Queneau: *Il pleut*
- Eluard: *Un compte à régler*, etc.
- Yves: *Bonnefoy*

France and its history:
Topical and cultural questions in the French-speaking world:
- Political institutions
- Minorities
- Corsica
- Nouvelle Calédonie
- La 'francophonie'
- Education, media, people and their environment
- Youth, tomorrow's world, advertising
- City life, art, religion, drugs, sport

Practising the language:
Pupils' interpretations of subjects, people, scenes.
- Debating
- Translating from the viewpoint of comparative linguistics
- Noticing the 'genius' of the language
- Comprehension exercises
- Differences between verbal and written language
- Intonation and vocabulary

Exercises/written work:
- Free essays and discussion
- Reports, letters

Reference
1   See Kiersch, J., *Language Teaching in Steiner Waldorf Schools*, SSF 1997, chapter 3, and the Appendix by Norman Skillen, for an explanation of the importance of movement in language teaching.

GARDENING

Classes 6 to 10

General aspects and aims

Gardening gives young people a real understanding of nature because they gain experience through practical activity. Working and observing over several years, and reporting regularly on what has been learnt, they build up a feel for the way nature works. Through their communal work in the school garden they gain a foundation on which they can base judgment and responsibility. Gardening lessons begin in early puberty and can become a real educational help. The pupils' growing awareness of their increasing independence manifests initially in considerable psychological irritability and lack of equanimity. It is a time when they need help from a steady hand that can show them how to find their way. An important element of this is active work with nature. The teacher becomes an expert who can show them the processes and complexities of nature.

Every school has different possibilities for gardening, depending on local circumstances. The size, variety and arrangement of the school garden should be governed entirely by educational criteria.

Space permitting, the following facilities are necessary:
- Garden house with space for theoretical and practical work, especially in wet weather or in winter
- Tool shed. There must be several of each tool
- Greenhouse with pricking out and potting facilities, and also frames for early planting
- Tree nursery, herb garden, tree and bush fruit, flower beds, lawns
- Beds for annual vegetables, herbs and flowers for cutting
- Composting area

The gardening programme can culminate with a period of practical work in agriculture in Class 9 or 10, or with a forestry period in Class 10.

Points of view and general themes:

Getting to know and appreciate gardening skills and knowledge
Learning these skills can help the youngsters gain respect for the skills of others. They also learn to have confidence in their own skills and become better able to assess their own possibilities.

Earthly maturity (puberty): working with the earth is helpful
Gardening provides a degree of stability during this time of physical and psychological change. Meaningful work strengthens the limbs. Psychological qualities such as reverence, gratitude, endurance and wonder are awakened. The schooling of the senses and of causal thinking has positive consequences for the development of more subtle experiential capacities and also of the capacity to think clearly.

Laying the foundation for a practical sense of responsibility
This is best achieved by getting youngsters to care for domestic animals, but it is also experienced by them when they care for a plot of land for several years, improving the soil and learning how to make and use compost, or when they grow young plants and care for garden beds including harvesting their produce.

Harmony and peace are found through working in nature
The work can lead to a 'healthy tiredness' (especially in Classes 8 and 9). The beauty of the garden and the orderly interplay between natural things (plants, soil, animals, weather, sun etc.), and also experiencing the regularity of the seasons, can lead to harmonising soul experiences in the long term.

There is a specific educational problem that can lead to widespread feelings of helplessness, especially amongst the young: the creeping destruction of nature. The threat hanging over everything often appears insurmountable, and at an age when they are strongly oriented towards their own future young people often find their will paralysed by a fundamental feeling of resignation. This can be overcome through proper, caring work in the school garden, on a farm or during a practical period of forestry. The youngsters have a direct experience of how the situation in the garden, the farm or the forest makes direct demands on them and how their own personal efforts lead to the creation of 'new life'. Through this it becomes a matter of course for them to want to help and share responsibility. A practical period working in agriculture is especially important in this connection for Class 9 or 10.

The suggested tasks for the different age-groups are not a rigid list: the size of the school garden, its situation, soil, climate and other local factors influence how we can do gardening with the pupils, and suggestions about which new tasks to introduce at the different stages may be helpful. In keeping with real life, where necessary the older pupils should take on tasks they have already done when younger. This goes for all the routine gardening jobs such as weeding, which all pupils should be taught how to do.

Where possible the pupils can also learn about forestry and woodland work. One need not be in the country to do this, city parks offer a wide range of trees and hedgerow plants.

Content suggestions:

Suitable tasks for Class 6:

Getting to know and carrying out basic practical activities such as:
GARDENING
- Sieving soil and compost

- Preparing beds
- Cultivating and harvesting
- Hoeing, initially with the short hoe
- Mowing grass with the sickle
- Making bunches of flowers or herbs
- Weeding reasonably sized patches

WOODLAND WORK
- Seed collection and sowing
- Special composts
- Grading of seedlings

In Class 7 can be added:

GARDENING
- Growing crops that need more complicated care, pricking out seedlings, potting
- Making and spreading compost
- Mixing seeding and potting compost
- Knowledge of soil cultivation and digging
- Finding out the geological history of the ground underneath the garden
- Making new beds. Using garden line and drilling rake
- Harvesting and cleaning vegetables ready for market
- Marketing of garden produce and keeping accounts
- Harvesting herbs and herb teas and preparing them correctly
- Making advent wreaths
- Making straw or reed mats

WOODLAND WORK
- Tree planting
- Weeding and maintenance of seedlings and saplings
- Thinning out trees by felling
- Cutting firewood
- Greenwood work, hurdles, tool handles

In Class 8 can be added:

GARDENING
- General gardening jobs that require skill, endurance and physical effort
- Mowing grass with the scythe. Haymaking

- Repairing tools and buildings
- Manufacturing foods from produce (pickles, chutney, herb salt, jams; using wax if bees are kept)
- The study of cultivated plants and the soils they need. Simple crop rotation sequences and their advantages/disadvantages

WOODLAND WORK
- Establishing, maintaining and harvesting willow beds
- Coppicing hazel
- Charcoal burning
- Greenwood turning – poles for stools, chairs, ladders

In Class 9, which usually has a longer gardening main-lesson, the pupils get to know about landscape gardening, building paths, steps and fences, ponds, water re-cycling projects.

- Propagation techniques are studied in theory and practice
- Caring for soft-fruit bushes, fruit trees and decorative shrubs, pruning

In Class 10:

The pupils learn the mysteries of grafting (as suggested by Steiner). This subject can be dealt with in great depth, leaving little time for anything else. It depends how much time is available.

In the Upper School, environmental studies and ecology overlap with gardening.

Depending on the school's resources there is much scope from practical environmental and landscaping projects, especially involving the timber cycle, with the preparation of timber for carpentry and joinery. Managing nature reserves, biotopes and ponds can even be done on a small scale. Here scientific observation plays an important role. All this can lead to individual project work of a practical, scientific or artistic nature.

In the following the traditional Waldorf practical blocks are described. There is, however, much innovation and variation. The following examples should be taken as offering guidelines.

The child shows a motivation and striving to go out over the environment, to form a unique world image as a part of achieving a singular identity. This is part of humankind's yearning and capacity for individualisation. Every child must integrate a world image with a corporal awareness, in order to know where she is and who she is. [1]

Classes 1 to 3

General aspects and aims

Geography, in all its various aspects, forms a key integrating subject within the whole curriculum. Defined at its broadest it encompasses many aspects of the world around us. Learning about the world around us is a complex subject covering many fields that relate to many other subjects. Essentially though, the methodology of geography teaching in Steiner Waldorf schools has fundamental themes:

- Physical or natural geography
- Social geography
- Inner or developmental geography

The first systematically describes the phenomena of the earth, its surface, interior and atmosphere. The second considers the human influence on the environment, its economic consequences and the relationship between the particular character of a geographical region and the social and cultural development of the people who live there. The third refers to how individuals' awareness of their environment is reflected in how they see the world and experience themselves within it and follows how this process evolves through the child's development. The methodology of the Waldorf curriculum seeks to integrate these three approaches.

The core of this method is to proceed from the whole to the inter-related parts and to start in the known world and proceed to the unknown before returning to the known. It is a voyage of discovery. *"The regions of the earth are not to be studied as mere divisions of the earth's surface, but rather that the areas of the earth's surface are to be studied for their particular character which is a product of their phenomena. It is their inter-relationship with each other which fills the areas with their content... Geography in Steiner Waldorf education entails the use of a comparative method".* [2] Furthermore, as Alexander von Humboldt pointed out, geography must contain something aesthetic, which proceeds from a premonition of the inter-relation of the sensual with the intellectual towards a feeling of universality. *"Descriptions of nature can be sharply limited and scientifically exact without thereby losing the living breath of the power of imagination".* [3] This aspect is fundamental to geographical education.

The basis for geography teaching is the concept of the earth as morphological and physical totality, or the earth as an organism. This implies a consciousness both of the inter-relationships of the parts within the whole and also of the whole as a developing being. This highlights the importance of climatic geography in which we can readily see the parts as aspects of a whole earth climatic system (ocean currents are another related example). Exploring the characteristic phenomena of the different climatic zones can be done either generically, as types regardless of location (tundra or equatorial zones) or by specific reference to actual regions. Both methods belong within the Waldorf Curriculum.

The relationship to true regional diversity is also important. It is important for the pupils to be able to visualise both the similarities with what they know and the differences in distance and scale of unfamiliar parts of the earth. Steiner stressed this:

In dealing with space we densify the spirit and soul of the child, we drive it down to the ground. By teaching geography in such a way that the child sees what we are telling him we bring about this consolidation in him. But there must be the true seeing in space. The child must, for example, be conscious that the Niagara Falls are not the river Elbe! We must help him to realise that a vast space stretches between the two. [4]

Geography is a subject that can lead the children 'down to earth' and thus prepare them for earthly maturity. Before they go to school and even during their first two years at school, children have a rather dreamy awareness of the world as a totality. Learning about the environment leads them to more wakeful and differentiated perceptions. Up to the age of seven or eight this unity exists of its own accord; thereafter it needs cultivating by means of ever more contact with the world. This includes vivid and colourful descriptions of the archetypal professions, crafts and the locality. Such descriptions are complemented by practical activities such as farming, processing cereals, housebuilding, gardening. How this is done will vary in ways that depend on the nature of the locality. The production and processing of natural materials is the basis of human economy and this relationship to nature is an important aspect of geography.

If we want to help the children enter into a partnership with nature we must enable them to go beyond mere intellectual knowledge of the kind gained by learning of nature indirectly, such as through electronic media, and penetrate to real feelings for the natural world, feelings that will always lead to activity and a responsible relationship between human beings and nature.

For Classes 1 to 3 the general aim of learning about the environment might be formulated as follows: *Getting to know and feeling connected with one's surroundings and with the work human beings do.* In Class 4 differentiation begins to be more pronounced. Local knowledge of the immediate area widens spatially (to include geography, simple astronomy, and the study of human beings, animals and plants) and temporally (history). From Class 4 onwards the differentiated subjects are named accordingly, but they ought to remain integrated within an overall experience of the world around us.

Environmental studies would thus be part of history lessons, for example, how the consequences of the Greco-Latin culture, of the Middle Ages and of recent history, as well as the aftermath of the Industrial Revolution's inventions, still influence our life and environment today. Similarly, environmental studies in geography lessons would show how climate and soil are related to the transport and trade, the economy and way of life of different societies. Environmental studies also relate to English lessons in the form of business essays and to arithmetic lessons in the form of commercial arithmetic. Steiner even considered that religion lessons would also be a part of environmental education, as his suggestions that the steam engine or something astronomical might be included in them.

The general educational aim for the children's ninth to twelfth year is thus: *to meet the children's need to experience reality i.e. the overall meaning of the realities of nature and the world, so that they can develop their love for the world. This is a cross-curricular aim.*

Environmental studies also play an essential part in the sciences of nature (physics and chemistry). Steiner considered it important for the youngsters in Classes 7 and 8 to have physics lessons *about life*, lessons that give them an understanding of their relationship with their surroundings:

> *We are living in a world made by human beings, shaped in accordance with human thoughts, a world that we use while knowing nothing at all about it. That we do not understand something made by human beings, something that is, to all intents and purposes, human thought, is a fact that is of great significance in connection with people's mood of soul and spirit ... The worst thing of all is to share in the experience of this world made by human beings without taking trouble over it.* [5]

This leads, from the pupils' twelfth year onwards, to the formulation of the general educational aims with regard to the way in which *'the world and the life around us'* influences all lessons: *the children should attain elementary concepts, knowledge and skills with regard to the more important functions of life. This is not only to give them confidence but also to give them the longing to know all about what is going on around them.*

In summary one can say that up to the age of 12, the task of the geography curriculum is to bring the child down to earth; to awaken them to the world around them. From this point on the curriculum moves through cultural geography in Classes 7 and 8 to relating to the world as a whole living organism in the Upper School.

In some schools, Class 8 pupils carry out year-long projects in connection with which environmental studies offers them opportunities to deepen their knowledge of life subjects, thus satisfying their curiosity, or developing it further.

We should point here to environmental studies within the curriculum in the Upper School, as practised in the various practical projects, and also the subject 'technology and life' which Steiner introduced as early on as 1921. Some Steiner Waldorf schools have made this integrated environmental approach as the basis for developing quite new forms of the Upper School.

Class 1

Points of view and general themes:

Small children take their surroundings, i.e. other people, animals, plants, stones, stars, sun and moon, as well as the seasons of the year, for granted. If we can constantly renew this unity of the different realms, we shall strengthen the children's confidence, gratitude and self-assurance. In the basic mood of a child during its first seven-year period, these feelings can be expressed as: 'the world is good!'

During their first year at school the children should learn to see differentiation in the overall totality of nature while at the same time becoming increasingly more awake to the way everything belongs together. The children are encouraged to reflect on things through stories, through looking at nature, following the seasonal changes and through descriptions of experiences that emphasise what is special about what they see; what is huge or tiny, what is delicate or immensely powerful in nature. Such stories and observations will only get through to the children if they are told 'with soul', i.e. if they are filled with humanity through personification. This lets them sense that there is nothing in the world that is meaningless or without significance. These experiences are particularly important as a preparation for the real situation in which we find ourselves today because they not only lay foundations, but also set the pattern for the future.

Content suggestions:

The kingdoms of nature, the elements, the seasons of the year, the stars should be described as though they themselves were speaking. By this we do not mean unreal stories or inventions but imaginative tales that speak of the essence of things. They can be in the form of parables or nature legends.

Class 2

Points of view and general themes:

In Class 1 the children have learnt to see their surroundings through 'new' eyes and have begun to hear what these surroundings are telling them. Now, in Class 2, they experience how human beings are linked to the kingdoms of nature. The feelings that result from this, an active identification with nature – what could be called 'love for the world' – are very important. These feelings evolve until the children become 'mature for the earth' in Class 8, when they can be experienced as responsibility.

Content suggestions:

Fables, such as those of Aesop tell of the relationship between human beings and their surroundings in anthropomorphic form. Saints' stories, notably those of Celtic saints, express a similar quality. The figure of St. Francis of Assisi, with his reverence and humility towards all created things, can serve as a yardstick by which to measure the lessons. Such stories lay a foundation for morality.

During the first two years of school, environmental studies belong as an integral part of every lesson. Let the children talk about what is going on in nature, what they meet with on their way to school, what they discovered on an outing, and so on. Things they bring to school with them (bird nests, leaves, conkers, fruit, stones, animal horns, snails, etc.) can provide the starting point for talking about the world around us. This does not mean that there need not be specific main-lesson blocks for some of these subjects, but simply that in Classes 1 and 2 there is no need to make separate subjects out of nature studies. The 'outdoor classroom' should be regularly visited and experienced in all weathers and seasons.

Class 3

Points of view and general themes:

Children reaching the age of nine undergo a decisive alteration in their relationship with the world: the world that was a part of them becomes the world that surrounds them. The children need to understand and literally grasp, as far as they can at this age, the links they sense they have with the world. In the coming years this can develop into an understanding of nature, animals, human beings, work and technology. Complex work processes that take a long time to complete can be understood by the children, for example, through a house-building main-lesson, or a farming main-lesson that shows them the whole sequence from ploughing and sowing to the end result, bread. Their intelligence is schooled by means of concrete reality. It is important that at the moment when they meet and sense what they are working with, their links with it are not broken and turned aside into mere rational and factual abstractions, but that their own activity leads them to the wide-ranging implications.

Content suggestions:

- The human being and the earth: the farmer and the work on the farm, ploughing (the horse, harness, shoeing, the plough), harrowing, sowing (various kinds of cereal), different soils (drainage of wet ploughland), harvesting, threshing, milling, baking, dairy farming. Once traditional methods have been introduced, children should see what tractors, combine harvesters etc. do
- The miner and other traditional occupations to do with working the earth (turf cutter, stone mason, dyke digger)
- Making use of the elements in house-building:

brick making (drying, baking), preparing mortar, bricklaying, carpentry, roofing
- 'Archetypal' callings such as shepherd, hunter, fisherman, woodcutter, charcoal burner, baker, tailor, shoemaker, potter, carpenter, tanner, saddler, spinner, weaver, or blacksmith
- As much as possible, children should have direct, hands-on experience of these trades

The emphasis among these various possible themes will vary depending on the geographical location of the school.

Class 4 – Local Geography

Points of view and general themes:

Steiner's imperative: 'all lessons must give knowledge about life' and should be taken into account. *Local geography* is an important aspect of environmental studies. Previously the lessons have turned on general aspects (links with nature, knowledge of work processes), but now they focus the children's attention in both space and time. A new, more concrete source of knowledge opens up, encompassing both time and space.

The immediate surroundings of the school, the locality, the town or city are shown to the children in their geographical/spatial and historical/temporal development, right up to the present situation. Through these studies, their more generalised relationship with the world can be transformed into a sense of belonging, both socially and spatially.

Content suggestions:

- Observing the sun as a way of recognising the four compass directions
- The rising and setting motions of a few characteristic constellations round the North Star, and the movements of the moon
- Drawing of bird's eye view of the school (or the child's home) and the town or village it is in
- Descending from a high viewpoint (hill, tower) into the surrounding landscape changes one's view of what can be seen
- Different children's routes to school are described and drawn
- The children can make clay or papier mâché models of the immediate surroundings and shapes of the landscape
- The first simple maps are drawn
- Historical events and legends illustrating the development of the locality are told
- The different ways the local soils are tilled, local industry, workplaces and infrastructure are examined. Vivid descriptions of typical local industries and professions
- A visit to the local railway station, docks or airport can give the children a sense of how their home town is linked to other places, why people travel to their hometown, what commodities are imported and exported

Classes 5 to 12

General aspects and aims

As with all subjects, the task of geography lessons is to accompany and support the children in their physical, psychological and spiritual development. In addition to this, Steiner also wanted geography to occupy a central position because it can be linked up with so many other subjects (biology, physics, chemistry, astronomy, mathematics, history etc.) and thus provide a general sense of unity. He also stressed the moral component of geography lessons by saying that learning about people living side by side would help the children to love their fellow human beings. [6]

Geography must give the children an interest in the world and courage for life. They must learn to understand the earth as a natural space with specific life rhythms in which human beings are enveloped but which they can also change through economic and cultural activity. The foundation for responsibility and an awareness of ecology must be laid early.

General aspects and aims for Classes 5 to 8

The curriculum alters its emphasis in keeping with the stage of development the children have reached. Building on the local geography of Class 4, the children in Classes 5 and 6 are first led closer to the earth through looking at local ways of farming and industry in which human beings are in partnership with nature in different regions and their inter-dependencies. This helps them in their development. In Classes 7 and 8 they then get to know the character and culture of other peoples, particularly in other parts of the globe. Geography lessons thus have a sense of movement and counter-movement. During the middle period of childhood the children find their home on the earth in physical space, i.e. there is movement towards the earth. Then, as puberty approaches, when they attain earthly maturity, there is a movement towards the psychological and cultural differentiation of the earth.

Class 5

Points of view and general themes:

Teaching geography to children in the middle part of childhood means giving them many facts linked to experience. The pupils are to learn something about the world, but in such a way that feelings are linked to that knowledge. Original causes remain in the background. A selection of regions and landscapes of their own country are described. The important thing is to expand the study of economics and infrastructure begun in Class 4 to wider regions.

Content suggestions:

The children can go on 'journeys of discovery' along rivers, travelling beyond their immediate surroundings. They can 'travel to the coast' or into hilly regions.

- Contrast life by the sea, in the hills, in the lowlands
- Mining and other industries
- Continuation of map drawing, use of wall-maps, atlases
- The economic and geographic links between the home and neighbouring countries, stressing mutual interdependence
- The regional and physical geography of their country or larger region. In the UK this would usually be the whole of the British Isles

Class 6

Points of view and general themes:

In Class 6 there are two aspects to geography. On the one hand, the home country is related to the continent it belongs to. On the other hand, there will be a short but systematic overview of all the continents. These are contrasted with one another as to their main topography and morphology (outline, river systems, mountains, skies, climate, vegetation, etc.). *Astronomy* belongs here in the way it relates to the earth and the seasons. *Geology* and *botany* also come into the geography main-lesson. Industry and commerce are extended to include a few striking examples where global links are significant. The teacher will make careful choices, bearing in mind what he or she intends to bring into the discussions of other parts of the world in Classes 7 and 8.

Content suggestions:

a) The main-lesson on Europe (if the school is European)

In their earlier geography lessons the pupils will already have been shown contrasting landscapes and lifestyles. Now Europe as a whole can be seen from the aspect of polarity, e.g. by looking at the different influences of water, air, light/warmth and of the rocks and soils in different regions on landscape and economy. This may mean a comparison between a lowland country such as the Netherlands with an Alpine country such as Switzerland, or between regions with a traditional economy connected to the sea, such as Norway, with a landlocked country such as the Czech Republic.

b) Regarding the wider overview of the earth as a whole:

- Shape and distribution of the continents and oceans. Ocean currents. Relationship of the tides to the moon
- Dependence of the vegetation belt on the position of the sun and climatic conditions. Seasons in relation to the earth's orbit
- The rocky foundations, old and young parts of the earth
- Young folded mountains (e.g. the Alps, the Himalayas, the Andes), the rift valleys, e.g.

the Red Sea Jordan valley, Rhone Valley etc.
- The great rivers and their individual characteristics, e.g. the Rhine, the Danube, the Dnieper
- Tropical rainforest, savanna, the outback of Australia, salt deserts as ecosystems
- The globe should be looked at as a whole from different perspectives i.e. not only with Europe at the centre
- Breaking new ground, forest clearance and the creation of dustbowls, with striking examples of soil erosion
- Mineral deposits and trade relations
- Opening of transport routes (e.g. Trans Siberian Railway, the Suez and Panama Canals)

Obviously one cannot cover all these topics but a balance is sought that exemplifies as much of the whole as possible.

Class 7

Points of view and general themes:

In Classes 7 and 8 the transition is made from agriculture to industry and commerce to the cultural situation in different parts of the globe. This is one of the shifts of emphasis that Steiner recommended. [7] This necessitates the teacher selecting the material for both the classes. The cultural aspect, in turn, leads to history playing a part in geography lessons: in Class 7 particularly the Age of Discovery, including the transition from the Ptolemaic to the Copernican view of the world. This shows the children that today's view of earth and universe is one that has evolved and that it is not a system set in stone for all time.

So that the different characters and cultures of other parts of the world do not remain in the realm of ideas, Steiner suggested letting the children paint or do other artistic or practical work in the style of those cultures. Other main-lessons, too, can be enriched by biographies of discoverers and descriptions of other parts of the world.

In connection with the theme of discovery, the astronomy of the visible sky should be studied. Obsrvations should be made and charts showing the main constellations shown.

Content suggestions:

Since the Age of Discovery is the subject of history lessons in Class 7, it could be argued that America would be the obvious choice for geography, or Europe if the school is in America i.e. where did the Colonists come from? Africa, too, with its polarity between the black African and the Islamic cultures can be taken as a whole. In the following, therefore, we shall assume the sequence: Class 7 Old World, Class 8 New World. Class 7 might even have two geography main-lessons.

As well as the historical perspective connected with European Colonialism, the link between agriculture, raw materials (cotton, rice, wheat, coffee, tea etc.) and manufacturing industry should be stressed. This in turn should be placed in a context of global climate zones e.g. SE Asian rice, rubber, hardwoods, North American Prairie wheat, Caribbean bananas, South American beef, Australian wool and mining etc.

Building on the astronomy in Class 6, the visible night sky should be described and observations made of the constellations. The appearance and paths of the planets can be described and the cycles of the moon observed.

AFRICA:
The main geographical regions of Africa can be characterised from a climatic, topographical, plant zone perspective:
- North Africa, West Africa and the Equatorial Regions, the Sahara and Sahel, Eastern Africa and Southern Africa
- Different ways of life in black Africa and Islamic Africa in the different vegetation zones (e.g. Pygmies and rain forest peoples, shepherd nomads, Samburu, Masai, farmers and plantations, oasis populations, miners)
- The continuation of various religions and traditional African societies
- The Colonial and post-Colonial influences of France, Britain, Holland, Germany. Confrontation with Western world views. Examples of developing nations and their economic relationship to the developed world. The problems of famine and civil war in the Horn of Africa, the tensions between tribalism and modern commercial interests in West Africa, multicultural societies in Southern Africa etc.

ASIA:
- Main geographical regions, Himalayas/Hindu Kush, Indian subcontinent, Tibet/Mongolia plateau, North and South China, SE Asia, Thailand, Philippines, Indonesia, Japan, Korea
- Macro-landscapes in their cultural and geographical polarity (e.g. the influence of Buddhism, Hinduism, Islam and Christianity); SE Asia as a subcontinent of islands, the huge populations of Eastern Asia, the Pacific Rim as a rapidly developing region and the modern significance of the Asian tiger economies
- How the role of Asian peoples is changing in the modern world. The future of China and the Pacific Rim countries, in relation to the global economy
- Issues connected with rainforest exploitation

Class 8

Points of view and general themes:

As they increasingly enter into the world, Class 8 pupils want to come to grips with world problems. Conversely, their own problems also take on 'world' dimensions. So especially in geography lessons the interplay between 'me and the world' should be catered for. By concerning themselves with the cultural and soul life of other peoples, as well as their cultures and values, the pupils experience that psychological characteristics of peoples can differ greatly. This can help the youngsters find a foothold in their search for their own inner soul life.

Another approach to geography lessons in Class 8 is to ask oneself where metamorphoses, polarities and intensifications take place in geographical phenomena.

If America is the subject of lessons in Class 7, North and South America can be compared. This helps develop the pupils' powers of imagination. It helps prevent fixed ideas from creeping in, but leads rather to knowledge that can come alive and grow. The pupils should learn to understand how the different mentalities of Hispanic and Anglo Americans came about in a historical process.

A further theme in Class 8 is the moods and changing patterns of the weather.

Content suggestions:

• Introduction to typical landscapes of North and South America, e.g. by means of an imaginary journey, use of place names to show cultural influences
• Structure of the double continent and its diverse animal and plant life
• Arrival of the Native Americans and their adaptation to different geographical areas
• The Spanish-Portuguese and the Anglo-French occupations and their consequences (mineral wealth, technology, destruction of nature)
• Encounters between individuals in America. Different psychological make-up of the various social and ethnic groups. Development tasks and possibilities. The demographic issues in the USA
• Cloud formations observed and painted. Meteorological readings taken and charted: rainfall, humidity, air pressure, wind speed; including the use of instruments e.g. barometer, wind vane etc. High and low pressure, weather fronts. Cultural aspects of climate in Northern countries and the length of day; Mediterranean lifestyle and climate; desert peoples; arctic peoples; tropical environments.

If America has been studied in Class 7, a geographical and economic comparison between Africa and Europe, or Europe and Asia can be undertaken.

General aspects and aims for Classes 9 to 12

In the Upper School, geography and all the other subjects continue in their task of accompanying and supporting the pupils in their physical, psychological and spiritual development. At this age this is helped by looking at the earth as something whole, beginning with the physical consistency of the rocks and the life processes in the earth (vegetation zones as organs of the earth, rhythmical processes inside the earth and in its mantle of water and air). Then comes the transformation of the earth by human activity (human-geography). The earth should be understood as an organism, which means that this concept must be clarified and that a Goetheanistic or contextual approach taking the phenomena as the starting point must be developed. It is good to avoid giving merely abstract, value-free knowledge or overstressing physical and mathematical chains of cause and effect. Rather than conditions, it is processes that need to be described, leading on to the cultural situation of the population in different regions.

Geography in the Upper School must develop into *eco-geography*. Examples must show the ecological effect of human activity on the different life conditions in the world (rainy and dry seasons, steppes, rainforest, monsoon and Gulf Stream climates), and the highly adapted lifestyles and industrial practices of the various societies. The consequences of disregarding ecological and socio-cultural structures by colonial and neo-Colonial exploitation must also be described. Towards the end of the Upper School, geography can become *'study of the earth's evolution'*. By learning from the skills of indigenous populations we can sow the seeds for a 'partnership with nature'. Discussions of a social order that is in keeping with human dignity can open up perspectives for the future.

Class 9

Points of view and general themes:

In Class 9 the pupils become 'mature for the earth' to use Steiner's phrase, and their bodies are more weighed down by gravity. In biology, for example, this phase is accompanied by studying the most 'earthly' part of the human body, the skeleton and the sense organs. The corresponding element in geography is the 'earth's skeleton', the world of minerals and their formations (the rocky mantle of the earth). The crucial factor here is the vividness with which teleological forces can be described. The macro-cycles of continental movements, mountain building, vulcanism, faulting and earthquakes need to be experienced as dynamic processes and not reduced to abstract and therefore incomprehensible diagrams or graphics. The students have to be able feel the three dimensional forces, of rift valley formation for example, as something they can grasp with their whole bodies, not merely with their intellects. This calls for a lively, participatory kind of teaching, one which cultivates a living and plastic imagination of nature's forces. Although picture material will be essential, the students first have to create their own inner pictures of the processes involved.

Content suggestions:

• Shape and distribution of continents and oceans
• Morphology and formation of folded mountains
• The 'mountain cross' of the earth, the great rift valleys, volcanoes, mid-ocean ridges and ocean trenches. From continental drift to plate tectonics
• Mineralogy, rhythmical processes in rock formation
• An overview of the earth's history

- Geological layers showing former ice ages and the effects of glaciation
- A survey of the other main forms of erosion

Class 10

Points of view and general themes:

The view Class 9 pupils have of the world is fairly homogeneous. In Class 10 this begins to fragment into perhaps quite contrary aspects. The youngsters can lose some of their confidence and begin to doubt things. At the same time they begin to discover their own internal soul space and are thus able to approach worldly phenomena with a greater degree of subtlety. For example this is the time when the most vital organs are discussed in biology; the processes of these organs can be traced as having an effect even in the psychological realm. In the geography main-lesson the earth itself is seen as a living organism with vital processes going on inside the depths of the earth, in its rocky crust, in its watery and airy mantle and even in outer space. In each case the most rhythmical processes are the ones to be studied.

Content suggestions:

- The mantles of the earth: from the lithosphere to the stratosphere
- The inner structure of the earth
- Movements of the tectonic plates
- Characteristics of water and how it flows: rivers and ocean currents as living organs of the earth: interchange between deep and surface currents.
- The links between ocean currents and climate, e.g. the Gulf Stream, trade winds, el Niño, etc.
- The layers of the atmosphere: meteorology (with practical exercises): the planetary winds: the earth's magnetic field
- Interplay between climate and vegetation: the ecosystems of the earth as organs of an organism
- Movements and rhythms of the earth

Class 11

Points of view and general themes:

Pupils in Class 11 take a clear step towards finding themselves. They gain confidence in their own inner powers of thinking, feeling and willing. They can begin to understand subtle correlations in the web of cause and effect, the kind of thinking necessary to grasp complex phenomena such as ecosystems. This makes it possible to lead the pupils beyond what they have been able to imagine so far. In biology, for example, the pupils are asked to look at the world of the cell, and of unicellular animals, i.e. the world of the unimaginably small. In geography there can be an *astronomy* main-lesson, to enable the pupils to enter the world of the unimaginably vast. On the other hand *cartography* does justice to the pupils' new capacity for abstract thought through the task of depicting the round globe on a two-dimensional flat surface. (Steiner

suggested cartography for pupils of this age as a continuation of the surveying main-lesson.)

The specifically geographical theme for this class is *eco-geography*. It examines the interplay between outer space, the relief structure of the face of the earth, climate, vegetation and the human being. Following on from the geography main-lesson of Class 10 (the mantles of the earth), this new main-lesson would need to include more economic and social geography. These should not concentrate solely on negative developments such as pollution and ecological destruction, but must also show the beginnings of a *study of how the earth evolves*. Examples of the positive influence on ecosystems through increased bio-diversity in some traditional forms of land cultivation can be discussed with a view to the feasibility of replicating similar effects through modern land management programmes. The whole concept of what constitutes health in an ecosystem should be discussed so that it becomes clear that nature left to her own devices is not the only answer, that people can live on the land in sustainable ways. *Technology* lessons throughout the year can lend further depth to these subjects.

Content suggestions:

- The earth's landscape zones as ecosystems and the significance of bio-diversity
- History as a process of economic steps
- Mineral wealth and its exploitation: world trade
- Poverty in developing countries created by exploitative practices
- Aspects of a just economic/social system
- Examples and assessment of ecological industry today
- Tasks for the future
- Aspects of modern astronomy and cosmology (can also be done in Class 12)

Class 12

Points of view and general themes:

The young people's horizon widens in Class 12. They get a closer focus of their own life tasks, and they also regard the problems of the world with a greater sense of responsibility. The step towards maturity they are taking now requires a change in the style of teaching them. They want an overview; they look for links with other subjects; they discuss questions of lifestyle in a highly technical world. By the end of their time at school the young people ought to have reached the realisation that a new partnership between human beings and the earth is needed, and that every single individual must work towards this.

Content suggestions:

- Seeing the earth from the point of view of its natural as well as its cultural structures
- Early forms of humanity and the emergence of Homo sapiens sapiens: the significance of human evolution for the biosphere: language, technology,

culture, religion and history as factors determining the creation of different peoples and nations

- Geographical and cultural origins of society
- Population changes and what the earth can support: starvation and affluence
- The task of overcoming racism and nationalism. The importance of education
- Steiner's ideas about a threefold social order as one possibility. Successful projects and initiatives. Examples of responsible behaviour towards the earth with regard to nature and the socio-cultural structure

References

1 Brierley D.L., *In the Sea of Life Enisled: An introduction to the teaching of geography in Waldorf Education*, Antropos Akademi, Oslo, 1998.
2 Ibid, p13.
3 Ibid, p16.
4 Steiner, R., *Waldorf Education for Adolescence*, op. cit., lecture of 14 June 1921.
5 Steiner, R., *Practical Advice to Teachers*, op. cit., lecture of 3rd September 1919.
6 See Steiner, R., *Waldorf Education for Adolescence*, op. cit., lecture of 14th June 1921.
7 Steiner, R., *Practical Advice to Teachers*, op. cit., lecture of 2nd September, 1919.

HISTORY

Classes 5 to 12

General aspects and aims for Classes 5 to 8[1]
Leading up to history through early years and the Lower School

Initially the children find their home in the landscape and history of their immediate surroundings. For the first three years at school, the children relate to historical events in a non-chronological and mythical sense. The narrative content of many lessons gives them archetypal pictures of human relationships and life paths, challenges and quests whilst familiarising them with social relationships of older cultures, with kings, queens, knights, peasants, holy men and women. Such myths and legends also provide them with an implicit understanding of narrative, the primary mode of history itself.

The children's awareness of the past emerges out of the context of the present in an anecdotal, experiential way. They discover that things have occurred in the past, that what happens now has consequences for the future. They are aware through many layers of experience that time passes, that many things take time to occur. Anticipation of and preparation for the future are intrinsic to the celebration of the festivals of the year. They learn about the cycle of the seasons and of the major cycles of life and death in nature. In Class 3 they learn about traditional forms of economic relationships when they learn about farming, fishing and forestry, about house-building and the traditional trades of blacksmith, wheelwright, carpenter, stone mason and so on. In the legends of the Old Testament they learn, among other things, about one people's struggle for national identity in an archaic society and encounter the political structures of ancient civilisations such as Pharaoh's Egypt or Babylon. They do so not analytically but biographically and mythically, in other words in the medium of orality, that is, as tales told.

In Class 4, the historical pictures they glean from the study of their local environment give them a first sense of historical time. Discovering their locality also means hearing tales and legends about earlier peoples who lived and worked here. It involves visiting their buildings, temples or churches, finding their traces on the land, hearing their language in the place names, perhaps seeing their bones and artifacts in the museum. Local geography also reveals the economic roots of the local environment, be they ancient or recent and industrial. For the children this is all past, all ancient history.

Until they are able to grasp the abstract concept of linear time, the children are hardly able to awaken to the literacy of historical progression. Learning about measurement in Class 3 and the verb tenses in Class 4

certainly help this process. So too does the spatial awareness of geography itself. Just as some, perhaps all, earlier cultures identified their land with the biography of their people, so too children develop a consciousness of events in time through an understanding of place. In particular the relationship of human activity to nature reveals our story. It tells us why communities settled here, what they did, how they lived, and this tells us something about *who* they were and that is where history begins. This in turn reveals something of who we are too, and that is the point of history.

This aspect of geography, which includes human, economic and social geography, is a recurring theme throughout the curriculum, one that merges with the study of history itself. The relevance of history to us today has more to do with people and their relationship to the natural world around them, how they have transformed it and in so doing transformed the nature of human societies in their wake. The stories of kings and battles and treaties and religions and empires only become meaningful in the context of place and what people have made of themselves in that place, and later how they have related to other places.

In Class 5 proper history lessons begin. Gradually the children look outwards from their familiar surroundings, both in time and space. This four-year period, between Classes 5 and 8, begins with mythological images of earlier times in human evolution; from the high civilisations of ancient times, via classical antiquity and the Middle Ages to the reality of our present civilisation and its political and social situation. This path gives the pupils a sense that to be human means to evolve, and that the concept of the human race embraces the whole variety of all the peoples who have played their part in the processes of history. Over these four years it is most important that the emphasis should be on cultural and economic history. The way people actually lived and worked the earth is the important thing, leading finally to how so many inventions have transformed the earth and the life of human beings on it. The journey leads from myths to the steam engine and thence to the discovery of nuclear energy and the consequences of harnessing it.

In Classes 5 and 6 history is told in the form of stories up to and including the end of the Middle Ages. Biographical accounts are the main feature, but not necessarily only of 'great men'. In Classes 7 and 8 the pupils' interest is directed towards those aspects of modern history up to the present that can be depicted through descriptions of conditions, motivations, causes, effects and consequences: discoveries and inventions of the Industrial Revolution and its consequences. In other words the transition is made from depicting history in images and stories to a more causal and rational mode of depiction that is in keeping with the changes the pupils undergo as they develop. Nevertheless, the vividness, mobility and drama of the depictions must not disappear.

What history and why?

The history curriculum here outlined describes topics that *can and are* taken in the various classes as teaching content. Obviously it is impossible to cover all the themes described in the time normally allocated for history teaching. What criteria should we use to make the choice? Paul Law, formerly history teacher at Michael Hall School in England formulated an answer as follows: *"To teach history economically one should try at every point to present examples or 'pictures' that are symptomatic of the forces shaping historical development. Such symptoms are not selected because they are typical or obviously important, but because through grasping them in an imaginative way the pupil will be able to reach an insight into the forces at work below the surface."* [2]

This advice is most relevant for the Upper School but also applies from Class 6 upwards. Economical in this sense means on the one hand, effective use of time and resources but on the other alludes to the integration with other subjects. Clearly history involves geography, literature, science, art, technology, mathematics, foreign languages and so on. Wherever possible the teaching benefits when relevant aspects from all these subjects cross-reference and interpenetrate each other.

The other key methodological starting point is to begin discussions of history in the present. That means not only taking current issues and seeking their explanations, their origins, their backgrounds in historical processes, it also means starting from where the students are in terms of their interests and general development. Essentially history serves the primary purpose of helping us understand the world we live in. The past is really only of interest to school pupils inasmuch as it reveals the present, both in terms of providing insights into what is happening in the world around us, but also as a reflection of developmental processes in the children themselves. This aspect highlights the leitmotiv of the evolution of consciousness within the history curriculum. Essentially we are studying the past to discover the evolution of human consciousness at different times in different cultures in different places and comparing that with our own.

Furthermore, the future too belongs to the study of history. The unrealised potential within each human being is the resource that needs tapping. Ideals are an expression of this potential since ideals provide the motivation for change and progress. History as a subject has an important role in both showing how ideals have motivated in the past but also in activating young people to a sense of their own historical potential. It is not a question of sowing ideological seeds – indeed this past century has demonstrated drastically what can happen when whole generations are indoctrinated with the ideals of the 'ruling' generation, or at least those in power. History can be a dangerous instrument, even in most subtle ways, of creating mindsets that limit freedom of thought and action. History's contribution to the cultivation of the basis for human freedom lies not in directing the rising generation to think this or that thought, but to support the creation of the faculties of thinking, judgment, moral initiative and social awareness within them. By definition we cannot know what the next generation will make out of the world we have created in the past. But we should give them the tools to ensure that they can do what seems necessary out of

who they are and who they will become. History has to be a process of emancipation, otherwise it loads a millstone around their necks.

Class 5

Points of view and general themes:

The study of history proper begins in Class 5. Now the children are beginning to be interested in larger contexts and, as Steiner put it, to take on board historical 'concepts'.

Initially they are introduced to the ancient cultures of India, Persia, Mesopotamia and ancient Egypt. Though it is rarely taught, there is no reason why the ancient cultures of China, Meso- and South America cannot be added to this list. Following a background of Greek mythology comes Greek history from Homer's time up to its encounter with oriental culture at the time of Alexander's campaigns.

It is important that the methods used should give the children a vivid concept of space and time in a living and pictorial way through experiencing how very different and how far away these former times were and how those cultures related to their landscapes and climate. They should also be given many interesting examples of how our culture today is founded on the achievements of past ages. This can enable a feeling to arise in the children that the different flowers of human civilisation unfold in the many peoples of the earth, that every culture has its own essence and yet at the same time contributes to the history of humanity and to our own civilisation. In this way the horizon of the youngsters is stretched far beyond their own geographical boundaries, and the foundation is laid for an understanding of how culture belongs to humanity as a whole.

At this age the children still need to be told things in a mainly pictorial manner. So the emphasis is not on an entirely scientific, fact-oriented, chronological presentation. By presenting history in the form of vivid pictorial narrative, the teacher lets the children share and feel the deeds and sufferings of historical figures. The context should speak for itself without unnecessary interpretation. In this way history lessons have their effect on morality and conscience. This does not mean that a moralising tone should creep into the lessons, but it does have a bearing on the teacher's responsibility in deciding what material to present and how to put it before the children.

The pupils recite and sing texts and verses from the various cultural epochs. In connection with ancient Greek history they might also be introduced to the Greek language and script.

Content suggestions:

- Mythological content from the ancient Indian Vedas, Upanishads and the Bhagavadgita; how the caste system arose. The childhood of Krishna; Krishna and Arjuna. Though belonging to a very different historical time, the life of Buddha can be taught to show the evolution of the Hindu religion
- The ancient Iranian culture: development of

sedentary communities; beginnings of farming and animal husbandry; the life of Zarathustra; texts from the Avesta and the Bundahesh.

- The city cultures of Mesopotamia; the Epic of Gilgamesh; cuneiform script
- Motifs from the mythology of ancient Egypt; examples of the great achievements of Egyptian culture such as the pyramids, royal graves, irrigation systems, hieroglyphs; establishment of a state system; how the geography of the Nile Valley influenced the Egyptian feeling for life and death
- Ancient Greece: The Iliad, or Odyssey; the rise of the Greek polis (Sparta, Athens); figures and events from the time of the Persian Wars; the age of Pericles; Alexander and the spread of Greek culture
- Legends from the Pre-Columbian cultures of Central and South America; life of the Mayas, Toltecs and Aztecs
- Legends from Ancient China

Class 6

Points of view and general themes:

By the age of 12 the children are ready to experience causality in history. The period to be taken covers about 2000 years, the history of the Romans and the Middle Ages up to approx. 1400 AD, so there needs to be clear criteria for the choice of topics.

During this period, history makes the transition from the origins of civilisation to the dimension of human events. The leading historical personalities now emerge as representative of social groupings. Now that the pupils are beginning to understand cause and effect, it is important for them to encounter the duality that comes to expression between personalities, groups, institutions, power bases such as patricians and plebeians, Rome and Carthage, Romans and barbarians, Arabs and Franks, Emperor and Pope, monks and knights. The history of the Romans and the Middle Ages can be viewed from this perspective. By means of examples the pupils experience the beginning of a dialectical principle which they will come to understand fully when they go through history for the second time in the Upper School. The foundation for this has to be laid in Class 6. History focuses increasingly on human confrontation, even in religion.

The Latin language is one of the special aspects of Roman culture that the pupils should now encounter. In Class 5 they were introduced to Greek, and now, in Class 6, the same can happen for Latin. A central theme is to identify the way Greco-Latin history affects us right up to the present time so that the pupils can see the many ways in which modern society still reflects the qualities of 'Roman-ness' in , for example the idea of the citizen – the *res-publica*, in civil justice, in civil engineering – roads, aqueducts, sewage systems, heating, federal administration etc. This principle of identifying factors still at work in our times, albeit in transformed ways, also applies to the effects the Crusades had on cultural development during the Middle Ages e.g. through the influence of Arabic culture in the development of science, trade, banking and so on. The rise of Islam and its

factions can be paralleled with modern historical and cultural developments, including the rise of Islamic fundamentalism.

Content suggestions:

- Enable the children to form concrete concepts of linear time, through spatial representations, through sequences of generations, through vernacular history using the testimony of older people, the sense of distance in time must be almost physically experienced
- Roman history
- The dual aspect of Rome's founding; Romulus and Remus (Rhea Silvia-Mars), the seven mythical kings, patricians and plebeians
- The rise of the Roman Empire and its constitution, traditional Roman values
- The confrontation between Rome and Carthage (Hannibal and Scipio)
- The organisation of the Roman army
- Caesar and the beginning of a new system of imperial power
- Roman achievements in civil engineering, road building, aqueducts and viaducts, heating and sanitation systems, typical Roman villa, baths etc. Technical limitations, e.g. the lack of the harness and stirrup, poor shipbuilding and navigation skills, inability to feed large urban populations
- Visits to and study of Roman sites in the locality.
- The spread of Christianity in the Roman Empire (Paul, Early Christian church, catacombs, persecution, Constantine, Diocletian etc.)
- Decline of Rome: the Huns and Goths, migration of the peoples
- The Middle Ages
- Mohammed and the spread of Islam
- The Franks, Charlemagne and the re-establishment of the Roman Empire
- The Norman Conquest
- Monastic culture, contrast two of the Cistercian, Benedictine, Dominican and Franciscan Orders
- The rivalry between Pope and Emperor
- The Crusades. Richard the Lion Heart
- Chivalry and orders of knighthood
- The meeting of East and West (Frederick II). New vocabulary in European languages from Islam and the East e.g. cotton, alcohol, coffee, algebra etc.
- Beginning of city culture, guilds and cathedral building
- The Battle of Agincourt as symptomatic of the end of Feudalism
- Technological innovation in the Middle Ages e.g. water wheels, tidal mills and windmills, magnetic compasses, shipbuilding, use of steel for armour and weapons, gunpowder and clocks

Class 7

Points of view and general themes:

At this age, the children need to build bridges to the world based on their own personal powers of judgment.

Their relationship to a teacher as an authority declines. Therefore the type of teaching must change to enable them to accept the material of the history lessons through their own understanding. The pupils should begin to learn that historical events belong to a broader context and that the consequences of these events can be equally wide-ranging. The way cultural and technological developments influence historical events and how both express a changing consciousness is a central theme. The most important task is to awaken the pupils' interest in the world, and the main part in this is played by recounting history in the way it relates to individuals, events and experiences.

The period from the end of the Middle Ages to beginning of modern history is now at the centre of history lessons. In his lectures on the curriculum Steiner described the task for the seventh class as follows:

In the seventh class the object is to make it so that the child really can understand what kind of life modern man evolved with the advent of the fifteenth century, and then to describe the circumstances in Europe and outside of Europe, up to about the beginning of the seventeenth century. This period of time is of the utmost importance, and it must be treated with great care. It is even more important than what follows. [3]

By telling the pupils about the discoveries and inventions, about art, and about new forms of trade and of religious life we show the pupils what is new, what has never existed before. It is also important to show them the new way in which people of the Renaissance related to the world through their senses. They should learn how practical, mechanical, technical matters took an increasing hold of people's awareness, while their relationship to miracles and wonders, to holy things, waned. Since the pupils in Class 7 are going through a similar shift of relationship, history does not take place outside themselves, in a museum, but is always topical and contemporary. Bringing in this topical aspect is also one of the aims of history lessons.

Content suggestions:

- The history of European explorations of other continents and their consequences for the indigenous populations (including an initial understanding of the problematical aspects of colonialism, e.g. the testimony of Bartolomé de las Casas concerning the plight of the Indians of South America), Henry the Navigator and the Portolan mapmaking, Columbus, the Spanish Conquest, Magellan, the English Colonies in North America. Cultural and economic aspects of the New World and new commodity imports to Europe. The origins of the slave trade. Sir Walter Raleigh, Francis Drake
- The invention of printing (as an example of modern inventions: the consequences up to the present – example of cause and effect); other inventions such as commercial arithmetic and international banking
- The Renaissance, Rise of Florence. Humanism in its reflection of Classical values

- Examples of how modern science began (Galileo, Kepler, Copernicus, etc.)
- Joan of Arc and the historical consequences of her actions
- Jan Hus, Martin Luther as examples of a new inner religious independence, and at the same time of attitudes weighed down by tradition
- The rise of new kinds of trade and commerce (e.g. the Fugger family, the Medicis, the Hansa league)
- The English Reformation and Elizabethan Age, Henry VIII, Elizabeth I, the Spanish Armada, Sir Walter Raleigh, James I, Shakespeare's life
- The Thirty Years' War
- The Plague
- Land enclosures and the wool industry

Class 8

Points of view and general themes:

In Class 8 we should endeavour to bring history right up to the present day. Most of what nowadays passes for history lessons need be mentioned only as an aside. It is much more important for children to hear how the steam engine and the mechanical loom have transformed the world, than about such curiosities as the Ems Telegram (which contributed to the outbreak of the Franco-German War). [4]

The interplay between causality and purposeful human actions can be observed throughout the Industrial Revolution, and it would be good to clarify the difference between the two. This is an historical paradigm of the first importance. [5]

These two indications from Steiner and Christof Lindenberg respectively, offer criteria for teaching history in Class 8.

Examples of causality are to be found in the social consequences of the great inventions. Both the positive developments (medicine, chemistry, transport and social mobility, trade unions etc.) and the negative (poverty of the workers, child labour, slavery and serfdom, intensive exploitation of mineral resources, colonialism and conflict between imperial powers etc.) aspects should be treated. The emphasis in Class 8 is on the experience of the individual in a rapidly changing world. The ideologies that motivated them are usually left until Class 9. History can be taught through brief but colourful accounts of personalities whose lives portray the symptomatic signature of the times.

Content suggestions:

History is taken up to the present time with special emphasis on the way human life has been changed by the Industrial Revolution and new technology. As throughout the curriculum, history is taught symptomatically and thematically rather than through adherence to strict chronology and the quantity of fact. Key moments, symbolic images, typical biographies or eyewitness accounts, extracts from literature, journals, the press and media are all used as sources to exemplify the issues being presented.

Examples of important history themes include:

- Accounts from the Pilgrim Fathers or pioneers in the New World and the founding of the US, its political concept and the Constitution; the Slave Trade and the Civil War, the resistance and fate of the Native American peoples, the biographies of Red Cloud, Geronimo, the consequences of the Battles of Little Big Horn and Wounded Knee
- Accounts of life in the British Empire, from the 19th and 20th Centuries e.g. the Boer War, the life of Mahatma Gandhi, Florence Nightingale, Dr. Livingstone, Marcus Garvey etc.
- Social consequences of factory work, child labour, slave plantations, transportation
- Mass emigration, Irish Famine, the immigrant in America
- The invention of the steam engine, James Watt, George Stevenson, development of railways, canals, Arkwright's spinning machine, Eli Whitney's cotton gin
- Newer technologies; telegraph, telephone, gramophone, light bulb and their social consequences. Biographies of Edison, Madame Curie, Liebig, Fleming
- First World War, life in the trenches

The following biographies can provide a background for an outline sketch of historical events:

- Lenin and Russian Revolution
- Wilfred Owen (the poet)
- Hitler and rise of Nazism
- Mao Zedong and the Cultural Revolution
- Martin Luther King
- Nelson Mandela

These should be balanced with biographies of other participants, victims, and the use of literature e.g. Anne Frank, Jacques Lusseyran (*And There Was Light*, the autobiography of a blind hero of the French Resistance), Laurens van de Post (*The Seed and the Sower*, account of life in a Japanese prison camp), John Hersey, (*Hiroshima*, account of six survivors), Benjamin Wilkomenski, Primo Levi, (concentration camp survivors).

- The Berlin Wall and the Cold War, Korean and Vietnam Wars. Revolutionary movements in South and Central America, The Fall of the Wall, collapse of Soviet empire
- First World-Third World issues, North-South problem (using concrete examples e.g. the coffee trade, oil exploration and rise of pan-Arabism, famine cycle in Horn of Africa)
- Environmental issues, rainforest, nuclear testing, environmental pollution
- Freedom and independence movements, regional conflicts: The Civil Rights Movement and Martin Luther King, Nelson Mandela, Fidel Castro, Vietnam, Israel-Palestine, Northern Ireland

General aspects and aims for Classes 9 to 12

In Classes 5 to 8, history lessons have depicted the progress of humanity from a mythical, pre-historical cultural stage up to the development of a material civilisation and its religious, social, political and ecological consequences. This has brought the pupils more and more practically into the present time. This progress is now repeated and deepened at a new level, in keeping with the developing capacities of the young people. The transition in consciousness from Class 8 to Class 9 with respect to history has been likened to the transition from the Middle Ages to Modern times. [6] The analogy is not to be taken literally but does characterise the shift in perspective.

The content and method of the lessons take account of the pupils' growing capacity to understand ideals as the moving forces in history and their developing capacity to take in overall insights. Rather than giving them finished images, it is now more a matter of appealing to their own capacities to form judgments. The teacher becomes the helper in bringing to birth knowledge that arises out of the young people's own forces of personality. History lessons should help them tread the path from *passing* judgments to *forming* judgments, which is the equivalent of building up a new relationship between their own individuality and the world.

In Class 9 modern history up to the present is reviewed once again. Class 10 brings a revision of the period from prehistory, through the Neolithic period and the origins of agriculture and the early urban civilisations up to Alexander the Great. And in Class 11 the Greco-Roman period up to the Middle Ages are looked at anew. This represents a second run through, at a new level, of the epochs of history. The final perspective comes in Class 12. Here the previous focus on the different periods of history is widened out to provide an overview of human history, universal history, as a whole. The students learn to understand themselves as active participants in the evolution of humanity; they learn to understand the historical position they themselves occupy in history. They come to see themselves as inheritors of the past, yet at the same time they should have the feeling that their destiny bears the seeds for future evolution and that through their own destiny they are also linked with the future destiny of humanity as a whole.

On entry into the Upper School the students expect to learn new tools for learning about history. They have a need to experiment and this means learning the various methodologies of historical research. This means above all emphasising the questioning role of the historian. Material can be presented anew, not simply as factual information but as a source that needs interpretation. Particularly important in understanding contemporary history is the awareness of the absence of a moral dimension, of materialism and its consequent loss of higher meaning. This realisation needs to be counter-balanced by the perspective that each individual is called upon to act out moral intuition based on insight, rather than on any external authorities.

The corollary to the element of questioning and

experimentation is the adolescent's need for security and certainty. For this reason the teaching should avoid being too abstract and intellectual. The teaching material should be as concrete and factual as possible, it should in a sense 'speak for itself'. The methodology used, however, should cultivate a critical and questioning attitude. The basic criterion is whether one can move from facts to thoughts. One method, which combines both of these processes, is to extract the facts from original sources, or for the teacher to present the facts in imaginative ways (e.g. in a fictional interview with one of the chief protagonists). The information gathered can then be interpreted by presenting it from a variety of perspectives, from the viewpoint of opponents, from the view of worker or factory owner, from the 'terrorist' or 'freedom fighter', etc. 'Stories' can be presented in the style of different kinds of newspaper or reportage. This exercise can lead to discussion of the role of the media in relation to world events and to the formation of what constitutes history. At any rate, history must avoid the impression of being an unfolding tapestry that records objectively what happened. Like the Bayeux Tapestry itself, it records a particular perspective, that most common view in history, namely that of the victors and the literate classes, and must of necessity be interpreted to reveal its full historical value. The recent trend from history 'from the bottom up', that reveals the everyday lives, concerns and consciousness of the people, as opposed to the great and good, offers many rich veins to mine for the symptomatological approach.

Class 9

Points of view and general themes:

The task of this class is to study recent history up to the present, that is the period covered in the previous class, but this time the emphasis is on the ideas that motivated and drove historical development. Steiner's suggestion was to take a key motive for each century from the 15th up to the present:

- For the 15th/16th Centuries the theme of humanity's expanding horizons and the significance of this
- For the 17th Century, the dissolution of old social structures and their replacement by new political ones
- For the 18th Century, the ideas of the Enlightenment in Europe and America
- For the 19th Century, the *"flowing together of the history of the various peoples"* [7]

To this we must add the 20th Century. The motifs for this past century must involve the antagonism of Communism, Fascism and Capitalism, the emergence of a global economy and the tensions between First and Third Worlds, including the emergence of the Pacific Rim economies as well as the incomplete consequences following the end of the Cold War. The 20th Century cannot be so easily encapsulated.

The purpose of studying these dynamic historical processes is to understand the present world as it can

be perceived by a 15 year-old. Furthermore history for this age only has meaning if it identifies ideas which lead towards the future. An analysis of modern history can lead to a picture of social dysfunction, disintegration and pathology, of injustice, of suppressed and violated civil and human rights, of inexorable, of unmanageable historical forces. This would, however, only be part of the picture. If history lessons are to engage the student's interest and inner activity, then they must offer not only a key to interpretation, they must offer the possibility of redemption. History also has to reveal in its inner progressive nature that human beings always have the potential for creating social health as well as social sickness.

Within the key themes that this period of history reveals, each has a shadow and a light side, even if historical events appear to over-emphasise the dark side. Technology is a classic example. Ideology and propaganda can always be countered by the possibility of freedom of thought; state control by individual initiative; fear by courage; injustice by justice; power by the balance of checks and balances; pessimism by optimism; utopianism by applied insight. History provides enough examples of all these balancing forces. Only when the students discover that each one-sided force in history can be countered by another and that the individual possesses ultimately the only source of social renewal, can the present be understood in terms of the future. History in Class 9 must be future orientated!

The aim of awakening interest and motivation in the students is not achieved by overt moralising but by developing historical judgment based on the recognition of the appropriate guiding principles for each aspect of the social organism. Specifically this means the recognition that the functional principle for the spiritual, intellectual and religious realm is freedom, without which this realm cannot function, to the detriment of social health. It means the recognition that public life, politics, the legal and justice system, social contracts and so on cannot function healthily unless the equal rights of each individual are respected and protected and that fairness and transparency are the prerequisites of this. Finally it must be recognised that economic life depends on the principle of mutuality and co-operation between people, organisations, industries and nations, as well as commitment to a non-exploitative attitude to the natural world. The students can well grasp that these functional social principles, if applied to the wrong realm, can lead to social instability and dysfunction. Freedom applied to the economic realm leads to gross injustice and the survival of the strongest. Mutuality in politics leads to corruption. Equality in intellectual life leads to stultifying conformity.

It is important to balance the domestic history of one's home country with wider perspectives of world history. The home country serves best as a specific example of global processes.

Content suggestions:

- Starting with current affairs (that morning's news headlines for example), the major themes of contemporary history can be introduced. The best advice is to start where the pupils are, what they know and understand and then trace the roots back into history. Many of these can quickly be traced back to the end of the Renaissance, if not earlier, e.g. the idea of nation states and its development, the dissolution of tradition societies, industrialisation and the post-industrial world of the developed nations, the formation of empires and the consequences of their disintegration

- Motifs for the 20th Century might be: the collapse of empires, post-Colonialism, totalitarianism, Fascism, Communism and its collapse, Pax Americana and the Cold War, the move away from the Eurocentric view of the world, the rise of the Pacific region, the arrival on the scene of developing countries, in short, the globalisation of our picture of the world

- The emergence of a worldwide consciousness is beginning to form not only in culture, commerce, technology and politics but also with regard to ecological factors. The historical events of this century mirror both the negative and the positive aspects of these processes. It is important for the pupils to get to know not only unhealthy tendencies and catastrophes but also the positive forces at work in ideas about social forms and a healing partnership with nature. The 20th Century is now the main focus of history lessons

- Emancipation of the individual at the beginning of modern times; humanism and the Renaissance as expressions of individual development, invention and discovery

- British history as an example

- The English Civil War, the Rise of Dissent and Non Conformists, Quakers, Levellers, Diggers etc.

- The 1688 Restoration, Constitutional Monarchy, the rise of Parliament

- The Enlightenment and the effects of the Enlightenment on politics (Locke, Montaigne, Rousseau)

- The background of the Irish Question

- The American Declaration of Independence and the founding of the USA, the structure of the American Constitution (figures like Benjamin Franklin, Tom Paine, Thomas Jefferson); the American Civil War, mass immigration to North America, the Monroe Doctrine, US foreign policy from the First World War to the present

- The ideas of the French Revolution (liberty, equality, fraternity); the course of the Revolution leading up to Napoleon, including leading figures before and during the Revolution e.g. Rousseau, La Fayette, Danton, Robespierre

- The idea of human rights and the fight for their realisation up to the present day

- Development of the modern state, absolutism, parliamentarianism, US Constitution – checks and balances on power

- The rise of national states in the 19th Century in the dynamic tension between opposing interests (e.g. history of unification and independence of Italy, Argentina or Germany): nationalism and liberalism as forces that build societies and states

- The development of industrialisation and the associated social question: the spread of European interests across the globe (worldwide transport and communication systems, world economy, imperialism)

- The rise and realisation of socialist ideas; Marx and Engels; the rise of trade unions; Communism in the 20th Century; the Russian Revolution, origins and outcome, Stalin; the collapse of the Soviet Empire

- The First World War, its consequences in and outside Europe

- Steiner's idea of a threefold ordering of society

- The Second World War, its political background, summary of main campaigns, its end and consequences

- The United Nations, European Union, NATO, ideals and problems

- The problems of post-imperial age: rise of national, ethnic, religious conflicts in many regions

Class 10

Points of view and general themes:

A primary concern of Class 10 age students (16 year-olds) is the question of causality and origins. How things came to be as they now are, is a fundamental question that young people ask of the world. The possible answers to this question require us to go into deep history, into earlier, radically different modes of consciousness. It is necessary to see in a broad sweep, the transition from hunter-gatherer lifestyles to highly structured urban civilisation and to reflect on the changing human consciousness that accompanied such transitions. Rather than a simplistic view of the march of technical and political progress, the students should learn to see different kinds of socio-economic organisation as the reflection of different kinds of mentality and consciousness. Furthermore such change also reflects a fundamental shift in human relationships to the natural world.

The evolution of human consciousness that this major period of pre- and early history expresses, qualitatively reflects the changing consciousness of each individual in the course of his or her biography. Thus the exploration of the origins of human society is also a process of self-discovery. In terms of consciousness this period spans the shift from a participatory consciousness in which the external world is experienced as being, as 'Thou', to an observer consciousness in which the external world has become inanimate, has become an object of study and thinking has become internalised.

This is the time for a second look at the cultural history of humanity from prehistoric times, through the Neolithic revolution to the high civilisations, ending with the decline of the Greek city states and the spread of Greek culture by Alexander the Great. The archaeological techniques involved in gaining knowledge about remote periods in history offer examples both of deductive and inductive thinking as well as discovery through doing (making stone tools from flint for example). It is important for the pupils to use their own thought processes, so that they have a genuine experience of the matters they have come to understand. A central theme for this main-lesson period is the inter-relationship between human societies and the environments they live in. Ideas and technologies, religions and social structures have their roots in the deepest human experience of the environment, of the earth, the sky, the cycles of the seasons, of the rise and fall of the life-giving river, of night and death and the heavenly constellations. This is hard for modern consciousness to grasp since we are so detached from these realities. The Class 10 student, in his or her inner development, is very much in tune with the forces of the earth, yet needs to awaken to the realm of ideas that articulate these relationships. This period of history reveals the emergence of nature forces as creative numinous realities in the imagination of human beings in particular times and places. These natural formative forces, transformed through human consciousness were harnessed to incredible feats of city and temple building, to vast irrigation systems and to complex religious activity. At the end of the period, these forces have become increasingly individualised and internalised. This transformation is mirrored in the souls of the 16 to 17 year-old students.

Content suggestions:

- The Human Revolution of the Upper Palaeolithic: Ice Age societies, culture and art, new technologies and the expansion of humans into all continents and new environments, Australasia, the Pacific Islands, North and South America, Siberia, North West Europe

  Ice Age art can be seen as a flowering of the highest cultural level, in a very specific context. In Ice Age art we can see not the beginnings of culture but an already advanced stage of development, in which the idea of ritual, religion, and the sacred place were well established. The images can be seen as equivalent to vivid mental images – the ability to produce them marking a significant stage in evolving human faculties. They can also be seen to contain the fundamental elements of conceptual or symbolic language

- The end of the Ice Age, rise in sea levels and corresponding loss of land in many parts of the world: Mesolithic societies, diversification of cultural and economic life, with a loss of artistic quality in a return to very primitive forms in art. The significance of the invention of the bow, which belongs in the period

- Neolithic Age: origins of agriculture in the Golden Crescent, Catal Huyuk, Mesopotamia, Nile Ganges, Yellow River, Yangtze, MeKong river valleys, Central and South America

- From settlement to city: centralisation of authority, writing, bureaucracy, trade, state religion

- A comparison between the Egyptian culture and the European Megalithic culture

  It is important when dealing with these issues to avoid the classical concept of progress. Firstly many of the developments that we traditionally associate with civilisation were established long before, e.g. animal husbandry, temple and ritual structures, production of ceramics, metallurgy and probably writing. Secondly the transition to settled communities based on farming lead initially to a decline of living standards and life expectancy, an increase in disease and greater human conflict. The so-called advantages of civilisation were a long time coming. It is more appropriate to see these steps as wrestling from a change in consciousness, than as the result of material progress

- Ancient Hindu culture and the radical changes it underwent as exemplified by the Bhagavad-Gita and later Buddhism. The origins of the caste system

- The ancient Persian culture and the mythical figure of Zarathustra

- Chaldean culture and the Epic of Gilgamesh

- The ancient Hebrew civilisation and its development of a script culture.

- A survey of the Old, Middle and New Kingdoms of ancient Egypt, showing the key elements of its religious and socio-economic structures, their consistency and stability interspersed with chaotic and dramatic change

- Bronze Age societies. Hallstadt and Celtic cultures in Europe, the Toltec and Maya cultures in Central and South America, Ancient Crete

- The origins of Chinese culture and its Neolithic revolution, the Zhou Dynasty in China, Lao Tzu, Confucius. The nature of traditional Chinese society

- Rise of ancient Greek city state. Examples of world views from the main schools of philosophy.

Class 11

Points of view and general themes:

In Class 11 the students usually make significant steps in their inner development and maturity. This very inwardness and capacity for reflection, the potential for love, devotion and service that awakens at this age finds a significant reflection in the esoteric streams flowing through the Middle Ages, notably those historical forces associated with the Celtic Christian Church of Iona and Lindesfarne, of learned scholasticism, the aesthetic and devotional qualities cultivated by the Minnesänger or Troubadour tradition, of Sufi mysticism, of Franciscan poverty and selflessness, of chivalry and knightly virtues, of Knights Templar and St Martin of Tours, of master cathedral builders and so on. However, the Medieval period also gives expression to the forces of the will, migration of peoples at the end of the Roman Empire, to Viking raiders, to the rise of Islam and the East-West conflicts that arose, to forces of power struggle between church and state, Emperor and Pope.

Several strands run through the historical period covered in this class, which spans the transition of Antiquity to the Middle Ages. Many of the themes flow artistically together in Wolfram von Eschenbach's *Parzifal*, which is studied in literature, and in Medieval art, studied in the Art History lessons. The history lesson can culminate in these subsequent studies.

The history lessons in this class show the way the world of the Middle Ages came about as the heritage of a Greco-Roman, a Germanic and a Judeo-Christian stream of evolution. Furthermore the medieval world with its tensions between state and church, and between Western and Eastern culture, provided the preparation for modern individualism in the culture of the city.

Content suggestions:

Since there is such a wealth of material to draw on, the history teacher will have to decide on some points of emphasis.

- An overview of main themes of Greek Philosophy
- Spread of Christianity, e.g. the life and travels of Paul
- Rise and spread of Islam, its contribution to Western culture
- The migration of the peoples following the fall of the Roman Empire e.g. Angles, Saxons, Jutes, Vikings
- Development of countries, local politics, feudalism
- The significance of the monasteries and their influence on economic and cultural life
- Secular and ecclesiastical power, Emperor and Pope
- West and East; the Crusades
- The town with its special relationship to trade and crafts, development of the towns, the plague, social problems
- Gothic cathedral building
- The Medieval world picture (Augustine, Thomas Aquinas, Meister Eckhart, Nicolas of Cusa). Also the views of the common people e.g. as described in works such as *Montcullou* by E. Le Roy Ladurie, or *The Cheese and the Worm* by Carlo Ginzburg
- The transformation of the Medieval world view e.g. development of maps from Mappa Mundi to Toscanelli's world map

Class 12

Points of view and general themes:

There are three main motifs for Class 12. Firstly there is the requirement that the pupils gain an overview of world history. Secondly by taking specific individual cultures or peoples as examples, the pupils should be shown 'the biography of a culture' (which can be one that reaches its culmination, or that breaks off, is incomplete, or gets stuck at a particular stage). Thirdly they must come to understand that, as history has proceeded, individual human beings have tended to become independent earlier and earlier and that their further development has become less and less a matter of

external norms or social conventions, in other words that individuals are becoming progressively more free.

The first motif gives the pupils an experience of being a member of humanity and shows them the reality of the idea of evolution. The second motif gives them a sense of belonging within their own destiny. The third motif points to their own path towards the future.

Content suggestions:

- Overview of the main epochs of world history from pre-history to modern times
- An understanding of contemporary history, of developments that have taken place since 1945, and of daily history, and a capacity to form judgments about these
- Showing the inner laws of great cycles of evolution (e.g. Jaspers' Time Axis Model)
- Various forms of government, economic recovery, making and implementing laws, administration, social and political problems
- Human rights, citizens' rights, development of political awareness, being ready for democracy
- Creating an awareness that every individual is history and creates world history through his or her deeds
- Collaboration amongst different nations
- International law
- Present developments, changes, situations and tasks of different nations
- Present changes in Europe: peace politics
- Present economic orders and possible ways of structuring social organisms, state or economic situations
- Topical events: united Europe; EU; development of a pluralistic, democratic order of society
- History of different nations from the point of view of their developmental dynamic (e.g. Greece, China, Japan, USA, Russia)
- Philosophy of history and changing trends in what each period understands history to be

References
1 The outline of history given here is based on practice in British Steiner Waldorf schools. However, more space has been given to the general principles than to the content, which will naturally vary in other countries.
2 Law, P., *Notes on Teaching History in the Upper School*, SSF, 1979.
3 Steiner, R., *Three Lectures on the Curriculum*, op. cit., lecture of 6th September 1919.
4 Steiner, R., *Practical Advice to Teachers*, op. cit, first lecture.
5 Lindenberg, Ch., *Teaching History*, AWSNA, 1989.
6 Law, P., *Notes on History Teaching in the Upper School*, SSF, 1979.
7 This is quoted in Lindenberg, Ch., *Teaching History*, 1989, p121.

Classes 9 to 12

Summary

There is no question that Steiner Waldorf education has to come to terms with the present and future important subject of computer technology. There is, however, as yet no firmly established understanding as to the appropriate ages for introducing the different aspects of this. Some aspects relate from physics, others from technology, whilst others relate to social and cultural aspects. There are three important aspects of information technology that belong in the curriculum:

a) Use of the computer and basic computer literacy; basic word processing and typing skills, how to use basic software to produce, edit, store and retrieve text, how to use databases, spreadsheets, graphics, desktop publishing etc.; the use of the computer as an instrument in support of other tasks and how to access and use the Internet.

b) An understanding of the basic principles of information systems in relation to the history of information storage (e.g. going back to the origins of writing and looking at its cultural significance); understanding how hardware and software relate; how software programs are designed and how file systems work; safe working practices and legal aspects such as copyright.

c) The social, cultural and personal influence of computers, including both the time-saving, liberating aspects as well as the possible negative, obsessional and anti-social aspects.

Crucial to the above is cultivating a sound understanding of the computer as a tool with its advantages and disadvantages. Ultimately the contribution of Waldorf education to computer use is to cultivate the qualities of literacy, problem solving, the formation of judgment and creativity. These skills are developed through the whole education but need in the Upper School to be consciously. The ultimate aim is to equip the students to be able to make judgments for themselves how best to use the computer as a tool in the service of real perceived needs.

A curriculum orientation

Class 8

The computer needs to be introduced as new technology in the history lessons. Simple banks of light switches can demonstrate (in physics) how the binary system can be applied in technology, thus showing the electrical basis for calculating machines. A general introduction through demonstrations can be given showing what computers can do.

Classes 9 and 10

Basic keyboard skills and touch typing should be taught to all pupils as a core skill. This includes saving and finding files, making spreadsheets, using data bases and simple graphics.

The use of computers for information and communication can be taught i.e. how to use e-mail and access the Internet. As most students will be familiar with this already, the social and cultural aspects of computer use need to be discussed. Especially important is how to select information and how to use it fruitfully. This work can continue into Class 10.

Classes 11 and 12

Analysis is a key theme in Class 11, in electronics, atomic theory, inorganic chemistry, the theory of functions. These experiences are necessary to develop the faculties needed to understand how computers and programming actually work. Only then does it make sense to use computer programs to teach about cascades and fractals, path curves and chaos theory.

The creation of a comprehensive curriculum for information technology has yet to be completed. Much research is necessary into the three key aspects out lined above.[2]

References
1   Steiner, R., *Waldorf Education for Adolescents*, lecture of 16 June 1921, SSF, 1980.
2   See *Computers and Waldorf Education: Report on a conference with Waldorf Educators and Prof. Joseph Weizenbaum of M.I.T.*, Sloan, D., Fink, A. and Mitchell, D. (eds.), AWSNA; and *A Draft Waldorf Computer Curriculum* by R. Jarman, *Paideia* No. 13, SSF, 1997.

THE LIFE SCIENCES

General aspects and aims

The whole structure of the Steiner Waldorf Curriculum is profoundly ecological.

The teaching method itself, going from the whole to the parts, confirms this and encourages children to keep the widest perspective on their studies at any age. As examples: in the Kindergarten an active awareness of the seasons, in the Middle School a sense of the wisdom revealed by the intricate relationships of plants and animals, in the Upper School an appreciation that analytical thinking and holistic thinking each make their different contribution to our understanding of living processes.

The themes taken up in different classes within the Life Sciences relate organically to the curriculum throughout the school, subconsciously nourishing a sense of unity within the whole.

As with other aspects of the Steiner Waldorf Curriculum such as writing and reading, what is recognisably learning in the conventional sense does not appear until much later than is usually the case. Nevertheless, as with writing and reading, the skills only seem delayed to the superficial eye and closer attention will show that seed preparations are being made in the soil of earlier consciousness for the faculties to germinate and grow rapidly in later years. It is hard to avoid such growth metaphors to explain the richness and depth of the curriculum and the teaching process.

It is remarkable that, many years before public awareness of environmental issues arose, the Steiner Waldorf Curriculum had laid the basis for the cultivation of an ecological consciousness in children.

Kindergarten

As elaborated in the section on Early Years, Steiner Waldorf education perceives the very young child as having a qualitatively different consciousness from that of the adult or even the older child. There is not the same separation or distance between self and the world. The consciousness is much more within the environment and within what attracts attention, with sense impressions deeply absorbed and played out through the limbs as activity and imitation.

Any study of the life sciences needs to have its foundation in such intense experiences but modern life does not provide much time for young children to be actively present in a natural and living environment.

A Steiner Waldorf Kindergarten lays the basis for this in number of ways.

The celebrations of the festivals make the rhythms of the earth, moon and sun an integral part of the child's awareness of the world.

The time spent in creative play (working with wood, wool, water and sand, for example) brings a wealth of sensory experiences which cultivate keen observation in later years.

Their teacher's care for the beauty and orderliness of the Kindergarten environment, inside and outside, will encourage those same qualities in the children. It will also go deeper, nurturing a respectful and precise attitude to their investigations of nature when they are older.

Stories, fairy tales, verses and artistic activities develop the imaginative faculties, without which the foundations of scientific method are barren and the holistic quality of thinking necessary to comprehend the complexity of the living world is stunted.

Classes 1, 2 and 3

The underlying mood of these classes carry all the themes relevant to the life sciences. The stories that are chosen during these stages of development reflect the changing relationship of the young child to the living world.

In Classes 1 and 2, the stories carry themes of transformation – the frog changing into the prince, the death of the snake and the appearance of the princess. They allow the children to understand the language of the animals and to be aware of other beings – gnomes, fairies – that guard secrets or protect life. Such imaginative elements are not fanciful, but lay foundations for a healthy feeling relationship towards the complexities and intricacies of animal/plant relationships and the hidden qualities of the biosphere studied in the Upper School through the faculty of clear thinking.

In Class 3, Creation stories give an holistic image of the origins of the earth, plants, animals and human beings. Other stories relate how particular people, holy people or saints, cultivated a special relationship with the animal world (e.g. St. Francis). In the farming main-lesson, the children learn how the farmer works with the forces of nature. As well as ploughing, sowing and harvesting there are hedges and fences to maintain, lambs to protect, land to drain and crops to weed.

All of this forms the prelude to a more conscious study of the living world in the following years, as well as unconsciously confirming that an ecology which respects and cares for the Earth has its ethical basis in the moral development of human beings.

Classes 4 to 8

There is a distinct threshold in the inner development of the nine year-old and in Class 4 this establishes itself with the children experiencing more distance to the people and the world around them. The imaginative faculties are still deeply drawn by a story, but the content now needs a sharper definition. Observations and descriptions of the living world which combine accurate detail with a sense of the character of the plant or animal and the environment in which they live, form a bridge to Classes 6, 7 and 8.

The characterisation of a cow in Class 4, for

example, can allow the particular quality of the animal to emerge from the details of its physical form, its movements, its diet and its whole way of life. The gaze, the movements, the chewing, the teeth, the chambered stomach, the digestive power which creates the richness of milk from its unlikely source, the birth and development of the calf – all these characteristics do more than define the cow as an 'herbivorous mammal'. They allow a feeling relationship to the cow, which is neither sentimental nor a fantasy, but a healthy union of the artistic, feeling faculty and exact observation. This can include those ways in which a creature's behaviour seems to reflect inner qualities such as greed, loyalty, pride, cunning and determination. At this stage of a child's development it is an appropriate step towards objectivity for the children to recognise that to be human is to be aware of these qualities and to keep them in balance.

Teaching Class 5 about the oak tree, for instance, with its unique characteristics and gestures, through lively description, painting, and poetry leads their own experiences towards an accuracy of observation which does not degrade the essential nature of the oak into a mere category such as 'deciduous'. Intellectually accurate though that may be, the whole emphasis on categorisation which is so common with the use of 'keys' to identify species, the definitions of mammal/reptile etc. and the study of isolated and dissected 'specimens', is a one-sided appeal to analytical thinking. The natural empathy that children have for the living world, the foundation of holistic thinking, is undermined when such studies come so early.

The Class 6 geology, the Class 7 health and nutrition themes and the Class 8 study of the human body increasingly draw on the children's own observations. The emphasis is on the phenomena as they can be experienced (through direct observation or the description of the teacher) rather than on the theories that may be current in contemporary science.

Gardening as an activity emerges from the general care for the classroom plants to the cultivation of a plot, where flowers and vegetables can be grown, compost can be made and responsibilities for the land awakened in a practical way. Weekly lessons can accompany all life science main-lessons through to Class 8.

Upper School

The threshold between puberty and adolescence gives birth to the faculties of thinking in a new way. While the early trials of adolescence have strong physical and emotional characteristics, it is the awakening thinking which guides the young person towards some clarity on the great issues of identity and meaning which rise up before him increasingly: who am I?; what is life for?

The emphasis of the life sciences in Classes 9 and 10 is on the human body and the processes that provide the physical basis for consciousness, health and reproduction. A reductionist biology which states or implies that the human body is a machine, the human

being an animal and the human condition a meaningless outcome of chance events, is not one which nourishes the adolescent's deepest concerns and unspoken questions. The current theories are just that – theories. They have not been in existence long and although they are usually presented as 'truth' they will inevitably change and the task of teaching adolescents should not be to suggest that such theories are true. They are models and should be treated as such. Meanwhile, adolescents need to exercise their burgeoning thinking capacities on understanding the processes within the body, recognising its complexities and mysteries and to facing the issues that arise through medical advance.

Alongside these studies, practical work with plant and animal should include field studies and bring a direct environmental and ecological emphasis to the life science curriculum.

By Classes 11 and 12, the adolescents' faculty of thinking has strengthened and matured to become more deeply engaged by ideas. The life science curriculum meets this with a study of botany and zoology in which current cell theory, genetics and Darwinism play a major part. This emphasis is echoed in a study of atomic theory, light wave/particle duality and astronomy in the chemistry and physics main-lessons. Young people's thinking is now mature enough to appreciate that there are alternative scientific viewpoints than the ones currently portrayed in the textbooks or through popular science and technology. Through an historical approach to scientific ideas and the consequences of technology, they can gain the perspective to recognise that a healthy science sees theories rise and then fall as new phenomena are explored.

The Life Sciences curriculum in a Steiner Waldorf school can lead young people to a clear understanding of contemporary scientific theory, an awareness of the human and environmental issues, issues raised by technology, as well as leaving them with a lively, open-minded attitude to the future of both.

Class 4

Points of view and general themes:

The focus of this main-lesson is the unique quality of the human being, which is to a large extent free of the instinctive behaviour of the animal world and whose physical body lacks those special features which allow the animals to live so intricately in their environment. The self-consciousness of the human condition is in part gained through the harmonious balance of those physiological features which are found as specialisations within the animal world. For example, the human arm and hand reflect this – their freedom of use and movement arises from *un*specialised joints and digits. The apposition of thumb and forefinger and the ability of human arms to open wide arises from this.

The characterisation of particular animals, as already described above, brings this principle to bear on the organs of the body as well. It can become very clear, by observation alone, that the metabolic system is brought to a particular, one-sided emphasis in the cow or other ruminant. The senses are particularly acute in the ever-active mouse or other small rodent – a vole quivers with nervous sensitivity. The form of the head is emphasised in the sea-urchin, while its close relation, the star fish shows itself as more of a 'limb' creature. There is no intention here to impart such comparisons as a theory, but to use this approach to unite what appears to be an overwhelming diversity and to relate it to the human being in an artistic and meaningful way.

Above all, the children need to gain a feeling for what is truly human through having the body upright, the hands free, with the power of speech and self-awareness.

Rudolf Steiner gave many examples to illustrate how the threefold dynamic inherent in the physiology of the human body can be seen displayed in a one-sided way in the animal world. His writings deepen this approach to include the spiritual basis of the human being and these give a teacher the widest possible context out of which to teach as well as examples to use in the classroom.

Content Suggestions:

- The polarity of the human head and limbs with the mediating form of the trunk
- A small selection of familiar and unfamiliar animals to use as the basis for the characterisations and relationships referred to above. Examples: the cow, mouse and lion (or animals from similar families) illustrate diverse tendencies as do the octopus, snail and sea urchin from quite a different world. It is far better to create a rich experience with a few well-chosen creatures than to attempt too many, with the danger of the lessons becoming just 'nature study', valuable as that may be
- Different animal limbs illustrate the theme described above concerning the human hand, etc.
- The human hand and arm as a picture of human freedom – not the physiology of joints and bones, but the gesture and practical reality of their movement. Similarly, the human foot, femur and spine in relation to uprightness, leading to the theme of uniqueness in the human being
- Examples of how the limitations of the human body are balanced by technological and cultural achievements. From the spade to the aeroplane, human invention achieves what the instinctive behaviour of the badger and the birds achieve, with their specialised limbs
- Animals which reflect fundamental soul qualities and inner faculties: the eagle's perspective from the heights; the bull's power of will; the balance of strength, lithe grace and fearlessness in the lion

These characterisations of the animal world continue through Classes 5, 6, 7 and 8, with choices of animal-related topics moving from characterisation to observational nature study as the causal thinking of Class 8 approaches. The emphasis continues to be on qualities, contrasts and relationships of creatures with the human being and with one another, with observations that avoid the usual ponderous Darwinian insistence on interpreting all animal behaviour as 'survival strategy'.

Class 5

Points of view and general themes:

This is the relative calm of puberty before the storm of adolescence.

Elegance and harmony are visible in the children's running and gymnastics. It is an appropriate time for the study of plants, whose growth and movement has a quiet beauty of form, gesture and colour. Feelings of respect, gratitude and interest need to permeate this main-lesson and deepen the children's sensitivity for the earth as a living organism.

Every plant needs to be observed in the context of its relationship to the landscape, the soil and the climate. A single plant in a pot or, worse, cut up and examined under a microscope, speaks of isolation and fragmentation and such studies belong to the Upper School. Children of this age need to appreciate the range of plant forms over the earth, the gestures of typical plant species, the relationship to insects and soil, and the development from seed to flower and fruit. While observation and naming of plants should play its part, any systematic identification of species cuts across the warm familiarity that local trees and flowers should engender at this age. While plant parts can be named, emphasis on the polarity and contrast of root and stem, leaf and flower, seed and fruit is more nourishing to the interests of Class 5 than the details in the usual textbook.

The study of plants requires quiet, accurate observation, a sense for movement in growth and the appreciation of transformations of form and metamorphosis of organs. Goethe's studies of the plant and recent research that has taken the same direction are a rich source of material for leading the children into such an holistic approach.

Content Suggestions:

- Familiar local landscapes and the types of plants that grow there; it is important that children learn the common names of local plants and trees
- The contrasts of different regions over the earth: desert, forest, tundra; the progression from pole to equator and from the ascent of a mountain in the tropics
- Some of the major plant types (e.g. fungus, lichen, moss, ferns) considered more as gestures of form in relation to the flowering plant than in detailed comparisons and evolutionary considerations
- Observation of the germination and growth of seeds, again with more emphasis on form and gesture than on technical details
- The concepts of root, stem, leaf and flower discovered through their polarities in different plants
- Trees as communities of plants and animals and

their relationship to the weather, the soil and the landscape; starting a tree nursery which could be maintained through the following classes to culminate in the planting out of the seedling in a suitable location, could be a long term project

What has begun here should continue into Classes 6, 7 and 8, linking naturally and practically with the gardening curriculum. Geography and geology also provide opportunities. As with the continuing animal main-lesson, the aspects of the plant world chosen and the method of teaching will meet a more causal mode of thinking as Class 8 approaches.

Zoology

Taking up the methodology of Class 4, several groups of animals can be studied in greater detail, showing how within one group polarities occur as specialisations. These can include:

THE BIRDS
- Birds of prey with their heightened sense of sight and sound, including eagles, buzzards, falcons and kestrels and owls
- Carrion birds such as vultures and crows
- Song birds
- Water birds; swans, geese, ducks; sea birds such as albatross, gulls, petrels, cormorants; waders such as oyster catchers, herons; penguins and diving birds
- Terrestrial birds; chickens, ostrich, emu

THE CARNIVORES
- Bears
- The big cats, compare the lion as generalist with the cheetahs as specialists, cats of tropical forests such as tigers, mountains – wild cat, panther
- Wolves and foxes

THE HERBIVORES
- Mountainous goats, steinbock
- Deer, compare antler with horn formation
- Giraffe and antelope with their specialised anatomies and grazing habits
- Hippos, pigs, rhinos

Study can be made of animals that have small litters and invest time in rearing their young and those with larger litters and a shorter period of intensive nurture.

Class 6

Points of view and general themes:

The study of minerals is at the heart of this class as they meet the 'threshold of causality' and the children's thinking seeks for how one thing affects another as a 'cause'. The relationship between plant structure, environment and the seasonal life-cycles can be made explicit.

Geology provides the physical basis for soil types, mountain flora and fauna. Geography gives every opportunity of widening appreciation for climate, vegetation zones and the economic aspects of plant cultivation, while the beginning of woodwork brings them experience of the qualities of different woods.

From Class 6, a gardening curriculum needs to involve the children with the plant world in a direct and practical way. There need to be weekly or twice-weekly lessons which can continue right into the Upper School. The emphasis is on the care of the soil and the tending and harvesting of flowers and vegetables. The opportunities will vary according to the school's location and the resources available, but the primary need is to maintain and develop the children's connection with the plant world. The practical reality of the rotation of crops, composting, pest control and winter storage are met with over the years as well as long-term projects such as a tree nursery, where seeds germinated in the early years could be planted in the Upper School.

Zoology

MAMMALS
- Elephant – as highly intelligent social animal with specialised development of trunk (as hand) and ear – relationship to humans
- Dolphins and whales – as intelligent social animals of the ocean
- Seals – as specially adapted aquatic mammal (highly oxygenated blood formation)
- Kangaroo – as marsupial with highly developed foot form

REPTILES
- Snakes – dominant quality of the vertebral structure
- Tortoise – dominant quality of hardened skin plates

FISH
- Describe several typical fresh and saltwater fish
- Migration of salmon and eel
- Problem of over-fishing

MOLLUSCS, BRACHIOPODS AND BIVALVES AND GASTROPODS
- Mussels, common sea shells
- Snails
- Worms – earthworm in connection with gardening

INSECTS
- In connection with botany studies – life cycle of the butterfly
- In connection with gardening – beetles, woodlice, etc.
- A threefold approach to insects; metabolic types – beetles, nerve sense types – butterflies, rhythmic types – bees
- Life cycle of bees – including care for and cultivation of bees – honey, wax, etc.
- Ants and their colonies

Botany

FLOWERING PLANTS
- Monocotyledons – lilies with their bulbs and rhizomes

- Cruciferous plants
- Grasses, unbellifers, papilionaceous flowers, chichoriaceae and the compositae groups
- Labiate flowers and other composites as examples of a concentration in the inflorescence
- Crowsfoot and roses and their many variants

The progression of these flowering plants can be followed throughout the year. The seasonal 'waking' and 'sleeping' of the year can be discussed.

Class 7

Points of view and general themes:

At this age, the emphasis on the human being through Classes 4 and 5 becomes a conscious focus.

A main-lesson in health and nutrition provides what Rudolf Steiner described as the last opportunity to draw on a healthy instinct for what is 'good for you' both in food to eat and nourishment for the senses. The parental role and influence that has guided the younger children now needs consolidation before the more adolescent attitude takes a hold. There is also opportunity now for touching on areas of personal hygiene and sexuality before the adolescent stage of acute self-consciousness.

Nourishment through the senses, through the lungs and through food relates this main-lesson to the whole environment and to the developing responsibility of the young person for their own health.

Responsibility for oneself includes respect for the other. In a way appropriate to the particular class, conversation about the responsibilities involved in sexual relations and parenthood, and discussion around topics like contraception and love need to be cultivated during this time. This could begin simply through explaining the basis of menstruation or it could develop through a discussion about the media and teenage magazines.

If the class teacher has had conversations at parents' evenings through Classes 4, 5 and 6 so that there is an awareness, understanding and respect between parents of the different ways in which they all handle these topics in the home and the different levels of awareness that their individual children have, the classroom contribution can be a more fruitful one. Behind such issues lie the profound questions of freedom, instinct and the nature of the human being.

Content Suggestions:

- The care of the senses: practical knowledge about eyesight (e.g. reading in good light), hearing (walkmans and discos), taste and smell (synthetic flavours and perfumes) touch (fabrics and allergies)
- The care of the lungs: basic knowledge of the heart and the circulation with enough detail to be practical (e.g. protection of the trachea by cilia; the intimate relationship of air and blood through the delicate membranes of the alveoli) but not with the goal of an anatomical study
- The care for diet: basic knowledge of the digestive

system but, as above, emphasis on what is needed to appreciate factors for long term health (e.g. the need for roughage to stimulate the intestinal lining, the need for rhythms in eating, avoiding exercise and baths after a heavy meal): protein, carbohydrates, fats, minerals and vitamins but with the sense that the health of the whole body is more than the sum of these constituents in a numerical balance: other nutritional philosophies (e.g. vegetarian, macrobiotic, vegan); organic food; fast food: the issue of 'dieting': the role of regular exercise
- The need for sleep and a balanced day's activities
- Related illnesses (e.g. lung cancer, emphysema, obesity, anorexia, diabetes)
- Substance abuse: alcohol, nicotine and those that seem most relevant to the class and their experience (e.g. opiates, hallucinogens): the fundamental nature of addiction (whether to caffeine, chocolate and sugar or to bad habits like biting the fingernails) and the steps to recognise it and change
- Healing plants (e.g. camomile, calendula); their uses in ointments, teas etc.
- Personal health and hygiene: sweating, care of teeth and breath, skin, scalp (and the media manipulation around these): washing the hands, touching food and their connection with health (e.g. bacteria, headlice, roundworm infection)

Class 8

Points of view and general themes:

This age sees such a transformation within the whole being of the child that one can refer to the end of childhood. Rudolf Steiner describes this life phase as 'earth maturity' (Erdenreife). As well as new spurts of bodily growth and maturity, far-reaching new psychological dimensions open up, with a loss of orientation in relation to home, school and friendships. The dissonance between bodily and psychological processes raises the unconscious existential questions that lead young people across a threshold into Class 9.

The educational task is to accompany this important maturational step and the focus is the outer physical body.

Bringing attention to the 'deadness' of the mineral skeleton in an artistic and practical way, grounds the young people into their new bodily experiences. The details of the skeleton need not be pedantically correct anatomically; it is more important to show how bones confront gravity and resist it with uprightness or transform it into movement (e.g. the unique arch of the foot and curve of the spine, the mechanics of locomotion) and how mathematics (e.g. Golden Ratio) and physics (e.g. the role of lever principles) have relevance. The gesture of individual bones (e.g. femur) can be related to the whole architecture of the skeleton if drawing and modelling keep the artistic element alive through observation.

The structure of the eye and/or the ear is another way to make conscious how the outer becomes inner, transformed through their form and function.

Content Suggestions:

- The form and function of the spinal column and its relation to uprightness
- The shape of the foot, its arch and its relation to uprightness
- The Golden Mean and its relation to the skeleton
- The polarities and contrasts of form in head, chest and limb bones
- The relationship of bones and muscles in major joints and the lever principles involved
- A study of the forms of particular bones, e.g. contrasting vertebrae, femur
- The form and function of the human eye and/or ear

UPPER SCHOOL LIFE SCIENCES

Classes 9 – 12

Points of view and general themes:

The essential question in Upper School teaching is not how to spread the enormous range of content in the Life Sciences over the timetable, but rather: what best serves the developmental process of adolescence? What role can the Life Sciences play in helping the young person in their discovery of themselves and their understanding of the world? The pupils are not there for the subject, rather the subject is there for the pupils. Adolescence engages a deep range of hidden questions that young people become aware of and opportunities are needed throughout the curriculum for them to be articulated.

One area of immediate interest to the adolescent and one that holds the potential to address fundamental questions about life, death and the human condition is the study of what is conventionally known as human biology. However, biology implies the study of organisms, so this sets up an expectation that real knowledge about the human being comes through a study of the human physical body and its constituent parts and processes, cells and genes, all of which add up to make a person. Biology implies animals and plants, human biology being the particular study of a particular organism, a species of mammal whose nature can be explained as any animal can be – reproduction, survival etc. A higher animal, but animal nevertheless.

Classes 9 and 10

The title 'Human Science' already allows the possibility that such a study can include all human experience from self-awareness, creative genius and inner feelings, to bruises, sweating and digestion. This approach can engage Classes 9 and 10, and the question of whether humans evolved from animals needs to be left as an open question for study in Classes 11 and 12, rather than treated as an assumed truth all along.

Alongside the Classes 9 and 10 human science main-lessons (10/12 weeks over the two years in blocks of 3/4 weeks), other life science studies are taught.

Class 9 need to engage in practical fieldwork with observations and projects which have an emphasis on the care and renewal of the land – composting, planting trees, tending ponds and hedgerows, for example. These would then become the basis for classroom studies, which could retain their link to the whole context of the environment from which they arose.

In Class 10, the increased powers of thinking are well met through laboratory-based studies of a more conventional kind, where the control of different variables in the growth of plants or the relationship of water to soil, brings the forming of an hypothesis and the concept of experimental proof into focus. By postponing the usual early emphasis on hypothesis, measurement and proof until Class 10, intellectual clarity will not be at the expense of a much wider perspective on the living world.

Another feature of life science study in Classes 9 and 10 is the introduction of biographies through which scientists can appear as real human beings with whom young people can identify. The qualities that are needed in real scientific investigation, rather than cardboard textbook cameos, come to life: single-minded dedication, passion, meticulous observation, inspiration, creative and lateral thinking, co-operation with others, fortuitous meetings and conversations, as well as practical ability and clear thinking.

Class 11

In Class 11, young people's thinking powers have matured to form the basis for a power of judgment, which had been all too easily clouded by the passions and extremes of adolescence or swayed by peer group pressure.

With their thinking more in hand, they are ready for a focus on the ideas and ideals in contemporary science, such as cell theory and genetics (parallelled by the atomic theory in the earth science curriculum). By taking an historical approach, there is a context for the theories showing how they arose out of the previous ideas through particular personalities and key experiments.

The study of botany provides a good basis for this, with practical work on plant cells and use of the microscope and with practical genetics through the germination of seeds. Narrowing the view of life through the microscope needs to be balanced by a macroscopic perspective. The study of landscape and of the major vegetation zones of the earth can provide this, and help in translating from one realm to the other can be given by projective geometry. The history of science provides a context, too, in which analytical and classificatory thinking (e.g. Linnaeus) rose to prominence, spawning a growth in knowledge about plants and a technology that advanced from fertilisers to genetic engineering. At the same time it reduced our relationship with the biosphere to a mosaic of factors, but no real wholeness.

The problems of the environment are the direct result of a certain way of thinking about the living world, which can be contrasted with Goethe's in a study of his method and approach to plants which emphasises exact observation, while retaining the context of the plant in its environment and its relationship to the whole.

The study of botany also provides the basis for consideration of the theory of evolution in general and Darwin's in particular, a theme to be taken up more strongly in Class 12.

Class 12

An holistic life science curriculum needs to make the human being central to enquiry into the nature of life. This has been an implicit theme throughout the Steiner Waldorf curriculum from the Kindergarten, articulated in ways appropriate to the age of the children.

Now, in Class 12, the issue needs to be raised in the fullest possible way so that environmental and ecological aspects can find their context within fundamental questions about the nature of the human being and the evolution of the earth. Social, political, spiritual and moral questions lie at the heart of an environmental education and all the Class 12 curriculum themes are relevant. The focus in life science for Class 12 is zoology. The immense range of animal life is examined through considering the architecture of the main Phyla. Each Phyla establishes a new aspect of independence (e.g. from the water in reptiles, from the temperature in mammals) and consciousness (e.g. amoeba, insect colonies, dolphins). The question of evolution and a detailed study of Darwinism lead inevitably to the issue of the responsibility of the human beings for the earth and for all life, now that they possess the commercial power to exploit it to extinction and the technological power to manipulate it down to the gene. The Darwinian mechanism delivers clarifying power within a certain range of phenomena, but it is rooted in reductionist thinking and Victorian ethics and young people need to emerge from school with a clear sense of its limits and the sure knowledge that new ways of interpreting nature are always being nurtured among small groups of scientists. The history of science shows that these will replace current ideas during their adulthood. The nature of the human being needs to receive the fullest consideration – a naked ape or a spiritual individuality clothed in a physical body?

Class 9

Content suggestions:

The rationale is elaborated with some examples out of the wide range of topics that could be chosen for a particular class.

STUDY OF THE SKIN AND SENSE ORGANS
Adolescents are exploring inner and outer boundaries. They are also intensely occupied with their surface appearances and their senses. The skin and the sense organs have a natural interest for them.
* Structure of skin, eye, ear, organs of smell, taste,

movement and balance: adolescents are exploring inner and outer boundaries. They are also intensely occupied with their surface appearances and their senses. The skin and the sense organs have a natural interest for them.
* Health and social issues: sweat, spots, cuts, bruises, fingerprints, skin colour (and racism), eye care, glasses, blindness, deafness (how do we relate to those we meet who are deaf and blind? How does society treat them?)

STUDY OF THE RHYTHMIC SYSTEM –
HEART AND LUNGS
Heart beat and breathing are very direct bodily experiences and carry health issues which are relevant to an adolescent (e.g. smoking, fitness).

The central heart and the peripheral circulation need equal emphasis, with heart and capillaries as polarities. The circulation of blood is not a closed system and the pump model is not sufficient to understand the circulation of the blood or the sensitivity of the heart to the emotions and the circadian rhythms of the hormonal and nervous systems.

* Structure and function of the heart, veins, arteries and capillaries
* The embryology of the heart and circulation
* Structure and function of the pulmonary and systemic circulation
* Composition and function of blood
* Structure and function of respiratory organs
* Lung disease – smoking and industrial disease, air pollution

This could lead on to consider many ethical/rights issues such as:
* The change of attitudes to the protection of workers over the last century
* Our personal involvement in buying products from other countries where safety and health standards are well below what we now expect
* Present laws about the age at which people can buy cigarettes
* 'Passive' smoking
* The predicament of young children whose parents smoke
* The rights of non-smokers in any house community
* Air pollution and the fact that air recognises no national boundaries.
* Blood transfusions, heart, lung and other transplants: the reality that foreign proteins are rejected by the immune system leads to the topic of blood groups, 'rhesus' babies, vaccination, AIDS and the whole nature of disease
* Illness and health: the limitations of the 'germ' theory, which omits the part played by the immune system and the degree to which this is strengthened by exposure to illness. Can some illnesses (e.g. childhood illnesses, common colds) actually be necessary? What should the role of medicine be – to 'knock out the invader' or to strengthen the immune system? Is health the same as the absence of illness?

Class 10

Content suggestions:

The rationale is elaborated with some examples out of the wide range of topics that could be chosen for a particular class.

The increased maturity of Class 10 goes hand-in-hand with a new stability in their thinking. They can follow more complex and abstract processes such as those in the digestive tract, where different food substances are subject to a sequence of breakdowns through the action of different enzymes. A study of the metabolic system is an appropriate challenge for them.

The anatomy and physiology of the skeletal and muscle systems have received some attention in Class 8 and it may be better to leave this topic to Class 10. Although the teaching approach is different, a Class 9 that has just entered the Upper School may not be keen on material that seems to take them back to their previous year's work. This is not necessarily so, but leaving the skeleton until Class 10 also allows comparative studies with animals, which raise evolutionary considerations which can be handled in more depth at that age.

STUDY OF THE METABOLIC SYSTEM
- Food and nutrition – including cultural and philosophical values (e.g. macrobiotic/vegan)
- Organs and biochemistry of digestion – nourishment as an active process, not a passive filtering of lists of chemicals
- Liver, gall bladder, pancreas, spleen: diabetes, medically and socially
- Kidneys – no passive filtering but active, selective re-absorption

STUDY OF THE SKELETAL SYSTEM
- Anatomy and physiology of the skeleton and muscles – polarities of form and function; those features that allow uprightness and freedom of the arms
- Comparative study of human and mammal skulls
- Joints and levers
- Bone formation and growth – ageing and bone disease
- Personal health in posture (e.g. sitting and lifting)

STUDY OF THE NERVOUS AND HORMONAL SYSTEMS
This is another topic where it is hard for most adolescents to grasp more than a crude 'electric cable/computer' model until Class 10. Similarly, the endocrine system, where crude 'chemical switch' models can prevent any real appreciation of the subtle and powerful interactions of glands and organs.
- Structure of brain/central nervous system; cerebrospinal fluid
- Nerve function – inadequacy of telephone/electric cable model; limitation of the motor/sensory model
- Latest research on brain function – inadequacy of the 'mapping' approach and the computer analogy
- The open questions: memory, thinking and consciousness
- The endocrine glands – sensitivity of the body to hormones; (e.g. growth, excretion); special influence of the pituitary; ovulation and menstruation

STUDY OF EMBRYOLOGY
Hormone influence leads naturally into a study of human embryology, a rich area for Class 10, and again one which demands the emotional and intellectual maturity that has been achieved by most pupils by the end of Class 10. The ability to follow the development of several features at the same time, to appreciate the transformations of shape and size, to relate to the responsibilities and the issues involved in sexual relationships and parenthood, demands that the young people have emerged from a general phase of sexual knowledge and interest. A number of young people in Class 10 will have entered a serious relationship and for those who have not, the prevailing mood of a Class 10 is usually one in which both sexes can feel comfortable in asking questions and stating their opinions, without fear of the crudities that are more prevalent in Class 9. While it is assumed that all young people of this age are fully conversant with 'the facts' it can also be surprising to find there are confusions and misunderstandings, too. If the mood of the main-lesson is one of genuine respect for the developing body of a unique individuality, deep questions can stir in the young person, along with the sense of wonder for the way in which conception, gestation and birth take place so smoothly.

Child development and the idea that we continue to grow inwardly our whole lives, with new crises and new opportunities, can help to balance the picture young people can have that 'growing up' is all about getting to be 18 or 21. The knowledge that their mother and father may be going through the physical and psychological passage of menopause and mid-life, could contribute to their finding a new relationship with their parents. It would also help to change their perception of old people, whose inner needs are not so easily perceived as their more obvious outer ones.

- Pregnancy and birth – physical and emotional changes for mother and father.
- Implantation and the development of the embryo from conception to term along with the surrounding membranes.
- Conception, abortion, embryo research, surrogacy and similar topics.
- First three years of physical and emotional development; standing, speaking, memory
- Child development, personality, temperaments
- Adulthood – what is it?
- Old age

Class 11

Content suggestions:

Some examples out of the wide range of topics that could be chosen for any one particular class:

HISTORY OF THE MICROSCOPE
From the early Dutch lens makers (e.g. Lievenhoek)

to the electron microscope. The scanning electron microscope reveals the richness of form, even at a magnification of 50,000. Experience in the preparation of slides allows pupils a more critical appreciation of the magnification, clarity and the colour of the images and diagrams seen in books etc.

THE PLANT CELL

A detailed study of its main features
- The importance of the cytoplasm in relation to the nucleus
- Mitosis and meiosis
- Sexual and asexual reproduction
- Boundaries of plant/animal (e.g. Euglena, Chlamydomonas)

GENETICS
- Mendel's experiments and their modern interpretation in breeding
- Chromosomes, genes, DNA: the essential features of genetic engineering

CLASSIFICATION
- Features of some of the major phyla: algae, fungi, lichens, ferns, mosses, grasses, conifers, flowering plants

ECOLOGY
- The role of plants in photosynthesis, decomposition and nitrogenation within the carbon and nitrogen cycles and in the hydrosphere
- Relationship to animals (e.g. seeds/herbivores/pollination)

PLANT/INSECT RELATIONSHIPS
- Examples of unique inter-dependent relationships

PLANT AND LANDSCAPE
- The precious nature of soil structure and its community of organisms.
- Trees, grasses and soil erosion, on a small and large scale
- Diversity in forests and animal habitats
- Monoculture and overgrazing

EARTH AS BIOSPHERE

Consideration of the whole Earth provides a balance to the microscope and genetic details.

GOETHE'S BOTANICAL STUDIES

An historical and practical introduction to a Goethean approach to plant and landscape observation. Current research along the same line.

AGRICULTURE AND FORESTRY

A consideration of the degree to which cultivation of the plant world has been distorted by other values (e.g. consumerism) and how the distribution of plant resources (e.g. food, timber) over the world is subject to commercial and political factors (e.g. the patenting of genes and terminator technology).

Class 12

Content suggestions:

Some examples out of the wide range of topics that could be chosen for any one particular class.

Some of the Botany could be carried over from Class 11, but the main focus for Class 12 is Zoology, with an introduction to the main phyla and their diversity.

The opportunity should also be taken to select detailed features which touch key issues in biological theory and raise fundamental questions about the relationship of human beings to the animal world.

Some examples below:

- *morifera* (sponges) – the sieving of a sponge through a nylon mesh and its ability to regenerate as a colony with form and function
- *coelenterata* (hydra) – the ability of the sea slug to ingest hydra without triggering the nematocysts, then to use those nematocysts within their own skins as a defensive mechanism
- *mollusca* – the unexpected complexity of the eye of the squid, which anticipates the mammalian eye well before the evolution of mammals
- *arthropods* – the complex structure of hives and colonies; metamorphosis and the re-constitution of living organisms
- Echinodermata – the embryonic development of the starfish shows that lateral symmetry (fundamental to the architecture of higher animals) develops first before radial symmetry overwhelms it
- Vertebrate development from the point of view of an increasing independence from the environment e.g. regulation of warmth and the internalisation of organs such as the lungs
- Evolution, including an historical appreciation of the development of a Darwinian interpretation of evolution, the fossil record and such anomalies as the Burgess Shale
- Comparative embryological development and the polarity of precocial and altricial development
- Ethical questions of biological and medical intervention in human, animal and plant life
- Conservation and human responsibility for stewardship of the earth's biological resources – philosophical, economic, political, social aspects of environmental degradation. The task of education and the urgency of changing attitudes. The role of tourism and consumerism on world habitats

General aspects and aims

- The overall aim of the movement curriculum is to support the central process of integrating the child's soul-spiritual being with the bodily organisation through the medium of movement.
- This aspect of the curriculum assists the development of the child's sense of movement, spatial awareness, sense of balance and inner equilibrium and sense of bodily well being through fine and gross motor control. The movement curriculum seeks to help the child to form and differentiate her overall awareness and control of her movement organisation and be able to marshal its energies in the places at the right time, thus enabling the child to direct those forces in a meaningful way.
- The curriculum aims to assist the child to transform the activity of the movement organisation, thus bringing inner mobility to thinking, feeling and willing, thus enabling a more complete expression of individual intention.
- The curriculum works to support the child's developmental path in age-appropriate ways.
- The nature of the movement organisation is such that an imagination of an action occurs before the actual movement is physically carried out. The relationship between the movement organisation and imagination is an intimate one. Thus the teaching method requires that the children be given meaningful and age-appropriate pictures as an impulse to movement or activity.
- In supporting the child's developing movement organisation, a basis is formed for social interactions, social skills through awareness of other people in relation to the self and thus to real social competence.
- The movement curriculum seeks to support and complement other aspects of the curriculum.

The movement curriculum takes up the central developmental process that every human being has to engage in, that of coming into, taking hold of and expressing themselves though the physical body. This process begins in the womb and continues intensively throughout childhood. From the earliest focusing of the eyes and turning of the head, through the child's learning to raise herself, manipulate the hands and grasp the world around her, through the long process of becoming upright and on and out into the world, the stream of movement is the medium through which the spirit of the individual enters the world. This stream of movement is essentially spiritual in nature. It is a force that literally mobilises the child and places her into a meaningful relationship to the world. Through movement the individual enters the world physically and so its primary instrument is the physical body.

Movement as a continuum

The movement curriculum works with and helps form the individual's path into her movement organisation and helps facilitate her finding a secure centre from which to reach out into the world. Since this entire process is a continuum and one that is individual, the curriculum should respect this process and not restrict it or artificially limit it to specific stages. The movement curriculum in this sense has to be an entirely open system that responds to the perceived changing needs of the children, rather than an enclosed one that predetermines what should happen when – a point which also applies to the whole curriculum. The indications given here are divided into age groups merely as points of reference and not seen in any sense as binding to specific classes.

Three factors inform but do not determine this process; insight into the archetypal nature of child development, insight into the nature of movement itself and the external circumstances, resources and possibilities.

The cultivation of movement in the pre-school setting

In pre-school settings the educational task is to support the establishing of behaviour patterns and sequences as habit (which includes everything from dressing, behaving in groups, listening to others, doing the washing up and tidying up after play). All these habits school the movement organisation in meaningful ways. Through practical activities and age-appropriate work in Kindergarten, the children learn archetypal activities and the movements that belong to them, such as baking bread, laying the table, doing simple handicrafts, gardening etc. The process of growing from the periphery into the bodily organisation from the fingertips and toes inwards, is strengthened by finger games, gesture accompanying song and speech, skipping, drawing, painting and so on. In all these activities the child learns through imitation both of the conscious intention of the adult and the activities themselves. Thus the imagination is stimulated from without, as it were. The imaginative content lies in the activity itself.

The key elements in the pre-school setting are providing a sense of security and continuity, a meaningful context for meeting, working and playing together. Balance and equilibrium are necessary not only for sound movement but for the perception of sound, for speaking and listening. Rhythm is the living balance of inner and outer and consists of repetition of the similar, rather than strict repeating of the same. Rhythm involves progression, it moves on. Manual dexterity and nimbleness of foot take years to establish but are the essential prerequisites for inner mobility. Many activities at home and in the Kindergarten contribute to the development of all these qualities.

The transition to school

Children enter school when they are ready to begin formal learning. In movement education the transition is marked by several changes of emphasis. In activities such as form drawing, the dynamic of movement is progressively internalised from outer movement in space to the ability to picture the movement inwardly until it can be translated through the hand and arm onto the paper as lines, the 'traces' of movement itself. The ability to 'read' such movement from the paper is an important preparation for the process of reading text. Form drawing and the letters and numerals themselves explore in two dimensions what has been experienced spatially in three. Literacy itself is the ability to translate the inner movement of thoughts and feelings into structured form (writing and sequences of numbers) as well the obverse; the ability to recreate in the soul the movement which has been 'frozen' in the letters.

The teaching approach

Imitation is translated movement. In the pre-school years this is largely an unreflected process. Once the child is able to begin to form independent mental images, imitation has to be transformed. Once the child begins formal schooling, imitation remains an important part of learning, not least in movement, but the process undergoes an important change. Rather than taking part in what the adult does (implicit learning), the child has to be stimulated to act out her own inner picture of the task. That means the teaching takes place through pictures. The teacher engages the child's imagination with a (usually) verbal picture and the impetus to act comes from the child's understanding and translation of the picture. In other words they are imitating the gesture or impulse of the picture which they have formed in their own souls, stimulated by the teacher's words. The children are invited, as it were to climb into the picture and be part of it. The child can only really move once a picture has been given. Otherwise the movements become unfocused, self-gratifying or formless. The movements children make in response to rapid, discontinuous, fragmented images, such as those given by television, accurately reflect these very qualities.

As well as working through pictures, movement education becomes increasingly task-orientated, which means more focused and placed within a more limited context. In a game involving rabbits and foxes, the task is for the rabbits to run away and the fox to catch them. The logic of the context is given; that's what rabbits and foxes do. Defining parameters through the rules of the game, equally focuses the task. The steam of movement can be channelled by simple and direct instructions, such as, *run over to those trees, jump over the stream, climb on the rock.*

A further element in the first school years is to provide the children with opportunities within games to gradually leave the security of the group, be chased and separate themselves. Initially a high degree of security needs to be provided by available safe places. Progressively throughout the Lower School the safe places become fewer and further apart and the challenge correspondingly greater. Tension and excitement are very much part of this challenge to leave the safe place. Tension increases attention and focus and is an awakening

experience. Games like Grandmother's Footsteps in countless variations are classic examples. The children are drawn out, away from the safe place and need to be very alert not to be caught. The possibility of scampering back to safety remains important. The rhythm of excitement and relaxation is an important element too. The rules of the games provide scaffolding within which the children can take the risks they are ready and willing to take. The teacher can extend or contract the scope of the scaffolding as needed.

Another element in movement education in the first two classes is rhythm. Rhythm has many dimensions in the whole life of a class of children but especially important are skipping games, clapping games, which also school hand co-ordination and sequencing, bean bag exercises involving passing, throwing and catching. Where songs, rhymes or chanting accompany such exercises, the movement is kept light and closely linked to the breathing. Music also provides a group experience in which the song carries the activity and is less focused on the individual. In such activities co-ordination, dexterousness, spatial orientation, rhythm, learning to follow instructions and increasing confidence are exercised.

Given that all these activities can be incorporated into the young child's holistic experience of learning through the main-lesson, foreign language and handwork lessons it is not necessary to have separate movement lessons in the timetable. However the movement teachers should work closely with their colleagues in advising and supporting movement education throughout the curriculum.

The essence of the teaching approach is direct observation in the classroom or gymnasium. Out of this arises the possibility to directly respond to the situation of the children by adapting the activities and the mood in which they occur to the children's actual needs. The key lies in the way the child is engaged in challenge and how far in front of him or her it is placed, i.e. how far the children have to reach beyond themselves. This goes for all teaching but especially for movement education.

In what follows the elements of the curriculum and key exercises are outlined. Details of the games and exercises referred to and their many variations are to be found in the recommended literature.[1] Unless otherwise stated the games named in the curriculum contents are described in Kim Brooking-Payne's book, *Games Children Play*. The Bothmer gymnastics exercises referred to by name only in the curriculum refer to specific exercises developed by Fritz von Bothmer, the original gymnastics teacher in the first Waldorf School. These are described and illustrated in Bothmer's book *Gymnastic Education*.

Class 3

General aspects and aims

Class 3 involves a progression to more formal movement education, often accompanied by the introduction of specific subject lessons dedicated to movement taught by specialist teachers, where previously movement was an integral part of main-lessons. Even where this step is taken earlier or later, the transition to more formal and longer periods of movement education is nevertheless important.

This transition involves a number of changes in the teaching approach, which lay the foundation for the methodology for the subsequent classes. These include:

- The gradual separation of movement from speaking, singing or listening. The children are encouraged to focus on the movement, that is not speak along with the teacher or other children whilst doing the activity.
- A change of context from the classroom to a games hall or gymnasium. This provides more space and new equipment. The children have to first feel at home in the new space and familiarise themselves with its specialist equipment, safety aspects, social rules of behaviour, appropriate clothing, hygiene. The gymnastic equipment is introduced to the children in an imaginative and play-orientated way, so that they become familiar with it before using it for formal exercises (parallel bars can be used as bridges; mats as islands, walls and pools of water; vaulting horses as horses etc.)
- A key aspect of the above point is learning to be a coherent group within a large space, coming together in 'huddles' for discussion, presentation of new tasks, leaving the huddle to enter the space and returning to it once more. This rhythm of coming together, separating into the activity and returning to base once more is fundamental to the practicalities of the movement curriculum and is crucial to developing social competence.
- The moral dimensions of the movement education are established through the dynamic of playing games. The separation of the individual from the group, the formation of separate, sometimes rival groups, poses the question of how the whole group and the individuals within it meet again. Separating, interacting and joining again highlights the importance of relationships and their moral basis. This is facilitated by the rules of engagement, the rules of the games. In many respects the rules *are the game*. Many social and moral skills are called for such as honesty (was I tagged or not? did I step over the line or not?), commitment (supporting my team, trying my best to achieve the objective), tact (how hard can I tag my classmate? What means can I use to play the game but avoid hurting someone? When is the game over?), recognition of appropriate authority (accepting the judgment of other players or the referee/teacher), fairness, co-operation and so on.
- The progressive separation of the individual from the group and the cultivation of the ability to act alone or with others, is a primary aim of the curriculum and this passes through various stages. In Class 3 the emphasis is on the experience of 'we', that is a sense of the collective group going into the world to face group challenges.
- The tasks are given using verbal pictures that are strong in imagery. Such pictures (you are going to walk over this narrow bridge but be careful not to fall into the snapping jaws of the hungry sharks below!) enhance the challenge, provide simple rules, generate the warmth of excitement and provide an imaginative and highly effective approach to discipline. Such images involves the kind of willing suspension of disbelief on the part of the pupils that characterises play itself, whilst leaving the individual essentially free. At a later stage the children can themselves suggest images to embrace the game or tasks involved.
- The groups activities and the qualities of the tasks engage the children in their warmth organisation. This means activities in which strong sympathy is awakened and the teachers' approach to the children should be hearty, encouraging and generous.

Content suggestions:

- Bothmer's First Roundelay, *We come, we come...* which involves running in a circle, doing the activities and gestures described in the text, such as galloping, trotting, leaping, stepping rhythms and standing still
- Practising coming into a huddle for instruction and returning after the activity
- Tag games involving all against one adversary. Typical examples, *stuck in the mud, sharks and octopuses, dragon tag*
- 'Jungle' games, using images such as climbing through the jungle, climbing the castle walls, being on a ship in storm etc., the children clamber over a course of obstacles made by gym equipment, which represents outdoor challenges not usually available to children today and involving climbing, jumping off, leaping across, rolling, crawling through confined spaces, balancing etc.

Class 4

The emphasis shifts from 'we' to 'I', in the sense of *here am I, there are you*. This also involves experiencing polarities such as dreaming and waking, weak and strong, safety and danger or creation and destruction. The rhythm of such polarities emphasises the breathing element of contraction and expansion. The principle of separation becomes stronger in games that involve one against the group. More tension is involved in games in which the children need to awaken from the picture that the teacher has bedded the game in and those still dreaming get caught or tagged.

At this age the children may begin to regularly challenge adult authority or feel themselves isolated from the group context. Here the social and moral aspects of learning and respecting the rules become very important. As the individual increasingly becomes aware of his or her own space, both in a literal and inner sense, the curriculum needs to respond by beginning to formally school the child's sense of the qualities of the dimensions of space, above and below, left and right, front and back and their integration through self-activity.

Content suggestions:

- Bothmer's Second Roundelay, the exercise, *I stand. I walk. I run...*, in which the experience of the archetypal elements of spatial awareness and the planes of movement are introduced and integrated in a playful rather than formal way. An iambic (short-long) is used to give the exercise a strong rhythm. The strong swinging movements emphasise a different element of rhythm. The child experiences their own self-activity of placing themselves into their own space.
- In gymnastics the children are introduced to more formal elements. The teacher demonstrates before the children. Pictures are still used to describe the elements of the exercises, such as forward and backward rolls.
- Tag games involving chasing and catching, rapid changes of role – from chaser to chased, games that involve focusing on achieving a specific goal. Typical examples include, *fire and ice, scarecrows, hunters and hares.*
- Games that involve some image of confrontation with negative forces, e.g. *river bandits, shark's jaws.*
- Games involving listening and attentiveness e.g. *MacPherson.*
- Simple throwing and catching games in increasingly difficult situations (e.g. balanced on a bench).
- Activities which introduce build-up games to softball and its basic principles e.g. *clocks, trains and stations, Swedish rounders.*
- Playground games can be re-introduced or taught if the children are unfamiliar with them, e.g. wall tennis, four-square, hop-scotch, marbles, reflex games such as knuckles, crocodile jaws, jacks, noughts and crosses, leap frog etc.
- More difficult jungle challenges.

Class 5

This age very much marks the heart of childhood, the last year before the onset of physical puberty starts in earnest. The child lives strongly in the processes of the blood and the dynamic between the pulse and the measure of the breathing. The children like to roam around in an unruly way as much as they seek the measured discipline of rhythmic movement. They also want to be challenged. Both courage and caution, both risk and circumspection are valued at this age. The loss of childhood innocence is to be compensated for through powerful grasping of reality. Rhythm in movement is important at this age. There needs to be a balance between levity and gravity, between imagination and intellect, between individual and group challenges. Holding the centre in a rapid alternation of rhythms strengthens the child's self-activity. This is an important transition stage before team games are introduced. Without the ability to hold the middle, to stay in their own space, positional sense in team sports is much harder to achieve and one sees the phenomenon of both teams chasing here and there after the ball as a whole group.

The Ancient Greek Olympic ideal stands as a leitmotiv for Class 5. The original games were rituals in which the individual sought to give expression to the creative powers of the Gods. The ideals of truth, beauty and goodness must permeate the activities and the five classical exercises, running, jumping, throwing the discus and javelin and wrestling, mirror the archetypal inner movements which form a basis for moral education.

The exercises are now given with much more matter-of-fact picture images and the children no longer stand in the circle. They face their teachers in rows.

Bothmer gymnastics: the *light beat* exercise, which involves a rhythmic interplay between lightness and weight.

Gymnastics: trend to more individual exercises; leap-frog, straddle vault; vault over the buck using the spring board; forward/backward roll over symmetric bars; cartwheels; balancing, swinging, jumping with increasing challenge (e.g. with eyes closed). The five classic Greek exercises are introduced.

Games: at this age there is a transition between play and sport, the games being neither. Typical games include: cat and mouse house, ship shark shore.

Swimming: many schools introduce regular swimming lessons at this age.

Class 6

The soul experience of the children at this age penetrates into the muscles, which hold a balance between fluid and solid. The human being seeks a new level of balance at this age when the physical processes of puberty cause rapid growth of the limbs, leading to clumsiness and greater individual diversity of physique among a class of children than at any other age. Uprightness is important and that requires an inner balance of forces. The play element now gives way, the principle of specific exercises and exactness, clarity of form, order and structure is striven for in the exercises. The element of objectivity comes to the fore, through measurement, keeping scores in games and acknowledging the teacher as referee/umpire. The pupils can stand in lines for exercises, ordered by height, tallest at the back.

Bothmer gymnastics: *triangles*; the main element being the fall out of levity and the transition to an alert uprightness. Rod exercises strengthen the experience of uprightness in relation to stretching up, whilst standing firmly on the ground.

Gymnastics: formal stations in the build up of the exercises, handstands, handstand to handspring, some work on the bars, rings, with increased need for health and safety awareness. Outdoor athletics including running and jumping disciplines.

Games: the transition to team sports. This requires the

preparation of the following skills: having winners and losers, outwitting opponents, sometimes physical contact, keeping scores. Dodge ball games are a good preparation, involving contact, direct encounter (having a ball thrown directly at you). Typical games include: wall ball, soft ball, prisoner, over-the-net ball games, invasion and territorial games, hitting field games.

Class 7

General aspects and aims

The pupils now have the strength and supple flexibility to move quickly from one activity to the next. This mobility is an expression of the fact that they already have good muscle development but are not yet fully engaged with the static properties of the bony skeleton. This is an age in which the children express their movement development through the ligaments and sinews.

They have the ability to separate themselves from the group and sufficient personal standing in the world to be ready for the challenge of competitive sport. They are capable of the individual standpoint, which not only enables them to take and maintain a position but the perspective to begin to oversee the game and its tactics. In order to really participate in team sports the pupil must be able to form a clear picture of where they are in relation to their surroundings, they must be aware of the dimensions and boundaries of the field. This requires good sensory integration. One of the reasons team sports are not introduced earlier in the curriculum is the danger of this exact conception of spatial relationships may inhibit the imagination. If the pupils at this age do not have a strongly established sense of imagination or inner picturing ability, they can be overwhelmed by the emotional forces which are awakening in them at this stage of puberty. When such forces are drawn in without the ability to channel them, it can cause considerable emotional distress. The imaginative and mental picturing element works to channel and order surges of emotionality.

Bothmer gymnastics: swinging movements lead to an experience of centre and periphery. The individual finds his or her own rhythm and discovers the moment of impulse to movement. The exercise *The Rhythm* complements the exercise *Fall into Space*, which was specifically created to take hold of the spatial experience in puberty. Bothmer originally suggested that the exercise *Jump into the Middle Point*, should precede the *Fall into Space*. This is very much a matter of judgment for the teachers concerned.

Gymnastics: the somersault, falling off a box onto mats, learning to enjoy weight through many swinging and pendulum exercises, such as hanging from the bars and using the swinging to experience the new centre of gravity (new because of the stretching growth that comes with puberty); vaults, such as handsprings, through vaults, straddle vaults over the length of the box, handstands. Wrestling in various forms can be practised, such as Indian wrestling, Greek/Roman

style wrestling (as described in Brooking-Payne).

Games and sport: games are used as warm-ups to sport. Half the session is given over to training, to learning and practising new technique. The individual skills are separated out and given specific focus. The main sports include basketball, hockey, softball, tennis or cricket. In athletics running, including cross-country – often in connection with orienteering using maps and marked out courses, and jumping. The pupils should start playing in tournaments.

Class 8

General aspects and aims

At this age the pupils encounter the full weight of their physical bodies and their sense of movement penetrates to the skeletal structure. They feel both burdened by the new weight of their bodies as well as energised by new physical strength. They need much opportunity to explore and experience this new combination of weight and strength and so there should be more emphasis on gross motor movement than on too much fine technique. From a movement and physical point of view, this age really marks the end of childhood.

Many outdoor pursuits can be introduced at this age including rock climbing and abseiling, canoeing and kayaking, hiking, mountaineering, skiing and so on. In all these examples the activities provide their own challenges, depending on the local resources of the school. What now becomes important, apart from the self-reliance and survival aspects of the sports is the relationship to the environment. The students must learn that outdoor pursuits are most rewarding when they enhance our experience of nature. Sport must never contribute to environment degradation, nor should the attitude develop, which sees the mere overcoming of the natural environment as an objective.

At this age gender differences need to be especially respected. The manifest differences in physical strength and size need to be acknowledged in contact sport as well as the quite distinct energy resources of the two genders. There is a need for a balance of integrated and separate activities. The integrated activities have a very different but essential character. Both genders need some time on their own, the boys needs to be able to explore the limits of their strength and power, the girls need protection in the bodily intimacy of many gymnastics exercises involving being held or exposed positions.

Bothmer gymnastics: the exercise *Jump into the Middle Point*.

Gymnastics: continuation of Class 7, though the exercises have a different quality because of the pupils' development. Somersaults and handsprings and vaults are continued. The main difference in Class 8 is that the pupils are often more hesitant and need to more consciously gather up the dynamic of their forces before the run-up to a vault. In circuit training correct and age-appropriate techniques are learned. There is an emphasis on fitness and developing strength e.g. through press-ups.

Games and sport: the sports played in Class 7 are continued and volleyball is introduced. There is a measured graduation of competition, which is seen as an important pedagogical instrument. Competition is an element used and controlled by the teacher to cultivate teamwork, as a catalyst for stimulating engagement, for pushing individuals to new levels of achievement, for drawing the best out of individuals by calling on their potential. Computation remains healthy as long as it is within an ultimately secure, trusting environment in which emotional and literal safety nets are available as needed.

Class 9

General aspects and aims

At this age the students need to learn to take responsibility for the consequences of their own actions. The frontal plane of the will, meeting and 'con-fronting' the world, needs to be encountered and a breakthrough made. The individual must literally take the plunge and break into the future with a new and conscious step. This takes both courage and new levels of consciousness. A certain laziness, often the expression of emotional uncertainty needs to be overcome. The students at this age need to leave childhood behind them and stand on their own feet.

In the Upper School it is necessary to make provision for more movement than the timetable actually permits by encouraging after school clubs in which the students simply have more time to develop their abilities but in which students with specific abilities can develop their full potential, which is not always possible in whole class situations because the socially inclusive element takes priority. Adolescents also need a healthy alternative to less appropriate movement activities such as martial arts or extreme sport. Ultimately the provision of meaningful activities offers youngsters an alternative to many less useful activities they may otherwise be drawn into. Regular competitions and matches with other schools are also important.

Bothmer gymnastics: the exercise *The Plunge* exemplifies what the Class 9 student needs to experience, involving a facing of the world, a plunge or leap, literally into the space before them, a fall into gravity, a breakthrough with a conscious stepping into the present/future with certainty. Other exercises at this age may include, *Rhythm of two interlacing circles (frontal walk)*.

Gymnastics: the new emphasis is a conscious overcoming of obstacles through courage and inner focus. Continue forward and backward somersaults, more challenging vaults e.g. through vaults, floor work, parallel bars, handsprings.

Sport: the sports already introduced are progressed with an emphasis on timing and more focused

application. Volleyball plays an increasing role in the Upper School. In athletics shot put, discuss and javelin can be practised. Other sports include archery and fencing.

Class 10

General aspects and aims

At this age the students need to develop a new awareness of their surroundings. The archetypal activity of throwing the discuss embodies many of the qualities the Class 10 students need to develop; the encounter with the object, engaging in dialogue with the world, going within into oneself but emerging and proceeding from the centre to the periphery without loss of inner balance, giving something to the world but following the consequences, retaining the connection. The key element is finding dialogue with the world. This entire activity is also about finding a goal and uniting oneself with it.

The curriculum from Class 10 onwards essentially builds on what has been established, practising and developing technique and competence.

Bothmer Gymnastics: *The Discus* exercise, also *Walking with Circling Arms (horizontal walk)*: all these exercises have a strong relationship to the consciousness of the horizontal plane and holding the middle.

Gymnastics: continuation of previous classes with an emphasis on finding a rhythm in the flow of movement and an experience of uprightness. An aesthetic element can be important at this age, and movements can be increasingly seen as an integrated sequence.

Sport: continuation of the sports already introduced with an emphasis on social play.

Class 11

General aspects and aims

At the age of 17 young people need to set themselves aims and ideals to strive towards. This requires the ability to make judgments and choices. A certain decisiveness is called for to follow a chosen path between competing, and destabilising alternatives. The archetypal gesture of throwing the javelin expresses this well. Symmetry and balancing left and right are key elements to be exercised at this age. Many sports, such as cricket offer opportunity to develop skills requiring strong symmetry, in batting or bowling for example, both of which require a strong sided-ness to be maintained in overall balance. The same is true of many racket games such as tennis and badminton. Accuracy and precision can be consciously practised. Rapid reflexes, sharp perception for an opening, a sense for tactics, as well as overall control are needed as essential skills in most sports. At this age the students are now mature enough to take all these into consideration. The students also need to be able to take increasing responsibility for sports through thorough understanding of the rules, as well as the health and safety aspects. Being able to understand the essence of a particular game is now important.

Bothmer gymnastics: the exercise *The Javelin*, also *Distorted Height (Eagle), Symmetry Walk*.

Sport: continuation of sports already introduced, with an emphasis on tactical skill.

Class 12

General aspects and aims

At this age the young person should be able to attain a freedom within the planes of space and hence an integration of thinking, feeling and willing. They should now be able to form and experience an overview of the whole range of possibilities within spatial awareness and with it the ability to see the wood for the trees.

Bothmer gymnastics: The human form is experienced in its threefold spatial qualities culminating in the exercise *The Cross.*

Games and sport: the sports introduced so far should be practised to a high level of skill. It is particularly interesting to the students to be led through the movement curriculum of their entire school career from the Lower School onwards, playing the games and practising the full range of exercises once more, with opportunity to reflect on the development processes involved.

Reference
1   See the following three reference books:
    Brooking-Payne, K. 1996, *Games Children Play; How games and sport help children develop.* Hawthorn Press; von Bothmer, F., *Gymnastic Education,* translated by Olive Whicher, available from Michael Hall School movement department or RSP;
    van Haren, W., and Kischnik, R., *Child's Play* volumes 1 and 2, Hawthorn Press.

Classes 1 to 12

General aspects and aims for Classes 1 to 8

Music speaks to human beings and they experience its language in their soul. As with language, music has a realm belonging to understanding and knowing which is grasped through music theory, a realm of feeling comprising everything to do with harmony, moods (major and minor), tension and relaxation, and a third realm, that of movement involving rhythm. All three realms mirror the soul life of human beings.

Music lives in the moment, in becoming. It consists of transitions, of the space between, of the formed flow of time. Its arising and its disappearing belong to its nature. What remain are inner space impressions; expectations, fulfilment, memory, are its constituent forces. The picture nature of music is at the same time moved and moving picture. The picture nature is of a flowing quality. The plastic nature of music is similar: the plastic qualities are in flow, in constant change. Architectural space and music stand as polar opposites, though in a way they determine each other: movement become form and moved-moving 'form'. How can music understood in this way be grasped, experienced and cultivated? [1]

From this point of view writing a curriculum for music teaching is indeed challenging. Given that the fundamental approach to Waldorf education is a pedagogical one, that is to say one that is directed towards the development of the child through music, then the task could be described as one of matching the nature of music to the nature of the child. Method and content are inextricably woven together.

So both the nature of the child and the nature of music are the starting point for any music curriculum. *"Active immersion in musical substance, experience through practice of its nature, progressive, step by step awakening to musical principles and finally proceeding to a basis for knowledge based on direct experience."* [2] These are the main goals of music teaching in the Waldorf school.

Music is not a subject on the timetable, it is a state of mind, to paraphrase an experienced music teacher. This state of mind has to be created in every lesson. It means diving into the stream of structured time we call music. Music learning is a process involving actively being in the music, experiencing the musical element, being responsible for musical development and the art of pedagogy. Only in this sense can

a music curriculum arise. The following curriculum is of necessity brief, no more than points of reference. Thus the activity of each music teacher is challenged.

Aspects of child development

Up to the age of about 9, the soul life of the child including thinking, feeling and willing is a homogeneous whole; the three faculties are not separate but work with and in each other.

In music, the 'mood of the fifth' conforms with the child's soul configuration. In this mood (i.e. in the *quality* of the fifth), the phenomena of melody, harmony and rhythm weave together. There are as yet no harmonic chords, just as there is no keynote or rhythm bound to a beat.

Just as a pentatonic melody is not bound to a keynote, so a freely swinging rhythm can find its orientation in the qualities of inhalation and exhalation of the breath.

We are frequently perplexed by so-called modern music and do not know how to evaluate it. This has something to do with our listening habits. These have been formed by a Classical and, later, Romantic understanding of music with harmonies strongly oriented towards a keynote. The language of a-tonal music remains foreign to us so long as we continue to expect music to make statements about the world. An abstract painting can challenge us to become creative ourselves and join in with continuing the painting process. The listener can be similarly challenged by an a-tonal composition.

Listening to music today we have to grow up and accept the challenge to share in making the music, or indeed to become a musician.

So if instruction in an art is intended to lead to an understanding of modern art, the growing 'co-artist' (for only as such can we hope to reach an understanding of today's art) must be taught about the basic elements of the art, in this case music.

By taking the mood of the fifth as the starting point, we help to create organs that will be needed later on for the comprehension of modern music.

After their ninth year, children experience an 'interruption'. Harmony of soul is no longer always present and they begin to turn unequivocally towards the earth and physical things. To help them find their orientation there we turn to the past, for to some extent the present can be understood out of the past. The same goes for music, so we now look for the traditional harmony of the third. The leading note that forces us to seek the keynote, and also a rhythm that is based on beat, now gain in importance didactically. Having first worked out of what was already there in the children, the teacher now leads them to music that has already 'found itself': *"Begin by working in conformity with the child's physiology. Then work in a way that compels the child to conform to the music."* [3] What the teacher has to do in the music lessons is prepare the transition from 'It sings in me' to 'I sing'.

Something objective enters into the music when the children play musical instruments. Since music mirrors the human soul it is an excellent medium for forming and educating.

It is becoming increasingly important to experience music not as something separate from life but as an archetypally human element. This means that music belongs not only to actual music lessons but also to other subjects.

That skill comes from practise is a primary experience for children when they learn a musical instrument. The reward for this, however, is not the good report or praise from the teacher, but beauty itself. In creating beauty the youngsters should feel themselves right at its centre. In music this can only be achieved through active, alert playing combined with immediate correction, and, in this, music differs from the other arts. Music lessons thus provide an elemental experience of being within the art. *"In sculpture and painting we look at beauty and experience it; in music we ourselves become beauty."* [4]

Class 1

Points of view and general themes:

The transition from pre-school to school is characterised by the expectation that the children will join in. Imitation remains a strong factor in music teaching throughout, indeed correcting by demonstrating is the most effective method of teaching. Thus the teaching methods consist on the one hand of the teacher playing or singing and the children joining in, whilst on the other hand the teacher empathetically corrects 'mistakes' such as wrong notes, phrasing or rhythms.

Stories create the mood for listening to music and feeling it; the melodic element is in the foreground. Singing and movement often still go together. By alternating between getting the children to make music or sing, and then letting them listen, music can have an awakening, harmonising effect on the soul. Active listening is cultivated through singing and movement with moments of 'pure' listening. Group work is important for the cultivation of social feeling, while solo singing or playing has an awakening effect.

Simple instruments are introduced in Class 1, as described below.

Content suggestions: [5]

SINGING, PLAYING INSTRUMENTS:
- Freely floating melodies in pentatonic mode (DEGAB); these are learnt by imitation. Pitch can be indicated through hand movements
- In addition to singing, each child learns to play the child's harp, lyre, cantele or descant recorder by ear. The children learn the simple melodies that have been sung first
- Tuned and untuned percussion can be used e.g. tambourine, gong, guitar, ocarina, cow-bell etc.
- Ear-training through listening to music played by the teacher or by groups within the class
- Training of finger skills using the instruments and through finger games
- The child's harp, for example, can be used for

experiencing moods through improvising
- Simple rhythms are not yet tied to a beat, nor are they practised separately from the song through clapping, stamping, walking or jumping. Dancing can be done in the circle.

INSTRUMENTAL:
- Preparations are gradually set in train for all the children to have individual lessons on an instrument (Class 3) as they move up through the school

Class 2

Points of view and general themes:

Continuation and intensification of work in Class 1. More attention is paid to the rhythmic element. Rhythm is still not related to beat and is a component of the melody.

Content suggestions:

SINGING, PLAYING INSTRUMENTS:
- New songs are introduced, including some for different times of day, and some that have a latent element of a keynote E/G. Singing melodies within the range of up to an octave. Repertoire; singing some traditional folksongs not necessarily restricted to the pentatonic scales
- To train the ear, songs are sung and also played on the recorder or other instruments (alternation between activity and listening)
- Work with instrumental groups now becomes possible
- Free conversations in music showing different moods
- The primary experience of the notes as light or dark is taken further and becomes a spatial experience of high or low
- Through imitation, rhythm and melody are gradually made more conscious (e.g. let the children show the pitch of notes with their hands while their eyes are closed etc.)
- Rhythm exercises on one note

Class 3

Points of view and general themes:

The psychological development of the children now makes it possible to begin introducing musical notation. Given the predominantly pictorial mode of the children's thinking, the introduction of musical literacy needs to recognise this in how notation is introduced. The keynote becomes more prominent in songs. The choice of individual instruments should be finalised during Class 3. The main instruments are violin, cello, piano, lyre and treble recorder.

Content suggestions:

SINGING, PLAYING INSTRUMENTS:
- Singing is still in unison. Pentatonic material gives

way to medieval modes and the diatonic scale

- Singing the major scale
- Main emphasis: songs with a sacred element
- The diatonic recorder is introduced and C major scale learned. Folk tunes provide good material
- Work with groups of instruments continues, and the instruments learnt individually are included in this
- Violin is introduced
- Cultivation of listening e.g. by letting the class listen to children play pieces learnt in their private lessons
- Percussion instruments can be used e.g. bells, triangles, glockenspiel etc.
- The melody of tunes can be drawn using pictures showing pitch (rising and falling line), long notes and pauses

STUDY OF MUSIC:
- Musical notation is introduced: the stave, the treble clef. Imagery is used to introduce pitch notation; the place of Middle C. Notation is best used initially for recorder playing

Class 4

Points of view and general themes:

In connection with fractions learned in main-lesson, the focus is on fixing the length of notes. The children write down what they have heard and then read this to make it audible (they should also sense the intervals). The children's feeling for music should from now on be 'earthed' i.e. it should find a secure base in the diatonic mode. The keynote now comes into its own. The children are more conscious towards the world around them. By the end of Class 4, all the children should be able to sight-read simple melodies.

Content suggestions:

SINGING, PLAYING INSTRUMENTS:
- Folksongs, travelling songs, trade songs, songs for times of day and seasons of year – including the reading of notation. The emphasis is placed on strongly rhythmic modal songs. The repertoire should also include art-composed music suitable to the age both in content and musically (e.g. Papageno's bird-catching song from Mozart's *Die Zauberflöte*, *John he was a piper's son* from the *Beggar's Opera*, Schubert's *Das Wandern* from *Die Schöne Müllerin*)
- Sight reading. This requires much practise to acquire the skill level required
- Rounds are introduced, including easier canons, descants and quodlibets
- The instruments learned in private lessons should be integrated into regular ensemble work. Recorders and bowed instruments accompany the singing and are very important for the cultivation of making music together. Identification of the notes of the scale and their pitch names. Reading notation

from the board, progressing to sheet music. Two and three part music on the descant recorder (not singing). Strings and fingering of the violin are learned
- Conducting: the children should have opportunities to conduct the class in pieces that have simple tempi. The emphasis at this stage is on time-keeping and is done without score and confined to pieces that are known

Number of lessons:
One singing lesson a week with another for Lower School choir

STUDY OF MUSIC:
- Stories (short episodes) from the lives of composers
- First studies of intervals
- Fixing note lengths
- Simple types of beat, also elementary conducting (one child over against the group)

Class 5

Points of view and general themes:

Once proper polyphony of 2 to 3 voices has been practised, more harmonic settings can be tried. The children now have a new need for harmony, and this makes it possible to do a lot of very beautiful singing with them; this provides an inestimable foundation for all their later musical activities. The children must begin to practise adapting to the requirements of the music. They continue to learn valuable music by listening. More songs are added to the repertoire.

Content suggestions:

SINGING:
- Folk ballads are used to practise songs with harmonic accompaniments in alternating listening and singing
- Part-songs in manageable two and three-part songs sung without accompaniment
- Exercises including identification of specific intervals, sing lower intervals up to a perfect fifth. Scales: diatonic keys should be studied and practised
- First attempts at singing in three voices (Palestrina, Mendelssohn)
- More rapid sight-singing can be expected

Number of lessons:
A minimum of one music lesson, plus one lesson in the Lower School choir.

INSTRUMENTAL:
- Building up a class orchestra (possibly an orchestra for the Middle School)
- Strings: introduction of viola and cello to those chosen by the teacher in consultation with the parents

STUDY OF MUSIC:
- Introduction to simple forms of songs

- Identifying the location of the key note from the key signature
- Simple keys and those they relate to are discussed and written, and simple modulations are improvised. Exercises based on the theory of music such as group improvisations on the three 'key' chords of tonic, dominant and sub-dominant
- The major scales
- The pupils should be systematically made conscious of musical terminology e.g. stave, da capo, allegro, first time bar, C clef, octave, timpani, double sharp, slur, up-beat, concerto etc.

Class 6

Points of view and general themes:

The lessons are increasingly guided towards aesthetic appreciation. First attempts at music drama (e.g. Mozart) can be introduced. The children should be singing in a formal choir. Through the acoustics main-lesson, the children become aware of the scientific aspects of music e.g. vibrating Chladni plates, exploring the timbre of different materials.

Number of lessons:
Ideally there should be two choir lessons a week and one instrumental lesson. The main-lesson can incorporate recorder ensembles.

Content suggestions:

SINGING:
- Taking music over into movement through folk dances
- More folksongs in several voices and ballads
- Intensive choral work

INSTRUMENTAL:
- Introduction to the class of orchestral wind instruments
- Some children will move on to orchestral instruments such as brass and woodwind
- Instrumental groups or class orchestra, or possibly a Middle School orchestra

STUDY OF MUSIC:
- Continuation of music theory, intervals, arpeggios, the experience of the octave, major and minor scales, major and minor chords diminished, modal scale, cadence, dominant 7th etc.
- Study of instruments (percussion, plucked, orchestral, wind)
- Working with parallel keys and reading key signatures
- Transposition of melodies
- Inventing melodies through improvisation and writing them down
- Understanding of music as an art begins at this age e.g. the children learn how different motifs belong to different epochs of music history. This does not have to be systematic

Class 7

Points of view and general themes:

The children should enjoy their music and see it as an end in itself. A beginning can now be made in helping them form judgments about music. They learn to distinguish the characters of different compositions e.g. from Haydn to Beethoven etc. The pupils should be exposed to a wider range of music by encouraging attendance at concerts. Rhythm becomes increasingly attached to beat. Cultivation of voices is important at this age and especially care of the boys' voices as they begin to break.

Number of lessons:
Two lessons of choir, two lessons of instrumental music

Content suggestions:

SINGING:
- Question-and-answer ballads (e.g. Carl Loewe, Robert Schumann)
- Duets, piano accompaniment (Monteverdi, Carissini, Purcell, Mendelssohn, Brahms)
- Simple Kunstlieder and arias, including pieces from opera e.g. *The Magic Flute*
- World music can be approached through songs from different cultures and related to the geography lessons

INSTRUMENTAL:
- Instrument group or class orchestra, as well as Middle School orchestra
- Begin with the guitar (the whole class). Cadenzas etc.
- Literature still mainly Baroque (overture, suites by Purcell, Telemann, pre-Classical (Bach and sons) and Classical (Mozart, Haydn)

STUDY OF MUSIC:
- Experiencing the intervals in chromatic scales (and relationship of fifth, connections with major and minor – transposing)
- Introduction to bass clef
- Rhythmical improvisations, musical pieces with spoken text
- Biographies of important composers

Class 8

Points of view and general themes:

Continue cultivating musical appreciation and judgment. Questions of musical style and character can now be discussed. Feelings of the search for truth, loneliness and growing individuation can be met by solo songs and ballads from the Romantic period. Experience of the octave is accented as a search for one's own spiritual quest and discovery of one's centre (e.g. the tritone problem). Continued care of boys' voices is needed as they break.

Number of lessons:
Two choir, two instrumental.

Content suggestions:

SINGING:
- Songs in 2 to 4 voices, a capella and accompanied
- Among others: older polyphonic folksongs, songs about death, songs criticising contemporary life, songs with strong rhythms. Humorous pieces are also appropriate at this age
- Spirituals, ballads, Kunstlieder with piano accompaniment (e.g. by Mendelssohn and Brahms)
- Melodramatic ballads (Schubert: *Die Winterreise*)
- Contrasting major and minor

INSTRUMENTAL:
- Various, including work on the music for the class play
- Literature should include arrangements of Romantic orchestral works (Schubert overtures, Tschaikovsky *Swan Lake* or pieces from his collection *Album for the Young*

STUDY OF MUSIC:
- Theory of melody (genuine and non-genuine melodies); improvisation
- Rhythmical and melodic musical dictation; rhythmical improvisation; improvisation of cadenzas
- Continuation of biographical descriptions

General aspects and aims for Classes 9 to 12

Progress through the Upper School begins in Class 9. It may be seen as leading the pupils from 'egoism' to sociability as they become more mature individuals able to make their own decisions. At the same time this is a historical path from baroque (self-orientated/single themes) via Classical (dualism/dialectic) and Romantic (transitions, entry into spatial thinking, awakening of social awareness) to the twentieth century and the urgent questions of the present time, and anxious searches for clarity about what is important ... Musically one might speak of a metamorphosis of the moods of fifth, third and octave: the 'emptiness' beginning with the fifth (Class 9), the third opening up towards the other person (Class 11), and the subjective, psychological mood turned towards knowledge in the octave (Class 12). [6]

Music is a valuable social component of education in the Upper School, providing a beneficial compensation, as the young people become more strongly individual. This is important in itself, but there is more to it. For the period in question, music is also a field of experience and activity that challenges individual young people to make their contribution to the whole in a fully conscious manner.

Youngsters in Class 9 display symptoms of egocentric, existential questioning and critical attitudes that do not yet have a proper focus. Seen together, such symptoms and attitudes have a certain 'Baroque' quality. This is not yet a subject that can be examined with them. It is an open motif around which proper themes can be developed later on, a motif that can bring new life to the forces of death now felt physically right down to the skeleton. It prevents the youngsters' own feelings from growing cold and rigid in the stereotypes of the rock and pop worlds to which pupils nowadays are especially susceptible. The desire to shackle the immaterial art of music to the skeleton must be transformed by music itself, so that it can once again become an art that is open to the spirit ...

Class 9 bears the rather Baroque stamp of egocentricity and single-track mindedness, endless doodling, loneliness and yet being part of the crowd, solo/tutti. In Class 10 the young people can begin to listen to one another again, which is a prerequisite for objective discussion and a willingness to consider, or at least respect, opposite views. A breath of new air blows through the class community. The youngsters are no longer exclusively searching by means of criticising everything like a kind of out-breathing process. They are also finding answers, moments of containment in hearing each other's views, like a kind of in-breathing that allows them to come to themselves and remain within themselves ...

In Class 10 the pupils have the opportunity to enter intensively into the form language of Classical music and follow its development from Haydn via Mozart to Beethoven's later works.

For the most part indicative (diatonic) forms have determined processes in the class. Having once encountered one another by means of an objective discussion, we can in Class 11 then approach the possible, the indeterminate, the vague, the irrational i.e. the subjunctive as a new reality between sense experience and knowledge. A new mood provided by the interval of the third as the sixth is now a sign of turning towards the other: 'Participating in the inner life of the other.'

... We must also take a new look at the 'programme music' of the Romantic period. It is not merely a matter of repeating a non-musical content by means of music. It is music awakening in images, a process that can bring in imaginative associations, even though these are initially external and materialistic. We follow the path from materialistic images (Smetana Vltava) to the imaginatively inspired works of the great impressionists (Debussy La mer). This path is also a way of practising what Steiner described as the feeling for the octave. Pupils sense that their subjective feelings (stuck in tonality) begin to let go and loosen, so that they can be led to a light of consciousness of which they have an inkling ...

In the composition and improvisation exercises we try to use the more important style elements of the Romantic period. By means of non-harmonic modulations new and unsuspected spaces are opened up that call tonality and orientation towards a keynote into question. The way is then open for an art that can take responsibility for itself. The score no longer offers any security. Art becomes a space for the essential, enabling it to appear – untouched – in a space that is etheric and spiritual. The prerequisite for this is that the wish for art to become artistic knowledge should enable us to extricate ourselves from subjective, dreaming imprisonment within. T. S. Eliot coined the phrase for this: "Precise emotion". [7]

Pupils in Class 12 experience that their feeling for the world and for themselves has changed. They no longer feel so much obligation towards the dreamy, warm life of the group. Instead they take on responsibility more and more for themselves and their life's motifs. This is not so much an 'awakening' as a 'resurrection'. Young people look for this not only in themselves but also in contemporary art. They hope for the genuinely new, the future-oriented, the unknown, the unheard-of – in music also. So in Class 12 music lessons one can begin to find a way towards a-tonal music. Harmony theory provides no safety net here; the only thing that counts is:

... to be open and ready to search out the musical phenomena and the inner logic of their unfolding, to sense the truth they contain, and to practise and school a new kind of 'thinking' in connection with them. As an example of this one need only look more closely at the last of Schönberg's Six Little Pieces for Piano, *Op. 19. ...*

When we examine the development undergone by music during the twentieth century from that point onwards, we discover that as music has grown more materialistic on the one hand and less materialistic on the other, there has nevertheless not occurred again a transparency, and transcendence (an openness for the spirit to flow in) carried by such a high degree of awareness as was experienced at the beginning of the century...

Seen from this angle, music is indeed an essential ingredient in education, essential because outwardly music, the least material of the arts, is without purpose; it speaks directly to the inmost core in every human being. [8]

Class 9

Points of view and general themes:

The pupils learn to understand and perform simple vocal and instrumental works in appropriate styles. Basic structures of some works are studied, and a beginning is made in looking at some of the streams in music history. Many schools form an Upper School choir combining all classes and an orchestra involving those capable of contributing. Large choral works are studied and performed, often together with staff and parents.

Content suggestions:

STUDY OF MUSIC:
- General studies: the line system and notation of music, scales, circle of the fifth, intervals, chords and inversions are continued both in instrumental and choral work and in improvisation and composition exercises
- Works are described, characterised, compared and assessed
- Look for links with history and the other arts e.g. the connections between music and society
- Experiencing phenomena of contemporary music

MUSIC THEORY:
- Rounds, fugues, suites, cantatas, oratorios, introduction to counterpoint style
- Differences between homophone/polyphone, temperate mood
- Study of the different instruments e.g. the organ and other keyboard instruments

BIOGRAPHIES:
- E.g. comparing Mozart/Beethoven, Bach/Handel

CONCERT AND OPERA VISITS:
- Classical works, with preparation and subsequent assessment

SINGING, CHOIR:
- Voice work.
- Extending the repertoire (choir): folksongs, Lieder, examples of light music, political songs etc., a capella, with accompaniment, unison and in several parts
- Singing songs in the foreign languages the pupils are studying

UPPER SCHOOL CHOIR:
- All the classes in the Upper School form this choir to work on pieces that can be performed in public

INSTRUMENTAL MUSIC:
- In the school orchestra or chamber music groups pupils work on pieces for performance to the rest of the school or in public
- Improvisation e.g. with the school's collection of percussion instruments

Class 10

Points of view and general themes:

Work is done on the formal structures of sonatas, fugues etc. The pupils learn about the significance of the sonata in Classical music, especially in the way this relates to the human being. The students can take a more active role in performing music in concerts, dealing with publicity, programme notes, front of house activities and taking music into the local community.

Content suggestions:

STUDY OF MUSIC:
- Forms of instrumental and vocal music: motifs, themes, sonata, symphony, concerto, opera
- Basic harmony studies
- Studies in composition, the students can be encouraged to compose their own pieces in harmony and counterpoint

BIOGRAPHIES:
- The pupils work up biographies of well-known composers or interpreters including good jazz and pop musicians [9]

CONCERT AND OPERA VISITS:
- Classical works, with preparation and subsequent assessment

SINGING, CHOIR:
- Voice work
- Expanding the repertoire of songs
- Folksongs, Lieder, opera arias, songs from musicals, chansons, a capella or accompanied
- Singing songs in the foreign languages the pupils are studying

UPPER SCHOOL CHOIR:
- All the classes in the Upper School form this choir to work on pieces that can be performed in public
- Classical choruses in four voices

INSTRUMENTAL MUSIC:
- In the school orchestra or chamber music groups pupils work on pieces for performance to the rest of the school or in public
- Improvisation

Class 11

Points of view and general themes:

The pupils learn to perform Lieder in an appropriate way. They also learn to recognise Romantic forms by ear or by reading the score.

They develop an awareness of the new view attained by musicians in the 19th Century and discover how the 'universal language' of Classical music relates to the origins of national folk music and jazz.[9]

Content suggestions:

STUDY OF MUSIC:
- Music main-lesson. (See also Art Studies in Class 11)
- Apollonian/Dionysian: expressions and forms of a musical work of art
- Development periods in the history of music from early days up to the 20th Century
- A look at the harmony of Pythagoras
- Using chromatic scales
- Significant works from important epochs with emphasis on the Romantic period

- Describing, comparing, categorising various works
- Programme music

MUSIC THEORY:
- The form of the main sonata movement

BIOGRAPHIES:
- Reports by the pupils on great Romantic composers: Schumann, Chopin, Brahms, Wagner, Verdi etc.

CONCERT AND OPERA VISITS:
- Classical and Romantic works, with preparation and subsequent assessment

SINGING, CHOIR:
- Voice work
- Solo singing
- Expanding the repertoire of songs: folksongs, Lieder, Romantic choir works, chamber ensembles (also solos) a capella or accompanied
- Singing songs in the languages the pupils are studying
- Four-part choral works (including Romantic ones)

UPPER SCHOOL CHOIR:
- All the classes in the Upper School form this choir to work on pieces that can be performed in public (seasonal and festive themes)

INSTRUMENTAL MUSIC:
- In the school orchestra or chamber music groups pupils work on pieces for performance to the rest of the school or in public
- Improvisation

Class 12

Points of view and general themes:

The pupils should be able to recognise and describe characteristic phenomena of twentieth-century music. Interest in the directions composition is taking in our time must include interest in the current situation in which human beings find themselves. The pupils should study examples of how musicians today, also with the electronic means at their disposal, can be responsible for music's continuing development. An understanding of the main streams of music history should help the pupils develop an awareness of today's relevant questions.

Content suggestions:

STUDY OF MUSIC:
- An overview of music history: music in the past, present and anticipated future trends, viewed both from the past and from the twentieth century
- Theory of harmonies
- Development of music after World War Two
- Important works of the twentieth century (e.g. Stravinsky, Hindemith, the New Viennese School, Schönberg, Berg, Bartok, Arvo Pärt etc.) are

described, characterised, compared and categorised
- Music and technology (electronic, synthetic and computer-supported music)

BIOGRAPHIES:
- Pupils' studies on 20th Century composers, or
- Pupils' projects on music and the human being

CONCERT AND OPERA VISITS:
- Classical and modern works, with preparation and subsequent assessment

SINGING, CHOIR:
- Voice work
- Expansion of song repertoire
- Choral works, folksongs, Lieder of the 20th Century, and solo singing, a capella or with accompaniment

UPPER SCHOOL CHOIR:
- All the classes in the Upper School form this choir to work on pieces that can be performed in public. Difficult works are tackled

INSTRUMENTAL MUSIC:
- In the school orchestra or chamber music groups

pupils work on pieces for performance to the rest of the school or in public
- Improvisation
- Solo work of gifted pupils
- School-leaving concert

References:
1   Ronner, S., Was Bedeutet Lehrplan für die Musik?, *Lehrerrund brief*, No. 67, November 1999.
2   Ibid., p4.
3   Steiner, R., *Three Lectures on the Curriculum,* op. cit., third lecture of 6th September, 1919.
4   Steiner, R., *Practical Advice to Teachers* op. cit., lecture of 23rd August 1919.
5   A detailed compilation of the indications on music teaching by Rudolf Steiner can be found in Dr B. Masters, *Steiner Education and Music*, 1999. This curriculum draws on Brien Masters' music curriculum, except where indicated.
6   Riehm, P. M., 1989, in Beilharz, G. (ed) *Erziehen und Heilen durch Musik*. Trans. J. C.
7   Ibid., p83.
8   Ibid., p90.
9   Steiner made no mention of jazz in his curriculum indications, though he must have been aware of its existence. Some music teachers may feel it unworthy of consideration. Dr. Brien Masters certainly dissociates himself from this curriculum indication. The editor, however, feels it certainly should be included as it is a theme regularly taught in the Upper School and can be justified as such.

PHILOSOPHY
Class 12

There are many opportunities to explore philosophical questions in the context of other subjects such as history, art, science, literature, religion and even to an extent in foreign language lessons. The philosophy main-lesson in Class 12 provides an opportunity to explore basic philosophical issues and methods. A starting point is to establish that people have been motivated by ideals throughout history and that these ideals often express changing worldviews. This forms a basis for all real knowledge. Highly complex and important concepts are accessible to everyone when they are presented in an appropriate way.

General aspects and aims

Philosophical questions arise as a matter of course in many subjects in the Upper School. Philosophy serves as a link to other lessons taught by the literature or the history teacher.

Young people of 18 or 19 are particularly open to philosophical questions. They want to survey what they have learnt from a 'higher vantage point'. Finding oneself now gains a larger dimension; personal perspectives widen to include humanity as a whole. Philosophy in Class 12 is much more than dry academic learning; it is rather, the 'love of wisdom', as the name implies.

Points of view and general themes:

Differing philosophies can suggest a variety of answers to basic human questions. The students learn to reproduce, classify and evaluate different philosophical trains of thought by means of text analysis, open discussion and essays for homework. These tasks are intended to provide a context for initial answers to the pupils' own, usually unconscious, questions. As Kant might have said, *"rather than learning about philosophy we should learn to philosophise."*

The following suggestions are guidelines only. It is obviously not possible to cover all or even most of these topics in one three week main-lesson.

Content suggestions:

INTRODUCTION:
- Origins of philosophical questions
- The special position of philosophy in relation to the humanities and sciences
- Taking up philosophical questions arising in other subjects such as English, history, art studies, religion, etc.

THE KNOWING HUMAN BEING:
- Fundamental questions in philosophy, theories of Knowledge and endeavours to answer them, e.g. by critical rationalism, positivism, scepticism etc.
- Theories of truth

THE ACTING HUMAN BEING:
- The initial question of human freedom
- Absolute and relative values
- Considerations of freedom as dealt with by various philosophers (Socrates, Plato, Kant, Nietzsche, Jaspers, Steiner)
- The responsibility of the scientist

A CHOICE OF THEMES:
- *The philosophy of history:*
  - The history of human consciousness as shown in the philosophical questions raised.
  - Lessing's *Education of Mankind*
- *The philosophy of language:*
  - Comparison of older and newer theories of language (e.g. Humboldt, Whorf, Chomsky, Pinker)
  - The nature of language as taken from the pupils' own experience (with a side glance at modern lyric poetry)
- *Philosophical anthropology:*
  - The nature of the human being in various cultures and religions
  - Gender issues
  - The problem of death
  - The tragedy of human limitations
- *Aesthetics:*
  - Matter and form in art
  - Schiller's *Letters on the Aesthetic Education of Mankind*, selected passages
- *Philosophy of the state:*
  - Comparison of various views of state, law, power in the history of philosophy (Plato, Aristotle, Macchiavelli, Rousseau)
  - Consideration of Utopias (e.g. Plato, Thomas More, Karl Marx etc.)

Principal aspects and general teaching aims for physics in the Middle School

The main aim of science teaching is to grasp the core of science that is relevant to the human being as well as presenting it in an imaginative way to appeal to the emotions. This means developing a faculty of observation for the real gestures of nature. Indeed science lessons begin at the age when the child gains an ability to see the world causally and they must serve to cultivate this thinking faculty. Indeed this can occur in such a way that a qualitative thinking is developed that continually considers the changing connection between the human being and the world.

Through the limiting of science to size, number and weight (as Galileo did), that is, to the purely quantitative, the question of the *being* of natural phenomena has been lost. During the rise of the modern age, man began to ask how he could control nature, and finally to see this control as what is essential. This trend has been connected with the development of causal and theoretical model views, because it is only possible to have absolute mastery over natural processes when you can explain them causally. If this is not initially possible, phenomena are reduced conceptually to explainable processes.

The danger is that these concepts of imposed quantitative and particle-like models of nature are taken up by pupils as objective reality. From this experience for example a curriculum formulated in 1977 already has this warning: *"It is essential to use models which are not too perfect when beginning teaching. There must be elementary phenomena which cannot be explained by the models used. Only by this means do the pupils altogether gain the insight into the principle of the insufficiency of models".* [1]

What is more valuable from a pedagogical point of view are however the following principles:

1. In place of models which cannot be experienced, should be thought processes which have their basis in real perception.
2. Initially an emotional connection to the phenomena must be awakened in the child. This must then be raised from the subjective level in order that the intrinsic qualities can be grasped in cognitive activity.
3. Thereby science teaching in the Waldorf school takes its departure from the sense qualities. Indeed it can in this respect even be described as an extremely sense-orientated method. This plays an important role and has a hygienic-pedagogical aspect. The lively joy in cognition is healing for the student aged between 12 and 14 years, and can even possibly lighten the tendency towards all-too-strong self-pre-occupation.

The phenomenological world view, the creative forming of thought connections with natural events requires, however, even more. It should not only be done out of an honest pedagogical endeavour towards a human-centred acquisition of knowledge. Rather it involves a epistemological discussion of the basic ideas of the empirical method of science.

The active participation of the individual person in the world characterises Rudolf Steiner's theory of knowledge. In his basic books on this subject *A Theory of Knowledge* and *The Philosophy of Freedom* [2], Rudolf Steiner described the connection between sense impression and thinking. *"Our whole being functions in such a way, that it flows in reality towards the elements of each thing observed from two sides; from the side of perception and from that of thinking."* [3]

Science teaching in the Waldorf school seeks to do justice to this basic rule

Classes 6 to 8

Principal aspects and general teaching aims:

The whole of physics teaching does not start from theories or models, but from the experienced and observed phenomenon. Wherever opportunities offer themselves, contrasts should be demonstrated for comparison. Even though the single disciplines of this subject are defined, one should try not to go through them in isolation but to cultivate the aspects common to other subjects where they appear in an interdisciplinary way. It is therefore self evident, that connections to art and technology should be presented, when they offer themselves and are appropriate to the age being taught.

The Middle School attempts to provide a rich experience of physical phenomena upon which the Upper School can conceptually build.

Class 6

Possible teaching content:

The experience of phenomena in simple, very clear experiments leads the pupil into the realm of physics.

For this purpose acoustics can be placed at the beginning. Various entries offer themselves; to name but two:

a) Introduction to basic acoustic phenomena (vibration, pitch, volume, tone colour)
b) Beginning with familiar musical instruments, pupils can recognise vibration as the physical equivalent of tone
   * The connection of the sounding body to volume, pitch and tone colour is presented
   * Intervals on the monochord
   * Sound transmission
   * Resonance

The pupils anyway get to know the physical – physiological qualities of the larynx (compare – biology in Class 8).

From experiences in painting they go on to:
* Colour studies
* Simple optics (i.e. studies without theory).

- The point of departure is the contrast: light – darkness
- The observation of illuminated coloured surfaces gives rise to after images in the eye, these lead to the concept of complementary colours (Goethe's 'summoned' colours)
- Colourful and coloured shadows are demonstrated and the conditions under which they arise are shown
- The phenomena of colour derived in an opaque medium when illuminated from behind and from the side
- The goal in colour studies is the observation of coloured fringes on dark/light borders as seen through a prism
- Fringes appear on dark/light borders
  Apart from colours shadows are an area of study. Magnetism is presented starting with naturally occurring magnetite
- The question "how is something magnetised?" is answered and which materials have (ferro)-magnetic properties

Ordinary magnets are presented and the compass (without casing) demonstrated. This leads to discussions on:
- The concept of north and south pole
- The concept of magnetic attraction and repulsion
- The magnetic field of the earth

Electricity is dealt with as regards the phenomena of attraction and repulsion in electrostatics, using charges obtained by friction.
  Heat studies considers the contrast of:
- Warmth and cold
- Sources of heat and cold are demonstrated and discussed together with the possibility of creating cooling (still without any technical details).
- Combustion and friction are looked at more closely as heat sources.

Class 7

Possible teaching content:

Mechanics is central to the teaching after which the further contents of acoustics, optics, thermodynamics, magnetism and electricity are discussed. In mechanics, levers are studied. Here it is clear that the concept is dominant. The content is in key words:
- Levers in several variations: effort arm and load arm
- Digital balance (which is decimal and sensitive)
- Inclined plane
- Winch
- Pulleys, block and tackle
- Wedge, screw, linkages, gears

Combinations of these 'basic machines' should be discussed and the aim is to arrive at the understanding of the means by which a weight-driven clock works.
- The development of formulas for the lever and inclined plane

- As summary, the Golden Rule of mechanics (i.e. that gain in force is paid for by greater distance travelled formally known as 'velocity ratio')

ACOUSTICS
- Chladni plates [can also be done in Class 6]
- Rotating plate with holes and air jet
- Gramophone
- Sound directing. Echoes [can also be done in Class 8]

OPTICS
Observation of:
- Shadows and images (combined with drawing)
- Light images on planes and curved mirrors practised
- The pin-hole camera (compared with the human eye) [can also be done in Class 8]
- Camera obscura

WARMTH
- Conduction
- Thermometers

MAGNETISM
- Declination and inclination of the earth's field
- The basic phenomena of magnetism
The new subject of electrodynamics comprises approximately:
- Sources of current (cells, dynamo)
- Electrical appliances in relationship to flow of current
- Magnetic effects, electromagnets.
- Technical applications: electric ovens, boilers, irons, fuses
- Indications of the dangers of electric current, also in lightening must be given

Class 8

Possible teaching content:

The new areas of hydrostatics, hydrodynamics, aerostatics and aerodynamics with a strong practical bias stand primarily in the foreground for this age. In detail:
- The Archimedes principal (for water and air)
- Hydrostatic buoyancy (depth pressure)
- Connected containers (hydraulic scales)
- Cartesian diver
- Specific weight of solid, liquids and gaseous bodies
- Stability (e.g. of ships)
- Static pressure (in water compared to air)
- Principal of pumps (especially leading to the hydraulic ram)
- Laminar and turbulent flow
- Vortices and resistance (in water and air in connection to the resisting forms which they pass)

In the area of meteorology (this is often taught in connection with the geography main lesson, some of which comes also in Class 10, see geography curriculum) the following can be done:

- Air moisture content and cloud formation (dew point)
- Cloud types (Cumulus, Cirrus, Stratus, Nimbus and their combinations)
- High and low pressure areas (with fronts developing over time)
- Cyclone alleys
- Weather maps, weather forecasts
- Wind force according to the Beaufort scale, special winds such as the Mistral, Föehn, trade winds, monsoon and typhoon. Climatic phenomena such as maritime and continental climate, tropical and sub-tropical and polar climate.

In acoustics one investigates for instance:
- Speed of sound (also in other media than air)
- Sound directing: reflection (echo) and absorption [can also be done in Classes 7 and 9]
- Kundt's tube
- Acoustics in building, acoustics in various musical instruments

In thermodynamics the content could be for example:
- Change of state of liquids, solids and gasses, evaporation.
- Anomaly point of water and its significance for nature [can also be done in Class 9]
- Warm and cold water pipe systems, convection, radiation
- Conduction and insulation mediums in various materials [can also be done in Class 7]

PROCESSES AND LAWS OF ELECTRICITY
- Warming effect, chemical effect of electric currents.
- Conduction properties of various materials, also earthing
- The magnetic effect of a current and its applications:
  Electro-motor, dynamo (possibly generator, in any case this should be dealt with in more depth higher up the school), measurement (Ohm's law).

Classes 9 to 12

Principal aspects and general teaching aims for physics in the Upper School:

In Classes 6 to 8 science lessons were given by a generally trained class teacher who taught many subjects. In particular, the relationship of the subject matter to the human being was presented in its physiological, economic, and ecological aspects. The starting point generally for teaching was experiments. Investigations were kept simple, so that the children could recall most of them at home. Where possible the children were encouraged to observe physical phenomena. Experiments and demonstrations of phenomena were arranged, and the pupils went on to deliver independent, written descriptions.

In science lessons in the Upper School, the impressions based on experience of the Middle school are

then ordered further by thinking and finally grasped as laws. The pupils should thereby be protected from valuing half understood theories above their own experience and judgment while building up their picture of the world. From this it should be clear that theoretical content, which today as a rule is considered the basis of subjects – and for this reason is often placed at the beginning of a teaching programme – is only taught in the Upper School in Waldorf schools. Therefore the model of the atom is only dealt with in the Classes 11 and 12. Where theories enter into the teaching, they should at least be elaborated as thought spheres about phenomena, as for instance the atomic theory which comes from the quantitative laws of chemistry, the emission of light etc. Otherwise the world appears, as it surrounds mankind, as meaningless compared to an elaborate model of it and the ability to judge retreats when confronted with the given content.

The aims for physics teaching in the Upper School are:

KNOWLEDGE AND UNDERSTANDING OF
- Fundamental physical phenomena and the attempts to describe their processes
- Physical dimensions and concepts defined – with consideration of aspects relevant to man – as well as the main laws of measurement and defining equations; estimates of the order of magnitudes of physical results
- Understanding of certain phenomena of daily life by means of physical processes
- Understanding of the physical basis of technical apparatus
- A knowledge of the main lines of historical development in physics and the biographies of significant scientists
- A knowledge of the idea of physical models and their capacity to predict

ABILITIES AND SKILLS
- To observe precisely and formulate observations
- To carry out simple experiments and interpret their results
- To construct independent concepts from observations
- To construct independent experiments so as to make observations
- To recognise uncertainties and evaluate their influence
- To present measurements graphically and evaluate them
- To understand physical processes with the help of known laws
- To recognise the possibilities and limitations of physics in describing reality
- To be able to judge the real component in models
- To produce independent reports of what is taught
- To look at things in their entirety, holistic observation, and present their connection to human life

INSIGHTS, EVALUATIONS AND ATTITUDES
- Readiness to communicate and co-operate in

observation, investigation and experimenting
- Recognition of the difference between quantitative and qualitative investigation and their results
- Insight into the meaning of dynamic and feed-back processes (change-causing-relationships) and their challenge to human thinking
- Arrival at an awareness of environmental and energy issues on the basis of their own insight
- Insight that the physical method of thinking must be constantly modified
- Insight that science and within it physics represents and important part of human culture
- The ability to judge information and presentations of the mass media thoroughly
- The ordering of different scientific investigative methods and their significance for the interpretation of results
- The evaluation of the wisdom of nature – also as an example for human endeavour

Class 9

Viewpoints and general teaching aims:

The pupils are guided in experiencing so that they can understand the processes of the surrounding world, especially those of technology. For this reason questioning thinking and judgment is practised especially in practical things from the realm of technology. The manufacture of materials should feature particularly in experiment description. A mathematical formulation of the rule is usually only given for certain examples e.g. for exercises to do with the area in hand, where a meaningful calculation is possible, and where the pupil can gain a feeling for quantities. Understanding for physics and its methods should be deepened and a glimpse of the physical content of everyday objects and technology be given.

Possible teaching content:

- Transformer
- Introduction to Potential difference, current, resistance
- Morse transmitter (telegraph)
- Bells, relays
- Washing machine

HEAT AND ENGINES
This is mostly built up on the suggestions of Rudolf Steiner, leading to the understanding of the steam engine, but a more contemporary development is advisable.
- The investigation of air pressure by Otto von Guericke
- Historical development of the steam engine and its importance in the historical development of Europe
- The function of the boiler
- Comparison of the heating value of various fuels (in ideal combustion situations)
- As regards basic laws thereby you can arrive at:
  - 1st and 2nd law of thermodynamics

The development in new areas of technology could for example take the following themes:
- Absolute zero; the Kelvin scale
- The steam turbine
- Fridges and the contrasting function of the heat pump
- Internal combustion engines – 4-stroke, 2-stroke, diesel, perhaps the Stirling motor
- Radiation
- Rocket propulsion

ELECTRICITY AND ACOUSTICS
Here one begins with the suggestion of Rudolf Steiner's, to present everything that will make a telephone comprehensible.
- Introduction or recapitulation of the concepts of potential difference, current, and resistance (see Class 8)
- Ohm's law with examples involving calculation
- Introduction of the concept of electrical work, electrical output and their units
- Calculation of electricity costs
- Function of the telephone; acoustically, and electronically
- Dialling technology
- Business significance of various communications technologies
- Fax machine
- Photocopier

For the Acoustic Doppler effect one can use Rudolf Steiner's suggestion:
- The treatment of relative motion of binary stars with the help of the Doppler effect (can also be done in the geography main-lesson)

Further possible themes:
- Principle of the electric motor
- Comparison of the efficiency of various machines
- Biographies of important physicists or alternatively independent presentations by pupils on Watt, Guericke, Papin, Morse etc.
- Optional energy requirement and inquiry into the means of energy saving
- Comparison of the readily available energy sources
- Solar energy and its possible significance in the future (could otherwise be done in Class 10 or 11, see technology curriculum)
- Hydrogen as possible energy carrier

Class 10

Viewpoints and general teaching aims:

The pupils experience their relationship to their surroundings increasingly consciously and thus stand in a tension between high ideals and uncertainty of appropriateness. In many subjects one can address the question of origins. Through transparent and fundamental concepts in mechanics one can attempt in various ways to give conscious clarity and security. For this the mathematicisation of physics is handled in an experiential way. The pupils can experience satisfaction in the dominance of statements won through mathematics using observation and measurement (for instance in the parabolic trajectory of a thrown object).

Discovering the principles, proportions and conditions with equations of quantities is practised.

The pupils receive a living, conscious vision of the great spiritual scientific turning point of the late Renaissance and the birth of physics by grappling with decisive historical questions as found in the biographies of significant personalities (Galileo, Bruno, Kepler, Tycho Brahe). They thus grasp how the human being as observer is caught in the facts of the physical world, its laws, from the outside, and in the lawfulness of logic, in thinking, from the inside. By their own development in consciousness as well as the recognition of their own mistakes the students learn the conditions of research and see the "great spirits" of earlier times in the correct light. They also learn the value of learning from failure for all research and development. So the pupil experiences, how security of understanding comes about, and learns, to connect himself to the earth and its laws in a new way.

Possible teaching content:

Classical mechanics
Kinematics (uniform movement)
* Measurement of speed
* The concept of average speed
* How to represent speed using vectors
* Parallelogram of velocity
* The concept of acceleration
* Development of the laws of motion for constant acceleration using an inclined plane v=at, s=1/2att
* Free fall, acceleration due to gravity, units of force
* Vertical and horizontal motion perhaps diagonal motion
* Principle of independence (of perpendicular motion)
Statics
* Hook's law; application to balances
* Measurement of forces, force equations
* Representation of forces by vectors
* Elastic and plastic deformation, pressure, stress
* Centre of gravity of a body
* Force and reaction of a body on a slope
Dynamics
* Concept of mass, force
* Newton's laws of motion
* Go into the historical development of these concepts and the biography of Newton
* Law of conservation of energy
* Recapitulation of the golden rule of mechanics
* Mechanical work
* The concept of energy
* The law of conservation of energy
* Friction and static friction and cohesion
* Rotary motion
* The rotation of the earth
* Centrifugal and centripetal force
Optional, Coriolis effect (see geography in Class 10)
* Law of moments and balancing using moments

* Impulse and momentum, elasticity
* Newton's law of gravitation
* Kepler's laws
  Optional: Kepler's *Harmonices Mundi* (or in astronomy main-lesson)
* Pendulums
* Rhythms in the solar system
* Wave motion in mechanics
* Mechanical oscillation and waves
* Superposition of waves (constructive and destructive interference, if not in Class 11)

An astronomy main-lesson could be considered (although otherwise covered in physics; Rudolf Steiner did not expressly require a main lesson) with the themes:
* The protective covering of the earth
* The solar system heliocentrically
* The 9 planets, asteroids and comets
* The sun and its rhythms
* Solar effects on the earth – life-history of a star
* Kepler's "Harmony of Worlds"
* Sun and moon and their rhythms in relationship to the earth
Optional:
* The golden section as rhythmical principle of form in the solar system
* Telescopes, microscopes, cameras, (human eye) (and Class 11)

Class 11

Viewpoints and principal teaching aims:

Following Rudolf Steiner's indications, which were to handle the modern discoveries of physics (at that time alpha, beta and gamma rays), electrical theory, electromagnetic theory, and the basic phenomena of radioactivity as well as the conceptual development in physics in the 19th and 20th Centuries should be worked through. Electrical and magnetic fields in particular are investigated. With this the students' intelligence, which has been schooled in observation and measurement, is turned to areas requiring mathematical thought. The principle of taking experiments as the point of departure, should, however, remain as in earlier classes.

Possible teaching content:

ELECTRICITY
* The history of electricity
  Optional: electrostatics (revision)
* Concept of the electrical field
* Capacitors
* Van de Graaf generators (as examples for electrostatics)
* Current induced magnetic fields
* Faraday's motor principle
* Revision work on the concept of potential difference, charge, current, resistance but on a more general level
* Connection between potential difference, current, resistance, force

- Warming effect of a current
- Conduction rules in various materials
- Induction: Inductive resistance, Lenzes rule, Lorenz force,
- Eddy current breaking effect
- Superconductivity
- Energy as calculation standard (extension of the energy laws from Class 10)
- Induction due to reciprocally acting currents; polarity of the electric and magnetic field
- Change in time of current and potential difference of a charging and discharging capacitor
- Capacitor rules, units, calculation of capacity, dielectrics
- Oscillatory discharge
- Current (quantitative)
- Potential difference and current diagrams for damped electrical oscillations
- Phase in electrical oscillations
- Undamped electrical oscillations, synthesiser
- Length of vibration and frequency; Thomson's wave formulae

SIGNAL GENERATOR, BOUNDARIES OF AUDIBILITY
- Transmitters and receivers; to which belong resonance, triodes, electron tubes (cathode ray tube), emission spectra (continuous, hot wire spectra); development of the concept of the electron as well as Millikan's investigations, transistors
- Transmission dipole, dipole laws, electromagnetic vibration fields, electromagnetic wavelengths
- The history of transmission
- Radio broadcasting, applied radio building possibly

ATOMIC PHYSICS
- High tension spark inductors; gas emission (emission tubes)
- Cathode rays, x-rays (details of subatomic particle of moving positive and negative charge carriers – ions, electrons) and their counterparts in alpha, beta and gamma rays, oscilloscope
- Radioactivity, natural occurrences of radioactivity, radioactive fallout; fission, nuclear reactors, man made radioactive isotopes, means of detection; (Geiger-Müller-tubes, cloud chambers
- History of the technological development of the atom bomb (dangers, protection from radiation)
- Atomic fusion
Optional: semiconductors, diodes, transistors (see IT).

Class 12

Viewpoints and principal teaching aims:

By now the maturity is reached which permits the young person awareness of how he or she acquires concepts. Now theoretical scientific questions can properly be addressed; for example the significance of the physical model of inductive and deductive thinking etc. Thereby one attempts to develop not blind belief in science but rather a personal capacity for judgment. This can be a decisive aid to the development of the personality. This can be done in optics – if not already done in Class 11 – or in the development of the atomic model. Besides conveying important basic knowledge a survey of the phenomena and ideas which characterise modern scientific knowledge should be given.

The various ways in which light meets matter can determine the approach to teaching.

The domain of optics can be used to show:
- Phenomena starting from their surroundings
- Analytical thinking in the domain of a complete manner of observation
- A symptomatic approach
- A discussion of points of view – development of judgment
- Building bridges between optics, man and art
- Cross curricular teaching is especially worthwhile here

Possible teaching content:

OPTICS (see list in Class 8)
- Aspects of geometrical optics
- Concept of shadow, umbral, penumbral
- Brightness
- The concept of contrast and its significance for vision
- Comparison: Eyes – photo cells; qualities, quantities, objectivity also in the domain of qualitative investigation
- After images and coloured shadows (successive contrast, simultaneous contrast) and their physiological basis
- The human eye and equivalent technical apparatus (e.g. lenses, aperture in a camera); short- and long-sightedness, spectacles
- The Weber-Fechner law (properties of optical stimulation and perception, geometric and arithmetical consequences
- Sense perception and consciousness, sensory deception
- Goethe's theory of colour (prismatic colours); colour qualities
- The polarity between the green and red spectrum, its counterpart in plant and the human being
Optional: Chlorophyll, haemoglobin: chemical structure
- The basic phenomena of chromatography according to Goethe; the Goethean method in science. Polarity of light and darkness according to Goethe and its significance for the creation of colours through darkening (Rayleigh scattering)
- Additive and subtractive colour mixing (use of technology) – difference in brightness
- Spectral and physical colours
- Plane mirrors
- Convex and concave mirrors
- Mirror laws: mirror plane (technical application)
- Microscope – electron microscope (resolution capacity)
- Refraction, total internal reflection (laws) (critical angle), Newton's basic experiment with prisms
- Diffraction (point light, laser; laser light – sunlight)

- Wavelength of light, spectroscope, spectrometer
- Polarisation – double refraction (technical application in tension/compression optics), asymmetrical structure of space – concept of isotropy
- Atmospheric colour occurrences in nature and their causes through diffraction, interference, refraction, polarisation
- The rainbow and its cause; perhaps indications about the golden section applied to the rainbow
- Photo-electric effect (technical application)
- Electron volt, Plancke's quantum effect
- Wave-particle duality and its significance for the consciousness of physics in the 20th Century (the development of models in science); regarding the methodology in dealing with borders of physics; making hypotheses
- The three models of light: wave, particle, ray, their significance and evidence for them
- Theory of relativity, quantum theory
- Biographies of significant researchers of the 20th Century (e.g. Einstein, Planck, Hahn, Schroedinger, Bohr, Heisenberg)

The pupils learn here by example to know about modern consciousness questions and the problem of science and ethics

- Mathematicisation of physics and fallibility law
- Formula structures, energy equivalence of mass; light and matter

Optional:
- Line spectra in emission and absorption, spectral analysis, meaning of spectral lines
- The measurement of potential difference by means of a photoelectric cell and the sequence of wavelengths
- Millikan's experiments (if not in Class 11 in connection with the electron), Rutherford's ray experiment, wave-particle dualism in matter.

In optics the following are taken up:
- Colour generation using prisms
- Lenses, focal points
- Virtual and real images
- The means of collection sunlight using a magnifying lens or concave mirror

References

1. *Materialen zum Unterricht (Material for Teaching)*: Hersisches Institut für Bildungsplanung, Frankfurt, 1977.
2. Steiner, R., *A Theory of Knowledge Implicit in Goethe's World Conception*, AP, 1968; *Intuitive Thinking as a Spiritual Path: A Philosophy of Freedom*, AP, 1995.
3. Ibid., Chapter 5, p67.

Classes 9 to 12

Agriculture Practical

Class 9

General aspects and aims

It is increasingly becoming necessary to give young people, while still at school, the opportunity to undertake practical tasks and prove themselves in the world of real work. Especially after puberty both boys and girls need experiences of concrete conditions in modern working situations.

For Class 9 pupils an intensive immersion in the life of a *farm* is in keeping with their age, when questions about life in general are beginning to awaken in them: What is the relationship between human being and earth, plants and animals? What problems result from technology and modern social conditions? Existential questions are rephrased as the youngsters become increasingly aware of them. Linked with their elemental urge to use the strength of their limbs, youngsters of this age want to test their will and fulfil tasks that require energy, care, courage and presence of mind. They also have a healthy natural urge to go out and experience nature, an urge that all too frequently remains unsatisfied in industrial regions. Such activities must appeal to their interest in understanding, their energy and their idealism.

Points of view and general themes:

Through concrete work on a farm the pupils should concern themselves intensively with the production of agricultural raw materials, and with the care of the earth and the landscape. Singly or in groups they work on a farm where, usually for the first time, they gain insight into the work and livelihood of one of the archetypal occupations. It is helpful if the farmers can be persuaded to explain the economic realities of produce prices, the capital costs of new equipment such as tractors, EU Subsidies etc.

Suggested fields of work and experience:

Getting to know all activities from planting, weeding, fertilizing, to harvesting and storing. Initial experiences of animal husbandry, including milk processing. Getting to know the farm in its full extent as an organism, including the prevalent social conditions. Working with people and machines. Suitable farms are those using organic, biodynamic or ecological methods while also being favourably disposed towards

young people. In 'contrast', a conventional farm might also be considered.

A diary is kept describing the farm, its geographical, commercial and social situation, and also its daily routine. This is to help the pupils work consciously on their experiences. It is also helpful to have a general discussion in the class, following such a practical, in which the students can exchange views and describe what they have learned.

Alternative work experience:

As an alternative to farming, Class 9 students can undertake practical projects involving building work or ecological work (clearing ponds, hedging, stone walling, path laying, protecting natural habitats etc.). The emphasis should be on practical skills, manual work, socially relevant and useful tasks, teamwork and accountability.

Surveying

Class 10

General aspects and aims

This subject, a part of 'Technology and Real Life', has the following aims:

- The pupils should learn that mathematics is not only about understanding links between things but can also be used for making accurate calculations which can be confidently checked. The mathematics content involves logarithms, sine and cosine and the procedures these involve
- Pupils who find it difficult to understand complicated situations can gain a new access to mathematics through this practical aspect that places more emphasis on confidence and reliability
- Sixteen-year-olds who are not only interested in understanding how things relate but also want to have concrete experiences can gain an objective independence through this subject, which taxes intelligence as well as physical will
- The pupils learn how to make accurate maps

Points of view and general themes:

All the main steps from surveying the land to plotting the map are covered in practice. The pupils gain an idea of how an ordinary object in daily use is made and they learn the importance of surveying as a basis on which buildings can be planned. The pupils learn that they have to subject themselves to the requirements set by the aim of the work, the measuring method used and the measuring apparatus. Care, patience and critical self-appraisal are called for. The youngsters discover all sorts of possible mistakes and gain a practical idea of what it means to work with accuracy.
- Most measuring is done in groups
- Agreement has to be reached as to who is going to do what
- Space and time both play a part in the measuring

process, and individual pupils have to be aware of the whole process so as not to miss the point when their own contribution has to be made

- Drawing the map requires care and accuracy
- The ability to make a mental picture and to think abstractly is strengthened
- The concept of accuracy is widened as it becomes clear that both measurement and drawing have to be accurate
- Mistakes, their causes and ways of correcting them can be discussed and made plain

The surveying period varies both in planning and emphasis, depending on the location and possibilities of the school. Duration is one to two weeks. If only one week is available, preparations are made in a number of preliminary lessons, and the map is not drawn on site, but later in additional lessons during the course of the school year.

Various related topics can be touched on, such as: national grid surveying, cartography and projection, geography and astronomy.

Forestry Period

Class 10

General aspects and aims

This period can also be taken in Class 9 or Class 11, the emphasis being different. Qualitatively though, the forestry period comes between the surveying period and the social period. Surveying involves techniques of understanding geomorphology through measurement while social work involves devotion to the needs of one's fellow human beings; forestry leads over from the one to the other.

Field ecology and forestry techniques help research the ecosystem of a woodland so that it can be properly understood and the necessary forestry measures carried out. The following framework curriculum for forestry will need adapting to local possibilities.

Points of view and general themes:

The youngsters need to extend their knowledge to include the way of life and needs of plants and animals, in order to expand their understanding of the forest as an ecosystem. In addition, practical work within the forest gives them a close experience of what the forest needs.

Suggested fields of work and experience:

PRACTICAL WORK IN THE FOREST

Together with forestry personnel responsible for the woods in question, a programme of forestry tasks is worked out, possibly with input from the pupils as well. Some suggestions:

- Reforestation (e.g. after storm damage)
- New planting
- The timber cycle
- Revitalising ponds, streams, dry meadows or other selected micro-biotopes

- Setting up forestry installations (feeding places, lookout towers, fencing, etc.)

SUPPLEMENTARY ECOLOGICAL SCIENCE

- Climatic measurements
- Microclimate: comparative measurements at various exposed sites (middle or edge of forest, meadow) of air and soil temperatures (daily round), atmospheric humidity, use of the hygrometer and evaporation (evaporimeter), soil humidity, wind direction and speed, precipitation
- Accompanying observation of the macroclimate
- Practical application of surveying knowledge: setting up climatic measurement sites and botanical and zoological test areas
- Botanical investigations
- Zoological investigations: birdsong, bird nests etc., small mammals, game (tracks, droppings etc.)
- Soil studies: digging soil profiles

Ecological themes are discussed in the group and recorded in workbooks (ecosystems, biotopes, food chain, food pyramid, etc.).

GENERAL SUGGESTIONS

Let the pupils work in small groups. Each day begins with a consultation about the day's work and ends with an exchange of day reports. Each group keeps an accurate record of work done and observations made. All these reports are combined in a final report. If the forestry period takes place at the same time each year, observation of annual changes should be aimed for. Previous reports serve each new class as a basis for their work.

Experience of the workplace, Class 10

This is a good age for students individually to choose a workplace and do a 3-week work experience. The range of workplaces can be broad. It is important that the students' visits are well-prepared and that their temporary employers have a suitable programme for them. At the end of the 3-week block the students should have 2 – 3 days in which to share their experiences with each other. Their reflections on work, different professions, human relationships in the workplace etc. can be most rewarding for the others. A daily work log should be kept. It is very useful if the students receive at least one visit from the teacher responsible during their working hours.

First Aid

Class 9 or 10

General aspects and aims

Knowledge of human anatomy and physiology gained in biology lessons is applied from the viewpoint of saving life or health in accident situations.

The theoretical basis for efficient first aid methods is established. Accident prevention is also emphasised. Practice is as important as theory. Resuscitation is practised on a dummy. Bandaging techniques and lifting are practised on each other. The pupils discover through theory and practice that giving first aid is an important service to one's fellow human beings.

Points of view and general themes:

Theoretical and practical knowledge of first aid in accordance with the training guidelines of the Red Cross, St. John's Ambulance or other organisations.

Suggested fields of work and experience:

- Need for and obligation to give help
- Tasks of the first aider
- Chain of help
- Danger zone: assessment, making secure, giving aid
- Lifesaving measures when victim is unconscious, has stopped breathing, has no circulation, is bleeding heavily or is in shock
- Wounds and how to treat them. Bandaging
- Animal bites, acid burns, burns, frostbite, hypothermia, bruising
- Joint damage, fractures, chest wounds, abdominal wounds
- Poisoning

Industrial Work Experience

Class 10 or 11

General aspects and aims

By studying and working with the newest technologies and their effects on the earth and human beings, the pupils learn to be aware of the age in which they are living, and for which they will share responsibility. The industry period gives them an insight into work carried out by large groups of people on a scale that could never be achieved by single individuals. On the other hand they also learn how, through co-ordination, individuals contribute to these large-scale achievements without which modern society would hardly be able to function. They see the social problems that arise with regard to the individual's self-realisation. All this, and the attempts that are made to solve these problems are experienced by the pupils in one setting. In discussions following on the industry period the pupils come to realise how an individual's own cultural and spiritual endeavours are his own private affair (liberty), how legal regulations have to apply to everyone (equality), and how economic measures and the physical and psychological worries of one's fellow human beings have a brotherly basis (fraternity). This is the principle of a threefoldness in human life that is experienced again and again throughout the pupils' time at school. It should lead to an understanding of society and a motivation to work at shaping it.

It may be that large industries are not available or accessible to the students. Placements can be in a variety of small businesses, preferably in manufacturing. Experience in the service industries (shops, restaurants, clubs) should follow. Many students already know this area from part-time work.

Many schools, notably in Switzerland, have developed Upper School programmes involving regular training and placements in the work place (e.g. two days a week) from Classes 10-12. This involves some reduction of the school timetable and long working hours. The motivation through this interface with the world of work has proved very rewarding. Other schools, particularly in Germany, have long offered apprenticeships within the school, in practical subjects such as childcare, nutrition, woodwork, metalwork or textiles. These programmes are integrated within the school timetable.

In countries such as Britain the demands of the public examinations take upwards of half the timetable, thus limiting the scope for practical work experience. The need for these experiences is becoming increasingly urgent.

During the industry period the pupils are under the special guidance of the works staff member who is responsible for them and of the specialist teacher at their school. Timewise the pupils participate in the routine of the establishment to which they are temporarily attached.

Points of view and fields of work and experience:

Learn from experience about:
- Industrial production
- The social situation of employees
- Strain caused by onesided work (or dust, noise, temperature etc.)
- Insight into wider implications
- Management questions
- Help in finding one's own way

Social Practical

Class 11 or 12

General aspects and aims

Sensitivity to others, responsibility and presence of mind in action are practised in a social setting and unaccustomed situations have to be dealt with.

The attitude at work requires the ability, or the effort, to disregard one's own interests, to enter entirely new social situations, and to devote oneself to others by noticing what they need and helping them.

Practical work in a social setting helps the pupils unfold a new kind of awareness. They participate in shaping human social life and experience the importance of each individual for the life and development of others.

The pupils' work timetable and tasks are the responsibility of the institution's staff member who is their monitor.

Preparation and supervision are carried out by a teacher or other adult connected with the school. During the social period the pupils meet for an internal weekend to share their experiences in discussion groups and to prepare for when they leave the institutions where they are temporarily working.

Points of view and general themes:

- Experience gained by working with groups marginalised by society
- Getting to know the biographies of people who have special needs or are socially deprived
- Experiencing the daily routine in social institutions
- Working with people who have special needs or are disabled
- Taking responsibility for others
- Not panicking; taking appropriate action
- Getting to know the professional problems of caring and teaching personnel
- Experiencing different types of social responsibility and integration

Suggested fields of work and experience:

- Sharing and playing a part in the daily life of the institution
- Taking on simple caring tasks such as washing, bandaging, feeding, dressing, going for walks, playing
- Finding out the history of the institution
- Finding out the structure of the institution and its connections with other establishments

Possible institutions

Hospitals, care homes, old-people's homes, establishments for people with special needs such as schools, workshops, homes, kindergartens, children's homes ...

Theatre Practical

Class 12

General aspects and aims

With the guidance of a professional or drama teacher, Class 12 work on a full-length play (opera, musical or cabaret) for public performance. In many schools plays have also been performed in Classes 9, 10 and 11, perhaps including a foreign language play. The difference is that, at the latest by Class 12, the pupils should be producing the play themselves with professional guidance.

One view is that the pupils should organise the whole project themselves as far as possible, taking responsibility not only for their parts in the play but getting into groups to prepare all the different aspects. The aim is to reach a standard, at latest by the first night, at which they would be capable of going on tour as an independent ensemble without any director. The

different teams, possibly with the occasional assistance of specialist teachers, prepare every aspect of the project (lighting, scenery, decorations, props, costumes, masks, music, sound, advertising, graphics, posters, photos, programme design, production, calendar planning, back-up, box office, prompting, scene changing etc.). The full educational effect of a project like this is reached through the whole complex range of tasks to be carried out before, during and after the performance, on the stage and behind the scenes. The aim is to produce a complete work of art involving not only a successful performance but also all the preparation and accompanying work. The pupils' powers of perception and will are put to the test in the social arena where the purpose is not to bring gifted individuals to the fore but to let all the participants – with all their strengths and weaknesses – take part in creating a 'social work of art'. Usually Class 12 plays are produced with a teacher or specialist director. Nevertheless, the students should be as involved creatively at all levels as much as possible. It is not particularly pedagogical if the students are merely players, instruments of the director's artistic will and self-image. We stress this point, as there is often the danger that due to shortness of time, the director simply drives the thing to completion and afterwards the pupils are exhausted.

This Class 12 play may be regarded as the climax and culmination of the English lessons. The pupils have to develop not only a theoretical understanding of the text but have to interpret it through gesture, facial expression and speech.

Many of the exercises carried out in English lessons during preceding years can be drawn on in achieving this:

- The speech exercises have schooled clarity and power of articulation.
- Daily recitation (and also, in eurythmy lessons, making the gestures for the sounds of speech) has schooled the pupils' feeling for speech sounds as soul gestures.
- The games lessons have cultivated a sense for spatial awareness and fluency and power of movement.

During rehearsals they continue to work at experiencing qualities of speech:

- The way a sentence spans tension and relaxation.
- The exclamation, the rhetorical question etc., as dramatic high points.
- The dramatic pause, and much else.

The pupils have to transform these qualities of speech into individualised movements, gestures and facial expressions in a way that contributes to the achievement of the overall concept of the performance. They must avoid both overplaying and unprofessional clichés. The aim is that the pupils should make their own interpretation and that they should put their all into creating the play and also enjoy doing so. This should arise through the way their fellow pupils see them (as themselves and as the character they are playing) combined with the way the play is directed (as an overall work of art) and the individual role (through working on the role itself and with the way it fits in with the play as a whole).

Art Trip

Class 12

General aspects and aims

Not only in botany but also in art it is correct to say: 'You only see what you already know about.' Art is such a wide field, constantly changing, that more than anywhere else a capacity to form judgments is needed. It is not only a question of cultivating the narrow range of sympathy and antipathy. In fact the temporary and preliminary nature of these two extremes needs to be overcome before a process of perception and discovery can really begin.

What the pupils have learnt in the Upper School has lead them up to the ability to apply their aesthetic sense in forming judgments. This is now experienced and exercised 'in situ'. Obviously many of the items found in museums and art galleries during the trip are not in their original setting, but there is a difference between seeing and perhaps sketching a Rembrandt in London's National Gallery or the Rijksmuseum in Amsterdam. An important line to follow is to see how an artistic stream has continued to the present time, been renewed or broken off in its country or city of origin.

More important than visits to museums or concerts are architectural studies and visits to the studios of living artists. Some of the questions the pupils can ask themselves are:

- What can I discover about a building through its proportions, its historical period, its national, ethnic or geographical connections?
- What is the social, biographical or national background out of which a particular contemporary artist is working?

In this sense the art trip not only strengthens the community of the class (as do all class trips) but it also has a social function with regard to society at large through finding appropriate ways of understanding how the art of a nation, of a particular historical period, or an individual artist or group of artists comes about. Once more, and perhaps for the last time, the young people can feel themselves to be pupils, protected and supported in the group. But at the same time they are now free and individual personalities facing the challenge of making their own stand and finding their own opinions.

The Class 12 Project (whole year)

The following applies in schools where Class 12 pupils undertake a year-long project.

The pupils can choose a theme from a single subject or one that draws on several. They bring what they have learnt, including new material, together in a report that can also be presented in public. It can be their final task in school, consisting of a written, an oral and an artistic or practical part and it should combine intellectual, artistic and practical work.

The theme is chosen in consultation with a mentor in collaboration with the Upper School meeting. The pupils carry out their own research, observations, interviews, experiments, conversations and so on. This forms the basis on which further reading and researches into other sources of information can be built. The pupils should summarise various points of emphasis, recognise causes and effects and provide tentative answers for questions raised by the work. The form given to the written part of the project should approach that of scientific papers (quotations, sources etc.). The method should involve the pupil's own experience and formulation of his or her independent assessment of the material and facts arising from study of the subject. A general educational aim is that the pupils should experience their own capacity to work, learning how to plan, organise and sustain a project of some magnitude over a lengthy period of time.

By experiencing their own individual interests and capabilities at the end of their years at school, the young people begin to mature in their own self-confidence and self-knowledge. Their personality gains firmer contours and they can begin to look forward towards the path they are going to take through life.

When they present their project in public, they gain objective insights about how they have handled their subject matter from the way the teachers and audience react and the questions they ask.

The project should be evaluated by the students themselves, by their specialist mentors and perhaps by a panel of other teachers or appropriate individuals from outside of school. This written evaluation as well as documentation of the project itself should be accredited by the school and form part of the student's portfolio, leaving report or record of achievement.

SOCIAL SKILLS
The cultivation of social competence
throughout the curriculum

General aspects and aims

Social skills and social competence are not subjects that appear on any school timetable. However, their cultivation is a central aim of Steiner Waldorf education. Developing social understanding based on sensitivity for other people is a faculty that essentially involves educating the will. For this to happen children must experience an environment in which social competence is apparent in the relationships around them. Social competence is also dependent on the inner commitment of each adult within the school community to moral development.

Social awareness needs to inform the school organisation in implicit and explicit ways. This does not mean necessarily ensuring a working atmosphere of total harmony, which would be entirely unrealistic. It does, however, mean that everyone works to create conditions in which social awareness comes to the fore and that conflicts and misunderstandings when they occur are dealt with in an open and constructive way.

The primary organisational structures of a Steiner Waldorf school, the central element of collegial self-management, the conscious working with the functional principles of the threefold social order, should all provide a fertile environment for children to observe social skills at work.

The curriculum, however, also provides many opportunities in inter-disciplinary ways, of cultivating social awareness in age-appropriate ways.[1]

"Social competence is never merely a matter of knowledge".[2] Competence is based on sound judgment, which requires a living thinking founded on an experience of reality. Grasping the dynamic of social processes requires mobile thinking, which itself is based on pictorial concepts capable of growth, adaptation and development through on-going new experience and reflection. Social interaction also requires the ability to hear and understand the other person as well as being able to express our own views. Much of our social, political and commercial life depends on mutual understanding and agreements, often between a number of different partners. The ideas involved are also often highly complex. Developing a living thinking is the key to creating real social competence.

In an age in which electronic means of communication are expanding exponentially, the inability to communicate clearly or empathise with others appears to be increasing. Children need to have developed real communication skills before they are exposed to electronic communications media.

Another key social ability is that of self-directed initiative and the capacity to work at something.

Children's innate drive to be active needs to be focused into play, transformed from creative play into the capacity to work which enables the individual to recognise need in the world and be able to respond to it.

The theme of social skills weaves throughout the curriculum and the teaching method. In what follows, guidelines are given as to how social skills can be fostered. The individual teacher will find many other points of reference. Our intention of including this theme within the curriculum is to highlight its central position and to stimulate thought on the matter.

Classes 1 to 3

In painting and drawing the children learn to recognise that shape arises out of colour and that there are subtle boundaries between the colours. The colours are explored in their individual characteristics and their various encounters are experienced, described and reflected upon. This process is a vital basis for understanding that social processes are not sharply defined or arbitrary in their relationships. The most important fields of discovery concern the overlaps in which something new arises.

Through the experience of movement and form drawing, children experience different points of perspective, sometimes facing the world from 'inside', sometimes being on the 'outside' looking in. Meeting at the crossing point and negotiating rights of way are also important social experiences.

In learning to read and write, the children experience that the intrinsic relationship between symbol, sound and meaning is not arbitrary, that form and content belong together, another important social skill.

Number work is particularly social in its emphasis on going from the whole to the parts. Experiencing division as a sharing helps establish the principle of fair sharing of value added. This enables the individual later to think of wages not as reward for work done but rather as an agreed division of what has been mutually earned. *"On the other hand one must understand that all those who have shared in producing and marketing a product must be able to live from the final selling prince i.e. that each 'profit margin' represents a portion of the final price. Even the large questions concerning the share of the GDP taken by the state, by the cultural sector or by the social security system are in the end a matter of reaching agreement about fair shares."*[3] Other moral and social aspects of arithmetic involve number stories (see the section on maths teaching).[4]

Learning to sing and play the flute together is a wonderful schooling of listening skills and responding to others. This is equally true of foreign language lessons in which the child learns to understand what the other person means on the basis of non-semantic perception (tone of voice, gesture, body language) as well as through the language itself. This requires the cultivation of a specific kind of empathy and rhythmic exchange between speaker and listener.

The manual dexterity learned in handwork forms a basis for later conceptual grasping of complex ideas.

Handwork also reinforces a strong sense of mutual dependency between people (the farmer who shares the wool and the person who buys a woollen garment) and between the human being and the kingdoms of nature. This primary experience is the basis not only for ecological thinking but also for a sound grasp of economic principles.

Classes 4 to 7

As described in the sections on crafts and nature study, there are important social dimensions to the blocks involving farming, work skills and house building, especially regarding the basic principles of economics, namely mutuality, the meeting of needs and the transformation of raw materials into useful commodities. The important elements to stress to children at this age include:

- The experience that all economic activities are mutually inter-dependent. The farmer depends on the tractor factory; the factory on the production of steel and other raw materials; these often have an international source; all workers and their families need food, clothing and housing; commodities need transport; all these processes require banking, insurance, lawyers, advertising, health and safety regulation; above all these activities need research and development, which means human thought.
- The experience that all economic activity is based on the transformation of natural resources of raw materials and energy and that this has consequences for the natural world.
- The experience that the economic process is reflected in financial relationships of various kinds.

The children need to experience these primary principles in real and tangible situations and not merely as theory. The emphasis at this age needs to be on positive examples, rather than on the many negative examples of exploitation, injustice, corruption and incompetence.

Wherever possible experience needs to be direct and modern. Whilst introducing the archetypal professions of shepherd, woodcutter, fisherman, the children also need to see their modern equivalents. The study of the locality should include the links a city or region has to other regions and other parts of the world. This may mean a visit to a local airport to see what freight and what passengers arrive from which destinations or it may mean looking at the products on display on a supermarket aisle and exploring their countries of origin.

Arithmetic is applied to practical life and examples are chosen which strengthen moral and social awareness, rather than abstractions or hypothetical situations. In English, not only are communication skills practised but the study of grammar makes relationships more conscious. Who did what to whom, how, where and why? The relevance of direct and reported speech for social responsibility cannot be underestimated. Faithfully reporting another person's words and opinions is a real skill. Writing business letters was something Steiner felt strongly about as an antidote to sentimental, self-indulgent thinking.

If you stuff the children mainly with sentimental idealism between the ages of thirteen and fifteen, they will later develop an aversion to idealism and become materialistic people... If you want to gather children around you in order, in your religious fervour, to tell them about the glories of the divine powers in the world, then... what you say will go in one ear and out of the other and never reach their feelings. If, having written a business letter with a group of children in the morning, you have the same group again in the afternoon carrying in their subconscious what has been brought about by the morning's business letter, then you are fortunate if it is now a matter of teaching them some religious concepts, for you yourself will have roused in them the mood that is now calling for its antithesis. [5]

The concept of business letters includes a wide range of formal letters, enquiries, orders, booking requests, letters of complaint and so on. These combine objectivity, clarity, precise terminology and awareness of rights and obligations. In the arithmetic of Class 6, the introduction of compound interest and algebraic formulas forms a similar basis for later understanding of economic relationships.

In history lessons which begin in Class 5, the children learn about the forms of early societies and their close relationship to their specific environment, Catal Hayuk in the Fertile Crescent, Ur in Mesopotamia, Egypt and the Nile etc. With the history of ancient Greece comes the polis, the city-state with its colonies and hinterland. Roman history introduces the concepts of citizenship, civil justice and the 'voice of the people'. The transition from theocracy to republic, and from there to Empire provides important historical models of social and political processes.

The discussions in Class 6 about the Medieval period focus on the three realms of; the church and especially the monastic orders, courtly and knightly chivalry, the urban guilds, all of which offered models for social relationships. The encounter between the Christian West and Islam in both its positive and negative aspects is an important study in intercultural relations. Class 7 and the Age of Discovery provides many opportunities to explore culture clashes as well as grasping the seeds of modern economic processes. Steiner stressed that the economic changes in Europe following the Reformation were the most important factors in modern historical development, [6] and involved the transference of land ownership from the Church into secular hands.

Topics such as the invention of printing, the development of banking and early capitalism, the rise of public theatre, the new technologies of warfare and so on have important sociological implications.

Class 8 and Class 9 address the Age of Revolutions and central themes are the rise of national identity, the increasing demand for individual rights and freedoms, the dehumanising effects of industrialisation and urbanisation. Mass education and the media are also important themes, as are the economic relationships that arose out of colonialism and the post-colonial world. The social, rights and economic aspects of modern history form an important part of the history curriculum.

Geography has a central position within the curriculum. The main emphasis throughout the geography curriculum is on human geography. Up to Class 6, one could describe geography as essentially concentric, that is, it relates from the home locality progressively to ever broadening horizons. Physical geography, including topography, geology, climate, vegetation and so on influence the developing child in profound ways. In this period geography is about experiencing the soul-spiritual forces of the earth and assisting the children to gain a firm footing on the earth.

From the age of 12 onwards geography becomes global. *"It is an outgoing, out-reaching subject that fosters a fraternity towards the different regions of the earth."* [7]

The social significance of geography teaching within the curriculum was stressed by Steiner as follows:

> *Teaching the child in this way, we place him into space and he will be interested in the world, in the whole wide world. And we shall see the results of this in many directions. A child with whom we study geography in this way will have a more loving relationship to his fellow men than one who has no idea of what proximity in space means; for he will live to feel that he lives alongside other human beings, and he will come to regard and respect them.*
>
> *Such things play no little part in the moral training of the children, and the lack of attention to geography is partly responsible for the terrible decline of the brotherly love that should prevail amongst men.* [8]

The introduction of gardening in Class 6 and its development through to Class 10 involves not only an appreciation of the relationship between effort, work and produce but also hands-on experience of the value of ecological methods of agriculture. Nature study and the sciences likewise cultivate an ecological awareness but human biology, particularly topics such as nutrition and health, provides an important balance to the influence of advertising and consumerism.

Social Studies

In most of the suggestions given above, the emphasis has been on developing social awareness more indirectly, through the subject itself. From Classes 7 and 8 upwards, social issues can be discussed directly. In his meetings with teachers, Steiner made the following suggestion with regard to teaching Social Science, *"in*

Classes 7 and 8 you could give them what is discussed in Towards Social Renewal." [9] It is unlikely that Steiner meant literally reading the book but rather that the phenomena of the threefold social order could be discussed.

For Steiner, it was crucial that all teaching from the age of 13 onwards should be related to practical life and that this should be inter-disciplinary, to counter the tendency to specialisation that characterises so much of modern life.

Steiner also suggested that the study of life skills and skills related to practical life, should be taught, such as shorthand and typing (its modern equivalent would be using a computer) and double entry book-keeping, managing personal finances and similar topics. He further recommended that people directly involved in economic life should be called on to draw up such teaching programmes. [10]

Classes 8 to 12

With adolescence, school needs to be ever more connected to practical life in the modern world. This is probably even more necessary today than it was in 1919, given each child's access to global media.

Space does not permit a full description of the possibilities for cultivating social skills and awareness in the Upper School. The following list of brief references will have to stand as stimulation to extensive research. The following ideas need to be woven into the curriculum as motifs, linking and integrating the many subjects.

Class 8

- Study of other societies with an emphasis on pre-industrial cultures as a contrast to effects of industrialisation.

Classes 8 and 9

- Modern history from the perspective of contemporary issues.

Class 9

- Physics, the motor car and diesel engine, their social and cultural impact.
- Ecology main-lesson.
- Work experience, forestry or agriculture practical.

Lifeskills Classes 9 to 12

This subject can be taught within the arts and crafts blocks as it benefits from smaller groups. They can also be integrated into the main-lesson programme. The topics form into groups:
- Rights and Responsibilities – the legal system, the role of the police, solicitors, lawyers, courts.
- Substance Abuse – laws relating to drugs including the penalties; types of drugs and their effects

including alcohol and tobacco; aspects of addiction.

- Money Skills – how to keep a bank account, cheques, credit cards, currency exchange, budgeting, stocks and shares.
- Health and Nutrition – basic facts of healthy living and lifestyles; principles of good nutrition, practical experience planning quality, low-cost quality meals, cooking and catering.
- Personal and Social skills – personal relationships, responsibility and sexuality, homosexuality and heterosexuality and gender issues, marriage and long term relationships, parenting skills, HIV/AIDS, conflict avoidance and resolution, group skills.
- Citizenship – the political system and its structures, voting, political parties, the role of Parliament, issues of individual responsibility.
- The World of Work – the changing pattern of work in a post-industrial society, applying for a job, employment rights and obligations, careers, the students should experience different work places and have the opportunities to meet a wide range of people who explain their profession e.g. nurses, engineers, architects, designers, journalists, caterers, police etc.

Language Lessons Classes 8 to 12

Foreign languages should include detailed study of the land, climate, economy, history, traditions, political systems, justice systems, current affairs of the countries where the language is spoken. An emphasis should be given to languages as bridges to other cultures.

Active Responsibility Classes 8 to 12

Students should increasingly take on social responsibility within the school community such as; playground supervision, play support for younger children, manning road crossings, assisting at school events, conferences (and not merely as fundraising activities for Upper School classes), helping with local community with ecological projects, helping the elderly, disabled etc., generating support for refugees, Third World Projects etc.

CLASS 10

- History – the close link between geography and culture in the origins of early civilisations, the emergence of tribal structures and political forms.

CLASSES 9 TO 12

- Anthropology – discussion of the nature of the human being, the significance of uprightness and the relationship to the animal kingdom. The question of human evolution and origins of language, art, technology, social forms, religion, relationship to death, relationship to the environment. The nature of perception and cognition and how we know about the world. Steiner suggested that

studying the relationship between the physical organs and their connection to soul experience is necessary to understanding how the social organism functions. [11] This is also the best way to approach the questions posed by contemporary evolutionary psychology or sociology.

- The relationship between polarities of all kinds and their reconciliation through the Goethean approach is a process which can be explored in all the arts, but equally in the sciences and humanities. Likewise the threefold approach of recognising the distinctive qualities of thinking, feeling and willing and their correlation to the nerve-sense, metabolic-limb and rhythmic-circulation systems of the organism, is an essential part of understanding threefold social processes.

Work and Technology Classes 9 to 12

- All aspects of craft and technology should be related on the one hand to their geographic origins and natural resources, on the other to their economic aspects. Steiner was very concerned to awaken genuine interest and understanding for economic questions.
- Related to this is the importance of real work experience in the workplace with meaningful tasks.

Class Trips

Group artistic activities, performances, class trips and excursions are all fields of rich social experience, especially if these aspects are reflected upon.

CLASS 11 OR 12

- Economics main-lesson. Characterisation of the distinction between cultural sphere, rights – justice – political – social sphere and the economic sphere, through concrete examples. Introduction to basic principles of economics, production and distribution of goods and services to meet human needs. The concepts of price, income, value. The idea of work. The origin and function of money; how value arises, different kinds of money. Social relationships within the economy. Examples of real economic processes e.g. the true price of a cup of tea, tracing the packet of tea in the supermarket back to the grower.

Whilst some of these topics may have been covered during the class teacher period, it is important to deepen them in the Upper School by focusing directly on them for short concentrated periods. The lessons should consist of accurate information and discussion with students being required to do research and seek out direct experience. Bringing professionals in is always useful, though the support of the teacher is often necessary.

One criticism often heard from former Waldorf pupils is that they felt that their education was inspiring but too remote from real life. This would be a criticism that Steiner would take very seriously, given his maxim *all* teaching should relate to and be a preparation for real life. What was once possible effectively through implicit teaching, now needs a more overt approach, so that the students can experience the relevance of the topics. This makes great demand on teachers, not only to be very well informed but to be able to focus the discussion on the higher, moral principles whilst enabling the students to form their own judgments. Preaching does not work.

The Teaching Approach

The above suggestions make it clear that the social sciences permeate the whole curriculum in an interdisciplinary way. It places the human being and human society at the heart of the teaching. But it is more than just a question of teaching content.

As we have seen the school's self-management structures and collegial working practises are influential in setting the tone. When pupils experience the support teachers give each other, how they complement each other's strengths, how they deal with problems, how they strive to research and deepen their understanding and above all, how they enjoy their work, they could have no better social education. When pupils realise that teachers set themselves aims and objectives, review and evaluate their work, consult on changes, they receive a practical demonstration of good working habits.

In the classroom, the teachers' respectful attitude to each child, their courage for the truth, their authority and generosity, all profoundly influence the child's developing social attitudes. When the self-activity of the pupil is encouraged, when pupils are shown how to work, how to tackle challenges and above all, how to learn from mistakes in a positive way, that self-activity is fostered. As the pupils get older, the process of engaging self-activity must become more and more conscious. At the end of their school time, each pupil should be able to say: *"They taught me how to work and learn and how to work together with others."*

References

1   We are indebted to Dr. Christoph Strawe for first drawing up a coherent study of all the social elements embedded within the existing Waldorf Curriculum. See Strawe, C., "Developing Social Skills, Social Understanding and Social Sensitivity in Steiner Waldorf Schools", in *Paideia* No. 16, SSF, April 1998.
2   Ibid. p32.
3   Ibid. p37.
4   See also Harrer, D., *Maths Lessons for Elementary Grades,* AWSNA, 1985, and Jarman, R., *Teaching Mathematics in Rudolf Steiner Schools for Classes I – VIII,* Hawthorn Books 1998.
5   Steiner, R., *Practical Advice to Teachers,* lecture 3, RSP, 1979.
6   Steiner, R., Lecture of October 12, 1919. German title *Soziales Verständnis aus geisteswissenschaftlicher Erkenntnis.*
7   Brierley, D. L., *In the Sea of Life Enisled. An introduction to the teaching of Geography in Waldorf education,* 1999, p119.
8   Steiner, R., *Waldorf Education for Adolescence.* SSF Publications, 1993, p38.
9   Steiner, R., *Conferences with the Teachers of the Waldorf School in Stuttgart.* Vol. 1, conference of March 8, 1920, p71.
10 Steiner, R., *Conferences with teachers...,* op. cit. Vol, 1, conference of September 25, 1919, p47.
11 Steiner, R., *Von Seelenrätseln* (GA 21) partly translated in *The Case for Anthropsophy.* Tr. Barfield, O., RSP, 1977.

STUDY OF ART / AESTHETICS

Classes 9 to 12

General aspects and aims

The aim of this subject is to awaken the students' interest in and understanding of art. Working with art also helps to develop and deepen certain psychological skills, including a heightening of the powers of perception and the ability to form judgments. There are three main aspects that involve all four classes in the Upper School:

1. Making sense perceptions subtler and schooling a more intensive and more conscious way of seeing and hearing through the study of the visual arts. This involves activating a full range of sensory experience including the activation and transformation of the lower senses (sense of balance, sense of life, sense of movement) into the senses of word and concept as a basis for the cultivation of a living thinking.
2. Developing the ability to judge the aesthetic qualities of all the arts, both spatial and temporal. Schooling the capacity to perceive subtle qualitative differences. Developing a vocabulary of concepts and a terminology to discuss artistic qualities such as form, volume, tone, colour, movement etc.
3. Gaining knowledge of art and art history and their development in relation to the evolution of human consciousness.

The study of art appears as a distinct new subject at the beginning of the Upper School as an answer to the physical and psychological changes the young people are undergoing and the questions and needs that arise as a result of these. Just as the scientific subjects gain new emphasis now, so the study of art provides a kind of balance. In contrast to a world in which immutable natural laws reign, art provides a view of a realm in which human freedom can open up.

At the ages of 14 and 15 the students also begin to feel the heaviness of their bodies and therefore also come into closer contact with the forces of gravity. The images art gives them, can provide a contrasting experience of lightness, even levity. Their soul life also takes on a new character as puberty progresses. They become more inward, more personal, more enclosed. A world of wishes, urges and passions pours in on them. This initially chaotic and unruly world of desires is confronted through art by an orderly world of regular forms and harmonies.

But it is not only this new world of urges that is besetting them, for they now confront the world and themselves with high ideals, noble aims and other demands. Great works of art can provide some initial response to their desire for perfection. At least through pictures they can satisfy their longing for the ideal, and the thought may awaken that perhaps the appearance of the picture may be revealing a spiritual reality.

The themes from the world of art taken in these four classes arise out of the inner requirements and needs of the youngsters, but choice of subject matter and emphasis is entirely up to the teachers. They are free to use whatever realms of art they are familiar with or find particularly rewarding. How the teaching is done and making it suitable for the age of the youngsters are what is important; what is chosen is secondary.

Class 9

Points of view and general themes:

The visual arts ('the arts in space') of painting and sculpture are the main focus here. Studying great works of art is intended to awaken enjoyment and enthusiasm for the beauty and greatness in art. The feelings become more subtle and refined, observation more alert as the young people learn to see. Initially questions of composition and form are only hinted at. Developing an aesthetic sense is schooled first by getting to know and experiencing great works of art.

Another aspect lies in considering what is characteristic for the three great historical periods chosen: What did the ancient Egyptians find 'beautiful'? How did the Greeks experience beauty? What was the ideal and concept of beauty during the Renaissance? By seeing how art evolved, something can be understood about how humanity has evolved. The stages of Egypt-Greece-Renaissance can be seen as revealing steps in the evolution of Western consciousness.

Content suggestions:

ANCIENT EGYPT
A description of the special geographical conditions of the country (Nile Valley, desert) can provide a basis for an understanding of Egyptian culture. It is above all a culture of death, (though filled with a sense of the vitality of life) and Egyptian art is closely bound up with this. The statues (standing, sitting, kneeling, squatting figures) show the human being as belonging to the realm of permanence. The reliefs and paintings make only the essential visible. Architecture (mastaba, pyramid, temple) need only be shown peripherally, as the great framework in which the sculptures and paintings have their place. It is important to establish that the sacred script of hieroglyphics forms a conceptual basis and canon to architecture, painting and sculpture. Such art also has to be 'read' and marks a significant cultural stage towards a script culture and the emergence of literacy.

ANCIENT GREECE
Once again a description of the landscape and how it is experienced provides a good beginning (the multiplicity of islands, valleys and bays isolated from one another by mountains and sea, the temple in the landscape, being close to nature in worshipping the gods). Greek sculpture is studied by showing its development through various stylistic states: archaic, classical (stern style, 'soft' style), Hellenistic. It is a matter of showing this development as a process (in contrast to the timelessness in Egypt): the budding, concentrated potential of archaic times, then unfolding, flowering, ripening in

classical times, with both the over-elaboration and withering and dying in later times. For Greece, too, architecture is left as a unifying background rather than a separate subject.

RENAISSANCE

As an introduction, early Christian art can be shown (the catacombs, the Ravenna mosaics). Some sense of typical medieval art forms such as gold background panels, wooden carving, cathedral sculptures, manuscript illustration, should be given as a preparation for the innovations of the late medieval period. The Middle Ages, with its attitude of turning away from the world, is not particularly interesting for Class 9 pupils, so needs to be briefly characterised rather than dwelt on. Then comes the transition from late medieval art to the early Renaissance. Giotto, Ghiberti, Brunelleschi, Masaccio, Donatello, Uccello and Piero della Francesco can be shown as representatives of a new interest in the world (discovery of linear perspective, etc.). The life and work of Leonardo, Michelangelo and Raphael provide the climax of the main-lesson.

The examples used should be limited to key studies so that the pupils are not flooded with a wealth of images that can lead to an inflation of expectation and superficiality. It is better to take one picture per lesson for an intensive study, perhaps showing a few related works as a follow up in the next lesson. Given the volume of images young people have to digest these days, sitting in a darkened room looking at slides can become a very passive activity. Teachers must find creative ways of overcoming this if art studies are to engage the self activity of the students and not merely entertain them with culture, however highbrow.

Class 10

Points of view and general themes:

THE ART OF POETRY AND LANGUAGE

This main-lesson looks at the power of the spoken word, its use in art and its abuse when used to convey ideology. The study of the art of poetry explores the means by which poetry and language can become an art form. Time is now experienced as a dimension that plays a part in artistic formation. The polarity of 'spatial arts' and 'temporal arts' is looked at for the first time. Seeing and hearing are now experienced as two qualitatively fundamentally different, though intimately linked, modes of experience. Now form and style come to the fore. The young people are to learn that feelings can be given shape and form through poetry.

This main-lesson may begin by examining the origins of language and its essential nature as a means of communication, as symbolic representation and as revelation of qualities in the world. The relationship between movement and language on the one hand, and language and thought on the other is explored phenomenologically. The differences and transitions between orality and literacy are an important theme.

The main theme however is the study of the craft of poetry, its various meters and rhyme schemes.

Examples of poetic forms such as epic, ode, sonnet, ballad, lyric and so on are all studied using examples from literature as well as the pupils' own creations. One way of doing this is to take a basic text, such as a fable and reproduce its content in a variety of different poetic styles as varied as Japanese haiku style or limerick. The full range of moods created by these different styles will fascinate and entertain the pupils. This is a task that equally appeals to students who are gifted in literacy skills as to those who are not since poetry is essentially an oral skill and poetry is a medium that does not depend on correct spelling or even extensive vocabulary. It is important that each style is objectively evaluated as to the mood it creates and expresses, whether heroic or comic, deeply inward or superficial.

The possibilities of assonance, alliteration, onomatopoeia and their effects on poetic style can likewise be explored. So too can the effect of words of different etymological origin, such as the difference between words from Anglo-Saxon, Latin/French, classical Greek, Arabic origin, to name the main examples. This can lead to a study of modern expressionist poetry where the meaning of the words is often subsumed by the tonal quality of the sounds. Related to these topics is the study of slang, jargon, cliché and the power of words in advertising, political usage and the media generally.

This a main-lesson that should stimulate the students to intense levels of creativity in the realm of language.

PAINTING AND GRAPHICS MAIN-LESSON

This main-lesson looks at the techniques and expressive power of a wide range of graphic arts as well as painting. Here too, form, technique, composition and style come to the fore. In keeping with the students' wish for knowledge, the emphasis moves from getting to know to recognising, from seeing (or hearing) to understanding.

Content suggestions:

If there is enough space in the main-lesson timetable, there can be a second main-lesson on painting. One of the main motifs could be the contrast between northern and southern Renaissance and Baroque art. Emphasis is on the great masters of northern art in the 16th and 17th Centuries: Dürer, Grünewald, Holbein, Rembrandt. Another important theme is a study of the new reproductive techniques used by many of these artists in graphics (woodcut, copper-plate, etching) which can be linked to practical exercises in these disciplines. Only through practising the techniques, even in simplified form does the medium and its conceptual aspects become clear. The basic principles of reversing the images, of removing what later remains and vice versa, of building up images through the superimposition of different plates or different stages in the printing challenge the student's thinking as well as their artistic sensibilities. Copying the work of masters in pencil drawing can reveal the structure of the images. Studying a sequence of plates of one motif in altered states by Rembrandt (self-portrait etchings for example) can reveal the range of moods and forms of expression open to the artist.

The social and cultural significance of the ability to reproduce works of art and the relationship of art to books should be studied, leading to questions of modern means of reproduction and their significance for the role of art in society.

Class 11

Points of view and general themes:

As the young people withdraw into themselves at this age, music is a new subject that will suit them (Hegel called it 'the art of pure inwardness'). It is given either as a separate main-lesson or in combination with painting or literature. In the latter case, more general views gain more weight and the pupils are shown wider horizons. Similarities and polarities in art are examined. The way painting and sculpture contrast with speech and music can, for example, be taken as a motif.

Content suggestions:

MUSIC

If a separate main-lesson (usually given by the music teacher) is devoted to music, examples are given of how music has historically developed, and the students learn to analyse form and style through listening. They are shown how music is unique among the arts in the way it is 'form taking place in time'.

An overview of the history of music can be given from ancient cultures to the present day, including Greek modes, music in Medieval churches from plain chant to polyphony, troubadours and minstrels, the birth of opera, the Baroque – Bach and Handel, the development of tonality – Haydn, Mozart, musical patronage, the Romantic revolution and the birth of the artist as individual creator – Beethoven; Romanticism in music – the development of symphony, concerto, grand opera etc.; the lives of great composers in the 19th Century; the breakdown of tonality in the 20th Century, atonality, 12-tone systems; examples of 20th Century composition.

Nietzsche's concept of Apollonian and Dionysian as contrasting qualities can be applied to music. (Some examples of these polarities include: pentatonic/chromatic, sound/melody, Handel/Bach, Debussy/Wagner).

Looking at artistic phenomena from the perspective of the Apollonian/Dionysian polarity can also be helpful for the other arts, for example in a comparison between Impressionism and Expressionism in painting or in poetry.

PAINTING

This main-lesson begins with the Romantics: Caspar, David Friedrich, Constable, Turner, Blake, moves on to neo-classicism and then leads to modern painting. Impressionism and Expressionism are the first point of emphasis. Then the path leads on via the great innovators (Cézanne, Gaugin, Munch, van Gogh, Monet) to the school of the 'Blauer Reiter', the classics among modern painters. Consideration of these artists and their paintings should always include wider cultural context. Just as the contrasting pair 'Impressionism/Expressionism' links up with the polarity of Apollonian/Dionysian that is to be found in music, so can one's view also take in other, more general aesthetic polarities such as: classical/romantic, sculpture/music, music/painting, eyes/ears, space/time, etc.

If music and painting are treated in a combined main-lesson, then the close relationship between music and painting discovered by artists in the 19th and 20th Centuries can be a fruitful avenue of approach (Gauguin, Debussy, Scriabin, Klee, Kandinsky and others).

Class 12

Points of view and general themes:

In keeping with the requirement for this year to treat lesson material from a universal point of view, the framework here should be an overview of the totality of the arts. However, architecture is the main theme for Class 12. Only now that they have reached this age can the young people really understand architecture. Their bodies, or rather the static element of the skeleton has developed to a stage where they can 'feel' their way into and 'understand' inwardly the static and constructive laws of architecture.

Architecture is looked upon as the universal art that includes and integrates all the other arts within its realm. This can lead on to the idea of a total or all-encompassing work of art. In connection with this, one can attempt to satisfy the desire for knowledge in Class 12 pupils by bringing in a separate chapter on the philosophy of art (aesthetics).

Content suggestions:

Architecture is considered in the special position it holds amongst the arts. Its development will be looked at from three points of view: artistic shape and form, technical construction and social function. The great steps in the evolution of these will be shown using examples. There are various lines along which these considerations can be carried out, e.g. the appearance and development of inner spaces; space and building; the qualities of space (e.g. longitudinal or centrally oriented spaces), the character of a space as an expression of a religious attitude, and so on. The evolution of architecture should mirror the cultural and historical stages in the evolution of human consciousness. Obviously the study of architecture should lead right up to the present time.

One can also go more deeply into the meaning and essence of art. Schiller's *Letters on the Aesthetic Education of the Human Being* can provide a suitable point of orientation. This can lead on to thoughts about art in our century, e.g. Paul Klee, Joseph Beuys or John Berger and to the aesthetic problems of modern art.

A longer art trip can be very enriching in Class 12. In order to avoid being merely tourist consumers of art, it is good to get the young people to do something themselves, e.g. draw the buildings they see, or better still, take part in some small social project. Such a trip should be the culmination of four years of study of art. Italy is naturally a popular choice in Europe but there are many other possibilities.

TECHNOLOGY

Classes 10 to 12

General aspects and aims

Technology is seen as a process that cannot be separated off from the human beings who bring it about. Nor is it merely about producing artifacts. There are several dimensions and these therefore need to be taken into account through the curriculum:

- the natural dimension involving scientific, engineering and ecological perspectives;
- the human dimension involving anthropological, physiological, psychological and aesthetic perspectives;
- the social dimension involving economics, sociology, politics, cultural history, legal and ethical aspects.

With the division of labour now running through the whole of society, technology has become the concern of specialists and engineers. However increasing environmental problems have led to a greater awareness of the human and social implications and have led to the realisation that a multi-dimensional, integrated concept of technology needs to be elaborated. The isolation of the different specialisms makes it essential to attempt a reintegration of technology as a whole. The evolution of technology comes about through the human being's innate capacity for development.

Technology lessons build on the whole lower school involvement with materials, crafts, social, historical and economic studies. Key subjects include learning about farming and house building in Class 3, the geography curriculum from Class 4 on which explores human economic relationships to the local environment and its natural resources and the links between regions around the world. History lessons show the significance of technological discoveries for social, economic and cultural developments in a wide range of fields (navigation, energy production and use, weapons, means of communication, farming, raw materials, trade etc.). The craft and handwork lessons throughout the school also form a practical and experiential basis for understanding technology.

The Class 9 physics main-lesson is oriented towards primary technology and will have provided among other things a history of technology by means of a few examples (e.g. combustion engines, telephone, turbines, etc.). Technology as such has some quite specific pedagogical tasks to fulfil, namely to school accurate observation, practical thought processes and social awareness. The chemistry curriculum too provides an understanding of substances, materials and their production and application to technology, especially petrochemical and fossil fuels.

Work experience provides opportunities to see industrial and agricultural processes at work. A topic for study in technology lessons might be to investigate a nearby factory including discovering the firm's commercial profile and depicting the production process including preliminary phases (purchase of parts and material) and subsequent tasks (advertising, marketing, selling etc.). In their social and industrial work-experience projects the pupils will especially gain direct experiences of the social aspects of work and its results. The lessons can also take the form of excursions to power stations, re-cycling plants, water reservoirs, mines etc. Such visits are best preceded by and followed up with detailed discussion. The use of modern media such as film and video is especially suitable in the high-tech realm. Many industries provide excellent information on their technology.

Class 10

Points of view and general themes:

These lessons are intended to provide life experience rather than exact knowledge. *"Now it is important at this stage that the pupils should begin to have an understanding for practical life that is going on all around them...we must introduce into our curriculum subjects that will lead the students to come to grip with practical life, subjects that will bring them into contact with the external world. We should accordingly do some mechanics, not the mere theoretical mechanics we teach in the physics lessons, but the first elements of technical mechanics that lead to the construction of machines."* [1]

An overview of what the pupils have learnt in handwork and craft lessons (woodwork etc.) combined with theoretical concepts from physics and mathematics will help the youngsters develop in a holistic way. Technologies throughout human history should also be discussed.

Content suggestions:

- Spinning wool, flax and cotton
- Weaving using various types of loom
- The textile industry
- Production of man-made textiles
- Soap production

Class 11

Points of view and general themes:

Technology now deals with two very important realms: power/energy on the one hand (e.g. the electricity industry) and substance/material on the other (e.g. paper manufacture). Technology in Class 10 started in the traditional technologies of past times. In Class 11 it shows us the present time.

Content suggestions:

- Water wheels and water pumps
- Turbines: high, medium and low-pressure turbines
- The screw and its many applications
- Power stations and the energy industry (water, wind, calorific and nuclear)
- Automobile mechanics
- A study of the qualities of flowing water
- Paper manufacture
- Printing
- Bookbinding and use of cardboard (see handwork in Class 11)
- Reproductive media, particularly printing
- Information technology

Class 12

Points of view and general themes:

Steiner Waldorf education teaches the pupils about historically important stages of technological development in the treatment of materials, energy, information and chemical substances. At the same time they are also expected to learn about the newest technological developments. As these change so rapidly it may not be possible to include everything in the curriculum, but examples at least must be given. The pupils need a basic understanding of developments, principles and problems rather than a detailed knowledge of every new technology.

Content suggestions:

Chemical technology:
- Natural materials.
- Artificial fibres made from natural materials: (celluloid, resins etc.)
- Semi-synthetic products (classical resins)
- Fully synthetic materials (polymers, plastics), e.g. from natural rubber to synthetic rubber
- Environmental and recycling problems: quality controls (soil, water, air)

BIBLIOGRAPHY

INTRODUCTION

The purpose of this bibliography is to provide a comprehensive overview of the primary and secondary literature related to the Steiner Waldorf approach and curriculum. Obviously the range of literature that teachers can refer to in their research and preparation is vast. What has been included here are titles specifically relating to the Steiner Waldorf approach in the English language, which, as far as we know, are in print.

Despite extensive researches, it was not always possible to track down the date of publication or sometimes even the publisher for some titles. Nevertheless we have included them on the basis of recommendation that they are "worthwhile". Furthermore the bookshops assured me that, as of the date of publication of this book, all these titles were available.

The books listed here should all be available by mail order from:

Rudolf Steiner Bookshop, 35 Park Road, London NW1 6XT. Tel/Fax: 020 7724 7699.
Botton Bookshop, Botton Village, Danby, Whitby, Nr. Yorks. YO21 2NJ. Tel: 01287 661 279.
Rudolf Steiner College Bookstore, 9200 Fair Oaks Boulevard, Fair Oaks, CA 95628, U.S.A.
In the UK, AWSNA books are available from the SWSF, Forest Row.

Key:

AP	Anthroposophic Press
RSP	Rudolf Steiner Press
SSF	Steiner Schools Fellowship
AWSNA Publications	The Association of Waldorf Schools of North America
GA	The volume in Steiner's collected works in German (Gesamt Ausgabe)

1.   Basic works on Anthroposophy by Rudolf Steiner
2.   Educational works by Rudolf Steiner
3.   General Introduction to Steiner/Waldorf Education
4.   The Waldorf Curriculum
5.   Aspects of Steiner Waldorf Education: education studies, teaching skills, being a teacher
6.   Child Development
7.   Early Years
8.   Teaching Resources
8.1   General
8.2   Arts and Crafts
8.3   Drama
8.4   English Language and Literature/Mythology
8.5   Environmental Studies
8.6   Eurythmy
8.7   Foreign Languages
8.8   Form Drawing and Writing
8.9   History
8.10 Learning Support
8.11 Mathematics/Geometry
8.12 Movement
8.13 Music
8.14 Poetry
8.15 Science
9.   Organisational Development and School Community in Steiner/Waldorf Schools
10.   Journals

1.   BASIC WORKS ON ANTHROPOSOPHY BY RUDOLF STEINER

Intuitive Thinking as a Spiritual Path: A Philosophy of Freedom, AP, 1995 (GA4).
Theosophy: An Introduction to the Spiritual Processes in Human Life and in the Cosmos, AP, 1994 (GA9).
Towards Social Renewal, RSP, 1977 (GA23).

2.   EDUCATIONAL WORKS BY RUDOLF STEINER

The Foundations of Human Experience previously *Study of Man*, AP, 1996. 14 Lectures, Stuttgart, 1919.
    Allgemeine Menschenkunde als Grundlage der Pädagogik. Pedagogischer Grundkurs (GA293).
Practical Advice to Teachers, RSP, 1976. 14 Lectures, Stuttgart, 1919. *Erziehungskunst Methodisch-Didaktisches*
    (GA294).
Discussions with Teachers, AP, 1996. 15 Discussions, Stuttgart, 1919. *Erziehungskunst Methodisch-Didaktisches*
    (GA295).
Education as a Social Problem, AP, 1969. 6 Lectures, Dornach, 1919. *Die Erziehungsfrage als soziale Frage*
    (GA296).

The Spirit of the Waldorf School, AP, 1995. 6 Lectures, Stuttgart and Basel, 1919. *Die Waldorf Schule und ihr Geist* (GA297).

Rudolf Steiner in the Waldorf School – Lectures and Conversations, AP, 1996. Stuttgart 1919-1924. *Rudolf Steiner in der Waldorfschule, Vorträge und Ansprachen* (GA298).

The Genius of Language, AP, 1995. 6 Lectures, Stuttgart, 1919. *Geisteswissenschaftliche Sprach-betrachtungen* (GA299).

The Younger Generation, Educational and Spiritual Impulses for Life in the Twentieth Century, AP, 1984.

Conferences with Teachers, SSF, 1986, 1987, 1988, 1989. 3 Volumes 1919-1924. *Konferenzen mit den Lehrern der Freien Waldorfschule* (GA300).

The Renewal of Education, SSF, 1981. 14 Lectures, Basel, 1920. *Die Erneuerung der Pädagogisch-didaktischen Kunst durch Geisteswissenschaft* (GA301).

Education for Adolescents, previously *The Supplementary Course – Upper School and Waldorf Education for Adolescence*, AP, 1996. 8 Lectures, Stuttgart, 1921. *Menschenerkenntnis und Unterrichtsgestaltung* (GA302).

Balance in Teaching (first four lectures), Mercury Press, 1982 and *Deeper Insights into Education* (last three lectures), AP, 1988. 9 Lectures, Stuttgart, 1920, 1922, 1923. *Erziehung und Unterricht aus Menschenerkenntnis* (GA302a).

Soul Economy and Waldorf Education, AP, 1986. 16 Lectures, Dornach, 1921-22. *Die Gesunde Entwickelung des Menschenwesens* (GA303).

Waldorf Education and Anthroposophy I, AP, 1996. 9 Public lectures, various cities, 1921-22. *Erziehungs- und Unterrichtsmethoden auf anthroposophischer Grundlage* (GA304).

Waldorf Education and Anthroposopy II, AP, 1996. 9 Public lectures, various cities, 1923-24. *Anthroposophische Menschenkunde und Pädagogik* (GA304a).

The Spiritual Ground of Education, Garber Publications, 12 Lectures, 1 Special Lecture, Oxford 1922. *Die geistig-seelischen Grundkräfte der Erziehungskunst* (GA305).

The Child's Changing Consciousness and Waldorf Education, AP, 1996. 8 Lectures, Dornach 1923. *Die pädagogische Praxis vom Geischtspunkte geisteswissenschaftlicher Menschenerkenntnis* (GA306).

A Modern Art of Education, RSP, 1981 and *Education and Modern Spiritual Life*, Garber Publications, 1989. 14 Lectures, Ilkley, 1923. *Gegenwärtiges Geistesleben und Erziehung* (GA307).

The Essentials of Education, AP, 1997. 5 Lectures, Stuttgart, 1924. *Die Methodik des Lehrens und die Lebensbedingungen des Erziehens* (GA308).

The Roots of Education, AP, 1996. 5 Lectures, Bern, 1924. *Anthroposophische Pädagogik und ihre Voraussetzungen* (GA309).

Human Values in Education, RSP, 1971. 10 Public lectures, Arnheim, 1924. *Der pädagogische Wert der Menschenerkenntnis und der Kulturwert der Pädagogik* (GA310).

The Kingdom of Childhood, AP, 1995. 7 Lectures, Torquay, 1924. *Die Kunst des Erziehens aus dem Erfassen der Menschenwesenheit* (GA311).

3. GENERAL INTRODUCTION TO STEINER WALDORF EDUCATION

Barnes, H., Howard, A., Davy, D. and Leichter, H.J., *An Introduction to Waldorf Education*, Mercury Press.

Blunt, R., *Waldorf Education, Theory and Practice*, Novalis Press.

Carlgren, F., *Education Towards Freedom. Rudolf Steiner Education A Survey of the Work of Waldorf Schools throughout the World*, Lanthorn Press.

Childs, G., *Steiner Education in Theory and Practice*, Floris Books.

Clouder, C. and Rawson, M., *Waldorf Education*, Floris Books.

Edmunds, F., *Rudolf Steiner Education, The Waldorf School*, RSP.

Mattke, H. J. and Zick, S., *Waldorf Education World-Wide*, Rudolf Steiner College Bookstore, Rudolf Steiner Library & AWSNA Publications.

Margulies, P., *Learning to Learn. Interviews with Graduates of Waldorf Schools*, Rudolf Steiner College Bookstore.

Nobel, A., *Educating Through Art*, Floris Books.

Waldorf Waldorf Waldorf, Published by Freunde der Erziehungskunst Rudolf Steiners/SSF. Exhibition Catalogue on occasion of the 44th Session and the International Conference on Education of UNESCO in Geneva.

Wilkinson, R., *Commonsense Schooling*, Robinswood Press.

Wilkinson, R., *The Spiritual Basis of Steiner Education*, Sophia Books.

4. THE WALDORF CURRICULUM

Rawson, M. (edited by), *Steiner Waldorf Education in the UK: aims, methods and curriculum*, SSF.

Rawson, M. and Masters, B. (edited by), *Towards Creative Teaching*, SSF.

Rawson, M. (edited by), *An Upper School Curriculum for the UK*, SSF.

Stockmeyer, M., *Rudolf Steiner's Curriculum for Waldorf Schools*, SSF.

von Heydebrand, C., *The Curriculum of the First Waldorf School*, SSF.

5. ASPECTS OF STEINER WALDORF EDUCATION: EDUCATION STUDIES, TEACHING SKILLS, BEING A TEACHER

Aeppli, W., *Rudolf Steiner Education and the Developing Child*, AP.

Avison, K., *A Handbook for Waldorf Class Teachers*, SSF.

Barnes, H., *Religion in the Rudolf Steiner School,* Rudolf Steiner Library.

Chilton Pearce, J., *Evolution's End: Claiming the Potential of our Intelligence,* Rudolf Steiner Library.

Edmunds, F., *Renewing Education,* Hawthorn Press.

Ege, K., *An Evident Need of Our Times: Goals of Education at the Close of the Century,* Adonis Press.

Fentress Gardner, J., *Education in Search of the Spirit,* AP.

Finser, T. M., *Research: - Reflections and Suggestions for Teachers for Creating a Community of Research in Waldorf Schools,* AWSNA Publications.

Finser, T. M., *School as a Journey, the 8-Year Odyssey of a Waldorf Teacher and His Class,* AP.

Furness, C. J., *The Creative Training of the Will in Education,* Rudolf Steiner Library.

Gabert, E., *Educating the Adolescent, Discipline or Freedom,* AP.

Harwood, A. C., *The Recovery of Man in Childhood,* AP.

Husemann, Dr. A. J., *Knowledge of the Human Being through Art, A Method of Anthroposophical Study,* Mercury Press.

Lissau, M., *The Temperaments and the Arts, Their Relation and Function in Waldorf Pedagogy,* Rudolf Steiner Library.

Maher, S. and Bleach, Y., *Putting the Heart Back into Teaching. A Manual for Junior Primary Teachers,* Rudolf Steiner College Bookstore.

McAllen, A. E., *Sleep, An Unobserved Element in Education,* Hawthorn Press.

Mitchell, D. (edited by), *Developmental Insights: Discussions Between Doctors and Teachers,* AWSNA Publications.

Molt, E. and Murphy, C., *Emil Molt and the Beginnings of the Waldorf School Movement; Sketches from an Autobiography,* Floris Books.

Moffat, P. S., *Forward Toward What? For Ourselves and Our Children,* Rudolf Steiner Library.

Müller, H., *Healing Forces in the Word and its Rhythms,* SSF.

Piening, E. and Lyons. N., *Educating as an Art,* Rudolf Steiner Library.

Querido, R., *Creativity in Education,* Rudolf Steiner Library.

Rist, G. and Schneider, P., *Integrating Vocational and General Education: A Rudolf Steiner School (Case Study of the Hibernia School),* Rudolf Steiner Library.

Schwartz, E., *Adolescence: The Search for the Self Weaving the Social Fabric of the Class,* Rudolf Steiner Library.

Schwartz, E., *Gratitude, Love, and Duty: Their Unfolding in Waldorf Education,* Rudolf Steiner Library.

Schwartz, E., *Millennial Child,* AP.

Schwartz, E., *Seeing, Hearing, Learning. The Interplay of Eye and Ear in Waldorf Education,* Rudolf Steiner Library.

Schwartz, E., *The Waldorf Teacher's Survival Guide,* Rudolf Steiner College Press.

Sloan, D., *Education and Values,* Rudolf Steiner Library.

Smit, J., *The Child, the Teachers, and the Community,* AWSNA Publications.

Smit, J., *How to Transform Thinking, Feeling and Willing,* Hawthorn Press.

Smit, J., *Lighting Fires. Deepening Education Through Meditation,* Hawthorn Press.

Smit, J., *The Steps Toward Knowledge Which the Seeker for the Spirit Must Take,* AWSNA Publications.

Soesman, A., *Our Twelve Senses,* Hawthorn Press.

Spock, M., *Teaching as a Lively Art,* AP.

Steiner, R., *A Talk to Young People,* Mercury Press.

Tautz, J., *The Founding of the First Waldorf School,* AWSNA Publications.

Tautz, J., *The Meditative Life of the Teacher,* AWSNA Publications.

Taylor Gatto, J., *Dumbing Us Down, The Hidden Curriculum of Compulsory Schooling,* AP.

Weihs, T., *The Curriculum as Healer,* Rudolf Steiner Library.

Wilkinson, R., *Commonsense Schooling,* Robinswood Press.

Wilkinson, R., *Spirit, Basis of Steiner Education,* RSP.

Zimmerman, H., *Speaking, Learning, Understanding the Art of Creating Conscious Conversation,* Lindisfarne Press.

6.   CHILD DEVELOPMENT

Aeppli, W., *The Care and Development of the Human Senses,* SSF.

Aeppli, W., *Rudolf Steiner Education and the Developing Child,* AP.

Anschütz, M., *Children and Their Temperaments,* Rudolf Steiner College Bookstore.

Ayres, A. J., PhD., *Sensory Integration and the Child,* Rudolf Steiner College Bookstore.

Baldwin, R., Kahn, T., Masheder, M., Oldfield, L., Glöckler, M. and Meighan, R., *Natural Childhood The Practical and Holistic Guide for Parents of the Developing Child,* Gaia Books.

Baldwin, R., *You Are Your Child's First Teacher,* Celestial Arts.

Childs, G., *Understand Your Temperament! A Guide to the four Temperaments,* RSP.

Childs, G., *Your Reincarnating Child,* RSP.

Elkind, D., *The Hurried Child: Growing Up Too Fast Too Soon,* Perseus Books.

Frommer, E. A., *Voyage through Childhood into the Adult World,* Hawthorn Press.

Gardner, *Youth Longs to Know,* RSP.

Harwood, A. C., *The Way of a Child,* AP.

Holzapfel, W., MD, *Children's Destinies,* Mercury Press.

Kellog, R., *Analyzing Children's Art,* Rudolf Steiner College Bookstore.

Klocek, D., *Drawing from the Book of Nature,* Rudolf Steiner College Bookstore.

Klugman, E. and Smilansky, S., *Children's Play and Learning: Perspectives and Policy Implications*, Rudolf Steiner Library.

Koepke, H., *Encountering the Self, Transformation and Destiny in the Ninth Year*, AP.

Koepke, H., *On the Threshold of Adolescence, The Struggle for Independence in the Twelfth Year*, AP.

König, K., *Brothers and Sisters, The Order of Birth in the Family*, Floris Books.

König, K., *Eternal Childhood*, Camphill Books.

Large, M., *Who's Bringing Them Up? Television and Child Development: How to Break the T.V. Habit*, Hawthorn Press.

Lievegoed, B., *Phases of Childhood*, Floris Books.

Luxford, M., *Adolescence and its Significance for Those with Special Needs*, Camphill Books.

Riera, M., PhD, *Uncommon Sense for Parents with Teenagers*, Rudolf Steiner College Bookstore.

Salter, J., *The Incarnating Child*, Hawthorn Press.

Schmidt, G., *Nutrition and Education*, Rudolf Steiner College Bookstore.

Schwartz, E., *Rhythms and Turning Points in the Life of the Child*, Rudolf Steiner College Bookstore.

Sleigh, J., *Thirteen to Nineteen: Discovering the Light, Conversations with Parents*, Floris Books.

Staley, B., *Between Form and Freedom, A Practical Guide to the Teenage Years*, Hawthorn Press.

Strauss, M., *Understanding Children's Drawings*, RSP.

Wilkinson, R., *The Temperaments in Education*, Rudolf Steiner College Bookstore.

7.   EARLY YEARS

Almon, J. (Ed.), *A Deeper Understanding of the Waldorf Kindergarten*, Waldorf Early Childhood Association of North America.

Almon, J. (Ed.), *An Overview of the Waldorf Kindergarten, Volume One*, Waldorf Early Childhood Association of North America.

Britz-Crecelius, H., *Children at Play Using Waldorf Principles to Foster Childhood Development*, Rudolf Steiner College Bookstore.

Copple, R., *To Grow and Become*, AWSNA Publications.

Eliot, J., *Let's Talk, Let's Play*, AWSNA Publications.

Glas, N., MD, *Conception, Birth and Early Childhood*, AP.

Grunelius, E. M., *Early Childhood Education and the Waldorf School Plan*, Rudolf Steiner College Bookstore.

Haller, I., *How Children Play*, Floris Books.

Heckman, H., *Nokken, A Garden for Children*, AWSNA Publications.

Jaffke, F., *Work and Play in Early Childhood*, Floris Books.

König, K., *The First Three Years of the Child*, Floris Books.

Mathieson, A. (edited by), *the World of Childhood*, Antropos Forlag, Oslo.

Müller, B., *Painting with Children*, Floris Books.

Paterson, J. and Bradley, P., *Beyond the Rainbow Bridge*, Michaelmas Press.

Pusch, R. (selected and edited by), *Waldorf Schools: Volume I, Kindergarten and Early Grades*, Mercury Press.

Pusch, R. (selected and edited by), *Waldorf Schools: Volume II, Upper Grades and High School*, Mercury Press.

Querido, R., *The Wonder of Childhood*, Rudolf Steiner College Bookstore.

Scott, A., *The Laughing Baby Remembering Nursery Rhymes and Reasons*, Rudolf Steiner College Bookstore.

Steiner, R., *The Poetry and Meaning of Fairy Tales*, Mercury Press.

Steiner, R., *Understanding Young Children. Excerpts from lectures by Rudolf Steiner Compiled for Kindergarten Teachers*, AWSNA Publications.

von Heydebrand, C., *Childhood, A Study of the Growing Child*, AP.

Willwerth, K., *Let's Dance and Sing Story Games for Children*, Mercury Press.

Zahlingen, B., *Plays for Puppets and Marionettes*, Rudolf Steiner College Bookstore.

zur Linden, W., *A Child is Born. Pregnancy, Birth: First Childhood*, RSP.

8.   TEACHING RESOURCES

8.1   General

Mitchell, D., *Resource Material for Class Teachers – Grades K-8*, AWSNA Publications.

8.2   Arts and Crafts

Collot d'Herbois, L., *Light, Darkness and Colour in Painting Therapy*, Goetheanum Press.

Gerbert, H., *Education through Art*, Mercury Press.

Hart, F., *Art, the History of Painting, Sculpture, Architecture*, Rudolf Steiner Library

Jünemann, M. and Weitmann, F., *Drawing & Painting in Rudolf Steiner Schools*, Hawthorn Press.

Martin, M. (edited by), *Educating Through Arts and Crafts An integrated approach to craft work in Steiner Waldorf Schools*, SSF.

Müller, B., *Painting with Children*, Floris Books.

Petrash, C., *Earthways Simple Environmental Activities for Young Children*, Rudolf Steiner College Bookstore.

Strauss, M., *Understanding Children's Drawings, The Path to Manhood*, RSP.

8.3 Drama

Capel, E., *Collected Plays for Young and Old*, Temple Lodge Press.
Jaffke, C. (edited by), *Plays for the Lower and Middle School. Materials for Language Teaching at Rudolf Steiner (Waldorf) Schools*, Rudolf Steiner Library, Rudolf Steiner College Bookstore in US, available from Rudolf Steiner Bookshop, London.
Jaffke, C. (edited by), *More Plays for the Lower and Middle School. Materials for Language Teaching at Rudolf Steiner (Waldorf) Schools*, Rudolf Steiner Library, Rudolf Steiner College Bookstore in US, available from Rudolf Steiner Bookshop, London.
Mitchell, D., *25 Plays, Inspired by Waldorf Teachers*, AWSNA Publications.
Moffat, P., *Twenty-One Plays for Children*, Floris Books.
Pittis, A., *Pedagogical Theatre Dramaturgy and Performance Practice for the Lower and Middle School Grades*, AWSNA Publications, Rudolf Steiner College Bookstore.
Schwartz, E., *Plays for Children and Communities*, Rudolf Steiner College Bookstore.
Wilkinson, R., *Plays for Puppets*, Rudolf Steiner College Bookstore.

8.4 English Language and Literature/Mythology

Aiken, G., *Spotlight on Words*, Robinswood Press.
Debusschere, E. B., *The Revelation of Evolutionary Events in Myths, Stories, and Legends*, AWSNA Publications.
Harrer, D., *An English Manual Compiled from Lessons in the Elementary School*, Mercury Press.
Jaffke, C. (edited by), *Tongue Twisters and Speech Exercises. Materials for Language Teaching at Rudolf Steiner (Waldorf) Schools.* Rudolf Steiner College Bookstore for US, Rudolf Steiner Bookshop, London.
Jaffke, C. (edited by), *Rhythms, Rhymes, Games and Songs for the Lower School. Materials for Language Teaching at Rudolf Steiner (Waldorf) Schools*, Rudolf Steiner Library, Rudolf Steiner College Bookstore for US, Botton Bookshops for UK.
Jaffke, C. (edited by), *Poems for the Middle and Upper School. Materials for Language Teaching at Rudolf Steiner (Waldorf) Schools*, Rudolf Steiner Library, Rudolf Steiner College Bookstore for US, Rudolf Steiner Bookshop, London.
Jaffke, C. (edited by), *Riddles. Materials for Language Teaching at Rudolf Steiner (Waldorf) Schools*, Rudolf Steiner Library, Rudolf Steiner College Bookstore for US, Rudolf Steiner Bookshop, London.
Jaffke, C. (edited by), *Proverbs and Sayings. Materials for Language Teaching at Rudolf Steiner (Waldorf) Schools*, Rudolf Steiner Library, Rudolf Steiner College Bookstore for US, Rudolf Steiner Bookshop, London.
Kovacs, C., *Ancient Mythologies: India, Persia, Babylon, Egypt*, Wynstones Press.
MacKaye Barnes, C., *For the Love of Literature*, AWSNA Publications.
Matthews, P., *Sing Me the Creation*, Hawthorn Press.
Nash-Wortham, M., *Phonic Rhyme Time*, Robinswood Press.
Schmid, R., *An English Grammar – The Language before Babel*, AWSNA Publications, Rudolf Steiner College Bookstore.
Schwartz, E., *Wish, Wonder, Surprise*, Rudolf Steiner College Bookstore.
Schwartz, E., *Why the Setting Sun Turns Red and Other Pedagogical Stories*, AWSNA Publications.
Uehli, E., *Norse Mythology and the Modern Human Being*, (translated by Copple, R.), AWSNA Publications.
Winter, D., *The Art and Science of Teaching Composition*, AWSNA Publications.

8.5 Environmental Studies

Brierly, D. L., *In the Sea of Life Enisled*, Antropos Forlag.
Querido, R., *Geography and Man's Responsibility for the Earth*, Rudolf Steiner Library.
Querido, R., *On the Teaching of Geography: Excerpts from the Work of Rudolf Steiner*, Rudolf Steiner Library.
Wilkinson, R., *Plant Study*, Rudolf Steiner College Bookstore.
Wilkinson, R., *Teaching Geography*, Rudolf Steiner College Bookstore.

8.6 Eurythmy

Adams, F., *Eurythmy for the Elementary Grades*, AWSNA Publications.
Down, R., *Leaving Room for the Angels – Eurythmy and The Art of Teaching*, AWSNA Publications.
Lebret, E., *Allegro. Music for the Eurythmy Curriculum*, AWSNA Publications.
Marquis, F., *Eurythmy for the Lower Grades*, ASWNA Publications.
Steiner, R., *Eurythmy as Visible Speech,* RSP (GA279).
Steiner, R., *An Introduction to Eurythmy*, AP.
Stoehr, S. and Oates, I., *Eurythmy An Art of Movement for Our Time*, Robinswood Press.
von Heider, W. M., *And Then Take Hands An Anthology of Rhymes, Poems, Stories, Legends and Plays for All Those Who Work With Children*, Rudolf Steiner College Bookstore.

8.7 Foreign Languages

Jaffke, C., *Textes pour L'Enseignement des Langues Etrangères dans les Ecoles Waldorf, Recueil de Poèmes, Chants, Jeux et Comptines*, Rudolf Steiner College Bookstore in US, available from Rudolf Steiner Bookshop, London.
Jaffke, C., *Textes pour L'Enseignement des Langues Etrangères dans les Ecoles Waldorf, Poésies, Textes et Chansons*, Rudolf Steiner College Bookstore in US, available from Rudolf Steiner Bookshop, London.

Kiersch, J. and Skillen, N., *Language Teaching in Steiner Waldorf Schools*, SSF.

Stott, M., *Foreign Language Teaching in Rudolf Steiner Schools Guidelines for Class-Teachers and Language Teachers*, Hawthorn Press.

Stott, M., *Utopie A Story from the 16th Century for the 7th Grade with Exercises*, Hawthorn Press.

8.8   Form Drawing and Writing

Dinklage, H., *Therapy Through Handwriting*, Mercury Press.

Gladich, J. and Sassi, P. A., *The "Write" Approach. Form Drawing for Better Handwriting*, Rudolf Steiner College Bookstore.

Kirchner, H., *Dynamic Drawing, Its Therapeutic Aspect*, Mercury Press.

Kutzli, R., *Creative Form Drawing, Workbooks 1, 2, & 3*, Hawthorn Press.

McAllen, A. E., *Teaching Children to Write; it's connection with the development of spatial consciousness in the child*, RSP.

Niederhauser, H. R. and Frohlich, M., *Form Drawing*, Mercury Press.

8.9   History

Harrar, D., *Chapters from Ancient History in Biographic Vein*, Mercury Press.

Harrar, D., *Roman Lives*, Mercury Press.

Lindenberg, C., *Teaching History*, AWSNA Publications.

Staley, B., *Hear the Voice of the Griot! Celebrating Africa in Geography, History and Culture*, AWSNA Publications.

Wilkinson, R., *Teaching History*, Rudolf Steiner College Bookstore.

8.10   Learning Support

Holtzapfel, W., *Children's Destinies*, Mercury Press.

Holtzapfel, W., *Children with a Difference The Background of Steiner Special Education*, Lanthorn Press.

König, K., *Being Human: Diagnosis in Curative Education*, AP/Camphill Press.

McAllen, A. E., *The Extra Lesson*, Rudolf Steiner College Press.

McAllen, A. E., *The Listening Ear, The Development of Speech as a Creative Influence in Education*, Hawthorn Press.

Nash-Wortham, M. and Hunt, J., *Take Time*, Robinswood Press.

Steiner, R., *Education for Special Needs: The Curative Education Course*, RSP (GA317).

Uphoff, J. K., Gilmore, H. E. and Huber, R., *Summer Children Ready or Not for School*, Rudolf Steiner College Bookstore.

Wilby, M. (Ed.), *Learning Difficulties, A Guide for Teachers*, Rudolf Steiner College Press.

8.11   Mathematics/Geometry

Anderson, H., *Active Arithmetic!*, AWNSA Publications.

Edwards, L., *Projective Geometry: An Approach to the Secrets of Space from the Standpoint of Artistic and Imaginative Thought*, Rudolf Steiner Institute.

Edwards, L., *Projective Geometry Grades 9 – 12*, Rudolf Steiner College Bookstore.

Flansburg, S., *Math Magic*, Rudolf Steiner College Bookstore.

Franceschelli, A., *Algebra*, Mercury Press.

Franceschelli, A., *Mensuration*, Mercury Press.

Ghyka, M., *The Geometry of Art and Life*, Rudolf Steiner College Bookstore.

Harrer, D., *Math Lessons for the Elementary School Grades*, Mercury Press.

Jarman, R., *Teaching Mathematics in Rudolf Steiner Schools. How to Become Holistic and Imaginative*, Hawthorn Press.

Keller-von Asten, H., *Encounters with the Infinite*, Walter Keller Press.

Pappas, T., *The Joy of Mathematics Discovering Mathematics Around You*, Rudolf Steiner College Bookstore.

Pappas, T., *More Joy of Mathematics Exploring Mathematics All Around You*, Rudolf Steiner College Bookstore.

Schuberth, E., *Teaching First Grade Math in Waldorf Schools*, Rudolf Steiner Library.

Schwaller de Lubicz, R. A., *A Study of Numbers A Guide to the Constant Creation of the Universe*, Rudolf Steiner College Bookstore.

Setzer, V., *Computers in Education*, AP.

Sheen, A. R., *Geometry and the Imagination*, AWSNA Publications.

Sloan, D. (edited by), *The Computer Education: A Critical Perspective*, Rudolf Steiner Library.

Sloan, D., Fink, A. and Mitchell, D., *Computers and Waldorf Education*, AWSNA Publications.

Swanson, H., *Geometry for the Waldorf High School*, AWSNA Publications.

Ulin, B., *Finding the Path: Themes and Methods for the Teaching of Mathematics in a Waldorf School*, AWSNA Publications.

van Bemelen, D. J., *A Drawing Lesson with Rudolf Steiner*, Mercury Press

von Baravalle, H., *Geometric Drawing and the Waldorf School Plan*, Rudolf Steiner College Bookstore.

von Baravalle, H., *The Geometry of Shadow Movements*, Mercury Press

von Baravalle, H., *The Teaching of Arithmetic and the Waldorf School Plan*, Rudolf Steiner College Bookstore.

von Baravalle, H., *The Waldorf Approach to Arithmetic Grades 1 – 8*, Rudolf Steiner College Bookstore.

Whicher, O., *Projective Geometry*, AP.

8.12 Movement

Brooking-Payne, K., *Games Children Play How Games and Sport Help Children Develop*, Hawthorn Press.
Cole, J., *Anna Banana 101 Jump Rope Rhymes*, Rudolf Steiner College Bookstore.
Gryski, C., *String Games. Cat's Cradle and Owl's Eye*, Rudolf Steiner College Bookstore.
Gryski, C., *String Games. Many Stars String Games*, Rudolf Steiner College Bookstore.
Gryski, C., *String Games. Super String Games*, Rudolf Steiner College Bookstore.
Stark, D., *Coaching Team Sports in a Waldorf School*, AWSNA Publications.
van Haren, W. and Kischnick, R., *Child's Play 1 & 2*, Hawthorn Press.
van Haren, W. and Kischnick, R., *Child's Play 3. Games for Life for Children and Teenagers*, Hawthorn Press.
von Heider, M., *Looking Forward. Games, Rhymes and Exercises to help Children develop their Learning Abilities*, Hawthorn Press.
Willwerth, K., *Let's Dance and Sing Story Games for Children*, Mercury Press.

8.13 Music

Frongillo, C., *The Importance of Being Musical*, AWSNA Publications.
Jacobs, R., *Music for Young Children*, Hawthorn Press.
Jaffke C. and Maier, M., *Early One Morning. Folk Songs – Rounds – Ballads – Shanties – Spirituals and Plantation Songs – Madrigals*, Rudolf Steiner Library, Rudolf Steiner College Bookstore in US, Rudolf Steiner Bookshop, London.
Knierim, J., *Quintenlieder, Introduction to the Mood of the Fifth*, Rudolf Steiner College Bookstore.
Lebret, E., *Pentatonic Songs*, Rudolf Steiner College Bookstore.
Lebret, E., *Shepherd's Songbooks For Grades I, II and III of Waldorf Schools*, Rudolf Steiner College Bookstore.
Lebret, E., *Songs of Heaven and Earth*, Waldorf School Association of Ontario.
Lewis, M., *When the Green Woods Laugh*, Association for Waldorf Education in London, Ontario.
Lindenberg, C-A., *The Child's Praise of the Seasons Festival Music to Sing*, Rudolf Steiner College Bookstore.
Lindenberg, C-A., *In Praise of the Seasons*, Rudolf Steiner College Bookstore.
Logan, A. (compiled and arranged by), *Building the Chorus*, Rose Harmony Association.
Logan, A., *One, Two, Three, for the Rose Lyre*, Rose Harmony Association.
Masters, B., *A Round of Rounds for the 52 Weeks of the Year*, Temple Lodge Press.
Masters, B. (edited by), *The Waldorf Song Book*, Floris Books.
Masters, B. (edited by), *The Second Waldorf Song Book*, Floris Books.
Oram, P. and Forder, P., *A Change in the Year*, Starborn Books.
Society of Brothers, *Sing through the Day Ninety Songs for Younger Children*, Rudolf Steiner College Bookstore.
Society of Brothers, *Sing through the Seasons Ninety-9 Songs for Children*, Rudolf Steiner College Bookstore.

8.14 Poetry

Harrar, D., *Verses and Poems and Stories to Tell*, Mercury Press.
Jaffke, C. (edited by), *Six Romantic Poets. Materials for Language Teaching at Rudolf Steiner (Waldorf) Schools*, Rudolf Steiner Library, Rudolf Steiner College Bookstore in US, Rudolf Steiner Bookshop, London.
Masters, B., *Weft for the Rainbow*, Lanthorn Press.

8.15 Science

Bordear, S. P., *Volts to Hertz... the Rise of Electricity*, Rudolf Steiner College Bookstore.
Borjarsky, M., *A Demonstration Manual for Use in the Waldorf School Eighth Grade Chemistry Main Lesson*, Rudolf Steiner College Bookstore.
Davidson, N., *Sky Phenomena, A Guide to Naked-Eye Observation of the Stars*, Floris Books.
Edelglass, S., Maier, G., Gebert, H. and Davy, J., *The Marriage of Sense and Thought. Imaginative Participation in Science*, Lindisfarne Press.
Edelglass, S. and D'Aleo, M., *Sensible Physics Teaching*, AWSNA Publications.
Graf, R. F., *Safe and Simple Electrical Experiments*, Rudolf Steiner Library.
Grohmann, G., *The Living World of Plants A Book for Children and Students of Nature*, AWSNA Publications.
Grohmann, G., *The Plant, Vols. 1 & 2*, Bio-Dynamic Farming & Gardening Association.
Holdrege, C., *A Question of Genes*, AP.
Julius, F. H., *Fundamentals for a Phenomenological Study of Chemistry*, AWSNA Publications.
Kennish, G., *Chemistry in Classes 7 and 8*, Wynstones School Publication.
Klocek, D., *Weather and Cosmos*, Rudolf Steiner College Bookstore.
Kolisko, E., M.D., *Zoology for Everybody, Volume 1: General*, Kolisko Archive Publications.
Kolisko, E., M.D., *Zoology for Everybody, Volume 2: Birds*, Kolisko Archive Publications.
Kolisko, E., M.D., *Zoology for Everybody, Volume 3: Mammals*, Kolisko Archive Publications.
Kolisko, E., M.D., *Zoology for Everybody, Volume 4: Protozoa*, Kolisko Archive Publications.
Kolisko, E., M.D., *Zoology for Everybody, Volume 5: Coelenterates, Echinoderms*, Kolisko Archive Publications.
Kolisko, E., M.D., *Zoology for Everybody, Volume 6: Tunicates, Molluscs*, Kolisko Archive Publications.
Kolisko, E., M.D., *Zoology for Everybody, Volume 7: Insects*, Kolisko Archive Publications.
Kolisko, E., M.D., *Zoology for Everybody, Volume 8: Amphibians, Reptiles*, Kolisko Archive Publications.
König, K., *Elephants, Bears, Horses, Cats, and Dogs*, Floris Books.
König, K., *Penguins, Seals, Dolphins, Salmon, and Eels, Sketches for an Imaginative Zoology*, Floris Books.
König, K., *Swans and Storks, Sparrows and Doves, Sketches for an Imaginative Zoology*, Floris Books.

Krupp, E. C., *Beyond the Blue Horizon Myths & Legends of the Sun, Moon, Stars, & Planets*, Rudolf Steiner College Bookstore.

Masters, B. (introduced and edited by), *Science in Education (Waldorf Curriculum Studies Vol. 1)*, SSF/Lanthorn Press.

Mees, L. F. C., *Secrets of the Skeleton, Form in Metamorphosis*, AP.

Mirbt, C. R., *An Introduction to the Study of the Stars*, AWSNA Publications.

Mitchell, D., *Chemistry 7, 8, & 9*, AWSNA Publications.

Schultz, J., *Movement and Rhythms of the Stars A Guide to Naked-Eye Observation of Sun, Moon and Planets*, Floris Books/AP.

Trostli, R., *Physics is Fun!*, Hartsbrook Waldorf School, 173 Bay Road, Hadley, MA 01035, USA, Rudolf Steiner College Bookstore.

von Baravalle, H., *Introduction to Astronomy in the Sixth Grade of the Waldorf Schools*, Rudolf Steiner College Bookstore.

von Baravalle, H., *Introduction to Physics and the Waldorf School Plan*, Rudolf Steiner College Bookstore.

von Baravalle, H., *Introduction to Physics in Waldorf Schools The Balance Between Art and Science*, Rudolf Steiner College Bookstore.

von Baravalle, H., *On Teaching Physics and Mathematics*, Mercury Press.

von Mackenson, M., Dr., *A Phenomena-Based Physics Sound, Light, Heat Volume 1 for Grade 6* (edited by Mitchell, D. and translated by Petering, J.), AWSNA Publications.

von Mackenson, M., Dr., *A Phenomena-Based Physics Sound, Light, Heat Volume 2 for Grade 7* (edited by Mitchell, D. and translated by Petering, J.), AWSNA Publications.

von Mackenson, M., Dr., *A Phenomena-Based Physics Sound, Light, Heat Volume 3 for Grade 8* (edited by Mitchell, D. and translated by Petering, J.), AWSNA Publications.

Wilkinson, R., *Teaching Physics*, Rudolf Steiner College Bookstore.

9. ORGANISATION DEVELOPMENT AND SCHOOL COMMUNITY IN STEINER WALDORF SCHOOLS

Brüll, D., *The Waldorf School and Threefold Structure – The Embarrassing Mandate – About the Risk of Being an Anthroposophical Institution*, AWSNA Publications.

Gladstone, F., *Republican Academies*, SSF.

Lehrs, E., *Republican, Not Democratic*, AWSNA Publications.

Leist, M., *Parent Participation in the Life of a Waldorf School*, AWSNA Publications.

Mitchell, D. (edited by), *The Art of Administration*, AWSNA Publications.

Mitchell, D. and Alsop D., *Economic Explorations*, AWSNA Publications.

Pietzner, C., *Handling Public Relations*, Rudolf Steiner College Bookstore.

Spence, M., *A Context for a Renewed Economics*, AWSNA Publications.

Spence, M., *Freeing the Human Spirit. The Threefold Social Order, Money and the Waldorf School*, AWSNA Publications.

Zimmerman, H., *Speaking, Listening, Understanding*, Lindisfarne Press.

Steiner, R., *Awakening to Community*, RSP.

Lievegoed, B., *Developing Communities*, Hawthorn Press.

10. JOURNALS

Economic Extracts The Economic Basis for Waldorf Education, AWSNA Publications.

Multiculturalism in Waldorf Education, AWSNA Publications.

Paideia, SSF.

Renewal: A Journal for Waldorf Education, AWSNA Publications.

Research Bulletin, Waldorf Education Research Institute, Sunbridge College.

Steiner Education, SSF.

Waldorf Science Newsletter, AWSNA Publications.